Modeling, Measuring and Hedging
Operational Risk

Wiley Finance Series

Modeling, Measuring and Hedging Operational Risk

Marcelo G. Cruz

JOHN WILEY & SONS, LTD

Other Wiley Editorial Offices

John Wiley & Sons, Inc., 605 Third Avenue,
New York, NY 10158-0012, USA

WILEY-VCH Verlag GmbH, Pappelallee 3,
D-69469 Weinheim, Germany

John Wiley & Sons Australia Ltd, 33 Park Road, Milton,
Queensland 4064, Australia

John Wiley & Sons (Asia) Pte Ltd, 2 Clementi Loop #02-01,
Jin Xing Distripark, Singapore 129809

John Wiley & Sons (Canada) Ltd, 22 Worcester Road,
Rexdale, Ontario M9W 1L1, Canada

British Library Cataloguing in Publication Data

A catalogue record for this book is available from the British Library

ISBN 0 471 51560 4

Typeset in 10/12pt Times from the author's disks by Dobbie Typesetting Limited, Tavistock, Devon
Printed and bound in Great Britain by Biddles Ltd, Guildford, Surrey
This book is printed on acid-free paper responsibly manufactured from sustainable forestry,
in which at least two trees are planted for each one used for paper production.

Contents

Preface

Several years ago, when working as a derivatives trader, I started to notice that problems at the trading desk not related to the usual day-to-day market situations (e.g. asset volatility, liquidity, credit limits, etc.) were affecting the results. These problems were not coming from the revenue side, but from operational errors and, therefore, were difficult for traders to perceive. Examples of such problems are transactions that were not settled properly due to a lack of capacity in the back-office to deal with a higher transaction volume for complex products and, as a consequence, interest penalties were being paid to the counterparty. Often clients sued banks when they lost large amounts of money in "obscure" derivatives products. All this cost a substantial amount of money, and brought an extra undesirable volatility to the earnings of the bank (aside from the bad publicity). Trading derivatives bore more risks than those considered at the time, i.e. measuring the volatility of prices (market risk) and the capability of a counterparty to honor a transaction (credit).

Nevertheless when, in 1995, operational risk started to be discussed more publicly, the initial ideas were that "operational risk is an immeasurable risk" or that "just qualitative or subjective models can be used in operational risk". Since that time, I have begged to differ with these ideas. Readers interested in the subject may have seen me talking at industry seminars or universities around the globe. I initially proposed models to measure operational risk in a mathematically robust way. Then, working as a researcher (finishing my Ph.D. on mathematical models applied to operational risk) and as a senior executive responsible for operational risk for a couple of very large global financial institutions in London and New York, I was able to put my theories into practice in real-life situations, using real data. I then became a consultant, and have helped several large organizations to structure their operational risk areas and develop risk measurement and management models. I have also helped quite a few financial authorities to prepare for the new risk regulatory environment, training them on how to supervise operational models in banks. All this has given me significant exposure to many different control environments in many unrelated cultures, and to the diverse models that might be used for the risks involved. Such is the experience upon which this book has been based.

In terms of the book's structure, I propose one structured model to measure operational risk and a number of mathematical techniques that can be used in specific situations. Part I of the book deals with the modeling of an operational risk database.

This is crucial, and forms the basis of any scientific work. Part II introduces stochastic models that are used to measure operational risk. Since measuring operational risk is not the end of the game, Part III gives examples of causal models that might be used to manage operational risk. Managing operational risk is one of the most important tasks in this area. I continue in Part IV by presenting models to manage this risk, with the focus on how to predict extreme events that have never taken place. Part V briefly shows models and programs to hedge operational risk. This part should be very interesting to insurers and those involved in mitigating operational risk. The material prepared for this section was so vast that it was decided to spin it off into a separate book on the subject, to be published by John Wiley & Sons towards the end of 2002. Part VI deals with the new regulatory environment for operational risk, which is still to be finalized by the Basel Committee in 2002. Finally, Part VII deals with the last frontier of risks faced by financial institutions: strategic, business and reputational risks. I believe that, after the consolidation of operational risk measurement, banks will move towards a better understanding of these risks.

I have tried as far as possible to write this book in accessible language, but without losing the mathematical rigor. Therefore, I believe that the operational risk manager with a basic course in statistics should understand most of the chapters and have a good grasp of the ideas underlying the subject. More advanced graduate (M.Sc. and Ph.D. levels), or even undergraduate, students would also benefit from the models presented here.

Marcelo Cruz
New York, NY
January 2002

Acknowledgements

I am grateful to a number of professionals, academics and friends who encouraged me to combine my thoughts and years of experience in operational risk together in a structured book. Special thanks go to a number of colleagues who had the tough job of reading earlier versions of the chapters, providing me with invaluable comments and suggestions. Needless to say, the ideas expressed in this book are my own, and I obviously take sole responsibility for any errors and/or omissions.

Particular thanks are due to Dr Brendon Young, Chairman of the Operational Risk Research Forum (ORRF), Dr Rodney Coleman, Department of Mathematics/ Statistics, Imperial College, London, Dr John Carroll of the Financial Services Authority in the UK, Dr Colin Farquhar of Credit Suisse First Boston, Dr David Rowe, President of SunGard Risk Management Systems and Michael Haubenstock, global leader of the operational risk practice at PricewaterhouseCoopers.

I would like to thank Sam Whittaker and Carole Millett from John Wiley & Sons for their support during the long process of writing and producing this book, also Sarah Lewis for careful copy-editing of the manuscript.

1
Overview

Operational risk has evolved considerably in the last 5 years. The term "operational risk" was probably mentioned for the first time right after the infamous Barings bankruptcy event in which a trader brought the bank down by hiding futures and derivatives positions in Asia. This event brought awareness to the financial market that these, until then ignored, risks could affect considerably their results and could not be classified either as market or credit risk. A recent survey showed that currently banks estimate their risks are divided into credit (50%), market and liquidity (15%) and operational risk (35%). This is a rough estimate, because no bank currently has a reliable measure for operational risks.

In terms of a formal definition, operational risk has been defined by the Basel Committee as "*the risk of losses resulting from inadequate or failed internal processes, people and systems or from external events*". Therefore, operational risk is related to losses originated from operational errors of any sort that affect the earnings of the bank.

The importance of operational risk within risk management is increasing exponentially. I have lectured on the subject since 1996 and, from personal observation, at that time operational risk filled just a small and unpopular slot in risk management seminars, with attendance limited to no more than five or six persons. Currently, there are two-day seminars dedicated exclusively to the subject, with attendance limited to 100–120 due to auditorium capacity. Despite all the interest, the challenges in this area still mount, as little has been done so far, especially on the measurement side. Most lectures and publications in the subject are still very qualitative, and few have faced the challenge of measuring operational risk.

The objective of this book is to fill this gap by introducing several mathematical models that can be used to measure and model operational risk. I hope the reader will find it exciting to apply the mathematical models shown here and verify that they have an extraordinary performance in the measurement of this new risk.

Regarding the basics of measurement, in my view operational risk, rather than being linked exclusively to past internal or external losses, is a function of the control environment of the organization. In this case, an organization with a good control environment is less risky in operational risk terms than an organization with a poor control environment. Having that in mind makes it easier to understand the operational risk process. The Barings event, for example, happened because a trader was responsible for performing trades and, at the same time, controlling them. There was a clear lack of control and a misrepresentation of responsibilities inside the control organization. The extremely poor control environment was responsible for such an extreme loss.

For the reader's benefit, there is one basic structured model (as seen in Figure 1.1) and several other mathematical models that can be used to model and measure special structures or areas.

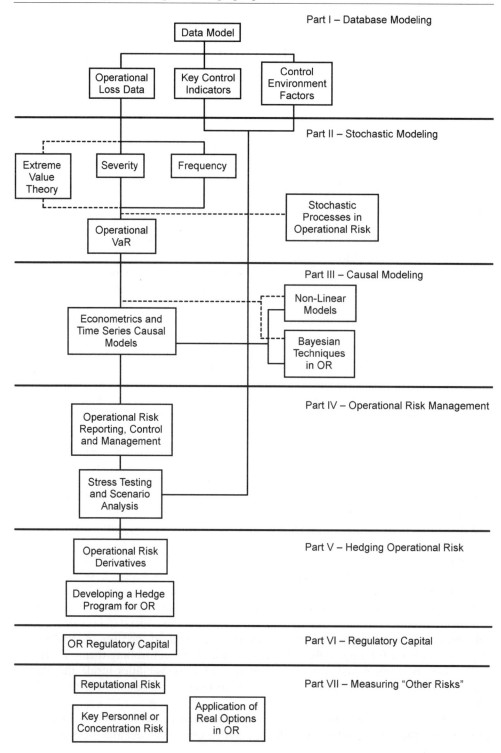

Figure 1.1   Book structure

In terms of the structure of the book, I have divided it into six parts and 18 chapters. I have tried as far as possible to put the theory in the simplest way and show examples throughout. The intention is to share my experience in modeling and measuring operational risk and allow even the operational risk manager who does not have a mathematical background to understand the concepts and exercises.

Part I of the book deals with database modeling. This is fundamental in any scientific work. An analyst needs to know what kind of data is necessary to develop his/her work before it starts. Every single institution with ambitions to model and measure operational risk will start in this area. I hope to provide quite a few ideas about operational database structure.

Part II presents the stochastic modeling of operational risk. Chapter 3 deals with severity models; Chapter 4 introduces extreme value theory, which is very important in this area; Chapter 5 shows frequency models. In Chapter 6, we see how to aggregate severity and frequency models to generate operational value at risk (VaR). Chapter 7 shows several other stochastic models and tools that might be useful in operational risk. This chapter can be skipped with no loss of continuity.

Part III of the book deals with causal models. The analyst would verify that getting to an operational VaR is not enough. One has also to understand what drives the VaR. The models presented in this section try to build a bridge between the VaR model and manageable causal factors. Chapter 8 presents linear models that use econometric and time series techniques. Chapter 9 introduces non-linear models in operational risk. Chapter 10 shows how Bayesian theory can play an important role in causal analysis.

In Part IV, having learned to develop an operational VaR model and also causal models that relate operational factors to these VaR figures, techniques are presented to use such models in active, passive and defensive operational risk management, as well as to develop stress tests and scenario analysis in operational risk. In Chapter 10 we see how operational risk can be inserted into an RAPM (risk-adjusted performance measures) framework for product pricing. There is also a brief discussion with examples showing how operational risk measurement can be useful to measure operational efficiency. In this chapter I show how to implement a sophisticated operational risk limit process in real time. Chapter 11 presents quite a few models, all based on the idea that operational risk is a function of the control environment, to develop scenario analysis and stress tests.

After measuring, establishing causes and managing operational risk, it is time to decide on financial hedging. Part V briefly shows how to use financial structures such as insurance to develop a financial hedge program for operational risk. Hedging operational risk is such an interesting and complex topic that it deserves a book on its own. This "spin off" should be released in 2002 ("Hedging Operational Risk and Integrated Risk Management"). Chapter 13 introduces a few financial engineering structures to hedge operational risk, called OR derivatives, and in Chapter 14 a program to hedge operational risk is developed.

Part VI discusses the new regulatory charges that will be determined by the Basel Committee in 2002. The rules presented in Chapter 15 are bound to change, but offer a good basis for how the charges will be calculated.

Part VII introduces models to measure so-called "other risks". These "other risks" in general are operational risk events that affect potential revenues rather than costs, and

---

Box 1.1   Fraud and Reputational Event: Nomura Securities[1] (Investment Bank), March 1997

Nomura Securities Co., the world's largest brokerage, released the news that two of its directors made unauthorized stock trades and funneled the profits to corporate customers. The executives passed the profits to a real estate company linked to "sokaiya" gangsters. Sokaiya refers to groups that blackmail companies by threatening to harass company executives at annual shareholders' meetings. The trades were made as early as the spring of 1993, and may have continued through the summer of 1996 when Japan's Securities and Exchange Surveillance Commission initiated investigations into the irregularities.

Nomura has been affected by similar activities in the past. In 1991, it was embroiled in a national scandal for compensating large clients for losses on investments. Nomura eventually named favored customers who received about US$ 1 billion in payments after the stock market tumbled in 1990. These payments were made at the expense of foreign clients and smaller domestic customers. The scandal also revealed links between Nomura and a famous leader of one of the largest criminal gangs in Japan. Japanese police investigated allegations that this gang leader made millions after Nomura lent him shares in the hotel operator Tokyo Corp. and then recommended the stock to other customers, driving up prices. Nomura was also accused in March 1997 by Australian regulators that its London-based subsidiary, Nomura International plc, manipulated futures prices in the Australian Futures Exchange.

The measurable loss in terms of reputation can be seen in the performance of Nomura shares on the stock exchanges. On release of the investigation in March 1997, the share price dropped by 10%. On the report of the Japanese Securities Commission, it plunged another 6%. The shareholders became considerably poorer, without considering the damage these events may cause to future business for Nomura, mainly related to deals with governments and large corporations, which are extremely conservative in terms of probity. Four days after the scandal was revealed, America's largest pension fund, the California Public Employees' Retirement System, Calpers, said it would stop trading with Nomura and joined a long list of Japanese pension fund managers, local government and other customers. This customer flight could have a cost to Nomura of US$ 413 million in lost revenue from trading commissions and underwriting new securities just in the month after the scandal was exposed. We are not considering losses from possible fines by market authorities.

[1]For a more detailed analysis of this case from a reputational risk point of view, please refer to Chapter 16.

---

are much more difficult to measure. Chapter 16 uses econometric techniques and market data to model and measure reputational risk, providing three real-life examples. Chapter 17 introduces models to measure concentration or key personnel risk in the front-office and the back-office, while Chapter 18 applies real options theory to measure strategic risk and also to evaluate operational risk at an e-bank.

The models presented in this book have been tested with real data from real operational events, and shown outstanding performance. I hope that the reader can benefit from my experience in adapting these mathematical models to operational risk by adapting them further to the particular operational risk environment in their organization. Many examples are presented throughout the book, using real or simulated data, as well as real cases that might help to illustrate how operational risk happens and how it can be avoided.

Part I
Database Modeling

2
Database Modeling

2.1 INTRODUCTION

One of the first and most important phases in any analytical process, and this is certainly no different when developing models to consider operational risk measurement, is to cast the data into a form amenable to analysis. This is the very first phase that an analyst faces when determining to model and measure operational risk. At this stage there is a need to establish what will (or will not) be included in the analysis. The early negative/complementary definitions of operational risk, stating "*it is every risk not included in market and credit risk*", still left analysts with the task of finding a converse, positive definition of operational risk. Although most banks in the industry now pursue a common broad definition, there is still no consensus on a single, precise definition. This makes the task of modeling an operational risk database even more difficult to achieve on a consistent basis.

Given this lack of absolute definition of operational risk, it is worth spending some time at this stage considering what might be classified as losses due to operational risk. Ultimately, for a financial institution, we wish to measure the impact of operational errors upon its profit and loss (P&L), where these give rise to an extra volatility not due to market and credit risk. Although this volatility has been present for as long as banks have existed, only recently have banks started to worry about measuring it in isolation from that due to market and credit risk. Additionally, banks are now becoming concerned with the volatility of the cost side of the P&L account, where previously attention had been focused upon the revenue side. Figure 2.1 depicts the idea of explaining the volatility of earnings by market, credit and operational risk and shows the results of a recent survey that estimates operational risk to be the second most important cause of P&L volatility in a financial institution.

In general, the situation faced by the analyst is that the problems related to developing a framework for classifying the causes of (and thereby quantifying the effects of) operational risk may seem abstract on first inspection. The usual classification of the causes of operational risk is either "system problems" or "poor controls". This kind of classification, however, may lead to mistakes or double interpretation. A more relevant way of defining the events to be included in the classification is to recognize that not all "system problems", for example, will generate an impact on the P&L (whilst appreciating the converse of this, i.e. it is possible that a "system problem" may generate several different impacts upon the results, e.g. in the areas of "interest expenses", "stock exchange penalties", and so on). A more meaningful/appropriate schema, therefore, is the classification of losses by the area of impact on the results, as the ultimate objective is to explain the volatility of the earnings arising from the direct impact of the losses on the results. Therefore, classification of the losses into items that directly affect the P&L, like "legal suits", "interest expenses", etc., is needed. Figure 2.2 depicts the situation.

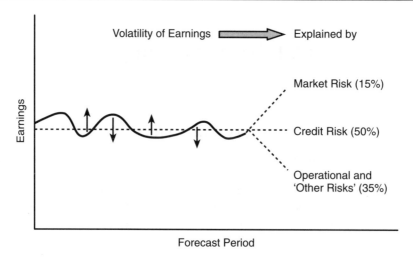

Figure 2.1   Earnings volatility and operational risk

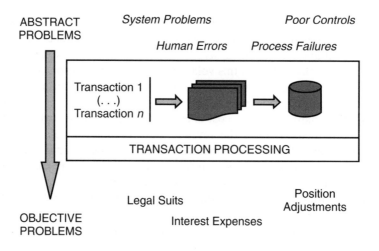

Figure 2.2   Modeling the OR database

Another decision to be made is in relation to the modeling design, which may be done either by process or for the system as a whole. Modeling by process can be quite frustrating, as large financial institutions have several thousand processes and modeling each and every one may be almost impossible to achieve. A more tractable approach is to choose a few types of operational errors and see how they apply to the processes, rather than the opposite. If a process is liable to failure, but brings no direct adverse monetary consequence, it may be left for a second or later round of the modeling process.

The analyst also has to decide on the reach of the model, i.e. how detailed the model is expected to be and what types of mathematical models will be used in the modeling process. If the objective is just to arrive at an operational VaR figure, the loss data alone will suffice. If the objective is greedier, in the sense that it wants to verify the impact and sensitivity that changes in manageable operational factors have on the operational VaR, a few more types of data are necessary. The data types are described in the following sections.

2.2 BUILDING THE DATA MODEL

Establishing a useful and robust data model is a crucial phase in the development of an operational risk measurement and management system. Therefore, the analyst should be very careful at this stage to determine the types of losses that will be of interest/ concern and, consequently, the data that should be collected inside the organization. As operational risk is a very broad concept that encompasses several different areas of an organization (most of them not used to risk measurement or risk control), it is very important to be as thorough as possible. A risk mapping exercise can take several weeks or even months to complete, depending on the size and complexity of the activities being considered, and it is very important that specialists are involved during the process. For example, it would be difficult for a non-lawyer to map legal risk, and this is compounded if the person doing the mapping does not work in this area. When mapping legal risk, therefore, the assistance of the legal department is essential.

2.2.1 Basic Framework and Initial Discussions

A few issues arise when the analyst is faced with the task of building a data model for operational risk. These are discussed briefly below.

Direct vs. Indirect Losses

Direct losses are those that impact directly on the results. For example, they can be a fee paid to a regulator for some irregularity, or an interest expense paid to a counterparty for late settlement. Indirect losses are those that arise from another cause. For example, the system crashes during the afternoon and consequently a number of transactions are not properly settled, resulting in reputational risk, interest claims, etc., which have an indirect impact on the costs and revenues.

In a paper issued in January 2001, the Basel Committee states that it requires capital to be held for both direct and *certain* indirect losses (without stating which). However, it is also clearly stated that the costs of improvement in controls, preventative action and quality assurance, as well as investment in new systems, will not be included.

Causes vs. Effect Classification of Losses

The causes and effects of operational events are very often confused. For example, it is common to see operational risk types such as "human or people risk" or even "system risk", although these types of events are merely the causes of the risk and not the effect, the effect being the monetary consequence. A classification based on causes is prone to errors/misunderstandings, especially when a large number of loss events are being considered, such as transaction processing risk. Where there are a significant number of loss events, it is very difficult to distinguish those errors caused by the system and human errors, or even to classify a human error as "inexperience" or "lack of supervision". Every classification that depends on subjectivity should be avoided at this stage.

Having said that, both cause and effect are important. In relation to market risk, when calculating VaR, the analyst may know that the volatility of a certain asset increases, and it is certainly important to understand the reasons for this, but the qualitative reason will not be incorporated into the VaR measure, except as a technical note. The same might be said about operational risk. The analyst might, for example, detect an increase in interest expenses, investigate and deduce that the problem is lack of understanding of a new settlement system or just a capacity problem.

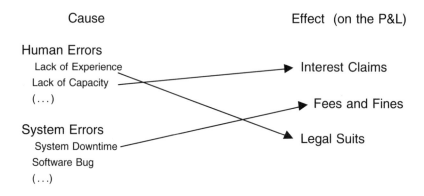

Transactional Level Modeling

The OR database should be modeled at the transaction level, instead of being aggregated on a daily or monthly basis, for a number of reasons. First, OR modeling is based on two underlying stochastic processes: the frequency and severity of losses. This will be explained in the following sections, but at the level of individual loss events it is fundamental that the bank knows when they happened, in addition to the more usually reported level of loss. Second, it is necessary to identify the root causes of losses arising from operational risk events, and attribute the losses appropriately. A numerical example will help to clarify the point.

Example 2.1   Suppose that an FX trader closed the following deal:

Buy US\$ 100,000,000 @ EUR 0.90 = EUR 90,000,000
Sell US\$ 100,000,000 @ EUR 0.9005 = EUR 90,050,000
Initial Trading Profit = EUR 50,000

Both transactions were made at almost the same time and the trader was obviously very satisfied that a profit of EUR 50,000 was made. In his/her excitement at the successful deal, however, the prices of the deal had been wrongly reported and, together with mistakes made in the back-office, the transaction was finally settled 3 days later than it should have been.

In FX it is typical that the tickets are of higher values to compensate the very low margins. This situation increases the scope for errors such as this. The counterparties obviously wanted to be compensated for the settlement delay of 3 days, and the bank also had to pay EUR 55,000 in penalties to the counterparty.

Looking at the overall picture now, it is not so good. There was a loss of EUR 5000 on aggregate due to operational errors. This is a realistic scenario arising in a trading environment. The actions of traders are recognized at the closing of the deal, and errors coming to light at a later time (e.g. mispricing, late settlement) are not linked back to the underlying cause. The error goes to an "error account" or the like and, in terms of OR management, those who contributed to the errors are never identified. Even worse, the real profitability of individual transactions is rarely understood. The cost side (and the operational risks involved) is in general ignored.

Knowing where these errors happen is very important for OR management. We will see examples like this throughout the book.

Automated Data Feeds

Considerable challenges exist in collating large volumes of data, in different formats and from different geographical locations, into a central repository, and ensuring that these data feeds are secure.

In gathering data from disparate sources, we need to avoid any operational risk in data collection. This might arise if, for example, the employee responsible for reporting losses did not send loss information to the central database, whether accidentally or not. The paper from the Basel Committee refers to this scenario, with the possible consequence that an institution which cannot prove loss data is flowing with a high degree of reliability to the central database(s) may not be allowed to employ more advanced techniques to assess the levels of risk.

Box 2.1 Misunderstanding a Trading Order: Large European Private Bank, August 2000

Despite the fact that we live in the "communication era", with technological devices such as e-mail, Internet and live-chats, many purchase orders still come via telephone. A very common mistake is the misunderstanding of the order, especially frequent when the counterparty is a foreigner. The world of private banking is still more conservative than that of investment banking, and voice purchase orders are the rule.

On a busy afternoon at the end of summer 2000, a client asked his private banker to purchase "60,000 of Swissair". The private banker passed this order to the trader, and at the end of the day the trader passed a bill to the private banker for several million Swiss francs. The private banker was absolutely stunned to see that they had bought a significant portion of the company. As a consequence of this transaction, the Swissair share price rose for a while and the bank decided to keep the shares and sell them little by little. The operational loss in this case was reflected in the value lost on returning the stocks to the market.

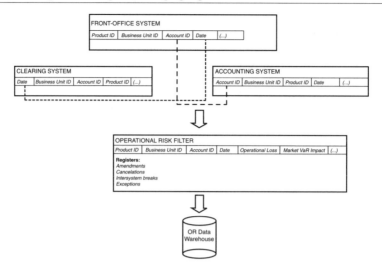

Figure 2.3   Developing an OR filter

The development of filters that capture operational problems and calculate the operational loss is one of the most expensive parts of the entire data collation process, but the outcome can be decisive in making an operational risk project successful.

Such operational risk filters will vary from bank to bank, depending on their systems, but work like a conduit between systems, collecting every cancellation or alteration made to a transaction or any differences between the attributes of a transaction in one system compared with another system. A typical example of filter design is shown in Figure 2.3. The transaction flow starts at the front-office system, which registers the transaction, passing it to the accounting and clearing systems. Any discrepancy, alteration or cancellation must be extracted by the OR filter. Also, abnormal inputs (e.g. a lower volatility in a derivative) can be flagged and investigated. The filter will calculate the operational risk loss event and several other impacts on the organization.

Operational Risk Data Warehouse

Data warehousing is an effort to combine all available sources of data and information relevant to an organization into a single, unified database structured to provide support for analytical decisions at all levels of the organization. More than an application, a data warehouse is a facilitator of applications by providing timely data on pre-established formats.

The main objective of the establishment of risk data warehouses is to assist the decision support system, storing different operational risk data types in one single framework, facilitating any kind of mathematical/statistical analysis that might be performed using all operational risk data available. An important concept within data warehouses is that of "metadata". In a literal sense, metadata means "data about data" and provides a complete profile of the data element, including sources, any eventual transformation or summarization, dimensions, time frame and any other information deemed to be important.

Particularly in large international organizations, where a term might have different interpretations or meanings, data warehousing might play a key role. In a risk data warehouse an operational loss will bear several different information fields, such as the time the loss took place, the time it was paid away to the counterparty, which departments were responsible, etc.

Truncation, Censoring and Inflation

It will often be necessary to perform changes in operational data due to, for example, inflation correction. Sometimes, for some calculations, we need to consider just the losses above a certain threshold. These changes usually occur in statistics and actuarial calculations.

Data truncation happens when observations that fall in a given set are excluded. In general truncations in operational data will happen from below, when the set of numbers excluded is below a certain threshold. An example of truncation is a deductible in an insurance policy.

Data is called censored when the numbers of observations that fall in a given set are known, but the specific values of the observations are unknown. An example of censoring is establishing a limit for coverage.

It is also important to correct events financially over time for inflation effects. This is very easy to perform and helps in understanding the real impact of events that happened a while ago. For example, suppose that in February 1995 a bank had a loss of US$ 30 million. Suppose also that the CPI index at the time was 22,123 and the CPI index at February 2002 is 30,640, showing an inflation of approximately 38.5%. The inflation-adjusted value of the loss February 2002 is in reality US$ 41.6 million.

2.2.2 The Data Model

Given the initial considerations, the data model that I propose considers several stages of operational risk, with the first stage being to collect data on the impact of operational losses in the results, although in itself this is not enough to form a complete understanding of how operational risk manifests itself. We need to understand the control environment as well. In order to model the control environment, we need to establish some quantitative factors—sometimes these factors can also be qualitative (control environment factors and key control indicators). See Figure 2.4.

Operational Loss Data

The losses attributable to manifestations of operational risk are obviously very important, as they reflect the direct impact on the results. There can be several distinct classifications. The list in Table 2.1 was developed in conjunction with the Industry Technical Working Group that helped the Basel Committee to develop the new capital requirements for operational risk. (It is noteworthy that all loss types mentioned in the table represent a direct impact on the results of a financial institution.)

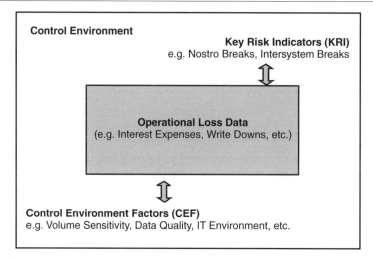

Figure 2.4   Operational risk data model

Table 2.1   Suggested list of OR loss types

Loss type	Causes	Monetary loss
Legal and liability	Lost legal suit	External legal and other related costs in response to an operational risk event
Regulatory, compliance and taxation penalties	Penalties paid to the regulator	Fines or the direct cost of any other penalties, such as associated costs of license revocations — excludes lost/foregone revenues
Loss or damage to assets	Neglect, accident, fire, earthquake	Reduction in the value of the firm's non-financial assets and property
Restitution	Interest claims. Note: Excludes legal damages which are addressed under legal and liability costs	Payments to third parties of principal and/or interest, or the cost of any other form of compensation paid to clients and/or third parties
Loss of recourse	Inability to enforce a legal claim on a third party for the recovery of assets due to an operational error	Payments made to incorrect parties and not recovered. Includes losses arising from incomplete registration of collateral and inability to enforce position using ultra vires
Write downs	Fraud, misrepresented market and/or credit risk	Direct reduction in value of financial assets as a result of operational events

Table 2.2   Suggestion of a few control environment factors

Business environment	Factor	Description
Systems	System downtime System slowtime Software stability (...)	Number of minutes that a system is offline Number of minutes that a system is slow Number of lines changed in a program
People/organization	Employees Employee experience (...)	Number of employees Average number of months of experience
Data flow and integrity	Data quality (...)	Ratio of transactions with errors to total transactions
Volume sensitivity	Transactions (...)	Number of transactions
Control gaps	Ratio of processes under control (...)	Ratio of processes under control–audit to total processes
External environment (...)	Counterparty errors Number of changes in regulations (...)	Number of errors caused by counterparties Number of changes in pertinent regulations over a period of time

Control Environment Factors

Another important type of OR information can be taken from the control environment factors. These factors are mostly quantitative and are used as a proxy for the quality of the control environment of a business. For example, in order to report the quality of the processing systems of an investment bank, we might create factors like "system downtime" (measuring the minutes that a system stayed offline), "system slowtime" (counting the minutes that a system was overloaded and running slow), etc. These factors will be extremely important in causal models (Part III). See Table 2.2.

Key Risk Indicators (or Key Performance Indicators)

Often just knowing where and how errors are happening, even without knowing the number or size of losses, might give a hint on how risky a financial institution is. For example, in transaction processing, if we know the number of breaks in the "nostro" account is growing, this might indicate that one of our processes has problems. Once again, this type of data will be used in causal models (Part III). See Table 2.3.

Business Units and their Risk Profiles

After deciding the form of the operational loss data model and the types of losses that need to be reported, it is useful to split the financial institution into different business lines, given that the operational risk profile is generally very diverse across the different businesses within a financial institution. While an asset management unit is more inclined to have legal/liability problems (although still having a few transaction

Box 2.2 System Crash: UK BACS System (Clearing House), March 1997

On March 25, 1997 telecommunication problems brought the BACS system (the UK clearing house for automated payments) to a standstill, threatening disruption to millions of salary cheques due to be paid the next day. Difficulties in the BACS telecommunications started at around 5:00pm with the result that thousands of companies faced problems transmitting their payroll instructions to the BACS processing center, culminating in a complete shutdown between 9:15pm and 10:00pm. (March 25 was the deadline for the monthly salary payments due to two imminent bank holidays.)

BACS did not release a figure for the associated losses, although it came up with an estimate on the order of several million pounds, based on the number of people who did not receive their salaries, business lost due to the delays, and reputational losses to the system. (BACS, a centralized utility jointly owned by the clearing banks, handles an average of nearly 10 million transfers a day, including direct debits and standing orders. However, towards the end of the month payment volumes can peak at well over 30 million transfers a day as payroll instructions come in.)

processing problems — in general, asset managers hold their positions longer than treasury managers), the investment bank arm is more inclined to operational errors in processing transactions. A large investment bank might process over a million transactions a day.

The list in Table 2.4 was developed by the Industry Technical Working Group and made public by the Basel Committee.

2.3 DURATION OF OPERATIONAL RISK EVENTS

Operational risk events will have a large range of different durations between the inception of the event and final closure, due to the large number of interacting factors, with the direct consequence of an operational error hardly ever being known immediately. In transaction processing risk, for example, when an event is not settled

Table 2.3 Suggestion of a few key risk indicators

Key risk indicator	Description
Transaction processing risk	
Nostro account breaks	Number of breaks in the "nostro" account
Intersystem breaks	Number of breaks between internal systems
Intercompany breaks	Number of breaks between coligated companies
Unmatched confirmation-fails	Number of failed process transactions
Legal and liability risk	
Open legal cases	Number of open cases
(...)	
(...)	

Table 2.4 Suggested list of business units

Business unit	Level 1	Level 2	Activity groups	Main operational risks profile
Investment banking	Corporate finance	Corporate finance Municipal/government finance Merchant banking Advisory services	M&A, underwriting, privatizations, securitization, research, syndications, IPO, secondary private placement	Legal/liability
	Trading & sales	Sales Market making Proprietary positions Treasury	Fixed income, equity, FX, credit funding, repos, brokerage debt, prime brokerage	Legal/liability, transaction processing, write downs, fees/fines, frauds
Banking	Retail banking	Retail banking	Retail lending and deposits, banking services, etc.	Legal/liability, transaction processing
		Private banking	Private lending and deposits, banking services, etc.	Legal/liability, transaction processing
		Card services	Merchant/commercial/corporate cards	Frauds, transaction processing
	Commercial banking	Commercial banking	Project finance, real estate, export finance, trade finance, factoring, leasing, lends, etc.	Legal/liability, transaction processing, write downs, fees/fines, frauds
	Payment & settlement	External clients	Payments and collections, funds transfer, clearing and settlement	Transaction processing
	Agency services	Custody	Escrow, depository receipts, securities lending, etc.	Transaction processing, frauds
		Corporate agency	Issuer and paying agents	Legal/liability
		Corporate trust		Legal/liability
Others	Asset management	Discretionary fund management	Pooled, segregated, retail, institutional, closed, open, private equity	Legal/liability, fees/fines Some transaction processing
		Non-discretionary fund management	Pooled, segregated, retail, institutional, closed, open	Legal/liability, fees/fines Some transaction processing
	Retail brokerage	Retail brokerage	Execution and full service	
	Insurance	Life insurance and benefit plans Property and casualty insurance Health insurance Reinsurance Brokerage and advisory		

Country	Offence Amount	Potential Amount	Final Loss	Open/ Closed	Ratio Offence/ Real	Date Opened	Date Closed
USA	10,000,000	5,000,000	1,000,000	Closed	10%	Nov-95	Dec-97
USA	50,000,000	10,000,000	500,000	Closed	1%	Oct-96	Jun-97
UK	1,000,000	100,000	ZERO	Closed	0%	Dec-97	Dec-98
USA	2,500,000	1,000,000	1,000,000	Closed	40%	Nov-98	Jun-99
USA	7,500,000	2,000,000	1,500,000	Closed	20%	Jan-98	Dec-99
Germany	500,000	100,000	200,000	Closed	40%	Feb-98	Dec-98
USA	5,000,000	2,000,000	7,500,000	Closed	150%	Mar-98	Nov-99
(...)	(...)	(...)	(...)	(...)	(...)	(..)	(...)

Values in US$.

Figure 2.5   Extract of a legal database

properly and interest expenses are to be paid to the counterparty, it will take several days until the right amount is calculated.

One of the challenges in assessing the level of operational risk is that in many instances an evaluation of the impact of an event may take months or even years to resolve. It is very important that a way is found to bring the consequence of the event to a certain "present value", utilizing as much of our experience in this area as possible.

Let us imagine that we have the database extract for a particular type of legal case as presented in Figure 2.5. (The number of fields in such a database would generally be much more extensive, but for this example we have selected a subset.) The "offence amount" is the amount that the third party sued the bank for. The "potential amount" is the amount that the specialists (lawyers in this case) reckoned would be appropriate recompense in the case. The actual loss can be crystallized when the case is closed. The ratio "offence/real amounts" is what we can work with to get to a loss estimate for a particular country, city or even court. The average experience in a certain region or case is important to bring a long duration case to a "present value". Suppose we separate out the events of this particular legal case in the USA and get the distribution shown in Figure 2.6. In this particular legal case, we must assume that, on average, the real loss is

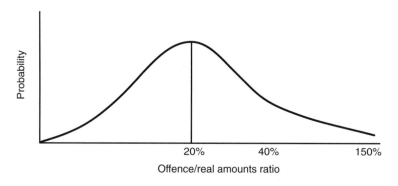

Figure 2.6   Distribution for the offence/real amount ratio for a particular legal case in the USA

Box 2.3 SBC Warburg (Investment Bank), October 1996

The Securities and Futures Authority in the UK (the former City of London regulator, since superseded by the Financial Services Authority) released partial details in March 1997 of an investigation that had commenced in October 1996 into rogue trading in a program trade at SBC Warburg. (A program trade is a transaction where one agent, generally a fund, chooses another agent, generally a bank or a broker, to sell part of its shares in the market at a day and hour determined by market prices.) The program trading error that made SBC Warburg the subject of the investigation is thought to have cost it no more than £5 million. Nevertheless, this program trade was one of the largest ever to be awarded to SBC Warburg, and the SFA investigation clearly embarassed it. The investigation relates to a mistake made during the execution of a £300 million program trade for an investment trust which caused the price of a number of French stocks to fall sharply. The investigation is being extended into whether this bank made a similar error when selling Spanish shares as part of the same program deal.

The SFA investigation focused on a 30-minute period during October 30, 1996. At some time around mid-day, SBC Warburg traders learnt that the bank had been awarded three contracts by Kleinwort Benson European Privatization Investment (Kepit) to execute a series of share sales—the so-called program trade—on its behalf. Contracts for program trades are often awarded just before the deal takes place, and the Kepit deal was no different. It involved SBC Warburg taking the £300 million-worth of shares onto its books just minutes later, at 12:30pm, and paying Kepit the mid-market price for each share at that time. In the remaining minutes before the 12:30pm deadline, SBC Warburg traders sought to sell some of the same shares they were about to get from Kepit in order to reduce the risk (this process is known as short-selling and is accepted as normal practice in a program trade, as long as the price does not fall too much).

Elsewhere at SBC Warburg, a trader was running an arbitrage position on Kepit, seeking to make money by exploiting differences between Kepit's own share price and the price of the shares the bank owned. SFA investigators were told that in the minutes before the 12:30pm deadline the SBC Warburg trader running the arbitrage position was seen on the trading floor making gestures with his hands for traders to get the price of the shares down. Nevertheless, a mistake by one of SBC Warburg's Paris-based traders attracted the attention of the SFA. Instead of selling as much as he could before 12:30pm, SFA investigators have been told that the trader misunderstood his instructions and instead attempted to sell at the strike time. The trader also failed to put a so-called down limit on his proposed share sales, effectively turning them into an unlimited sell order.

In the tapes passed to the SFA (all conversations on the trading desk are recorded), the London-based trader is heard talking with a colleague about how the price of the French shares had fallen much further than planned. The trader complained that a colleague had just told him, in hindsight after the share price had collapsed, that they should only have pushed the price down by 1%. SBC admitted in March 1997 that its short-selling had contributed to adverse price movements and dismissed several employees involved in the trade.

just 20% of what was asked for in the first instance. However, if we want to guarantee ourselves in 90% of cases, the ratio of losses referring to what was asked for in the first instance (the "offence amount") can be 150% (including external costs).

2.4   MODEL RISK — MODELS, INPUTS AND PRICE VERIFICATION

One important activity for many financial institutions is buying and selling securities and financial contracts. With the increased sophistication of these financial products, financial institutions rely evermore on very sophisticated and complex models to price these products and estimate the embedded market and credit risk.

In the modeling process, however, there is considerable scope for the introduction of operational problems that may give rise to potential losses. Figure 2.7 depicts this. The potential problems in modeling can be split into:

(a) Problems in inputs and feeds;
(b) Problems in the model itself;
(c) Problems in reporting the results.

We analyze them separately below.

2.4.1   Inputs and Feeds

The models that calculate prices and risks are fed with market data, usually provided by information agencies like Bloomberg, Reuters, Telerate, etc. Nevertheless, those with experience in the area will have noticed that problems sometimes arise with the price(s) quoted by these agencies, especially for less liquid instruments. Often they are not the same and, of course, the model output is liable to change substantially due to these price discrepancies.

Another complicating factor for global banks is the presence of business units in different time zones. For firms with offices in New York, London and Tokyo, for example, using a mark-to-market methodology, the end of the trading day in one center does not coincide with the end of the day in the other two centers. The bank has to

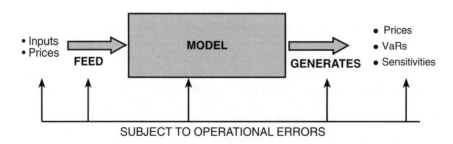

Figure 2.7   Model risk

decide how to value its global positions. If it decides to mark the positions locally (e.g. London prices for London, and so on), accounting issues might arise in cases like intracompany trades between Tokyo and London. If these trades are not marked at the same price (or the same end of business day price), the trades will not net out to zero and the consolidated balance sheet of the bank will show an exposure that in reality does not exist.

If the time of close of business in one center is used as the datum across all the centers that the bank trades in, e.g. we price a Brazilian bond at London closing time, we may have problems in finding an appropriate/representative price for a bond with the underlying based on a closed market (especially if there are liquidity considerations). This is especially true where a bank has illiquid instruments for which the price is hard to estimate. In general, the estimated price would come from a trusted broker, but there might be questions over how representative the price is of sentiment in the wider market.

In terms of derivatives pricing models, where traders are able to provide input parameters such as volatility and correlation, another source of operational risk variable may be added. An example of this happened in 1997, when a trader fed a lower volatility to a bank's pricing model just to get more clients (and increase his bonus, obviously). Checking if the inputs are too discrepant from a certain average might be advisable.

In terms of feeding data into the model, a seemingly trivial but potentially serious problem may occur in uploading prices from commercial suppliers to the model. For example, the feeds might be wrongly placed, the prices for 10 April being used on 11 April, with the obvious consequence that the model generates inaccurate results.

2.4.2 Model

This is a very complex and fundamental area in risk management. All pricing and risk models developed must be checked thoroughly. This review might be performed by an internal department (generally inside risk management and independent of the trading units and middle-office) or even an external auditor/consultant with expertise.

2.4.3 Results

An operational error due to a price, feed or model error will be crystallized in the output from the model. If a model is deemed inaccurate after a review for any of the reasons above, the operational loss is calculated as the impact on the P&L caused by the difference between the "correct" (or reviewed) model and the previous model. (In this case, the model might be "corrected" either for structural reasons or errors in parameterization.)

2.5 THE IMPACT OF OPERATIONAL RISK ON MARKET AND CREDIT RISK

A very important consequence of operational errors within a treasury function is that these will certainly impact on the measurement of market and credit risk. If the trade has incorrect terms, e.g. an incorrect price, the valuation of the position will be wrong,

---

Box 2.4 Model Inputs Fraud: NatWest, March 1997

One of the most famous cases in derivatives mispricing is what happened at NatWest in 1997. On February 28, 1997, a few days after the bank released its annual results, it announced a loss of approximately US$ 150 million caused by a junior trader who had already left the bank. The trader was said to be dealing in long-dated OTC interest rate options, used by companies that borrow at a floating rate and purchase a cap on the interest payments. The major problem in valuing these options is that they are relatively illiquid. The trader calculated the price of the options by providing his own estimates of volatility, which he apparently overestimated, creating fictitious profits that built up in the books over time.

The volatility estimates resulted in the options being underpriced. The trader attracted more clients, booking the requested premium, thereby increasing the apparent profitability of his desk (and, by extension, his remuneration). The loss was realized when the options were exercised.

---

as will be the level of market risk calculated using the erroneous figures. In Table 2.5 we show a list of operational errors and their impact on other risks.

Errors like these happen every day in financial institutions and there are parallels in traditional manufacturing industries, such as automobiles and electronics. Manufacturers in traditional industries know that from a certain number of products manufactured, in general a proportion will be defective. One of the cost control and quality benchmarks is to reduce this proportion to a minimum, and there is a substantial body of theory and practice on how to do this, built up over many years. Very few industries or factories claim to see a zero rate of defects, and the financial industry should recognize this.

On the other hand, the culture in financial institutions has always been much more towards revenue than costs or errors. Many senior traders do not recognize today the importance of such errors, with the result that these errors may happen considerably more often in banks as no preventive and/or remedial action is taken, with a potentially serious impact on the bottom line. A factory in a traditional industry, such as automobile manufacturing, might claim that their error rate is around 1%, i.e. from a million cars manufactured 10,000 would bear some kind of defect. A large investment bank might process more than a million trades a day and the error rate may be, for

Table 2.5 Examples of operational errors that affect other risk types

Operational error	Impact (cost/frequency)	Risk category affected	Risk type
Incorrect terms	Average/high	Market risk	'P&L adjustments'
Incorrect 'counterparty'	High/low	Credit risk	'Write-offs'
Wrong trade data integrity	Average/high	Settlement risk	'Interest expenses'
Corollary			
All above	Average	Cost basis	'Cost of correction'

Table 2.6 Adjusting positions, results and market VaR for operational errors

Business	Position	Adjusted position	P&L adjustment	VaR adjustment
Equities	$100	$95	($2)	$1.2
FX	$500	$620	$23	$2.1
Fixed income	$1000	$920	($10)	$2.0
(...)				

example, around 4–5%. In this case we would have 40,000–50,000 wrongly reported transactions every day. The cost of this inefficiency would be substantial, and the impact on the reporting of market and credit risk is of concern.

Consider a simple example. A trader buys 1000 shares of XYZ at $2.50. The total position bought of XYZ is $2500. When the transaction is registered, a mistake is made, 10,000 shares are booked and the value of the position is found to be $25,000. The error is noticed the next day but the original VaR calculation is completely wrong. Of course, in this case the amounts involved are not large, but if an event like this were to happen thousands of times a day we might expect a significant impact on the bottom line.

The consequence of these errors is that an investment bank treasury's position is summarized as follows:

$$P = \alpha_1 \text{Asset}_1 + \alpha_2 \text{Asset}_2 + \cdots + \alpha_n \text{Asset}_n + \varepsilon$$

where P is the bank's position, α is the price, Asset represents the quantity held of a particular asset, and ε represents the stochastic operational errors. Table 2.6 depicts an example with three assets.

These position adjustments will impact the VaR calculations, necessitating adjustments to these figures as well. The adjustments to the VaR figures should not be compared to *real* operational losses, such as lost legal suits, interest expenses paid to counterparties, etc. They are merely reporting errors, but understanding them will help us to improve our measurement of market and credit risk. An exception might occur when an event affects the figures for more than one fiscal year and therefore the results are misreported to the public due to this error. Figure 2.8 gives an example of how different the results may be after adjustment.

If there are errors relating to market positions, any measures based on these positions (such as VaR) will consequently be wrong and, by extension, any risk reports containing these figures. The influence of these errors in risk reporting is perhaps the most important effect that they cause. We would expect a very smooth curve for the market VaR and sometimes, due to inexplicable errors in the price or quantity, the curve is less smooth than it should be. Figure 2.9 depicts this.

As a first approximation, market risk measurement is done by verifying the volatility of market factors (like a particular interest rate, a stock, etc.) multiplied by the position. If the position is wrong, the VaR is obviously wrong too. This is important because the regulatory capital associated with a position is, in many instances, based on this figure and is checked periodically by the banking authorities. Of course, the less susceptible the VaR figure is to operational events, the closer this measure is to the concept which the financial institution uses to evaluate the riskiness of its positions.

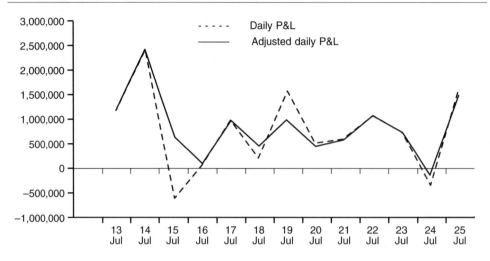

Figure 2.8 Daily P&L and operational errors adjusted P&L

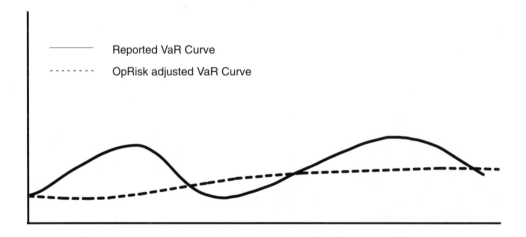

Figure 2.9 Market VaR adjusted for operational errors

The calculations for the adjustment are not simple though. We need to recalculate the risk of a portfolio by adding or deleting values to a past position. Jorion (2000) provides some ways of approximating these calculations.

Based on Jorion (2000), several VaR tools can be used to approximate the values of changes in a portfolio VaR, but as VaR is not just the sum of the risks but also incorporates the inherent correlations between positions, etc., to measure the effect of changing positions on the entire portfolio, adding or subtracting individual marginal

VaRs is not enough. When an asset belongs to a portfolio, what matters is the marginal contribution to portfolio risk, i.e. the change in portfolio VaR due to taking an additional dollar of exposure to a given position. It is the partial derivative with respect to the component weight, this being based on the proportion of the portfolio which the position represents. The formula can be seen as:

$$\text{Marginal VaR} = \alpha \frac{\text{cov}(R_i, R_p)}{\sigma_p}$$

where:

$$\sigma_p = \sigma \sqrt{\frac{1}{N} + \left(1 - \frac{1}{N}\right)\rho}$$

α is the standard normal deviate and N the number of securities in the portfolio. Perhaps a more simple way of seeing marginal VaR is:

$$\text{Marginal VaR} = \frac{\text{VaR}}{\text{Portfolio market value}} \times \beta_i$$

where:

$$\beta_i = \frac{\sum w}{(w' \sum w)}$$

with w the weight of the asset in the composition of the portfolio.

Another useful metric is the "component VaR", that allows an approximation to be made of how much the portfolio would change if a component were deleted. The component VaR would be calculated as:

$$\text{Component VaR} = \text{Marginal VaR} \times w_i \times \text{Portfolio market value}$$

A simple example might help us to understand how this works. An investment bank has two assets, stock XYZ and an (uncorrelated) position on a government bond (asset B). The position in XYZ is $8 million and that in the government bond is $10 million. The volatility of the stock price is 20% and that of the bond price is 5%. In a quick and dirty calculation, the investment bank VaR would be (figures in million dollars unless stated otherwise):

Variance position stock $\text{XYZ} = (20\%)^2 \times \$8 = 0.32$
Variance position asset $\text{B} = (5\%)^2 \times \$10 = 0.025$

Portfolio variance $= \$8 \times 0.32 + \$10 \times 0.025 = 2.81$. The volatility is $\sqrt{2.81} = 1.676305$
VaR@95% $= 1.65 \times 1.676305 = 2.765$ or **$2,765,904**

However, after the positions and the VaR were reported it was discovered that 10,000 shares of XYZ at $10 were bought and not recorded. Therefore, new calculations need to be performed. Using the formulas above, we can estimate the VaR "operational risk" adjustment:

Table 2.7   Consequences of changes in the position

Position adjustment	P&L adjustment	VaR adjustment
$100,000	**$20,000**	**$31,503**
10,000 shares @ $10	$12 (MTM)−$10 = $2	
	$2×10,000 = $20,000	

$$\text{VaR increment factor} = \alpha \frac{\text{cov}(R_i, R_p)}{\sigma_p} = 1.65 \times \frac{0.32}{1.676} = 0.315035$$

Given that the position adjustment was $100,000, the marginal VaR is simply:

Marginal VaR = VaR increment factor × Increment = 0.315035 × 100,000 = $31,503

Given that the additional shares were bought at $10, and closed the day at $12 (the mark-to-market price), the adjustments are as detailed in Table 2.7. This exercise, when applied as a rule every day, helps to make the market VaR model more reliable.

Similar calculations might be performed to adjust the figures reported for credit risk where it is believed that an operational event has occurred. The same problem in terms of an inaccurate VaR figure would arise if a bank believed that it was overexposed to a low credit client, due to operational errors, or vice versa. Problems may also occur due to errors in identifying the right counterparty, where counterparties are of different credit quality, or are subject to different settlement terms, etc.

2.6   BASIC DATABASE FRAMEWORK FOR THE INTEGRATION OF MARKET, CREDIT AND OPERATIONAL RISK

The assumption that market and credit risk are not correlated with operational risk is a fair one. Nevertheless, as we have seen before, operational errors may cause problems in the correct estimation of the level of market and credit risk.

The integration of the three types of risk is seen by some as the "Holy Grail" in risk management. This, however, is surely years away from becoming a reality. The problems, apart from finding the right model for integration, are quite numerous. If, for market risk, the losses are known on a daily basis due to the marking-to-market of prices, in the areas of credit and operational risk the losses are much more likely to show up on a longer time scale. In operational risk most losses will appear in the next few days (transaction processing risk), but other losses may crystallize over a period of months or even years (e.g. legal events). Nevertheless, building such a database may be useful on the road to developing (and then even backtesting) integrated models in the future. Figure 2.10 provides an idea of the basic data framework for risk integration.

2.7   INCLUDING INSURANCE/HEDGING IN THE DATABASE

To control for hedging efficiency purposes, it is important to include a field for individual transaction losses reporting how much of the loss was recovered. Table 2.8

Date:	13.March.2001		Results	
	Market Positions			
	Equity	200,000		**Upside and Downside**
	FX	(55,000)		**(Might have profits)**
	Credit Losses			
	(...)	(...)		**Downside**
				(Large time gaps)
	Operational Losses			
	Transaction Errors	(15,000)		**Downside**
	Legal	(20,000)		**(Shorter time gaps)**
	(...)	(...)		
	P&L	(...)		
	Market VaR	xx,xxx.xx		
	Credit VaR	xx,xxx.xx		
	Operational VaR	xx,xxx.xx		

Figure 2.10   Basic framework for risk integration

Table 2.8   Some fields for the hedging database

Loss amount	Type of loss	Date of loss	Date of loss reimbursement by insurance company	(...)	Coverage
$2431	Stolen computer — *loss or damage to assets*	12.March.2001	16.June.2001	(...)	$2431 (100%)
$16,910	Interest expenses — *restitution*	16.March.2001	–	(...)	$0 (0%)
$1,200,000	Settled discrimination case — *legal and liability*	22.March.2001	13.July.2001	(...)	$200,000 (16.7%)

shows an example of a few relevant fields in the database. The use of such a database will be seen in Part V.

2.8   PROVISIONING TREATMENT OF EXPECTED OPERATIONAL LOSSES

Unlike credit risk, where the calculated expected credit losses might be covered by general and/or specific provisions in the balance sheet, for operational risk, due to its multidimensional nature, the treatment of expected losses is more complex and restrictive. Recently, with the issuing of IAS37 by the International Accounting

Standards Board, the rules have become clearer as to what might be subject to provisions (or not). IAS37 establishes three specific applications of these general requirements, namely:

(i) A provision should not be recognized for future operating losses.
(ii) A provision should be recognized for an onerous contract — a contract in which the unavoidable costs of meeting its obligations exceed the expected economic benefits.
(iii) A provision for restructuring costs should be recognized only when an enterprise has a detailed formal plan for restructuring and has raised a valid expectation in those affected.

(The last of these should exclude costs, such as retraining or relocating continuing staff, marketing or investment in new systems and distribution networks, the restructuring does not necessarily entail.)

IAS37 requires that provisions should be recognized in the balance sheet when, and only when, an enterprise has a present obligation (legal or constructive) as a result of a past event. The event must be likely to call upon the resources of the institution to settle the obligation and, more importantly, it must be possible to form *a reliable estimate of the amount* of the obligation. Provisions should be measured in the balance sheet as the best estimate of the expenditure required to settle the present obligation at the balance sheet date. Any future changes, like changes in the law or technological changes, may be taken into account where there is sufficient objective evidence that they will occur. IAS37 indicates also that the amount of the provision should not be reduced by gains from the expected disposal of assets (even if the expected disposal is closely linked to the event giving rise to the provision) or by expected reimbursements (arising from, for example, insurance contracts or indemnity clauses). Only when and if it is virtually certain that reimbursement will be received should the enterprise settle the obligation, and this reimbursement should be recognized as a separate asset.

2.9   DEVELOPING AN OPERATIONAL RISK POLICY

Having defined the data feeds and planned the modeling of the central database, it is very important to communicate this to the organization. We should never forget that every person inside an organization is a possible source of operational risk and, therefore, the dissemination of such policies must be as wide as possible.

2.9.1   Operational Risk Mapping and Definitions

A clear risk mapping and definition of operational risk should be provided and fully described. The collection of data with which to populate the database starts from this exercise, and the organization should know very clearly which loss events are understood to arise from the manifestation of operational risk inside the institution. The risk mapping process has to involve the "experts" in the organization. (See Appendix B for comments.)

2.9.2   Operational Loss Directive

It is important also to establish an operational loss directive that will ensure consistency in the reporting of operational losses inside the organization. Thresholds should be set above which reporting of operational errors is required, with data going to the central database. An example of a simple loss directive is seen below:

Operational loss	Report to
<$1000	Direct Report
<$5000	Branch Manager
<$50,000	Area Director
>$50,001	Group Director

Note: This might require an estimate to be made at the outset of the likely impact of an operational risk event.

2.9.3   Operational Risk Measurement Policy

The guidelines for the quantification of the impact of operational risk should follow a similar approach as market or credit risk to facilitate integration into a single risk measure. In these two risk types, the probability and severity of an event are two important factors, and it is important to develop a similar methodology for measuring the level of operational risk. The guidelines for the development of such measurement methodologies should be detailed in the policy document.

The principles for measuring operational risk should include:

- *Risk Decomposition*
  Operational risks in any product/business unit should be identified.
- *Operational Risk Measures*
  An operational risk framework comprising the six operational risk types should be used to calculate the level of operational risk across all business units. (This is particularly important for operational risk due to its multidimensional nature.) If an operational risk type is not appropriate/present in any business unit, this must be clearly stated.
- *Probability-based Measures*
  As in market and credit risk, a probability-based methodology should be put in place to allow management to estimate the likelihood of an event occurring, considering both catastrophic and high-frequency occurrences, with the associated capital at risk for the firm.
- *Control Environment*
  Different from market risk but very similar to the "creditworthiness" principle in credit risk, an extra principle should be introduced in which the control environment (quality of a business unit's control) is evaluated by an independent function, e.g. the risk management function or the internal audit department.
- *Sensitivity Measures*
  Firms should be capable of measuring the sensitivity of their positions to individual operational risk factors.

Table 2.9   Comparison of principles to build market, credit and operational risk models

Key principles	Market	Credit	Operational
Risk decomposition	YES	YES	YES
Risk measures	YES	NO	YES
Probability-based	YES	YES	YES
External evaluation	NO	YES	YES
Sensitivity measures	YES	YES	YES
Position valuation	YES	YES	NO

Table 2.9 gives a comparison of the key components necessary in building models for measuring market, credit and operational risk.

REFERENCES

Dalkey, O. and Helmer, O. (1963), "An Experimental Application of the Delphi Method to the Use of the Experts", *The Management Science*, 9(3), 458–472.

Jorion, P. (2000), *Value at Risk — The New Benchmark for Managing Financial Risk*, 2nd Edition, McGraw-Hill, New York.

Linstone, H.A. and Turoff, M. (1975), *The Delphi Method*, Addison-Wesley, New York.

Oppenheimer, A.N. (1968), *Questionnaire Design and Attitude Measurement*, Heinemann, London.

APPENDIX A: EXTERNAL DATABASES

Since operational risk is growing rapidly as a risk management area, institutions find themselves having to start up specialist units from scratch, without expertise and/or data. Although suitable personnel may be recruited internally from the credit risk or internal audit areas, data presents a weightier problem, with none or very little being available internally. There are a number of external databases available in the market, but there are caveats to be borne in mind.

So far, the data collection is rudimentary and incomplete

Up to this point in time, financial institutions have not made this a high priority, delegating the task of gathering published data (e.g. from the *Financial Times*) to relatively junior people. In fact it is believed that most of these events are hidden by the financial institutions and even those reported might be wrong, in terms of realized losses. Most of these databases have no more than a few thousand events, whereas a large bank that processes over a million transactions daily may see significant losses due to operational errors in a few days.

Banks are still not prepared to provide loss information at this stage; therefore the data feed is still random

Even if banks join the same data consortium, they are not prepared at this stage to release reliable information on their losses to competitors, and may be selective in the information they do release.

How do you aggregate data from other institutions, cultures and countries to your model?

The next challenge is to assimilate/integrate a few extreme data points from the external database into yours. What is the validity of every single bank using the "Barings event" in their calculations? How do you explain to management that you are allocating a very high amount against their business because a bank on the other side of the world lost a significant amount a few years ago?

The modeling of these databases is still simplistic

One of the main sales arguments of these consortiums is that "the insurance industry uses similar databases to perform their rating". The reality is that the insurers use much more complex databases. For example, in motor insurance they collect several fields of information on losses. In a collision, for example, they collect the age and sex of the driver, the model of the car, year, if the car had ABS, air bags, the weather conditions at the moment of the accident, etc. Therefore, having information on all these risk factors makes it easier to price a new risk. The operational risk databases, on the other hand, just include the loss itself and the size of the bank. No underlying risk factors, such as processing capacity or control environment factors are provided, since banks are not prepared at this stage to provide such information.

APPENDIX B: RISK MAPPING ("SELF-ASSESSMENT")

A common stumbling block when starting an operational risk measurement project is the absence of an appropriate historical database that records data, allowing an assessment of the kinds of risk central to the project. This issue makes it difficult to approach OR through historical databases or regular statistical inference techniques. This is because many business units are unable to provide sufficient loss data in a standard format, at least at the outset.

Another important issue is that, given its multidimensional characteristics, even an experienced operational risk manager is highly unlikely to be able to foresee all the risks involved.

To circumvent these problems, the application of questionnaires and the Delphi technique may be employed to solicit the required data. The industry, in general, calls this kind of approach "self-assessment". This must not be confused with asking the business-makers of the organization what they think their capital figure is for covering risks, that is the job of the risk manager. For example, in market risk management a risk manager would never go to a trader and ask what his/her VaR was in a particular instrument; rather, the risk manager would calculate the overall level of risk and discuss this with the trader. Likewise, in operational risk it is also unacceptable for operational risk managers to ask their business counterparts what their risk is, since their job is to estimate the overall level of risk.

The Delphi technique, as defined by Linstone and Turoff (1975), "...*may be characterized as a method for structuring a group communication process so that the process is effective in allowing a group of individuals, as a whole, to deal with a complex problem*".

The Delphi concept is a spin off from defense research. "Project Delphi" was the name given to an American Air Force project, started in the early 1950s, making use of expert opinion (see Dalkey and Helmer 1963). The objective of the original study was to "*obtain the most reliable consensus of opinions within a group of experts*" by a series of intensive questionnaires interspersed with controlled opinion feedback.

The application of Delphi can be very important in assessing the current operational risks embedded in a bank's business. This is a one-off exercise in which the organization, using its experts, will identify the operational risks in its processes, products, etc.

Delphi has been tested and broadly used in several applications, such as:

- Gathering current and historical data not accurately known or available.
- Examining the significance of events.

Usually, one or more of the following properties of the problem to be solved lead to the need for Delphi:

- The problem does not lend itself to precise analytical techniques but can benefit from subjective judgments on a collective basis.
- The individuals needed to contribute to the examination of a broad or complex problem have no history of adequate communication and may represent diverse backgrounds in respect of experience or expertise.
- Time and cost make frequent group meetings infeasible.
- More individuals are needed than can effectively interact in a face-to-face exchange.

We thus require a group of experts in each business, in order to derive an estimate of operational risk occurrences at a given confidence level.

There are two ways of applying Delphi:

- *Conventional Delphi*
  This is the traditional way. A monitor (in the present case, a risk manager) designs a questionnaire that is sent to a large group of respondents. Afterwards, the questionnaire is returned, the monitor summarizes the results and, based on the results, may or may not develop a new questionnaire for the respondent group. The respondent group is usually given at least one opportunity to re-evaluate their original answers, based on examination of the group response.
- *Real-Time Delphi*
  In this form, the monitor is largely replaced by an internal system (generally intranet), which has been programmed to carry out the compilation of the group's results. This latter approach has the advantage of eliminating delay caused by summarizing each round of Delphi, thereby turning the process into a real-time communication system.

The implementation of Delphi can be customized. For example, the questionnaires would be supplemented by "operational risk workshops" with the business units. In these workshops the concept of operational risk would be spread throughout the organization, and the risk management would have the opportunity to discuss the possibility of retrieving data on operational risk losses and determine guidelines for future implementation of an operational risk database.

Delphi has a number of stages:

(1) In the first step, the subject under discussion should be explored with as many individuals contributing additional information as is believed can contribute valuably to the issue at hand.
(2) Given the information from step 1, feedback and a description of the issues are provided to the group.
(3) (Optional) The possible differences found in step 2 should be brought out and evaluated.
(4) A final evaluation occurs when all previously gathered information has been initially analyzed and the evaluations have been fed back to the respondents for consideration.

Compiling the Questionnaires

It may seem obvious, but one of the most important tasks when compiling a questionnaire is to understand what one really wants from the respondents. This can be done through a map where one states all the information one wants to have after the completion of the poll. The approach must typically be top-down, i.e. first the goals must be defined and then the best way to achieve them from the questionnaire must be determined.

Concerning the design of the questionnaire, Oppenheimer (1968) affirmed that *"questionnaire design cannot be taught from books; every investigation presents new and different problems. A textbook can only hope to prevent some of the worst pitfalls and to give practical, do-it-yourself kind of information that will point the way out of difficulties"*. The following guidelines should be followed when designing a questionnaire:

(1) Decide the aims of the study.
(2) Prepare a "map" containing all the information one would like from the poll.
(3) Design the questionnaire following some existing techniques (and with regard to the information required from the "map") to avoid common pitfalls.
(4) Define the sample size.
(5) Design or adapt necessary research methods and techniques, and prepare the pilot work.

The questionnaire might also have additional objectives. For example, to obtain information on operational events reporting and flow, or to confirm a business unit's accounting data, or to understand how the business unit's executives estimate their figures for economic capital compared to those measured statistically.

Part II
Stochastic Modeling

Different from market VaR, operational VaR is based on discrete stochastic processes rather than continuous ones. Therefore, operational VaR is generated through the aggregation of two processes: the severity and frequency of operational losses.

The need to separate severity and frequency can be verified with a simple example. It is quite common these days in most countries that the motor authorities demand drivers use safety belts while on the road. This measure, the use of safety belts, might impact the severity of car accidents, since arguably, drivers and passengers would tend to be injured less than when not using safety belts. However, the use of safety belts per se would not impact the frequency of car accidents. Accidents would not be avoided because drivers and passengers were using safety belts, so it is expected that the frequency of car accidents would be unaltered.

The same pattern should be expected in operational risk. Some managerial actions would affect just the severity of losses and some just the frequency. Therefore, we need to measure these two processes separately.

Chapter 3 presents the basis to analyze severity models and Chapter 4 introduces extreme value theory, which will be very helpful in dealing with operational risk events. Chapter 5 deals with the frequency models and Chapter 6 finally shows how to generate the operational VaR. Chapter 7 presents a few more stochastic models that can be helpful in operational risk.

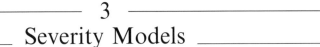

3
Severity Models

3.1 INTRODUCTION

In the previous chapter I presented ideas on how to develop an operational risk database. In this chapter we will start to see how to use these loss databases, how to use the data to fit statistical distributions and how to choose a model for the severity of losses.

3.2 GENERAL APPROACH

The approach followed in this section is the usual one for dealing with statistical distributions. One would not know prior to testing what pattern the losses follow. Therefore, we need to download data from the database and start testing some pre-specified models. See Figure 3.1. The models need to be fully tested to minimize model errors.

3.3 BASIC CONCEPTS IN PROBABILITY THEORY

Before we get to the distributions, let us review some basic concepts in probability theory. Readers with a statistical background could skip this section.

3.3.1 Probability Density Functions (PDFs) and Cumulative Distribution Functions (CDFs)

The use of random variables enables us to put questions of probability into a mathematical framework and thereby apply mathematical techniques.

A random variable X represents the hypothetical numerical value taken as the outcome of an experiment. A random variable is called discrete if it can assume only a finite number, or an infinite sequence, of distinct values. Frequently this would mean that X takes only positive integer values. Experiments involving counting or scoring are typical sources of discrete random variables. A random variable is deemed continuous when it may assume a value that can be measured to any degree of precision, such as length, time, etc.

If a random variable X is continuous, the probability of X having any precise value within that range is zero because we are allocating a probability of 1 amongst an infinite number of values. We define a PDF (represented by $f(x)$) as:

$$f(x) = \frac{d}{dx} F(x)$$

The meaning of the equation above is that $f(x)$ is the rate of change of the CDF (represented by $F(x)$), which is the mathematical formula describing the probability

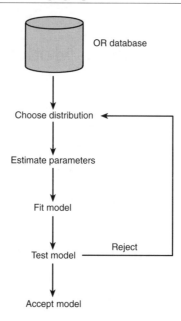

OR database

Choose distribution

Estimate parameters

Fit model

Test model ——— Reject

Accept model

Figure 3.1   General approach to fitting statistical distributions

that a random variable X takes a value less than or equal to x, i.e.:

$$F(x) = \Pr(X \leqslant x)$$

where $\Pr(X \leqslant x)$ means the probability of the event $X \leqslant x$.

A CDF has the following properties:

(1) $F(x)$ is always non-decreasing, i.e. $\dfrac{\mathrm{d}}{\mathrm{d}x} F(x) \geqslant 0$;

(2) $F(x) = 0$ at $x = -\infty$;

(3) $F(x) = 1$ at $x = \infty$.

Another important theorem on transformations for normal distributions says that if X and Y are normally distributed, then so is any linear combination $Z = aX + bY$. Understanding this will help us later.

3.3.2   Moments

Moments are a basic and important concept in probability theory. It is important to mention that not all distributions will have moments (or will have infinite moments).

In general, moments are represented by:

$$m_k = E(X^k)$$

The first moment of the population (the data) will be calculated by:

$$m_1 = E[(X - \mu)^1]$$

Put another way, the moments can be represented by the following estimate:

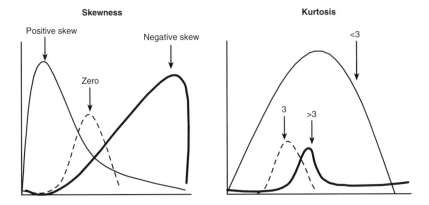

Figure 3.2   Skewness and kurtosis

$$m_k = E(\hat{X}_k) = \frac{1}{n}\sum_{j=1}^{n} x_j^k$$

Therefore, the first moment is simply the average of the sample:

$$m_1 = E(\hat{X}_1) = \frac{1}{n}\sum_{j=1}^{n} (x_j - \bar{X})$$

where $\bar{X}$ is the mean of the sample.

The second moment is the standard deviation. This is simply the square root of the variance and can be represented by:

$$\sigma = \sqrt{E(X - \mu)^2}$$

The third moment is the skewness and the fourth the kurtosis. The skewness can be calculated from the following formulas:

$$\text{Skewness} = \frac{\sum_{i=1}^{n}(x_i - \mu)^3 p_i}{\sigma^3} \qquad \text{for the discrete case}$$

$$= \frac{\int_{\min}^{\max}(x_i - \mu)^3 f(x)\mathrm{d}x}{\sigma^3} \qquad \text{for the continuous case}$$

The formulas above are easily available in spreadsheets and are calculated using "=skew (data range)". For any symmetric distribution the skew is zero. Positively skewed distributions tend to have most of the probability assigned to small values.

The kurtosis measures the nature of the spread of the values around the mean. A small kurtosis indicates a sharp peak in the middle. A population with high kurtosis is usually called *leptokurtic*. The kurtosis plays an important role in distinguishing those distributions that place additional probability on larger values. The kurtosis is calculated from the following formulas:

Table 3.1   Skewness and kurtosis for a few distributions

Distribution	Skewness	Kurtosis
Normal	0	3
Lognormal	0 to ∞	3 to ∞
Poisson	0 to ∞	3 to ∞
Binomial	$-\infty$ to ∞	1 to ∞

$$\text{Kurtosis} = \frac{\sum_{i=1}^{n}(x_i - \mu)^4 p_i}{\sigma^4} \qquad \text{for the discrete case}$$

$$= \frac{\int_{\min}^{\max}(x_i - \mu)^4 f(x)\mathrm{d}x}{\sigma^4} \qquad \text{for the continuous case}$$

Figure 3.2 represents the shape of skewness and kurtosis in a few cases. Meanwhile Table 3.1 reports the limits of skewness and kurtosis for a few popular distributions. From this table we see that, if a random population has kurtosis above 3, it cannot be represented by a normal distribution.

3.3.3   Measures of Central Tendency

Apart from the mean, which we have seen above, two other measures of central tendency are worth mentioning here: the mode and the median.

The mode is the value with the greatest probability $p(x)$ for a discrete distribution, or the greatest probability density $f(x)$ for a continuous distribution. The mode is not uniquely defined for a discrete distribution with two or more values that have equal highest probability. The median is the value that the variable has a 50% probability of exceeding, i.e. $F(x_{50\%}) = 50\%$.

If a distribution is right (or positively) skewed, these three measures of central tendency are positioned from left to right: mode, median and mean. On the other hand, if the distribution is left (or negatively) skewed, the reverse order occurs. For an absolutely symmetric distribution the three will be equal.

In Figure 3.3 I show two data sets, one absolutely symmetric and the other a bit skewed. The first set does not have a mode as two or more events would have equal probability of happening. The mean and the median are the same. As the second data set is slightly skewed to the left, the order of the central tendency measures is mean, median and mode. We can see that the first data set fits a normal distribution reasonably well, having skewness 0 and kurtosis < 3.

3.3.4.   Central Limit Theory

A very important theorem in statistics is the so-called Central Limit Theorem (CLT). It basically says that as the size of the sample increases, the distribution of the average of a random sample of n observations tends to be normal with first moment μ and standard deviation $\sigma/\sqrt{n}$.

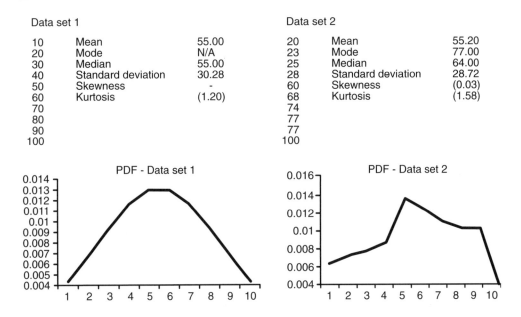

Figure 3.3   Symmetry in distributions

An application might help our understanding of the importance of the CLT. Suppose that a risk manager has a huge database of legal events containing over 20 years' of data for a financial institution. The average loss of this database is $72 and the standard deviation is $9.

(a) Determine the probability of a random sample of 10 events to show the average is higher than $80.
(b) Given that the population is normally distributed, calculate the probability of a certain event, randomly chosen, to be higher than $80.

To answer (a), we know that the CLT affirms the average of large populations to have approximately normal distribution. Therefore, we can calculate:

$$\Pr(\bar{X} > 80) = \Pr\left(\frac{\bar{X} - \mu}{\sigma/\sqrt{n}} > \frac{80 - 72}{9}\right)$$
$$= \Pr(Z > 2.81)$$
$$= 0.0025$$

To answer (b), knowing that the observation comes from a normal distribution, it makes the calculation even easier:

$$\Pr(X > 80) = \Pr\left(\frac{X - \mu}{\sigma} > \frac{80 - 72}{9}\right)$$
$$= \Pr(Z > 0.89)$$
$$= 0.1867$$

Although there is a reasonable chance of any randomly chosen event being higher than \$80 (approximately 19%), it is extremely improbable that, considering 10 random events, the average loss will reach \$80 (less than 1% chance).

3.3.5 Law of Large Numbers and Tchebysheff's Inequality

Averages are present on a day-to-day basis. When we read the newspapers there are a number of indices, economic data, providing relative information regarding growths, decreases or averages. To make inferences about the future behavior of these indices, it would be useful to understand how the sequence of these events behaved in the past. Usually we might have to simulate a model to verify this behavior. Nevertheless, we need to know if there is an average or if the sequence is mean-reverting, etc. What is the theoretical basis for this?

The law of large numbers plays an important role in probability and statistics, being the theoretical basis of Monte Carlo simulation. Let $X_1, \ldots, X_n$ be a sequence of iid random variables with common distribution function. We need to know the convergence of this sequence if we want to get a general idea of the fluctuations of $X_1, \ldots, X_n$. Suppose this sequence does not converge. Nevertheless, we can still get some information about how the sequence behaves in the mean.

One particularly useful theorem here is Tchebysheff's inequality. This inequality states that, for any number k greater than 1, at least $(1 - 1/k^2)$ of the measurements will fall within k standard deviations of the mean, or within $(\bar{x} - ks)$ and $(\bar{x} + ks)$ for random samples. This rule can help us to interpret the standard deviation of a data set or probability distribution that is non-normally distributed.

Based on this (and without digressing into mathematical formulas), the law of large numbers basically says that, over long periods of time, the average of a sequence converges to $E(X)$, or the expected value.

3.3.6 Methods to Estimate Parameters

There are two broad categories to estimate parameters. In the first category the parameters are estimated through a system of equations equivalent to the number of parameters to be estimated. Three methods are popular under this category: moments, percentile matching and probability weighted methods.

In the method of probability weighted moments, a random variable X with CDF $F(x)$ is defined by the quantities:

$$M_{p,r,s} = E[X^p \{F(x)\}^r \{1 - F(x)\}^s]$$

For a distribution that has a quantile function $x(u)$, the parameters α and β can be calculated by:

$$\alpha_r = \int_0^1 x(u)(1-u)^r du \quad \text{and} \quad \beta_r = \int_0^1 x(u)u^r du$$

Alternatively, in the method of moments the parameters are estimated by:

$$E(X^r) = \int_0^1 \{x(u)\}^r du$$

In the methods of percentile matching, the sample and model percentiles are forced to be equal at r arbitrarily selected points.

The overall problem with all the methods in this category is their incapacity to fit well the whole data range, concentrating instead on matching a few characteristics.

The other category of parameter estimation methods is optimization (maximum likelihood). In this case a likelihood function for a set of n independent observations is estimated as:

$$L(\theta) = \prod_{j=1}^n L_j(\theta)$$

Here we need to find the maximum likelihood of a function. In most cases, we will need to set all partial derivatives to zero and solve the resulting equations. This can be very difficult and, especially for small samples, the calculation might have no solution at all or present huge bias.

The commonest methods to measure the performance of a parameter $\hat{\theta}$ evaluate its bias and root mean square error (RMSE), defined by:

$$\text{Bias}(\hat{\theta}) = E(\hat{\theta} - \theta)$$

$$\text{RMSE}(\hat{\theta}) = \sqrt{E(\hat{\theta} - \theta)^2}$$

It is usually said that $\hat{\theta}$ is unbiased if $\text{Bias}(\hat{\theta})=0$, i.e. if the estimated parameters are equal to the real ones.

3.3.7 Transformation of Distributions — How New Distributions are Built

There are a huge number of distributions. A few are very popular and many not so popular but still important to define the behavior of a particular random variable. It would be interesting to have an idea of how distributions can be transformed, or new families of distributions created from existing ones (for more details please refer to Klugman et al. 1998).

There are a few ways of transforming a random variable to create a new distribution:

(1) Exponentiation;
(2) Multiplying by a constant;
(3) Mixing;
(4) Raising to a power.

In Table 3.2 I list a few simple transformations that relate the exponential distribution to other commonly used distributions (please refer to Johnson et al. 1994).

Table 3.2 Transformations of the exponential distribution

Transformation	$\bar{F}(x) = 1 - F(x)$	Distribution
$Y = \log X$	$\exp(-e^{y})$	Extreme value
$Y = \exp(X/\tau)$	$(1/y)^{\tau}$ $(y \geqslant 1)$	Pareto
$Y = 1 - e^{-X}$	$1 - y$ $(0 \leqslant y \leqslant 1)$	Uniform
$Y = X^{1/c}$ $(c > 0)$	$\exp(-y^{c})$ $(y > 0)$	Weibull

3.3.8 Empirical Distribution

The relationship between the order statistics and the empirical distribution function is direct: for $x \in \mathfrak{R}$, we might introduce the empirical distribution function or sample distribution function as:

$$F_n(x) = \frac{1}{n} \sum_{i=1}^{n} I_{\{X_i \leqslant x\}} \quad x \in \mathfrak{R}$$

In practical terms, the empirical distribution can be plotted using the simple formula below:

$$p_{k,n} = \frac{n - k + 0.5}{n}$$

where k is the order of the data and n the number of events in the sample.

3.4   TAIL HEAVINESS

It is also important to understand the behavior of the tails of the distributions, i.e. how far the extrapolation of the predictions will go. In the next chapter I present a set of theories that cover the "heaviest" distributions, providing a special analytical setting to deal with them. Meanwhile, Table 3.3 gives a few distributions ordered by tail heaviness.

Table 3.3 Comparative tail heaviness for a few distributions

Distri-butions:	Weibull $(\alpha > 1)$	Exponential	Pearson	Weibull $(\alpha < 1)$	Lognormal	Generalized extreme value, generalized Pareto
Form of $f(x)$ for large x:	$\exp(-x^{A})$ $(A > 1)$	$\exp(-x)$	$x^{A}\exp(-Bx)$	$\exp(-x^{A})$	$x^{-A \log x}$	x^{-A}

Heavier tail $\longrightarrow$

Source: Based on Hosking and Wallis (1997).
A and B are constants.

3.5   GOODNESS-OF-FIT TESTS

It is very important to test the fitness of the models and see which one is the most appropriate. There are a few tests to do this; we indicate some of them below. Initially, we present formal tests. Then we show how graphs can help us to analyze a model fit.

3.5.1   Formal Tests

Kolmogorov–Smirnov

There are a number of goodness-of-fit tests on the general lines of the Kolmogorov–Smirnov (KS) test. This test basically verifies the differences in fit between the empirical distribution and the fitted one. The test is based on the maximum observed distance between the two functions. To perform this test, one first has to estimate parameters for the distributions. The KS statistic is:

$$D_n = \max[|F_n(x) - F(x)|]$$

where:

D_n is known as the KS distance;
n is the number of data points;

$$F_n(p_{k,n}) = \frac{n - k + 0.5}{n};$$

k is the rank of the data point (the largest has rank 1);
$F(x)$ is the distribution of the fitted distribution.

Figure 3.4 depicts the KS statistic. We are basically getting the maximum distance between the empirical and the fitted distributions. The problem is that the KS statistic

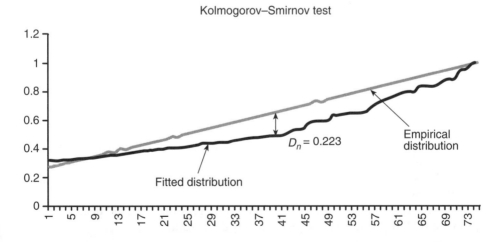

Figure 3.4   Kolmogorov–Smirnov test

Table 3.4 Significant and critical values for the Kolmogorov–Smirnov statistics

Critical value	Significance level (α)
$\dfrac{1.07}{\sqrt{n}}$	0.20
$\dfrac{1.22}{\sqrt{n}}$	0.10
$\dfrac{1.36}{\sqrt{n}}$	0.05
$\dfrac{1.63}{\sqrt{n}}$	0.01

cares only about the maximum level of discrepancies, without considering whether the distribution as a whole fits reasonably well.

The results from the test are checked against Table 3.4 to see whether they can be accepted or not.

The major problem with the KS test is its lack of power. It tends to overfit the data (i.e. be too lenient). This is especially true for small samples.

Anderson–Darling

The Anderson–Darling (AD) statistic is a more sophisticated version of the KS statistic. The AD statistic is computed by:

$$A_n^2 = \int_{-\infty}^{\infty} |F_n(x) - F(x)|^2 \Psi(x) f(x) dx$$

where:

$$\Psi = \frac{n}{F(x)(1 - F(x))};$$

n is the number of data points;
$F(x)$ is the CDF of the fitted distribution;
$f(x)$ is the density function of the fitted distribution;

$$F_n(p_{k,n}) = \frac{n - k + 0.5}{n}.$$

The increased power comes from the fact that:

- The vertical distances are integrated over all values of x, making maximum use of the observed data.
- $\Psi(x)$ balances for the increased variance of the vertical distances between distributions.
- The density function of the fitted distribution weights the observed distances by the probability that a value will be generated at the x-value.

The results are tested against the figures in Table 3.5.

Table 3.5   Significance levels for the Anderson–Darling test

Scaling	5% Significance level	1% Significance level
$1 + \frac{0.2}{\sqrt{n}}$	0.757	0.05
$1 + \frac{0.3}{\sqrt{n}}$	1.321	0.01

Table 3.6   Significance levels for the Cramer–Von Mises test

Scaling	5% Significance level	1% Significance level
$1 + \frac{0.2}{\sqrt{n}}$	0.124	0.174
$1 + \frac{0.16}{\sqrt{n}}$	0.222	0.338

Cramer–Von Mises

Another statistic is the Cramer–Von Mises (CVM). It is mainly a measure of the mean squared deviation of the distance between the data and the model, with a correction based on the sample size. The CVM statistic is given by:

$$W^2 = \sum \left[F(x) - F_n(x) \right]^2 + \frac{1}{12n}$$

The statistic is tested against the figures in Table 3.6.

3.5.2   Graphical Tests

QQ-Plots

A popular way of checking a model is through the so-called QQ-plots. The observations need to be ranked in descending order. Then, we need to find the fitted CDF and the respective quantiles against the empirical one through a plotting formula (such as $(n - k + 0.5)/n$). If the model is good, the points will lie very close to the line from 0 to 1 in the graph.

3.6   A FEW POPULAR PROBABILITY DISTRIBUTIONS

As we have seen before, new distributions are generally transformed from previous ones. They can be grouped into "families" of distributions. Figure 3.5 shows one example.

This family of distributions is quite useful, since several "members" have heavy-tail characteristics that might be useful for operational risk. Below I detail some of these distributions, also showing how to estimate the parameters by moments or percentile matching, which makes them easy to use in spreadsheets.

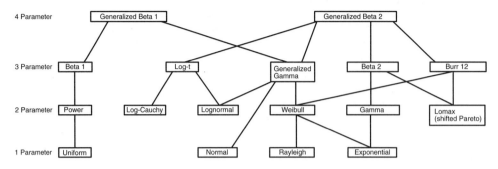

Source: Based on Cummings et al. (1990).

Figure 3.5   Generalized beta family of distributions

3.6.1   Normal (or Gauss) Distribution

Although the events in operational risk will hardly ever follow a Gaussian pattern, the normal (or Gauss) distribution is the most significant one, and its application in market and credit risk management is extremely important.

Early research in the 18th century regarded this distribution as just a convenient approximation to the binomial distribution. It was only at the beginning of the 19th century that an appreciation of its broader theoretical importance became clear, with the work of Laplace and Gauss. The normal distribution has a unique position in probability theory and can be used in other distributions:

$$f(x) = \frac{1}{\sqrt{2\pi}} \exp\left[-\frac{1}{2}\left(\frac{x - \mu}{\sigma} \right)^2 \right] \quad \sigma > 0$$

Let $Z = (x - \mu)/\sigma$. This random variable Z is called a standard normal variable. In this case, the CDF of Z is calculated by:

$$\Phi(x) = \Pr[Z \leqslant z] = \frac{1}{\left(\sqrt{2\pi}\right)} \int_{-\infty}^{z} e^{-x^2/2} dx$$

The moment estimation of the parameters is:

$$\hat{\mu} = \frac{\sum\limits_{j=1}^{n} X_j}{n}$$

and

$$\hat{\sigma} = \sqrt{\frac{\sum_{j=1}^{n} (X_j - \bar{X})^2}{n}}$$

3.6.2 Lognormal Distribution

The development of lognormal distributions followed the idea mentioned earlier that distributions could be transformed. If there is a number θ such that $Z = \log(X - \theta)$ is normally distributed, the distribution of X is said to be lognormal. The PDF of X is given by:

$$f(x) = \frac{1}{x\sigma\sqrt{2\pi}} \exp\left(\frac{-z^2}{2}\right) = \frac{\Phi(z)}{\sigma x}, \quad z = \frac{\log x - \mu}{\sigma}$$

The CDF is:

$$F(x) = \Phi(z)$$

The estimation of the parameters is made by considering $Z_i = (\log X_i - \mu)$. Then:

$$\hat{\mu} = \bar{Z} \quad \text{and} \quad \hat{\sigma} = \sqrt{\frac{\sum_{j=1}^{n} (Z_j - \bar{Z})^2}{n}}$$

3.6.3 Inverse Normal (Wald) Distribution

This distribution was derived by Wald (1947) as a limiting form of the distribution of sample size in certain probability ratio tests. The name "inverse Gaussian" was first applied by Tweedie (1947), who observed the inverse relationship between the cumulant generating functions of the Gaussian and this type of distribution.

A random variable X would have a Wald distribution if:

$$f(x) = \left(\frac{\theta}{2\pi x^3}\right)^{1/2} \exp\left(-\frac{\theta z^2}{2x}\right), \quad z = \frac{x - \mu}{\mu}$$

The CDF is calculated by:

$$F(x) = \Phi\left[z\left(\frac{\theta}{x}\right)^{1/2}\right] + \exp\left(\frac{2\theta}{\mu}\right)\Phi\left[-y\left(\frac{\theta}{x}\right)^{1/2}\right], \quad y = \frac{x + \mu}{\mu}$$

The parameters can be calculated (method of moments) as:

$$\hat{\mu} = \frac{\sum_{j=1}^{n} X_j}{n}$$

and

$$\hat{\theta} = \frac{\left(\dfrac{\sum_{j=1}^{n} X_j}{n}\right)^3}{\left(\dfrac{\sum_{j=1}^{n} x_j}{n}\right) - \left(\dfrac{\sum_{j=1}^{n} X_j}{n}\right)^2}$$

3.6.4 Exponential Distribution

The exponential distribution has been applied in a wide variety of statistical procedures. One of the most prominent is the field of reliability theory. This distribution is also very important in operational risk.

The random variable X has an exponential distribution if it has a PDF of the form:

$$f(x) = \lambda^{-1} \exp\left[-\frac{(x-\theta)}{\lambda}\right] \quad x > \theta, \ \lambda > 0$$

This is the two-parameter type of exponential distribution. Nevertheless, the most common type of exponential distribution is the one-parameter, assuming that $\theta = 0$, and this is usually represented simply by:

$$f(x) = \frac{e^{-x/\lambda}}{\lambda}$$

The CDF is represented by:

$$F(x) = 1 - e^{-x/\lambda}$$

The moment estimation for the one-parameter case is simply calculated by:

$$\hat{\lambda} = \frac{1}{\sum_{j=1}^{n} X_j/n}$$

3.6.5 Weibull Distribution

The Swedish physicist Waloddi Weibull used a distribution of the breaking strength of materials in 1939 that was later named after him. In his work, the close agreement shown between his observed data and that predicted by his model was very impressive. This is the distribution that has received the most attention from researchers in the past quarter of a century. Nowadays even spreadsheets contain the distribution, making it popular and easy to use.

A random variable will have a Weibull distribution if there are values of the parameters such that:

$$f(x) = \frac{\alpha}{\beta^{\alpha}} x^{\alpha-1} e^{-(x/\beta)^{\alpha}}$$

The CDF is given by:

$$F(x) = 1 - e^{-(x/\alpha)^\beta}$$

The percentile matching method provides the following method of calculating the parameters.

Initially we need to calculate an auxiliary parameter c:

$$c = \frac{\ln(\ln(4))}{\ln(\ln(\frac{4}{3}))} = -0.262167$$

Then, we use c to help calculate the parameters α and β:

$$\beta = \frac{c \ln(a) - \log(b)}{c - 1} \quad \text{and} \quad \alpha = -\frac{\ln(\ln(4))}{\ln(b) - \ln(\beta)}$$

where a and b are the 25th and the 75th percentile respectively.

3.6.6 Pareto Distribution

The Pareto distribution was named after the economist Vilfredo Pareto, who formulated an economic law (Pareto's Law) dealing with the distribution of income over a population.

The two-parameter Pareto distribution has PDF:

$$f(x) = \frac{\alpha\theta}{(x+\theta)^{\alpha+1}}$$

The CDF can be represented by:

$$F(x) = 1 - \left(\frac{\theta}{x+\theta}\right)^\alpha$$

The moment estimation of the parameters can be represented by:

$$\hat{\alpha} = 2 \frac{\dfrac{\sum_{j=1}^{n} x_j^2}{n} - \left(\dfrac{\sum_{j=1}^{n} x_j}{n}\right)^2}{\dfrac{\sum_{j=1}^{n} x_j^2}{n} - 2\left(\dfrac{\sum_{j=1}^{n} x_j}{n}\right)^2}$$

and

$$\hat{\theta} = \frac{\left(\dfrac{\sum_{j=1}^{n} x_j}{n}\right)\left(\dfrac{\sum_{j=1}^{n} x_j^2}{n}\right)}{\left(\dfrac{\sum_{j=1}^{n} x_j^2}{n}\right) - 2\left(\dfrac{\sum_{j=1}^{n} x_j}{n}\right)^2}$$

The single-parameter representation of the Pareto distribution is also very useful. It is very similar to the two-parameter one, but the value of θ must be set in advance. The distribution is represented by:

$$f(x) = \frac{\alpha\theta^\alpha}{x^{\alpha+1}}$$

The CDF is:

$$F(x) = 1 - \left(\frac{\theta}{\alpha}\right)^\alpha$$

The parameter α is estimated by:

$$\hat{\alpha} = \frac{\dfrac{\sum\limits_{j=1}^{n} x_j}{n}}{\dfrac{\sum\limits_{j=1}^{n} x_j}{n} - \theta}$$

3.6.7 Gamma Distribution

The gamma distribution first appeared in 1836, as obtained by Laplace. The gamma distribution gives a useful representation of many physical situations, for example in reliability theory, random counter theory, etc.

The PDF of the two-parameter gamma distribution is given by:

$$f(x) = \frac{\left(\frac{x}{\theta}\right)^\alpha e^{-x/\theta}}{x\Gamma(\alpha)}$$

where $\Gamma(\alpha; x)$ is given by $\Gamma(\alpha) = \int_0^\infty t^{\alpha-1} e^{-t}\, dt$.

The CDF is given by $F(x) = \Gamma(\alpha; x/\theta)$. The parameters are estimated by (method of moments):

$$\hat{\alpha} = \frac{\dfrac{\left(\sum\limits_{j=1}^{n} x_j\right)^2}{n}}{\dfrac{\sum\limits_{j=1}^{n} x_j^2}{n} \left(\dfrac{\sum\limits_{j=1}^{n} x_j}{n}\right)^2}$$

and

$$\hat{\theta} = \frac{\left(\dfrac{\sum_{j=1}^{n} x_j^2}{n}\right) - \left(\dfrac{\sum_{j=1}^{n} x_j}{n}\right)^2}{\left(\dfrac{\sum_{j=1}^{n} x_j}{n}\right)}$$

3.6.8   Cauchy Distribution

Although named after Augustin Cauchy (1853), it was Poisson (1824) who first noticed that the distribution with density $(1/\pi)[1/(1 + x^2)]$ has some peculiar properties, and could provide counter-examples to some generally accepted results and concepts in statistics.

The PDF of the Cauchy distribution is:

$$f(x) = (\pi\lambda)^{-1}\left[1 + \left\{\frac{x - \theta}{\lambda}\right\}^2\right]^{-1} \quad \lambda > 0$$

The CDF is:

$$F(x) = \frac{1}{2} + \pi^{-1}\tan^{-1}\left[\frac{x - \theta}{\lambda}\right]$$

The parameters are calculated (based on order statistics) by:

$$\tilde{\lambda} = (\hat{X}_{p1} - \hat{X}_{p2})\,\frac{1}{(\cot \pi p_2 - \cot \pi p_1)}$$

and

$$\tilde{\theta} = (\hat{X}_{p1}\cot \pi p_2 - \hat{X}_{p2}\cot \pi p_1)\,\frac{1}{(\cot \pi p_2 - \cot \pi p_1)}$$

where $p_{k,n}$ is an estimator of the rth order statistic, X'_r with $r = (n + 1)p$.

3.6.9   Beta Distribution

The PDF of the beta distribution is:

$$f(x) = \frac{\Gamma(\alpha + \beta)}{\Gamma(\alpha)\Gamma(\beta)}u^\alpha(1 - u)^{\beta - 1}\frac{1}{x} \quad 0 < x < \theta,\, u = \frac{x}{\theta}$$

The CDF is given by:

$$F(x) = \delta(\alpha,\, \beta;\, u)$$

The parameters are estimated by:

$$\hat{\alpha} = \frac{\theta \left(\dfrac{\sum\limits_{j=1}^{n} x_j}{n} \right)^2 - \left(\dfrac{\sum\limits_{j=1}^{n} x_j}{n} \right) \left(\dfrac{\sum\limits_{j=1}^{n} x_j^2}{n} \right)}{\theta \dfrac{\sum\limits_{j=1}^{n} x_j^2}{n} - \theta \left(\dfrac{\sum\limits_{j=1}^{n} x_j}{n} \right)^2}$$

and

$$\hat{\beta} = \frac{\theta \left(\dfrac{\sum\limits_{j=1}^{n} x_j}{n} \right) - \left(\dfrac{\sum\limits_{j=1}^{n} x_j^2}{n} \right) \left(\theta - \dfrac{\sum\limits_{j=1}^{n} x_j}{n} \right)}{\theta \dfrac{\sum\limits_{j=1}^{n} x_j^2}{n} - \theta \left(\dfrac{\sum\limits_{j=1}^{n} x_j}{n} \right)^2}$$

3.6.10   Rayleigh Distribution

Lord Rayleigh derived the Rayleigh distribution in 1880, in connection with a problem in the field of acoustics. Since then, the Rayleigh distribution has been used to model lifetimes in reliability theory, as it has a linearly increasing hazard rate.

A Rayleigh random variable X has PDF:

$$f(x) = \frac{x}{\alpha^2} e^{-x^2/2\alpha^2} \quad 0 \leqslant x < \infty, \alpha > 0$$

The CDF is:

$$F(x) = 1 - e^{-x^2/2\alpha^2} \quad 0 \leqslant x < \infty, \alpha > 0$$

The moment estimation of the parameter is calculated by:

$$\hat{\alpha} = \sqrt{\frac{\sum\limits_{j=1}^{n} X_j^2}{2n}}$$

The likelihood function is:

$$L(X_1, \ldots, X_n; \alpha) = \frac{1}{\alpha^{2n}} \left\{ \prod_{j=1}^{n} X_j \right\} \exp \left\{ \frac{-\sum\limits_{j=1}^{n} X_j^2}{2\alpha^2} \right\}$$

3.7   APPLICATION TO A LEGAL EVENTS DATABASE

Perhaps the best way to check our concepts is to apply them to an exercise. Below we apply three distributions (exponential, Weibull and Pareto) to a legal events database shown in Figure 3.6. The units are US dollars.

Database of Legal Events for a Business Unit

3,821,987.00	630,200.00	360,000.00	250,000.00	200,000.00	160,000.00
2,567,921.00	600,000.34	350,000.00	248,341.96	200,000.00	157,083.00
1,415,988.00	556,000.00	350,000.00	239,102.93	193,500.00	153,592.54
1,299,345.00	550,000.00	332,000.00	232,500.00	192,806.74	151,000.00
917,000.00	505,947.00	301,527.50	230,000.00	191,070.31	150,930.39
907,077.00	483,711.60	297,035.48	229,368.50	186,330.00	150,411.29
845,000.00	426,000.00	294,835.23	220,357.00	185,000.00	146,875.00
800,000.00	423,319.62	274,509.80	220,070.00	182,435.72	145,500.50
750,000.00	416,562.38	270,341.11	220,000.00	180,000.00	143,000.00
742,651.56	410,060.72	260,000.00	214,634.95	176,000.00	142,774.19
734,900.00	406,001.47	255,414.00	210,536.56	176,000.00	
660,000.00	400,203.01	252,000.00	204,450.00	165,000.00	
650,000.00	394,672.11	251,489.59	202,077.38	165,000.00	

Figure 3.6   Legal losses database

An initial analysis with this database shows that the first four moments are as seen in Table 3.7.

A normal distribution clearly would not be the case here, given that the database is leptokurtic and positively skewed. Given the heavy tail, it would be a good idea to start trying the application with exponential-like distributions.

The database histogram plotted in Figure 3.7 confirms that the data is more concentrated until $600,000 and then the tail becomes heavy.

The three distributions were fitted using the formulas provided above and the parameters stated in Table 3.8.

I also performed QQ-plots to see how the distributions fit the data. This is seen in Figure 3.8.

Apparently the best model is the Pareto, as it differs least from the empirical one. Nevertheless, it can be realized that none of these models seems to deal well with the largest events.

It is interesting to perform formal tests as well. Table 3.9 shows the results of the Kolmogorov–Smirnov and Cramer–Von Mises tests.

None of the models has proven to give a great fit to the data. Perhaps we will need models that deal more properly with extreme events (see next chapter). Meanwhile, the best model, seeming to confirm our visual test, is the Pareto.

Table 3.7   First four moments of the sample

Average	439,725.99
Standard Deviation	538,403.93
Skewness	4.42
Kurtosis	23.59

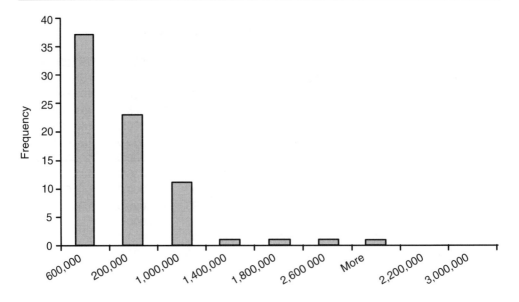

Figure 3.7 Legal losses histogram

The next step is to plot the quantiles (or the CDF solved for x: Weibull, $\beta(-\log(1-p)^{1/\alpha})$; exponential, $-(\log(1-p))/\lambda$; as a test, find Pareto's quantile formula). Once again, confirming the results above, the Pareto distribution seems to be the most adequate to fit the data, as seen in Figure 3.9.

Another way of testing it is to plot the estimated quantiles for the three distributions against the data. This is done in Figure 3.10.

The results are as expected. The Pareto distribution is the most aggressive but still not enough to cover the two largest events at extreme quantiles (98% and 99%). How do we deal with situations like this, where we need heavier tails?

In the next chapter I continue to show severity distributions, with the focus on extreme value theory, and how to deal with extreme events and skew/leptokurtic databases, typical in operational risk.

Table 3.8 Parameters for the exponential, Weibull and Pareto distributions

Distribution	Parameter(s)
Exponential	$\lambda = 0.00000227$
Weibull	$\alpha = 2.8312$
	$\beta = 380{,}225.32$
Pareto	$\alpha = 6.1737$
	$\theta = 2{,}275{,}032.12$

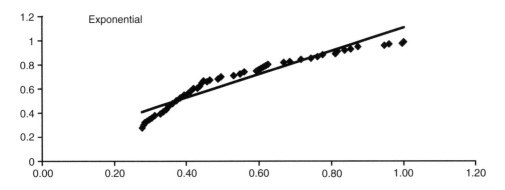

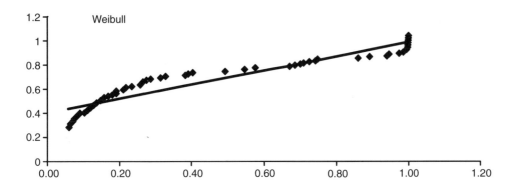

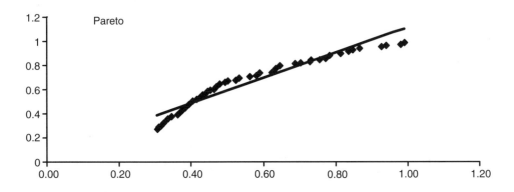

Figure 3.8 QQ-Plots of the fitted models

Table 3.9   Formal test results

Kolmogorov–Smirnov	
Exponential	0.2104071
Weibull	0.3687582
Pareto	0.1697013

Cramer–Von Mises	
Exponential	1.352537
Weibull	4.872570
Pareto	0.819777

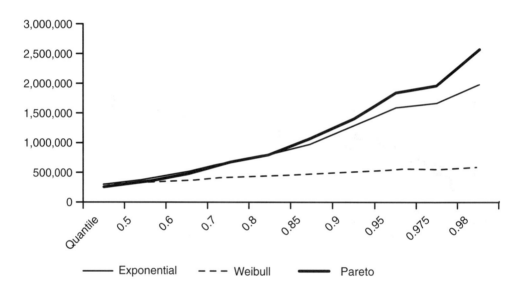

Figure 3.9   Quantiles for the exponential, Weibull and Pareto distributions

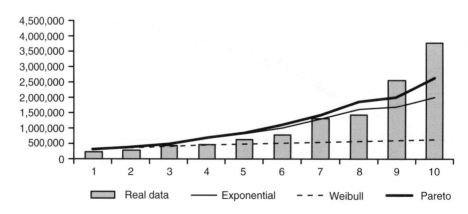

Figure 3.10   Quantiles plot for the exponential, Weibull and Pareto distributions

REFERENCES

Cauchy, A.L. (1853), "Sur les resultats moyens d'observations de meme nature, et sur les resultats le plus probables", *Comptes Rendus de l'Academie de Sciences, Paris*, 37, 198–206.

Cummings, J.D., Dionne, G., McDonald, J. and Pritchett, B. (1990), "Applications of the GB2 family of distributions in modeling insurance loss processes", *Insurance: Mathematics and Economics*, 9, 257–272.

Hosking, J.R.M. and Wallis, J.R. (1997), *Regional Frequency Analysis*, 1st Edition, Cambridge University Press, Cambridge.

Johnson, N., Kotz, S. and Balakrishnan, N. (1994), *Continuous Univariate Distributions*, 2nd Edition, Wiley Series in Probability and Mathematical Statistics, Wiley, New York.

Klugman, S., Panjer, H. and Willmot, G. (1998), *Loss Models*, Wiley Series in Probability and Statistics, Wiley, New York.

Poisson, S. (1824), "Sur la probabilite des resultats moyens des observations", *Connaissance des Tems pour l'an 1827*, 273–302.

Tweedie, M.C.K. (1947), "Functions of Statistical Variate with Given Means, with Special Reference to Laplacian Distributions", *Proceedings of the Cambridge Philosophical Society*, 43, 41–49.

Wald, A. (1947), *Sequential Analysis*, Wiley, New York.

Weibull, W. (1939), "A Statistical Theory of the Strength of Material", Report no. 151, Ingeniors Vetenskaps Akademiens Handligar, Stockholm.

4

Extreme Value Theory

4.1 INTRODUCTION

The application of the techniques shown in this chapter to operational risk arises from my interest in the study of extreme risks in the financial market. Extreme risks are, by definition, uncommon; nevertheless, significant statistical results can be obtained if the proper inference methods are applied and, especially, if we learn how to read the outputs of the model carefully.

The amount of data recording extreme events is, naturally, expected not to be large. Operational risk events, as disturbances of the regular day-by-day operations, will also frequently present a one-off characteristic, i.e. the events composing the database might not be frequent but could be significant in their impact relative to the size of the business unit. On the other hand, some business units or departments will also typically experience daily small events that, nevertheless, would also require economic capital to protect the business, and this might be calculated using traditional statistics.

The approach used here is very similar to that used in reliability studies and insurance. Indeed, the concept of risk management has been taken from the world of insurance. By choosing to use past events to estimate the future, we are building a framework very close to the methods used in reliability, insurance and even financial risk management.

One common difficulty with newly developed mathematical models is calibration. In extreme value theory (EVT), this is particularly important due to the number of variables, parameters and inputs coming from many different sources and frequencies of observation, as well as the likelihood of erroneous observations. Two special challenges for the models presented in this chapter are that they were the first to be presented formally to measure OR robustly, and the mathematical/statistical techniques found to be the most suitable are still relatively new.

The array of techniques presented in this chapter, consolidated under EVT, are typical of the above. There has been some criticism, mainly among statisticians, of what EVT claims to achieve; i.e. to provide reliable estimates of the chances of events that have never been seen before. I will try to show that EVT can do much better than empirical curve fitting, intuition or guessing. EVT relies on tested statistical techniques and its application to finance and insurance has to date proven worthwhile.

4.2 RISK MANAGEMENT AND STATISTICS OF EXTREMES

The concept of VaR, implemented by JP Morgan (see RiskMetrics 1995), has been considered to be the standard measure for market risk measurement and management. VaR measures the maximum estimated losses in the market value of a given portfolio that can be expected to be incurred until the position can be neutralized. In other words, VaR calculates an eventual extreme loss resulting from holding the portfolio for a determined period using as a measure the volatility over the last n days.

More precisely, extreme loss is the $100(1-\alpha)\%$ quantile x_p of the distribution. As a consequence, VaR estimates x_p for sufficiently low values of α. I will try to prove that a similar approach based on the same foundations of market risk management can be applied to operational risk (in this chapter used to estimate the severity of operational losses) by using EVT applied to "operational events" in a financial institution. Nevertheless, by applying EVT we will obviously be relaxing the Gaussian hypothesis of the market VaR models and the results would tend to be more conservative.

EVT has the mathematical tools to predict the chances of events that have never happened. This is very useful for several applications and, in this case, for measuring operational risk. It has been applied in reliability theory (Lawless 1982), insurance (Embrechts et al. 1997), telecommunications (Gumbel 1958), environmental monitoring (measuring sea levels, pollution concentrations, levels of rivers — Embrechts et al. 1997; Gumbel 1958) and more recently finance (Longin 1997). The application of EVT has been particularly important in the calculation of the probability of events connected to engineering (Davison 1983). In order to build a dam, for example, an engineer must calculate with a certain degree of confidence the level of a river in past years to infer possible future levels. In order to perform this calculation, just extremes (in this case floods) in determined time periods are considered. Another early application of EVT was in measuring human longevity.

The statistical aspects of reliability theory are very similar to those met in OR. Reliability, in itself, has many connotations. Applied to a person, it usually refers to his/her abilities to perform certain tasks according to certain rules and standards. The original use of the term was purely qualitative. In Crowder et al. (1991) an example is provided showing that initially, aerospace engineers recognized the desirability of having more than one engine on an aeroplane without any precise measurements of failure rate. No precise measure or quantitative estimate was attempted, other than the most basic qualitative measure. Today, reliability is usually a quantitative concept, and reliability theory deals with models and methods of measuring reliability. This is what might be expected to happen with OR, i.e. it will become increasingly quantitative.

The idea of linking reliability theory with OR has been tried before (see Chapter 7 for a discussion with examples). A financial institution reported the use of one "reliability" method called MTBF (mean time between failures) as a critical parameter to measure OR. The problem with this method is that it deals only with the frequency of the events. MTBF provides no measure of the impact of errors and frauds, only the mean interval between them, making it cumbersome to transform this into some monetary measure.

What makes extreme events in insurance and finance different from other extreme events is that they can (and should) be measured in monetary units. The use of EVT in this case is to forecast possible losses at certain levels of confidence, or to permit capital allocation in monetary units to guard against extreme conditions.

What EVT does in reality is to extrapolate, in a scientific manner, extreme past events to try and predict the future. For example, suppose that a bank has a database presenting two large events of similar size during the course of 5 years (see Figure 4.1). When EVT is applied to this database, it interprets that if an event of a certain magnitude happened twice during the last 5 years, one event of magnitude X should happen once every 10 years. This is a simple way of seeing it. That is exactly why, if an

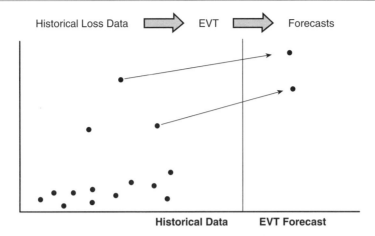

Historical Loss Data ⟹ EVT ⟹ Forecasts

Historical Data   EVT Forecast

EVT helps us to understand the patterns of events. If an event of magnitude X happens twice every n years, an event of magnitude Y should happen once every N years.

Figure 4.1   Simple view of EVT

analyst wants to know very high quantiles like 99.999%, i.e. events that happen once in 1000 years, the answer might be ridiculously high.

4.3   EXTREME DISTRIBUTIONS AND EXTREME VALUE THEORY

A typical operational loss database will present a distribution that is not Gaussian. In general, an operational risk database is composed of a few very large events and several smaller ones. Nevertheless, for some businesses, like an investment bank back-office, for example, due to the huge number of transactions processed daily, eventually a quasi-normal pattern of losses could possibly appear. For risk management purposes, we are interested in knowing the behavior of the tail of this curve (or the maximum losses). The question to be answered by the risk manager is: *"How much economic capital should I allocate to a particular business to protect against an eventual operational catastrophe?"*. The answer comes from analyzing the distribution of losses that arise from extreme value distributions.

The application of EVT, as the theory that supports this type of distribution, is known, but is still at an embryonic stage in risk management. A recent book with applications to finance was edited by Embrechts (2000).

Suppose that X denotes the operational losses in the database provided by the bank. Let $X_1, \ldots, X_n$ be the monetary losses observed in a certain period. Extremes are defined as maxima and minima of the n ordered random variables $X_1, \ldots, X_n$. Let $X_{1,n}, \ldots, X_{n,n}$ be the order statistics of this series, with $X_{1,n}$ denoting the highest value (the maximum) observed during the period; $X_{2,n}$ the second largest, and so on. To find a non-degenerate limiting distribution, the maximum random variable $Y = X_{1,n}$ is standardized by location, scale and shape parameters, chosen to give a proper distribution of standardized extremes. We therefore focus on the asymptotic behavior of the extremes.

Three important extreme value distributions are those defined by Frechet, Gumbel and Weibull. A convenient representation of these is given in the generalized extreme value (GEV) distribution. This three-parameter distribution $F_{\mu,\xi,\psi}$ arises as the limit distribution of normalized maxima of iid random variables. It can be represented (in the three-parameter form) as follows.

For the random variable $Y = X_{1,n}$, we let:

$$Z = (Y - \mu)/\psi \quad \text{and} \quad z = (y - \mu)/\psi \qquad (4.1)^1$$

where μ and ψ are location and scale parameters respectively. Then:

$$\Pr(Y \leqslant y) = F_{\mu,\xi,\psi}(y) = F_{0,\xi,1}(z) = \exp\{-(1 + \xi z^{\ 1/\xi})\} \quad 1 + \xi z \geqslant 0 \qquad (4.2)$$

where ξ is the shape parameter. Letting $\xi \to 0$ gives the Gumbel distribution; $\xi > 0$ the Frechet distribution; $\xi < 0$ the Weibull distribution.

$F_{\mu,\xi,\psi}$ arises as the limit distribution of normalized maxima of iid random variables. Standard statistical methodology from parametric estimation theory is available if the data consist of a sample:

$$X_1, \ldots, X_n \quad \text{iid from } F_{\mu,\xi,\psi} \qquad (4.3)$$

Proposition (4.3) above assumes that the X_i have an exact extreme value distribution F, which is maybe not the most realistic assumption. If a more justifiable supposition, that the X_i are approximately $F_{\mu,\xi,\psi}$ distributed, is assumed, we could interpret the X_i as belonging to a maximum domain of attraction (MDA). The X_i would belong to a suitable domain depending on the sign of ξ, the shape parameter.

Broadly speaking, GEV amounts to full parametric assumptions, whereas MDA is essentially semi-parametric in nature, having a parametric component ξ and a non-parametric component (a slowly varying function). Due to this difference, MDA is considered a better inference for heavy-tailed distributions than for GEV. For a more detailed discussion, please refer to Embrechts et al. (1997). The estimation under MDA of GEV is of relevance for heavy-tailed OR databases, leaving us with the job of estimating and testing just one parameter, the tail index.

Another very important distribution for measuring extremes is the generalized Pareto distribution (GPD). The three-parameter distribution $G_{\mu,\xi,\psi}$ can be defined by:

$$G_{\mu,\xi,\psi}(y) = \begin{cases} 1 - e^{-z} & \text{if } \xi = 0 \\ 1 - (1 + \xi z)^{-1/\xi} & \text{if } \xi \neq 0 \end{cases} \qquad (4.4)$$

where:

$$z \geqslant 0 \qquad \text{if } \xi \geqslant 0$$
$$0 \leqslant z \leqslant -1/\xi \qquad \text{if } \xi < 0$$

The GPD was introduced by Pickands (1975) and studied by Davison (1983) and Hosking and Wallis (1987) among others. It is often used in the modeling of large insurance claims and in reliability studies. The noticeable feature of the Pareto

---

[1]Due to the higher than the average number of equations in this chapter and to the fact that many of them are correlated, equations in this chapter are partionally numbered for convenience.

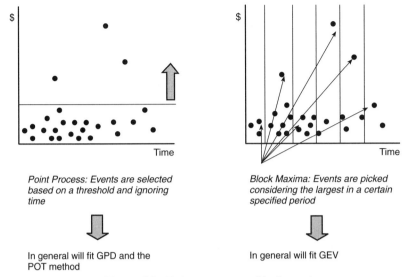

Point Process: Events are selected based on a threshold and ignoring time

Block Maxima: Events are picked considering the largest in a certain specified period

In general will fit GPD and the POT method

In general will fit GEV

Figure 4.2   Point process vs. block maxima

distribution is that the scale parameter is a function of a certain threshold to be determined by the analyst.

To simplify what has just been said, there are roughly two ways to proceed with the EVT analysis (see Figure 4.2). The first is based on the point process method, where we choose a threshold and ignore when the events happened. This approach is called peaks over threshold (POT) and in general would be fitted by GPD. The second approach takes time into consideration and in general would fit GEV (see Box 4.1 for an analytical test of the hypothesis for the GEV distribution—Zempleni's test). For risk management purposes the second approach might be better to sell to business unit managers. Otherwise, it is harder to justify that capital is being allocated to a unit for an event that took place many years ago.

The statistical tools to deal with both methods are basically the same. The POT approach is summarized in Appendix A and the block maxima are described in more detail later in this chapter.

4.4   APPLYING EVT TO OPERATIONAL RISK

The purpose of this book is to be as practical as possible. For this reason I would rather show many examples on how to deal with the basic techniques in EVT, providing some codes and examples in spreadsheets whenever possible, instead of purely showing the theoretical framework. With that intention, Figure 4.3 provides a summary of a fraud database in a major British retail bank. This data is provided on a monthly aggregate, instead of for individual fraud events. The reader might apply the techniques shown in this chapter to this database, and check if the concepts have really been understood.

This fraud data was provided by a large British bank concerning fraud events that took place between 1992 and 1996, resulting in 3338 observations (on a daily basis: the average is approximately three fraud attempts per day over 5 years). These are events

Box 4.1   Zempleni's Test of Hypothesis for the GEV Distribution

Zempleni (1991) proposed a test statistic to test the hypothesis of a CDF $G \in$ GEV against the general alternative of F being an arbitrary continuous CDF. The statistic is:

$$\Phi_n(X) = \sqrt{n} \min_{a,b} \max_x |G_n(x) - G_n^2(ax + b)|$$

where:

$$G_n(x) = \frac{1}{n} \sum_{i=1}^{n} I_{(\infty,x]}(X_i) \quad X = X_1, \ldots, X_n$$

The GEV fulfills the max-stability property (see Kotz and Nadajarah 2000), i.e. for any integer m there exist a_m, b_m such that:

$$G(x) = G^m(a_m x + b_m) \quad \text{for all } x \in \Re$$

Zempleni (1991) offered algorithms to optimize b for fixed a, finding afterwards an optimum value for a. First the optimal value is approximated via an iterative procedure, and then the exact solution is achieved through simple calculations. The results are checked against a table that is built based on the following calculation:

$$\Pr(\Phi_n(X) > r) \leqslant \Pr\left(\sqrt{n} \min_n \max_{x \in \{X_1,\ldots,X_n\}} |U_n(x) - U_n^2(x^a)| > r\right)$$

where U denotes the empirical distribution of the uniform sample.

Zempleni's test is conservative (see Kotz and Nadajarah 2000), and in the case that the shape parameter is $\geqslant -1$, the rejection is less frequent than expected. However, as the scale parameter increases the estimates become more accurate. The table with the critical values for checking the acceptance of the GEV model is as below (for several p and n).

Quantiles of the estimator $\Phi_n(\cdot)$

	$n = 50$	$n = 100$	$n = 200$	$n = 500$	$n = 1000$
0.1	0.583	0.604	0.616	0.630	0.635
0.2	0.636	0.664	0.676	0.693	0.699
0.5	0.775	0.800	0.808	0.826	0.834
0.8	0.919	0.956	0.976	0.988	0.997
0.9	1.015	1.044	1.065	1.088	1.094
0.95	1.078	1.126	1.147	1.174	1.177
0.99	1.226	1.282	1.303	1.338	1.350
0.999	1.43	1.46	1.49	1.53	1.54

Source: Kotz and Nadajarah (2000); Zempleni (1991).

	1992	1993	1994	1995	1996
1	907,077.00	1,100,000.00	6,600,000.00	600,000.34	1,820,000.00
2	845,000.00	650,000.00	3,950,000.00	394,672.11	750,000.00
3	734,900.00	556,000.00	1,300,000.00	260,000.00	426,000.00
4	550,000.00	214,634.95	410,060.72	248,341.96	423,319.62
5	406,001.47	200,000.00	350,000.00	239,102.93	332,000.00
6	360,000.00	160,000.00	200,000.00	165,000.00	294,835.23
7	360,000.00	157,083.00	176,000.00	120,000.00	230,000.00
8	350,000.00	120,000.00	129,754.00	116,000.00	229,368.50
9	220,357.00	78,375.00	109,543.00	86,878.46	210,536.56
10	182,435.32	52,048.50	107,031.20	83,613.70	128,412.00
11	68,000.00	51,908.05	107,000.00	75,177.00	122,650.00
12	50,000.00	47,500.00	64,600.00	52,700.00	89,540.00

Figure 4.3 Frauds in a major British retail bank

that happened in a single business unit. This financial institution has created a procedure in which all fraud events are reported to the risk management department in order to keep a useful database on these operational risk events.

The fraud report from which this data was extracted provides details of the potential and real loss of each fraud. We will use here the real losses caused by these frauds.

I next show, using the same data, how to estimate (and test) parameters, test the models and work with quantiles, the very basics of EVT.

4.4.1 Parameter Estimation

The most important parameter of extreme value distributions is the shape parameter ξ that describes the weight in the tail of the distribution. If the data fits an extreme distribution, the shape parameter would probably be significant. Otherwise, ordinary statistical distributions like the lognormal or exponential might suffice.

It will be important to determine, in addition to the shape parameter, the scale parameter ψ and a location parameter μ such that the distribution of standardized extremes $(x_{1,n} - \mu_n)/\psi_n$ (or Z as in equation (4.1)) is non-degenerate. The methods most used to estimate the parameters are: moments, probability weighted moments (PWM) and maximum likelihood (ML). I briefly describe how to estimate parameters using these methods, with clear emphasis on PWM.

Moments

This method is one of the simplest ways to estimate parameters. Nevertheless, the biases in the parameters are highly significant, and we do not suggest using this method. For the two-parameter GEV the formulas to calculate the parameters are:

$$\mu = \frac{\sqrt{6}}{\pi} S \quad \text{and} \quad \hat{\psi} = \bar{X} - \gamma\hat{\mu} = \bar{X} - 0.450041 S$$

Probability Weighted Moments

PWM consists of matching moments based on the GEV distribution ($F_{\mu,\xi,\psi}$) to the corresponding empirical moments based on the data. In order to estimate μ, ψ and ξ, we must consider the rth moment m_r and its estimator $\hat{m}_r$:

$$m_r(\mu, \psi, \xi) = \hat{m}_r(\mu, \psi, \xi) \quad r = 0, 1, 2 \tag{4.5}$$

We solve these three equations in these unknowns for $\hat{\xi}$, $\hat{\psi}$, $\hat{\mu}$. We can obtain in a straightforward way:

$$\hat{m}_r(\mu, \psi, \xi) = \frac{1}{n} \sum_{j=1}^{n} X_{j,n} U_{j,n}^r \quad r = 0, 1, 2 \tag{4.6}$$

where U is a plotting position (a distribution-free estimate of $F(X_i)$) for the sample that may be taken as $p_{j,n} = (n - j + 0.5)/n$, for example.

When $r = 1$, m_r would be the sample mean. To calculate for $r = 2$ and $r = 3$ we should plot the positions using the plotting formula provided above. The derivation of the formulas will not be presented here. This can be seen in several texts, such as Johnson et al. (1995). For the GEV, Hosking et al. (1985) derived:

$$m_r = \frac{1}{r+1}\left[\mu + \frac{\psi}{\xi}\left\{1 - \frac{\Gamma(1+\xi)}{(1+r)^\xi}\right\}\right] \quad \xi > -1, \xi \neq 0 \tag{4.7}$$

Since the exact solution for ξ from equation (4.7) requires iterative methods, the following estimators were suggested by Hosking et al. (1985):

$$\hat{\mu} = \frac{(2\hat{m}_2 - \hat{m}_1)\hat{\xi}}{\Gamma(1 + \hat{\xi})(1 - 2^{-\hat{\xi}})} \tag{4.8}$$

$$\hat{\psi} = \hat{m}_1 + \frac{\hat{\mu}}{\hat{\xi}}(1 - \Gamma(1 - \hat{\xi})) \tag{4.9}$$

$$\hat{\xi} = 7.8590c + 2.9554c^2 \tag{4.10}$$

where:

$$c = \frac{2\hat{m}_2 - \hat{m}_1}{3\hat{m}_3 - \hat{m}_1} - \frac{\log 2}{\log 3} \tag{4.11}$$

For the GPD the estimators of scale and shape parameters are:

$$\hat{\psi} = \frac{2\hat{m}_1\hat{m}_2}{\hat{m}_1 - 2\hat{m}_2} \tag{4.12}$$

$$\hat{\xi} = 2 - \frac{\hat{m}_1}{\hat{m}_1 - 2\hat{m}_2} \tag{4.13}$$

An example in a spreadsheet illustrates how easy this approach can be. See Figure 4.4.

Hosking et al. (1985) have also shown the asymptotic efficiency of the individual PWM estimators. It is important that the conclusion they reached was in terms of the

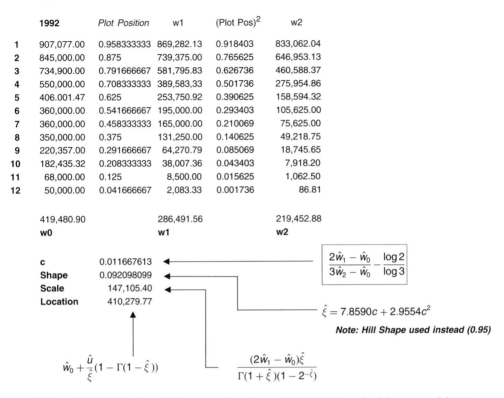

1992		Plot Position	w1	(Plot Pos)^2	w2
1	907,077.00	0.958333333	869,282.13	0.918403	833,062.04
2	845,000.00	0.875	739,375.00	0.765625	646,953.13
3	734,900.00	0.791666667	581,795.83	0.626736	460,588.37
4	550,000.00	0.708333333	389,583,33	0.501736	275,954.86
5	406.001.47	0.625	253,750.92	0.390625	158,594.32
6	360,000.00	0.541666667	195,000.00	0.293403	105,625.00
7	360,000.00	0.458333333	165,000.00	0.210069	75,625.00
8	350,000.00	0.375	131,250.00	0.140625	49,218.75
9	220,357.00	0.291666667	64,270.79	0.085069	18,745.65
10	182,435.32	0.208333333	38,007.36	0.043403	7,918.20
11	68,000.00	0.125	8,500.00	0.015625	1,062.50
12	50,000.00	0.041666667	2,083.33	0.001736	86.81

419,480.90   286,491.56   219,452.88
w0   w1   w2

c   0.011667613 ←
Shape   0.092098099 ←
Scale   147,105.40 ←
Location 410,279.77

$$\left| \frac{2\hat{w}_1 - \hat{w}_0}{3\hat{w}_2 - \hat{w}_0} - \frac{\log 2}{\log 3} \right|$$

$$\hat{\xi} = 7.8590c + 2.9554c^2$$

Note: Hill Shape used instead (0.95)

$$\hat{w}_0 + \frac{\hat{u}}{\hat{\xi}}(1 - \Gamma(1 - \hat{\xi}))$$

$$\frac{(2\hat{w}_1 - \hat{w}_0)\hat{\xi}}{\Gamma(1 + \hat{\xi})(1 - 2^{-\hat{\xi}})}$$

Figure 4.4   Estimating GEV parameters through the PWM method in a spreadsheet

small-sample properties of PWM. Most databases found in OR will present small samples.

Continuing, Figure 4.5 plots the scale and location parameters on a rolling 12-month period for the entire database.

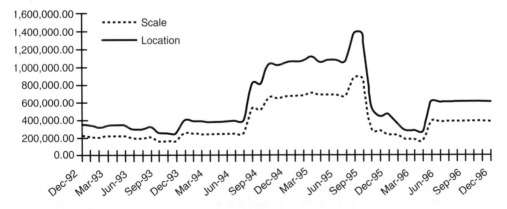

Figure 4.5   Scale and location parameters on a rolling 12-month basis using PWM

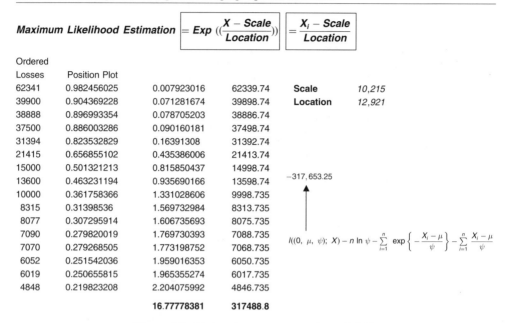

Figure 4.6   Estimating parameters through ML

Maximum Likelihood Estimation

ML is a very popular way of estimating parameters. It offers the benefit of flexibility, as the analyst can work with covariates or even redefine the likelihood function for special cases.

For the distribution $F_X(x) = \exp\{-e - (x - \mu)/\psi\}$, the log-likelihood function is:

$$l((0, \mu, \psi); X) = -n \ln \psi - \sum_{i=1}^{n} \exp\left\{ -\frac{X_i - \mu}{\psi} \right\} - \sum_{i=1}^{n} \frac{X_i - \mu}{\psi}$$

In Figure 4.6 we show how to estimate parameters using the ML method in a spreadsheet.

Performing ML in spreadsheets is very easy, however, it is also not recommended. All the sensitivity analysis is lost and the spreadsheets are not appropriate for this kind of task. Hosking et al. (1985) developed a FORTRAN algorithm for more efficient processing in this case.

Comparing PWM and ML

The advantage of PWM in relation to ML is its simplicity and straightforwardness. It also has a better applicability to small samples than ML (see Landwehr et al. 1979). As Hosking et al. (1985) noted, although probability weighted estimators are asymptotically inefficient compared to ML estimators, no deficiency is detectable in samples of 100 or less. The biases of PWM estimators are small and decrease rapidly as the sample increases. The standard deviations of the PWM estimators are comparable with those of the ML estimators for moderate sample sizes ($n = 50$, 100), and are often substantially less than those of ML for small samples.

		Shape $= -0.2$		Shape $= 0.2$	
		$Q_{.01}$	$Q_{.0001}$	$Q_{.01}$	$Q_{.0001}$
Bias	ML	0.01	24.84	0.78	$>10^3$
	PWM	0.08	0.47	−0.01	0.55
RMSE	ML	1.91	$>10^4$	$>10^2$	$>10^4$
	PWM	0.10	1.16	0.31	6.31
Median Bias	ML	−0.10	−0.15	−0.18	−0.08
	PWM	0.06	0.20	−0.14	−0.20

Note: GEV based on a sample of 15.
Source: Coles and Dixon (1998).

Figure 4.7   Comparison between ML and PWM parameters

In a study made in 1998, Coles and Dixon confirmed that PWM is less biased than ML for small samples. A summary of their findings is given in Figure 4.7.

Tail Index and Shape Parameter Estimation

The estimation of the shape parameter (ξ) is fundamental for the statistical inference of the tail of a distribution, especially if we consider using the distribution belonging to the MDA of the GEV and/or estimating quantiles above the sample.

The shape parameter is related to the tail index parameter (γ) by the relation $\gamma = 1/\xi$. Estimators for the tail index α do not assume that the observation of extremes follows an asymptotic distribution exactly, and in such a situation they can be more efficient than ML estimators.

A popular estimator of ξ was proposed by Hill (1975). It was proved to be a consistent estimator of $\xi = 1/\gamma$ for fat-tailed distributions (Pictet et al. 1996).

The estimator proposed by Hill is:

$$\hat{\gamma}_{k,n}^{(H)} = \left(\frac{1}{k-1} \sum_{j=1}^{k} \ln X_{j,n} - \ln X_{k,n} \right)^{-1} \tag{4.14}$$

Therefore, the estimated shape parameter becomes:

$$\hat{\xi}_{k,n}^{(H)} = \gamma_{k,n}^{(H)-1} \tag{4.15}$$

We provide below a simple program in Mathematica™ to estimate the shape parameter by the Hill method:

```
Create a variable r to include the data

r = { observation1, observation2, . . . , observation n}
lr = N [Log[r]]
k[i.] := lr [[i]]
X[i.] := Take [lr, i]
c[i.] := i − 1
```

$$\text{Hill}[i.] := \text{Plus@@} \left(\frac{X[i] - k[i]}{c[i]} \right)$$

In order to print a list of the Hill parameters along the database, I use the following code (in this example up to 20):

```
N[Do[Print[Hill[i]], {i, 2, 20}]]
```

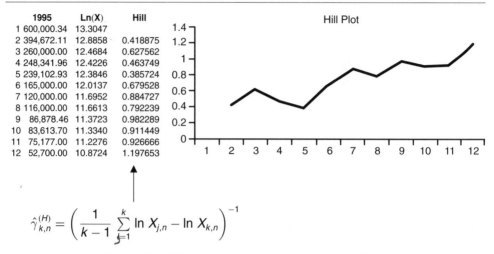

	1995	Ln(X)	Hill
1	600,000.34	13.3047	
2	394,672.11	12.8858	0.418875
3	260,000.00	12.4684	0.627562
4	248,341.96	12.4226	0.463749
5	239,102.93	12.3846	0.385724
6	165,000.00	12.0137	0.679528
7	120,000.00	11.6952	0.884727
8	116,000.00	11.6613	0.792239
9	86,878.46	11.3723	0.982289
10	83,613.70	11.3340	0.911449
11	75,177.00	11.2276	0.926666
12	52,700.00	10.8724	1.197653

$$\hat{\gamma}_{k,n}^{(H)} = \left(\frac{1}{k-1} \sum_{j=1}^{k} \ln X_{j,n} - \ln X_{k,n} \right)^{-1}$$

Figure 4.8 Hill parameter calculation in a spreadsheet

The Hill parameter can also be calculated in a spreadsheet on a one-off basis. For continuous calculation, we suggest using either the program above or another simple one in Visual Basic. An example of the calculation in a spreadsheet can be seen in Figure 4.8.

The Hill plot helps us to choose the data threshold and the parameter value as well. The parameter should be chosen where the plot looks stable. The example in Figure 4.8 uses a very short sample and therefore the parameter does not stabilize properly. Nevertheless, a value around 0.8/0.9 would seem to be reasonable.

The properties of the Hill parameter can be seen below. I refer the reader to Resnick and Starica (1996) for the weak consistency property, Deheuvels et al. (1988) for the strong consistency property and Embrechts et al. (1997) for the asymptotic normality property.

(a) weak consistency:

If $k \to \infty$, $k/n \to 0$ for $n \to \infty$, then $\hat{\alpha}^{(H)} \xrightarrow{P} \alpha$

(b) strong consistency:

If $k/n \to 0$, $k/\ln \ln n \to \infty$ for $n \to \infty$ and $X_{1,n}$ is an iid sequence, then $\hat{\alpha}^{(H)} \xrightarrow{a.s.} \alpha$

(c) asymptotic normality:

$\sqrt{k}\,(\hat{\alpha}^{(H)} - \alpha) \xrightarrow{d} N(0, \alpha^2)$

Other shape parameters and tail index estimators are those of Pickands (1975), Dekkers et al. (1989), Dekkers and DeHaan (1989).

In Figure 4.9 we plot the Hill shape parameter for frauds in a retail bank across the time.

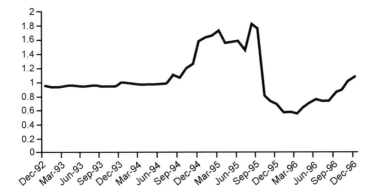

Figure 4.9 Shape parameter (Hill method)

Developing Confidence Intervals and Verifying Parameter Bias

Limiting the analysis to tail events in general means working with small samples. Therefore, the inclusion or exclusion of a single operational loss event may influence the shape of the tail, which is quite crucial in the analysis. Hence, it is important to test the robustness of the parameters estimated.

Two techniques may help in this sense: "bootstrapping" and "jackknife" (see Efron and Tibshirani 1993). Bootstrapping is used to obtain a description of the sampling properties of empirical estimators using the sample data themselves, rather than broad theoretical results, which are in general not yet developed for tails of the distribution. Let $\hat{\Theta}_n$ be the estimate of a parameter vector θ based on a sample of operational loss events $X = (x_1, \ldots, x_n)$. An approximation to the statistical properties of $\hat{\Theta}_n$ can be obtained by studying a sample of bootstrap estimators $\hat{\Theta}(b)_m$, $b = 1, \ldots, B$, obtained by sampling m observations, with replacement, from X and recomputing $\hat{\Theta}$ for each sample. The bootstrap sample size, m, may be larger or smaller than n. This is done a total of B times, and the desired sampling characteristic is computed from $\hat{\Theta} = [\hat{\Theta}(1)_m, \ldots, \hat{\Theta}(B)_m]$. We might approximate the asymptotic covariance matrix of the estimator $\hat{\Theta}$ by using:

$$\text{Estimated asymptotic variance } [\hat{\Theta}] = \frac{1}{B} \sum_{b=1}^{B} [\hat{\Theta}(b)_m - \hat{\Theta}_n][\hat{\Theta}(b)_m - \hat{\Theta}_n]'$$

The jackknife is a simulation technique similar to bootstrapping. In this technique we have to re-estimate the parameters by successively dropping a single observation from the operational loss events, getting n alternative parameter estimates $\{\hat{\Theta}_{-1}, \ldots, \hat{\Theta}_{-n}\}$. The pseudo-parameters originated by the jackknife can be useful to estimate the variance (or bias) of the parameters, as well as standard errors.

These techniques can be performed even in spreadsheets. I show a simple example in Figure 4.10, for an application using the normal distribution.

In the example I took a small (Gaussian) data set with 10 elements and estimated the location and scale parameters. After that, in the spreadsheet, I entered *Tools/Data Analysis/Sampling* and asked the spreadsheet to calculate 10,000 sets based on the

Data Set	Bootstrapping 1	Bootstrapping 2	Bootstrapping 3 (...)	Bootstrapping 10,000
1079.91	1638.01	1106.33	1710.59	1297.70
688.93	1638.01	1079.91	1297.70	1710.59
1297.70	1710.59	1079.91	1710.59	1079.91
1710.59	1638.01	1679.34	1893.25	1297.70
1679.34	1106.33	326.56	1893.25	326.56
1893.25	1638.01	1106.33	1679.34	1297.70
326.56	1710.59	326.56	1710.59	1297.70
1106.33	765.32	1079.91	1297.70	765.32
1638.01	1638.01	1106.33	326.56	1638.01
765.32	1638.01	1893.25	688.93	1710.59
Location	*1218.59*	*1512.09*	*1078.44*	*1420.85*	*1242.18*
Scale	*516.96*	*315.57*	*489.67*	*530.04*	*434.60*

Figure 4.10   Bootstrapping a data set

original data set (with reposition). Based on that, we can check the variability of the parameters. This can be extremely useful if you have limited availability of data.

An Analytical Method to Choose a Data Threshold

One of the most important issues when dealing with extremes is the definition of the threshold level. The establishment of this cut-off in the database seems to have no clear answer. Nevertheless, a few researchers have tried to develop methodologies that might help in suggesting a good threshold level.

There are a few methodologies available to calculate an "optimal" choice of k, such as Danielson and DeVries (1997), the text of Pictet et al. (1996) that provides a bootstrap method to estimate heavy tails, and the Monte Carlo simulations proposed by Jansen and DeVries (1991).

Below we show a simple algorithm proposed by Beirlant et al. (1996) that the reader might find easy to implement and, at least, suggests automatically a threshold level to be validated later by the analyst. The proposed algorithm works by choosing the estimator with minimal MSE and is processed as follows:

(1) Determine k_0 minimizing $\dfrac{1}{k} \displaystyle\sum_{j=1}^{k} \left(\log \dfrac{x^*_{n-j}}{x^*_{n-k}} \right) - H_{k,n} \log \left(\dfrac{k+1}{j} \right)^2$.

(2) Let $\xi_0 = H_{k,n}$.

(3) Plot $\left(-\log \dfrac{m}{n}, \log \left| H_{m/2,n} - H_{m,n} \right| \right)$ for $m = k_0, \ldots, n-1$ and determine m_0 by

     minimizing $\dfrac{1}{m-k_0} \displaystyle\sum_{i=k_0}^{m-1} \left(\log \left| \dfrac{H_{i(i/2),n} - H_{i,n}}{H_{i(m/2),n} - H_{m,n}} \right| - R_{m,n} \log \dfrac{m}{i} \right)^2$.

(4) For $\eta = 1, 2, \ldots$ perform:

     • determine k_η by minimizing $\dfrac{1}{k} \displaystyle\sum_{j=1}^{k} w^{\text{opt}}_{j,k} (\rho_\eta - 1) \left(\log \dfrac{x^*_{n-j+1}}{x^*_{n-k}} - \xi_{\eta-1} \log \left(\dfrac{k+1}{j} \right) \right)^2$;

     • let $\xi_\eta = H_{k,\eta}$;

- let $\rho_\eta = R_{m,\eta}$, with m_η determined by minimizing

$$\frac{1}{m - k_\eta} \sum_{i=k_\eta}^{m-1} \left(\log \left| \frac{H_{i/2,n} - H_{i,n}}{H_{m/2,n} - H_{m,n}} \right| - R_{m,n} \log \frac{m}{i} \right)^2 .$$

(5) Finally, let $\hat{k}_{\text{opt}} = k\eta$, where $\left| k_\eta - k_{\eta-1} \right|$ is smaller than a chosen tolerance level.

4.5 GOODNESS-OF-FIT TESTS

Having chosen a few models, estimated the parameters and fitted the data to them, we now need to find the best fit. There are two ways of proceeding: using graphical tests and analytical tests. I show a few of these below.

4.5.1 Graphical Tests for Extreme Value Theory

In these early stages of EVT the most reliable techniques to check the goodness-of-fit of the models are still graphical. Below we show a series of tests that will help the analyst to check the models.

Mean Excess Plot

At this point, the greatest difficulty we have in processing these shape estimators is in computing the appropriate number k of upper order statistics or, in other words, the number of tail observations for a set of distribution functions. From these estimators and the estimates of location and scale parameters we can (if we wish) estimate the distribution function and the high quantiles that will be necessary to allocate economic capital. There are some "goodness-of-fit" techniques that could help, among other attributes, in finding a suitable k. Mean excess functions (MEFs) can be used for various purposes, in particular to discriminate tails. The MEF of a random variable X can be seen as:

$$\text{MEF}(\tau) = E(X - \tau | X > \tau) \quad 0 < \tau < X_{k,n} \tag{4.16}$$

where τ is a chosen threshold.

A representation of equation (4.16) could be:

$$\text{MEF}_n(\tau) = \frac{\sum_{i=1}^{n} (X_i - \tau)}{\text{Card } \Delta_n(\tau)} \quad \tau > 0 \tag{4.17}$$

where $\Delta_n(\tau) = \{i : i = 1, \ldots, n, X_i > \tau\}$. (Note that $\text{Card}(x)$ denotes the cardinal number of x.) It should be plotted as:

$$\{(X_{\tau,n}, \text{MEF}_n(X_{\tau,n})) : \tau = 1, \ldots, n\} \tag{4.18}$$

As mentioned before, the choice of threshold is very difficult and could be helped by graphical techniques. As also pointed out by Embrechts et al. (1997), MEF can be used to choose an "optimal" threshold τ. Smith (1983) and Davison and Smith (1990) found it extremely valuable in processing the behavior of insurance claims.

One of the main uses of MEF will be in helping us to distinguish between light and heavy-tailed models. The steeper the line in the graph, the heavier the tail.

Taking τ when the graph looks linear makes it apparent that there is no single choice for the threshold. The researcher should compare the resulting estimates across several τ values.

QQ-Plot

Another graphical technique that can be used to verify the goodness-of-fit of a model is the so-called QQ-plot. This technique can be useful, among other things, to compare distributions. The plot should look roughly linear if the data were generated from a sample of the reference distribution. The heaviness of the tail of the distribution can also be checked. If the tail is heavy the plot will curve up at the right.

The QQ-plot formula is:

$$\{(X_{k,n}, F(p_{k,n})) : k = 1, \ldots, n\} \tag{4.19}$$

where $p_{k,n}$ is a plotting position formula that can be represented again by:

$$p_{k,n} = \frac{n - k + 0.5}{n}$$

I performed a QQ-plot on the 1995 database. The results are shown in Figure 4.11.

Z and W Tests

Smith and Shively (1995) developed a number of diagnostic techniques to check the fitness of the model. One of these techniques is called Z-statistics. These statistics are an indication of how closely the exceedances of a fixed level u are represented by a non-homogeneous Poisson process. They are calculated as follows:

$$Z_K = \int_{T_{K-1}}^{T_K} \Lambda_S(u)ds$$

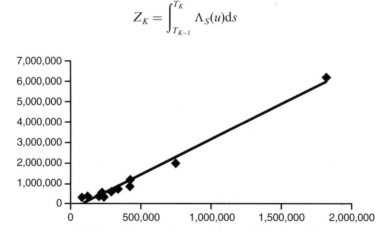

Figure 4.11   QQ-Plot for 1995 fitted to GEV

where:

$$\Lambda_t(x) = \left(1 + \xi_t \frac{x - u_t}{\psi}\right)^{-1/\xi_t}$$

and T_K denotes the time of the k exceedance. If the model is correct, $Z_1, Z_2, \ldots$ will be independent exponentially distributed random variables with mean 1. However, this statistic does not test the GPD assumption for the distribution of excesses over the threshold. This should be done through the W-statistic as below:

$$W_K = \frac{1}{\xi_{T_K}} \log\left[1 + \xi_{T_K} \frac{Y_K - u}{\psi_{T_K} + \xi_{T_K}\{u - \mu_{T_K}\}}\right]$$

where Y_K is the corresponding value of T_K. The model will be correct if $W_1, W_2, \ldots$ are also independent exponential random variables with mean 1.

Some plots using those techniques suggested by Smith and Goodman (2000) are:

(1) Serial correlation plots: showing if successive values of Z_K and W_K are independent.
(2) Scatter plots of Z_K or W_K against T_K: systematic variation of the Z or W values with time would indicate a trend not accounted for by the model.
(3) QQ-Plots, i.e. order Z_K or W_K in increasing fashion and plot them against the expected order statistics under the exponential distribution.

Box 4.2   Checking the Partial Results

In order to provide a better understanding of the methods, an application of PWM and Hill methods was carried out using the aggregated fraud database provided in this chapter. The shape parameter was estimated by the Hill method and the scale and location by the PWM. At this stage, it might be useful for the reader to check his/her understanding. The interested reader might test his/her skills by performing the analysis on the database and checking the results below.

Parameter estimation (PWM and Hill)

Parameter	1992	1993	1994	1995	1996
Shape parameter ξ	0.959265	0.994119	1.56577	0.679518	1.07057
Scale parameter ψ	147,105.40	298,067.91	612,300.60	25,379.83	361,651.03
Location parameter μ	410,279.77	432,211.40	1,101,869.17	215,551.84	445,660.38

The shape parameter was estimated by the Hill method and the scale and location by the PWM.

4.5.2   Formal Tests for Extreme Value Distributions

There are a few formal tests for extreme value distributions, noticeably the Sherman and an adaptation of the Kolmogorov–Smirnov. Most of these tests are based on testing the results of the model against a theoretical distribution. It must be highlighted that both tests tend to overfit (i.e. be too lenient), but can provide a rough basis for accepting/rejecting a model.

Sherman Test

Sherman (1957) developed a formal test based on the comparison of estimated and observed distributions. The test uses the series of ordered data denoted by $(X_{n,i})_{i=1,...,N}$. The statistic is computed as below:

$$\Omega_N = \frac{1}{2} \sum_{i=0}^{N} \left| F_{X_n}(X_{n,i+1}) - F_{X_n}(X_{n,i}) - \frac{1}{N+1} \right|$$

where $F_{X_n}(X_{n,0}) = 0$ and $F_{X_n}(X_{n,1}) = 1$. The variable Ω_N can be seen as the distance over the set of distributions and is asymptotically distributed as a normal distribution with mean $[N/(N+1)]^{N+1}$ and an approximate variance of $(2e-5)/e^2 N$. A low Ω_N suggests that the estimated and observed distributions are near each other and that the behavior of extremes is well described by EVT.

Kolmogorov–Smirnov Statistics for Extreme Value Distributions

As part of a statistical analysis that involves fitting a parametric model, it is always advisable to check the adequacy of the model. A formal test of goodness-of-fit or a more appropriate statistical analysis can be used. Here the application of Kolmogorov–Smirnov statistics is suggested for testing if the database originated from an extreme value distribution or not.

The test of fit presented here is based on the article of Chandra et al. (1981). They proposed a test considering the Kolmogorov–Smirnov statistics D^+, D^- and D and the Kuiper statistic V given by n observations $y_1, \ldots, y_n$.

It is important to mention that the test was originally prepared for the fitting of a two-parameter (scale and location) distribution and the inclusion of a third parameter (shape) could cause overfitting. Graphical goodness-of-fit tests such as QQ-plots (Embrechts et al. 1997) can be used to verify the fitness of the model but are handicapped by needing the intervention of the analyst in the tests.

The test is carried out by following the steps below:

(1) Put the observations in ascending order $y_1 < \cdots < y_n$.
(2) Calculate $F(y_i)$, $i = 1, \ldots, n$, where $F(y)$ is the GEV (as seen in equation (4.2) using the estimated parameters).
(3) Calculate the statistics D^+, D^-, D and V (defined as below):

$$D^+ = \max_i \left\{ \frac{i}{n} - F(y_i) \right\}$$

$$D^- = \max_i \left\{ F(y_i) - \frac{i-1}{n} \right\}$$

$$D = \max(D^+, D^-)$$

$$V = D^+ + D^-$$

(4) Compare the appropriate test statistic, multiplied by $\sqrt{n}$, with values in Figure 4.12. The null hypothesis that the data are from GEV should be rejected at level α if all the statistics exceed the corresponding table entry.

Statistics	n	Upper Tail Significance Level α			
		0.10	0.05	0.025	0.01
$\sqrt{n}D^+$	10	0.685	0.755	0.842	0.897
	12	0.694	0.764	0.848	0.907
	20	0.710	0.780	0.859	0.926
	50	0.727	0.796	0.870	0.940
	∞	0.733	0.808	0.877	0.957
$\sqrt{n}D^-$	10	0.700	0.766	0.814	0.892
	12	0.708	0.773	0.824	0.904
	20	0.715	0.785	0.843	0.926
	50	0.724	0.796	0.860	0.944
	∞	0.733	0.808	0.877	0.957
$\sqrt{n}D$	10	0.760	0.819	0.880	0.944
	12	0.767	0.827	0.889	0.954
	20	0.779	0.843	0.907	0.973
	50	0.790	0.856	0.922	0.988
	∞	0.803	0.874	0.939	1.007
$\sqrt{n}V$	10	1.287	1.381	1.459	1.535
	12	1.301	1.399	1.476	1.558
	20	1.323	1.428	1.509	1.600
	30	1.344	1.428	1.538	1.639
	∞	1.372	1.477	1.557	1.671

Source: Chandra et al. (1989).

Figure 4.12 Percentage points of statistics $\sqrt{n}\,D^+$, $\sqrt{n}\,D^-$, $\sqrt{n}\,D$ and $\sqrt{n}\,V$ when the parameters are unknown

Once again we use the fraud database to test the methodology presented in this chapter. The results are summarized in Figure 4.13.

The significance points given in Figure 4.12 were found for fitted values of μ and ψ, treating the estimate of ξ as exact. The test is thus less likely to reject than if a test — not yet available — allowed for the variability in the estimate of ξ.

There is no evidence for rejecting the GEV model even for very small significance levels α based on the Kolmogorov–Smirnov statistics. The parameters of the distribution were quite stable during the period considered, except for 1994 (which saw some exceptionally massive potential losses) and 1995 (when no major fraud was attempted).

4.6 WORKING WITH QUANTILES

With estimates of the parameters of the model we will be able to determine the quantiles, or the amount corresponding to the probability (p) of some OR event. In financial risk management the quantile chosen would be 90%, 95% or 99% in most cases.

From the point of view of the financial market practitioner, one of the most interesting questions is whether one has seen the largest event or if there are still larger ones. Risk management in financial institutions and the preservation of a stable

Statistics	1992	1993	1994	1995	1996
n (number of frauds)	586	454	485	658	798
ξ Shape Parameter	0.959265	0.994119	1.56577	0.679528	1.07057
ψ Scale Parameter	147,105.40	298.067.91	612,300.60	97,262.00	216,539.66
μ Location Parameter	410,279.77	432,211.40	1,101,869.17	215,551.84	445,660.38
$\sqrt{n}\ D^+$	0.110	0.090	0.287	0.105	0.156
$\sqrt{n}\ D^-$	0.002	0.085	0.065	0.045	0.095
$\sqrt{n}\ D$	0.110	0.090	0.287	0.105	0.156
$\sqrt{n}\ V$	0.112	0.175	0.352	0.150	0.251

For this example the largest fraud of each month of the year was taken to estimate the parameters for the respective year.

Figure 4.13   Kolmogorov–Smirnov test for fraud data (with fitted parameters)

financial system by regulators are indeed more concerned with what could happen under extraordinary market circumstances (say 1% or 5% of the occasions) rather than under normal market conditions (say 99% or 95% of the time). Once the parameters are known, the technique presented here can be applied outside our sample to consider possible extreme movements, guaranteeing statistical coverage of 95–99% of events.

Given that we have determined the parameters and chosen the size of the upper tail of the GEV distribution for the fraud data, the problem can be reduced to finding the amount of economic capital to cover operational risk. This can be achieved by determining the 100p% quantile for the GEV, and transforming to the 100p% quantile for the fitted fraud data distribution, namely:

$$\hat{x}_p = \hat{\mu} - \frac{\hat{\psi}}{\hat{\xi}}(1 - (-\ln p)^{-\hat{\xi}}) \tag{4.20}$$

An application can be seen using the parameters for the fraud database in 1992 at 95% confidence level:

$$\hat{x}_p = 361,092.23 - \frac{292,869.94}{0.98374}(1 - (-\ln 0.95)^{-0.989374}) = £5,656,815$$

Figure 4.14 shows the results based on the remaining years of the fraud database for various quantiles.

Due to the asymptotic characteristics of GEV, high quantiles such as 99% can present very high figures. Figure 4.14 shows that the quantile curve is very stable up to

p	1992	1993	1994	1995	1996
99%	28,113,271	26,992,371	144,659,944	1,012,706	38,023,601
95%	5,656,815	5,522,432	22,135,683	444,486	7,311,518
90%	2,808,238	2,760,593	9,693,673	335,950	3,547,268
85%	1,851,669	1,827,292	5,911,090	292,046	2,302,561
80%	1,370,670	1,356,118	4,124,980	267,195	1,682,761

Figure 4.14   Quantiles (£)

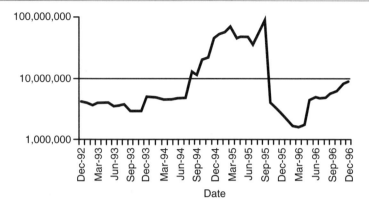

100,000,000

10,000,000

1,000,000

Dec-92 Mar-93 Jun-93 Sep-93 Dec-93 Mar-94 Jun-94 Sep-94 Dec-94 Mar-95 Jun-95 Sep-95 Dec-95 Mar-96 Jun-96 Sep-96 Dec-96

Date

Figure 4.15   Individual loss sizes (£) at 95% confidence level on a 12-month rolling period basis

the 90% quantile. The growth starts to be exponential-like after that. Given the asymptotic characteristics, our advice in this case is to avoid high quantiles such as 99.99%.

I also processed the results for a 95% confidence level of the 12-month rolling basis data (largest monthly event on a 12-month rolling basis). The results can be seen in Figure 4.15. It must be noticed that the y-axis is in log-scale.

4.7   BACK TO THE EXAMPLE AT THE END OF CHAPTER 3

At the end of Chapter 3, I tested the database below (repeated for convenience) with three distributions: Pareto, Weibull and exponential. The fit was not too good and I inferred that EVT would help us to improve the fit of such a database.

Database of Legal Events for a Business Unit					
3,821,987,00	630,200.00	360,000.00	250,000.00	200,000.00	160,000.00
2,567,921.00	600,000.34	350,000.00	248,341.96	200,000.00	157,083.00
1,415,988.00	556,000.00	350,000.00	239,102.93	193,500.00	153,592.54
1,299,345.00	550,000.00	332,000.00	232,500.00	192,806.74	151,000.00
917,000.00	505,947.00	301,527.50	230,000.00	191,070.31	150,930.39
907,077.00	483,711.60	297,035.48	229,368.50	186,330.00	150,411.29
845,000.00	426,000.00	294,835.23	220,357.00	185,000.00	146,875.00
800,000.00	423,319.62	274,509.80	220,070.00	182,435.72	145,500.50
750,000.00	416,562.38	270,341.11	220,000.00	180,000.00	143,000.00
742,651.56	410,060.72	260,000.00	214,634.95	176,000.00	142,774.19
734,900.00	406,001.47	255,414.00	210,536.56	176,000.00	
660,000.00	400,203.01	252,000.00	204,450.00	165,000.00	
650,000.00	394,672.11	251,489.59	202,077.38	165,000.00	

Given that I tested this database for GEV using the 12 largest events, fitting the data to GEV (through PWM for scale and location and Hill for shape), we find that the parameters are:

Location	1,085,091.15
Scale	305,088.17
Shape	0.60

The fit was indeed much better, as we can see from the QQ-plot in Figure 4.16.

That completes our example by showing that the operational risk analyst might always consider testing EVT for operational risk databases.

Figure 4.16   GEV QQ-plot for the Chapter 3 example

REFERENCES

Beirlant, J., Teugels, J. and Vynckier, P. (1996), *Practical Analysis of Extreme Values*, Leuven University Press, Belgium.

Chandra, M., Singpurwalla, N.D. and Stephens, M.A. (1981), "Kolmogorov Statistics for Test of Fit for the Extreme Value and Weibull Distributions", *Journal of the American Statistical Association*, 76, 729–731.

Coles, S. and Dixon, M. (1998), "Likelihood-based Inference for Extreme Value Models", working paper.

Crowder, M.J., Kimber, A.C., Smith, R. and Sweeting, T. (1991), *Statistical Analysis of Reliability Data*, Chapman & Hall, London.

Cruz, M., Coleman, R. and Salkin, G. (1998), "Measuring and Modeling Operational Risk", *Journal of Risk*, 1, 63–72.

Danielson, J. and DeVries, C. (1997), "Robust Tail Index and Quantile Estimation", *Journal of Empirical Finance*, 4, 23–32.

Davison, A. (1983), "Modeling Excesses Over High Thresholds, with an Application", in *Statistical Extremes and Applications*, T. de Oliveira (ed.), NATO ASI Series, Vimeiro, Portugal.

Davison, A. and Smith, R. (1990), "Models for Exceedances Over High Thresholds (with discussion)", *Journal of the Royal Statistical Society, Series B*, 52, 393–442.

Deheuvels, P., Hausler, E. and Mason, D.M. (1988), "Almost Sure Convergence of the Hill Estimator", *Mathematical Proceedings of the Cambridge Philosophical Society*, 104, 371–381.

Dekkers, A. and DeHaan, L. (1989), "On the Estimation of the Extreme Value Index and Large Quantile Estimation", *Annals of Statistics*, 17, 1795–1832.

Dekkers, A., Einmahl, J. and DeHaan, L. (1989), "A Moment Estimator for the Index of an Extreme Value Distribution", *Annals of Statistics*, 17, 1833–1855.

Efron, B. and Tibshirani, R. (1993), *An Introduction to Bootstrap*, Chapman & Hall, New York.

Embrechts, P., Kluppelberg, C. and Mikosch, T. (1997), *Modeling Extreme Events for Insurance and Finance*, Applications of Mathematics, Stochastic Modeling and Applied Probability No. 33, Springer-Verlag, Berlin.

Embrechts, P. (2000), *Extremes and Integrated Risk Management*, Risk Publications, London.

Gumbel, E. (1958), *Statistics of Extremes*, Columbia University Press, Columbia, OH.

Hill, B. (1975), "A Simple General Approach to Inference about the Tail of a Distribution", *Annals of Statistics*, 3, 1163–1173.

Hosking, J.R.M., Wallis, J. and Wood, E. (1985), "Estimation of Generalized Extreme Value Distribution by the Method of Probability Weighted Moments", *Technometrics*, 27, 251–261.

Hosking, J.R.M. and Wallis, J. (1987), "Parameter and Quantile Estimation for the Generalized Pareto Distribution", *Technometrics*, 29, 339–349.

Jansen, D.W. and DeVries, C.G. (1991), "On the Frequency of Large Stock Returns: Putting Booms and Busts into Perspective", *Review of Economics and Statistics*, 73, 18–24.

Johnson, N.L., Kotz, S. and Balakrishnan, N. (1995), *Continuous Univariate Distributions*, Vol. 2, 2nd Edition, Wiley, New York.

Kotz, S. and Nadajarah, S. (2000), *Extreme Value Distributions: Theory and Applications*, Imperial College Press, London.

Landwehr, J., Matalas, N. and Wallis, J. (1979), "Probability Weighted Moments Compared to Some Traditional Techniques in Estimating Gumbel Parameters and Quantiles", *Water Resources Research*, 15, 1055–1064.

Lawless, J.F. (1982), *Statistical Models and Methods for Lifetime Data*, Wiley, New York.

Longin, F. (1997), "From Value-at-Risk to Stress Testing: The Extreme Value Approach", Ceressec Working Paper, May.

Pickands, J. (1975), "Statistical Inference Using Extreme Order Statistics", *The Annals of Statistics*, 3, 119–131.

Pictet, O., Dacorogna, M. and Muller, U. (1996), *Hill, Bootstrap and Jackknife Estimators for Heavy Tails*, Olsen & Associates, http:www.olsen.ch

Resnick, S. and Starica, C. (1996), "Tail Index Estimation for Dependent Data", Working Paper, School of ORIE, Cornell University.

RiskMetrics (1995), Technical Document, JP Morgan, New York.

Sherman, L.K. (1957), "Percentiles of the *n* Statistic", *Annals of Mathematical Statistics*, 28, 259–268.

Smith, R. (1983), "Threshold Methods for Sample Extremes", in *Statistical Extremes and Applications*, T. de Oliveira (ed.), NATO ASI Series, Vimeiro, Portugal.

Smith, R. and Shively, T.S. (1995), "A Point Process Approach to Modelling Trends in Tropospheric Ozone", *Atmospheric Environment*, 29, 3489–3499.

Smith, R. and Goodman, D. (2000), "Bayesian Risk Analysis", in P. Embrechts (ed.), *Extremes and Integrated Risk Management*, Risk Publications, London.

Zempleni, A. (1991), "Goodness-of-Fit for Generalized Extreme Value Distributions", Technical Report, University of Sheffield.

APPENDIX A: PEAKS OVER THRESHOLD METHOD

Recently, with the popularity achieved by EVT, several alternative approaches have been considered for the application of these techniques. One very popular method is to look at exceedances over high thresholds rather than maxima over fixed time periods. This method is called POT, and has been used by hydrologists since the 1970s.

The mathematical development of procedures based on a determined number of extreme value statistics, as in the work of Hill (1975) and Pickands (1975), and the use of GPD as a stable distribution for excesses over thresholds, like in the work of Davison and Smith (1990) and Hosking and Wallis (1987), permitted the propagation of this method in several areas.

The POT method allows for fitting GPD models even with time-dependent parameters (scale, shape and location). The corresponding excesses over a certain threshold τ are independent and have a GPD. A simple and reduced way of describing the method can be seen below. A complete description of the approach is provided in the book of Embrechts et al. (1997), including a chapter on point processes of exceedances.

Assume that $X_{1,n}, \ldots, X_{k,n}$ are iid with distribution function $F \in \mathrm{MDA}(G_\xi)$ for some $\xi \in \Re$. Then, select a threshold τ. The number of exceedances to the threshold can be indicated by $M_1, \ldots, M_n$, $M_n < X_{k,n}$. The excess of the distribution function of X can be seen as:

$$F_\tau(m) = \Pr(X - \tau \leqslant m | X > \tau) = \Pr(M \leqslant m | X > \tau) \qquad (4.21)$$

Recalling the GPD function of equation (4.4), if and only if there exists a positive measurable function $\mu(\tau)$:

$$\lim_{\substack{\sup \\ 0 \leqslant x \leqslant xF}} |\bar{F}_\tau(x) - G_{\xi, \mu(\tau)}(X_{k,n})| = 0 \tag{4.22}$$

where τ must be chosen large enough and, subsequently, the parameters ξ and μ ($\mu = \mu(\tau)$) are estimated from excess data, so that the consequent estimates depend on τ.

Based on what we see in equation (4.22), we obtain as a natural estimator:

$$\bar{F}(\tau + X_{k,n}) = \bar{G}_{\xi,\mu}(X_{k,n})\frac{M}{n} \tag{4.23}$$

where M is the number of events above the threshold.

From the function above, a p-quantile estimator can be derived which will represent in reality the quantile with the formula (4.24) below:

$$\text{VaR}_p = \tau + \frac{\hat{\mu}}{\hat{\xi}}\left(\left(\frac{n}{M}(1-p)\right)^{-1/\xi} - 1\right) \tag{4.24}$$

5
Frequency Models

5.1 INTRODUCTION

In Chapters 3 and 4 we dealt with severity distributions and learned to estimate how severe operational losses can occur for individual events in operational risk. In this chapter, I show how to perform an estimation of the frequency of these events in the future.

This chapter starts with a list of probability distributions, and then we show how to apply the chi-squared test, with plenty of examples for operational risk databases. In the last part, state-of-the-art mathematical techniques are briefly discussed to deal with extreme events in frequency, similar to EVT for severity.

5.2 FREQUENCY PROBABILITY DISTRIBUTIONS, TRUNCATION, ZERO-MODIFICATION AND COMPOUNDING

The frequency distributions of interest for operational risk should be fewer than those for severity. One rough classification can divide frequency distributions into three classes: ordinary, zero-truncated and zero-modified. The ordinary are the usual Poisson, geometric, binomial, hypergeometric, etc. The zero-truncated are distributions in which there is no possibility of having the value zero, and therefore it need not be estimated. These distributions should only be used when a value of zero is impossible. As one can imagine, these types of distributions are not very useful in OR, but two are presented here for illustration, the zero-truncated Poisson and the zero-truncated geometric. Starting with a truncated distribution creates a zero-modified distribution in which is placed an arbitrary amount of probability at zero and the remaining probabilities are adjusted accordingly.

Frequency distributions can also be classified in terms of composition: simple or compound. Members of the latter class are obtained by compounding one distribution with another. In Section 5.2.6 we show the Polya–Aeppli, which is a type of compound (Poisson–geometric) frequency distribution that is very popular in OR.

Below are described a few of the most popular severity distributions.

5.2.1 Poisson

The Poisson distribution is certainly one of the most popular in OR frequency estimation due to its simplicity and the fact that it fits most of the databases very well. As truncation of databases is very frequently needed, the Poisson distribution proves to be an interesting and simple choice, since if a Poisson distribution fits an entire database, it will also fit a truncated database (with a different parameter). Poisson also has the interesting property of $Poisson(a) + Poisson(b) = Poisson(a + b)$. Therefore, it is easy to add or include more data without changing the analysis structurally.

The Poisson distribution (and process) is named after the French mathematician and physicist Simeon Denis Poisson. The Poisson distribution has probability mass function:

$$p_k = \frac{e^{-\lambda}\lambda^k}{k!} \quad k = 0, 1, 2,. . .$$

The cumulative function (a step function — discrete distributions do not have CDFs) is given by:

$$F(x) = e^{-\lambda t}\sum_{i=0}^{\lfloor x \rfloor}\frac{(\lambda t)^i}{i!}$$

The probability generating function is:

$$P(z) = e^{\lambda(z-1)} \quad \lambda > 0$$

The parameter is estimated by:

$$\hat{\lambda} = \frac{\sum_{k=0}^{\infty}kn_k}{\sum_{k=0}^{\infty}n_k}$$

The zero-truncated Poisson has probability mass function:

$$p_k^T = \frac{\lambda^k}{k!(e^k - 1)} \quad k = 0, 1, 2,. . .$$

where T is the truncated value.

The parameter λ can be calculated by:

$$\hat{\lambda} = \frac{\log\left(\frac{\sum_{k=0}^{\infty}kn_k}{\sum_{k=0}^{\infty}n_k}\right)}{n_1}$$

An example in a spreadsheet might be helpful to clarify this important distribution. Suppose we have the database of frauds in branches of a commercial bank as seen in Table 5.1.

The Poisson parameter λ estimated from this database is 4.88. Most spreadsheets will have the Poisson function predetermined. It is usually represented by "=Poisson $(x, \lambda$; True)" for the cumulative and "=Poisson $(x, \lambda$; False)" for the probability mass function. Using these functions, a plot can easily be drawn, as in Figure 5.1.

Just as an illustration, I again used the same fraud database (now yearly aggregated) as presented in Chapter 4, at this point, to determine the frequency of these extreme events over some specific threshold. With that intention an arbitrary threshold[1] of £100,000 was chosen. The results are shown in Table 5.2.

---

[1]All the maximum monthly frauds selected for Table 5.2 were above £100,000, indicating that a reasonable level for the threshold has been adopted.

Table 5.1 Number of daily frauds in a commercial bank

	No. of frauds in branches in a certain region
27-Mar-01	4
28-Mar-01	1
29-Mar-01	6
30-Mar-01	9
2-Apr-01	9
3-Apr-01	10
4-Apr-01	2
5-Apr-01	4
6-Apr-01	8
9-Apr-01	2
10-Apr-01	3
11-Apr-01	0
12-Apr-01	1
16-Apr-01	2
17-Apr-01	3
18-Apr-01	1
19-Apr-01	3
20-Apr-01	4
23-Apr-01	5
24-Apr-01	4
25-Apr-01	4
26-Apr-01	4
27-Apr-01	9
30-Apr-01	5
1-May-01	4
2-May-01	3
3-May-01	11
4-May-01	8
7-May-01	12
8-May-01	3
9-May-01	10
10-May-01	0
11-May-01	7

In cases like this one, where we truncate the data at a certain level, perhaps a transformed Poisson would be a better choice to work with. Some examples are provided below and a good reference for this type of distribution is Klugman et al. (1997).

5.2.2 Negative Binomial

The negative binomial distribution is probably the most popular in OR, after the Poisson distribution. Because it has two parameters, it has more flexibility in shape than the Poisson. In technical terms, perhaps most OR events will fit this distribution better than Poisson. The distribution has probability mass function:

$$p_k = \binom{k+x-1}{x}\left(\frac{1}{1+\beta}\right)^r \left(\frac{\beta}{1+\beta}\right)^k \quad k = 0, 1, \ldots, n; \, r > 0, \beta > 0$$

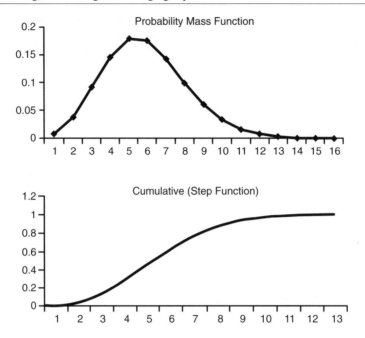

Figure 5.1 Poisson probability mass function and cumulative plot for the frauds in commercial bank database

Table 5.2 Frequency of extreme frauds ($>£100,000$)

Statistics	1992	1993	1994	1995	1996
n (number of frauds)	586	454	485	658	798
m (number over £100,000)	21	17	17	19	21
$\lambda = m/n$	0.03584	0.03744	0.03505	0.02888	0.02632

The cumulative function can be calculated by:

$$F(x) = \sum_{i=0}^{\lfloor x \rfloor} \binom{k+i-1}{i} \beta^k (1-\beta)^i$$

The parameters r and β are estimated by solving the following system of moment equations:

$$r\beta = \frac{\sum_{k=0}^{n} k n_k}{n}$$

and

$$r\beta(1+\beta) = \frac{\sum_{k=0}^{n} k^2 n_k}{n} - \left(\frac{\sum_{k=0}^{n} k n_k}{n}\right)^2$$

5.2.3   Binomial

Another important frequency distribution is the binomial. For samples in which the variance is less than the mean, the binomial might provide a better fit. The binomial portrays a situation in which a set of m risks is subject to a certain event. There are two parameters, m (independent and identical risks) and q (probability). The probability mass function is:

$$p_k = \binom{m}{k} q^k (1-q)^{m-k} \quad k = 0, 1, \ldots, m$$

The parameters (generally the value of m is known and fixed) are estimated by:

$$\hat{q} = \frac{\text{No. of observed events}}{\text{Maximum no. of possible events}}$$

$$= \frac{1}{\hat{m}} \frac{\sum_{k=0}^{m} k n_k}{\sum_{k=0}^{m} n_k}$$

5.2.4   Hypergeometric

The hypergeometric distribution reflects a process in which we are randomly sampling without replacement from a population and counting the number in that sample having some particular characteristic. The probability mass function is given by:

$$f(x) = \frac{\binom{D}{x}\binom{M-D}{n-x}}{\binom{M}{n}}$$

The cumulative function is given by:

$$F(x) = \sum_{i=0}^{\lfloor x \rfloor} \frac{\binom{D}{i}\binom{M-D}{n-i}}{\binom{M}{n}}$$

where M represents the number of groups of individual items, and D is a number that represents a certain number of a particularly desired characteristic.

5.2.5   Geometric

The geometric distribution models the number of failures that will occur before a success (p is the probability of succeeding). The probability mass function is given by:

$$p_k = \frac{\beta^k}{(1+\beta)^{k+1}}$$

The parameter β is simply estimated by:

$$\hat{\beta} = \frac{1}{n} \sum_{k=1}^{\infty} k n_k$$

The zero-truncated geometric is represented by:

$$p_k^T = \frac{\beta^{k-1}}{(1 + \beta)^k}$$

The parameter β is estimated by:

$$\hat{\beta} \left(\frac{1}{n} \sum_{k-1}^{\infty} k n_k \right) - 1$$

5.2.6   Polya–Aeppli (Poisson–Geometric)

An important compound distribution is the Polya–Aeppli. The probability generating function is:

$$P(z) = \exp \left(\lambda \frac{[1 - \beta(z - 1)]^{-1} - 1}{1 - (1 + \beta)^{-1}} \right)$$

The parameters are estimated by:

$$\hat{\lambda} = \frac{\hat{\mu}}{1 + \hat{\beta}} \quad \text{and} \quad \hat{\beta} = \frac{\hat{\sigma}^2 - \hat{\mu}}{2\hat{\mu}}$$

5.3   GOODNESS-OF-FIT TESTS

The goodness-of-fit tests for frequency distributions will have the same basic framework as for severity. We are basically trying to compare the discrepancies between the reality and what the distribution is predicting. We list one test below, the chi-squared test.

5.3.1   Chi-Squared Test

The chi-squared test is a very popular one and basically compares the actual result with the predicted one. The test statistic has the following formula:

$$Q = \sum_{k=0}^{n} \frac{(n_k - E_k)^2}{E_k}$$

The null hypothesis is rejected if Q exceeds $\chi^2_{d,\alpha}$ with $d = k - r - 1$ degrees of freedom (k is the sample and r the number of parameters). Spreadsheets also use this test applying $=$ CHITEST (actual_range, expected_range); the p-value is given by $=$ CHIDIST $(x$, degrees_of_freedom).

Continuing the earlier example of frauds in a commercial bank, we test the Poisson fit as in Table 5.3.

In Table 5.3 the Poisson fit is just the PDF $\times 33$ (the size of the sample). The fit looks reasonably OK, and a graph is plotted to confirm this in Figure 5.2.

Table 5.3 Testing the Poisson fit to the data

No. frauds/day	Count	Poisson fit
0	2	0.25
1	3	1.23
2	3	2.99
3	5	4.86
4	7	5.93
5	2	5.78
6	1	4.70
7	1	3.28
8	2	2.00
9	3	1.08
10	2	0.53
11	1	0.23
12	1	0.10
13	0	0.04

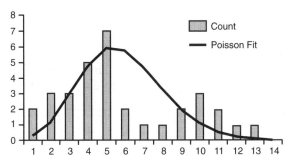

Figure 5.2 Real count vs. Poisson fit

Perhaps the differences found in the middle of the plot might indicate that eventually we should try and fit a few other distributions. However, applying the chi-squared test we get 0.000112521 and the p-value is 1. Bear in mind that small is good for the chi-test, and large is good for p-values. Formally, we might accept Poisson as a good fit.

5.4 APPLICATION TO THE FRAUDS DATABASE

It might be interesting to compare the fit of the Poisson and the negative binomial distributions to the frauds at the large British bank database, this time aggregated daily. As mentioned in Chapter 4, there are 3338 events distributed along the 1992–1996 period. The events, as per daily occurrence, happened as in Table 5.4.

I picked this database and estimated parameters for both distributions; the results can be seen below:

Distribution	Parameter(s)
Poisson	$\lambda = 2.379$
Negative binomial	$r = 3.51$
	$\beta = 0.67737$

Table 5.4 Frauds database — daily aggregation

No. of events/day	Observed frequency
0	221
1	188
2	525
3	112
4	73
5	72
6	44
7	40
8	14
9	7
10	2
11	2
12	4
13	3
14	2
15	1
Total	**3338**

Now we are able to fit the distributions and compare with the observed values. See Table 5.5 and Figure 5.3. The graph shows that both distributions reflect the observed data reasonably well.

The fit for the Poisson is slightly better than the negative binomial, although either can be chosen. Following Occam's razor principle[2], I picked the simplest. Picking the Poisson distribution also makes it computationally simpler to aggregate severity and frequency. Spreadsheets normally carry Poisson random number generators, but not negative binomial ones that would have to be programmed. We will see this problem in the next chapter.

5.5 EXTREME EVENTS FREQUENCY ANALYSIS

As seen before, estimating the frequency of operational events is very important to estimate the operational VaR. We have also seen in Chapter 4 that the study of the severity of extreme events is of particular importance to operational risk. In this section, we show that it is relevant in OR also to be able to estimate how frequently an event of a given magnitude may be expected to occur. Estimation of these frequencies is difficult, as for severity, because extreme events are by definition rare and the data record available is often short.

There is a branch of statistics, supporting especially hydrology studies, that is helpful in estimating extreme frequencies. In hydrology it is known as "regional frequency analysis" (for more details, refer to Hosking and Wallis 1997). Regional frequency

---

[2]"Descriptions should be kept as simple as possible until proved inadequate". *The World of Mathematics*, Vol. 2, J.R. Newman (ed.), Simon & Schuster, 1956.

Table 5.5 Poisson and negative binomial fit

No. of events/day	Observed frequency	Poisson	Negative binomial
0	221	309	543
1	188	736	657
2	525	875	531
3	112	694	357
4	73	413	216
5	72	196	122
6	44	78	66
7	40	26	34
8	14	8	17
9	7	2	9
10	2	0	4
11	2	0	2
12	4	0	1
13	3	0	0
14	2	0	0
15	1	0	0

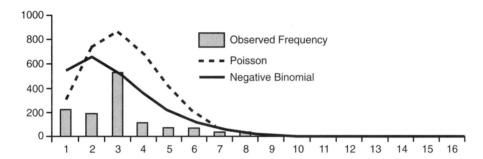

Figure 5.3 Poisson and negative binomial probability mass functions: frauds database

analysis aims at resolving the problem of estimating the frequency of extreme events by, as Hosking and Wallis stated, "trading space for time". In this case, data from several sites are used in estimating event frequencies at one site. In operational risk it can also be argued that the distribution for one sample can be estimated more accurately by using information from other related samples. At this stage, I think it is worth saying that I still do not believe external databases can be used in this case, because the samples originated from different organizational cultures, processes, etc. (without information on methods of data collection) and we might expect the results to be biased and irrelevant. Having said that, these restrictions might not apply for events inside the same organization. It is reasonable to assume that a global organization should follow minimal joint standards of processing transactions and dealing with externalities like legal suits and, for this reason, the pattern of the frequencies might be similar. In this case, if an operational risk manager is starting a measurement project and does not have enough extreme events in, say, London but does have in New York, they may be combined to perform reliable and robust measurements.

The study of the frequency of extreme events follows a few steps. Initially, we should perform an initial screening of the data to check for any gross inconsistencies. After that, we need to form the "clusters" or the group of businesses/products that will have similar frequency patterns (I will follow the name used in hydrology and call them "sites"). Following the methodology we will just fit (almost) regular distributions to the data.

One important difference in the estimation of parameters (the reason for the "almost" above) is that it would be interesting to use the method indicated by Hosking and Wallis to estimate the parameters of the distributions, the so-called L-moments method.

Nevertheless, the whole theory for using this methodology is extensive. I will cover just a small though relevent part. Below, I show how to create an operational risk index with the data available for similar sites, and then how to identify homogeneous sites for operational events.

5.5.1   Indexing Operational Losses

Indexing can be a convenient way to pool summary statistics from different samples. The most important assumption of this index would be that the sites form a homogeneous region, i.e. that the frequency distributions of N sites are identical apart from a site-specific scaling factor, which is this index. In hydrology, indices have been used since the 1960s (Dalrymple 1960; Hosking and Wallis 1997).

This procedure of estimating data assumes that the observations at the sites are not just independent but serially independent, and the frequency distributions are identical apart from a scale factor.

Suppose that an operational risk manager has data available from N sites, with site j having sample size n_j and observed data D_{ji}, $i = 1, \ldots, n_j$. If we assume $D_j(Q)$, $0 < Q < 1$, to be the quantile function of the frequency distribution at site j, we can then write:

$$D_j(Q) = \phi_j d(Q) \quad j = 1, \ldots, n$$

where ϕ_j is the operational loss index (OLI).

The OLI can be estimated by:

$$\hat{\phi}_j = \bar{D}_j$$

i.e. the sample average at site j. If we rescale the data as:

$$d_{ji} = \frac{D_{ji}}{\hat{\phi}_j} \quad j = 1, \ldots, N; \, i = 1, \ldots, n$$

we might assume d_{ij} as the basis for the regional growth curve $d(Q)$, $0 < Q < 1$. Assuming that the form of $d(Q)$ is known (we might know the underlying distribution) apart from p undetermined parameters $\theta_1, \ldots, \theta_p$, we can write $d(Q)$ as $d(Q; \theta_1, \ldots, \theta_p)$. Parameters can be estimated separately at each site. These at-site estimates can be put together in the regional estimate, using the following formula:

$$\hat{\theta}_k^{\mathrm{ALL}} = \frac{\displaystyle\sum_{j=1}^{N} n_j \hat{\theta}_k^i}{\displaystyle\sum_{j=1}^{N} n_j}$$

where "formula" means the at-site estimate of the parameters.

This formula is basically a weighted average of the at-site estimates. Replacing these estimates in $d(Q)$ gives the estimated regional growth curve:

$$\hat{d}(Q) = d(Q; \theta_1^{ALL}, \ldots, \theta_p^{ALL})$$

5.5.2 L-Moments in Estimating Parameters

L-moments, as defined by Hosking and Wallis (1997), are an alternative system of describing probability distributions. This method was derived from modifications in the probability weighted moments. The "L" means a linear combination of the expected values of the moments of a distribution multiplied by scalar constants.

As in operational risk, we might generally be dealing with events using order statistics (ascending or descending). It would be useful to have a justification for L-moments by considering linear combinations of the observations in a sample of data that has been displayed in order.

Suppose that we work with the sample in descending order, and call $X_{k,n}$ the kth largest event in a sample of size n.

Therefore, the L-moments of a probability distribution can be defined, in general, by:

$$\lambda_r = \frac{1}{r} \sum_{j=0}^{r-1} (-1)^j \binom{r-1}{j} E(X_{r-j,r})$$

where r represents the moments of the distribution. Using the notation above, the L-moments are defined by:

$$\lambda_1 = E(X_{1,1})$$

$$\lambda_2 = \frac{1}{2} E(X_{2,2} - X_{1,2})$$

$$\lambda_3 = \frac{1}{3} E(X_{3,3} - 2X_{2,3} + X_{1,3})$$

$$\lambda_4 = \frac{1}{4} E(X_{4,4} - 3X_{3,4} + 3X_{2,4} - X_{1,4})$$

The formula or system of equations to calculate the parameters will obviously vary from distribution to distribution. A short inventory of distributions and L-moment estimators can be found in Hosking and Wallis (1997).

Just as an example, the L-moments for the normal will be:

Moment	Parameter
1st	μ
2nd	$\sigma \times 0.5642$
3rd	0
4th	30π arctan

5.5.3 Identifying and Testing Homogeneous Operational Risk Event Frequency Clusters (Business Units, Products, etc.)

At this stage the analyst has already established a few plausible clusters of operational events. Now what is needed is to test if these clusters are meaningful and correctly chosen. A few formal tests might help us in this task.

A simple test developed by Hosking and Wallis (1997) can be constructed measuring the differences between at-site estimates and all the samples together. The test is:

$$S = \sum_{j=1}^{N}(\hat{\theta}^{(j)} - \hat{\theta}^{\text{ALL}})$$

In this test, the value of S is compared with a certain "null distribution" that S would have if the region is homogeneous. The calculation of this null distribution is made by inferring the form of the frequency distribution for the sites in the cluster. If the observed value of S lies far in the tail of its null distribution, the hypothesis of homogeneity is rejected because it is considered unlikely that such an extreme value of S could have arisen by chance from a homgeneous cluster.

Another formal test developed by Hosking and Wallis (1997) uses simulation to verify the likelihood that all the sites belong to a cluster or that the cluster was perfectly built. Basically we want to test:

$$\frac{\text{Observed dispersion} - \text{Mean of simulations}}{\text{Standard deviation of simulations}}$$

A large positive value of this statistic indicates that the observed L-moment ratios are more dispersed than is consistent with the hypothesis of homogeneity. Formally, the test will be given by:

$$H = \frac{V - \mu_V}{\sigma_V}$$

where H and V are calculated as below. Hosking and Wallis suggested that the cluster evaluation can be classified as:

H value	Classification
$H < 1$	Acceptable
$1 \leqslant H < 2$	"Possibly heterogeneous"
$H \geqslant 2$	Reject

In order to calculate V, we need to use the following formulas:

$$L - CV^{\text{ALL}} = \frac{\sum_{j=1}^{N} n_j t^i}{\sum_{j=1}^{N} n_j}$$

where $L - CV^{\text{ALL}}$ is the coefficient of variation (average/standard deviation) of the cluster and t^i are the L-moments.

Then we can calculate V as:

$$V = \sqrt{\frac{\sum_{j=1}^{N} n_j (t^i - L - CV^{\text{ALL}})^2}{\sum_{j=1}^{N} n_j}}$$

Now we have to simulate a number of times (500, 1000, etc.) a cluster with N sites, each having a particular distribution as its frequency distribution. From the simulations determine the mean (μ_V) and standard deviation (σ_V) of V and calculate H.

An example might help us to understand the approach. I provide loss data for a few sites in Table 5.6.

The criteria for acceptance are:

H	Decision
$H < 1$	Acceptably homogeneous
$1 \leqslant H < 2$	Possibly heterogeneous
$H \geqslant 2$	Heterogeneous

I initially calculated $L - CV$ (the L-moment coefficient of variation minus the standard deviation divided by the average) and found respectively 0.2411, 0.1219, 0.3160, 0.090 and 0.1695. Applying the formulas above, $V = 1.66$.

Following the methodology, I simulated another 500 sites based on the same distributional assumptions and the average (μ_V) was 1.56. The standard deviation (σ_V) was 1.26. Applying the H-test, we realize that:

$$H = \frac{1.66 - 1.56}{1.26} = 0.073529$$

Therefore, these branches can be considered homogeneous regions of operational risk.

5.5.4 Estimation for Sites with Data Not Available

Often, particularly at the beginning of a measurement project, loss events may not be available. Still, there is a need for measuring and understanding the risk profile of the unit. Suppose that a global bank is quite advanced in OR measurement in New York and the project is very slow in London. Typically some characteristics of the business unit in London should be known, as they would not be much different from those in New York, especially within the same organization. The few available data should then be used to assign the London business to a suitable cluster (it could be, for example, the Tokyo branch rather than New York).

Estimation of the OR index (ORI) for a business with the above characteristics may require further modeling. When the relation between the index and the business is not so clear, a more formal statistical model might be used. A simple example is a linear regression model relating ORI_i, or some function of it such as $\log ORI_i$, to a linear

Table 5.6   Loss data for five sites

Branch 1						
1506	1315	1135	1009	906	767	698
1394	1263	1133	969	883	759	667
1319	1140	1082	955	851	742	
Branch 2						
2100	1908	1729	1603	1499	1421	
1987	1856	1726	1562	1477		
1912	1734	1675	1548	1445		
Branch 3						
1321	615					
1129						
854						
Branch 4						
1678	1486	1307				
1565	1434					
1490	1312					
Branch 5						
910	718					
797	666					
722	544					

combination of the business characteristics measured at z_j:

$$\mathrm{ORI}_i = \theta_0 + \sum_{j=1}^{k} \theta_j z_j + \varepsilon_i$$

The model parameters can be estimated by fitting the model to businesses at which data is available. In this case, these business clusters do not need to form a homogeneous cluster given that the model represented above provides an adequate approximation for a wider range of clusters.

REFERENCES

Dalrymple, T. (1960), "Flood Frequency Analyses", Water Supply Paper 1543-A, US Geological Survey, Reston, VA.

Hosking, J.R.M. and Wallis, J.R. (1997), *Regional Frequency Analysis*, Cambridge University Press, Cambridge.

Klugman, S., Panjer, H. and Wilmot, G. (1997), *Loss Models: From Data to Decisions*, Wiley Series in Probability and Statistics, Wiley, New York.

Operational Value at Risk

6.1 INTRODUCTION

The VaR models, whose development began in the financial industry in the early 1990s, are currently considered the standard measure for market risk and used intensively in risk management. From a market risk viewpoint, VaR measures the maximum estimated losses in the market value of a given portfolio that can be expected to be incurred until the position can be neutralized. In other words, in market risk, VaR calculates an eventual extreme loss resulting from holding a portfolio for a determined period using as risk measure the volatility of the asset prices over the last n days. More precisely, extreme loss is the $100(1-\alpha)\%$ quantile x_p of the distribution. As a consequence, VaR estimates x_p for sufficiently low values of α.

In this chapter, I will show that a similar approach based on the same foundations of market risk management can be applied to operational risk, developing an "operational VaR", which is estimated by combining the severity and frequency models presented in Chapters 3, 4 and 5.

There are two fundamental differences in the market and operational VaR models. The first one is related to the fact that the application of EVT (or other fat-tailed distributions) makes us relax the Gaussian hypothesis on which market VaR models are based. Put another way, the stochastic processes underlying operational losses are by no means explained by a normal distribution, as one would expect in market risk (although this assumption is often questioned, even for market risk). The second main difference is that market VaR models are not concerned with the "frequency of events", as it is fairly assumed that asset prices follow a continuous stochastic process, i.e. there is always a price quote available for an asset while the markets are open. Operational losses follow discrete stochastic processes. By that, it is meant that they can be counted in a certain period, i.e. a certain operational event happens n times per day, which makes no sense in market risk measurement. Also, we measure by observed losses, not changes in MTM (mark-to-market) value.

For this reason, market risk managers are more concerned with the size of the losses than their frequency. In credit risk management the concern with frequency of default increases. Although the single use of the loss severity could be useful in indicating how large an individual loss may be, an operational risk model similar to that used in insurance mathematics and actuarial science includes the frequency and can be applied in operational risk to find the aggregate distribution for frequency and severity. This measure will designate the operational risk for a certain period.

A more simplistic approximation sometimes states simply that *total expected claims = frequency of the events × loss severity* (or, from a risk standpoint, *total unexpected claims = frequency of the events above a threshold × loss severity*). Nevertheless, this is a very crude measure and would not work for the job we are proposing, which is the parametric inference of losses generating a VaR measure. In this chapter we introduce a simple way to solve this problem, as well as several tests to check the reliability of the model. We also compare the operational VaR with more traditional market VaR models.

6.2   THE CONCEPT OF VaR AND THE DIFFERENCES BETWEEN THE MARKET AND OPERATIONAL VaRs

As the instruments in the financial markets become more and more sophisticated, and the impact they could have on financial institutions is devastating, banks have developed methodologies to combine all the risks into one single measure, called VaR. From a market risk point of view, this risk tool basically tries to answer the question "How much could we lose given our current portfolio, up to some given level of confidence, over a stated period of time?". This is perhaps the greatest advantage of VaR, trying to put into a single, easy to comprehend, measure the downside risk of a bank based on the financial market variables. In a few words, VaR summarizes the expected maximum loss over a target horizon within a given confidence interval.

In measuring market VaR, we need to set a confidence interval (99%, 95%, etc.), set a time horizon (10 days, 1 day, etc.), measure the volatility of the risk factors (6-month interest rate, a particular stock, etc.) and know the position of each asset marked-to-market.

Roughly speaking, considering that our portfolio is composed solely of 10 million shares of stock ABCD bought at $10 (and the market today closed at $10), with volatility 20% and for a 10-day period with 99% confidence, the maximum loss would be around $9.2 million.

This type of information is particularly important when increasing the sophistication of a portfolio, and helps with a number of decisions (for a discussion of these see Chapter 11).

Nevertheless, the differences from the operational VaR, that will start to be presented in the next section, are remarkable, although the benefits are the same. In the financial markets, in most cases, prices are continuous, meaning that you can have a price quote continuously as long as the market is open. In probabilistic terms, the events will, in general, follow a stochastic process known as Brownian motion.

On the other hand, in operational risk, the events follow a discrete pattern. The stochastic processes on which OR is based are Poisson processes, mixed Poisson processes, Cox processes, etc. (for a brief discussion of these see Chapter 7). These processes change the way risk is calculated relative to the market VaR, but the concept of VaR is unaltered by them. We are still going to be measuring how large the aggregated risk is for a certain time horizon and with a certain degree of confidence.

Another remarkable difference is that in market VaR we could know (or could stress test) how eventual changes in price OR risk factors would affect the entire VaR. In operational risk, as the factor changes are exogenous to the system, we will need an auxiliary model to stress test it. These models will be seen in Part IV.

6.3   AGGREGATED RISK MODELS

In actuarial science there are two basic risk models to estimate the total losses for the period: the individual and the collective risk models. The scheme can be valid for operational risk as well, with a few adaptations. The details of such models can be seen in Klugman et al. (1997).

In summary, the aggregated operational losses can be seen as a sum (S) of a random number (N) of individual operational losses ($X_1, \ldots, X_N$). This sum can be represented by:

$$S = X_1, \ldots, X_N \quad N = 0, 1, 2, \ldots$$

The collective risk model assumes the losses X_j are iid random variables. In this model the distribution of N (frequency) is independent of the values of X_j (severity).

The individual risk model characterizes the aggregate as a sum of a fixed number of losses. Such models are used in insurance to sum up the losses from a particular contract. In operational risk they can be used in terms of a fixed number of a particular loss type.

The separation of the severity and frequency processes is important because it allows, for example, a better understanding of the effect on the aggregate distribution of changing data threshold levels.

6.4   AGGREGATING THE SEVERITY AND FREQUENCY DISTRIBUTIONS

Having calculated separately both the severity and frequency processes (as seen in Chapters 3, 4 and 5), we now need to combine them into one aggregated loss distribution that allows us to predict a figure for the operational losses with a degree of confidence (see Figure 6.1). I provide below the formal theoretical results and a practical way of putting them together.

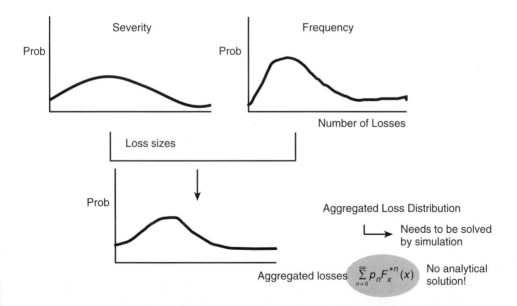

Figure 6.1   Aggregating severity and frequency models

6.4.1 Formal Results

The aggregated losses at time t given by $X(t) = \sum_{i=1}^{N(t)} U_i$ have the distribution function (where U represents the individual operational losses):

$$F_{X(t)}(x) = \Pr(X(t) \leqslant x) = \Pr\left(\sum_{i=1}^{N(t)} U_i \leqslant x\right)$$

The derivation of an explicit formula for $F_{X(t)}(x)$ is, in most cases, impossible. It is usually assumed that the processes $\{N(t)\}$ and $\{U_n\}$ are stochastically independent. Deriving the formula above, we see the following fundamental relation:

$$F_{X(t)}(x) = \Pr(X(t) \leqslant x) = \Pr\left(\sum_{i,k=0,1}^{\infty} p_k(t) F_U^{*k}(x)\right)$$

where F_U^{*k} refers to the kth convolution of F_U with itself, i.e. $F_U^{*k}(x) = \Pr(U_1 + \cdots + U_k \leqslant x)$, the distribution function of the sum of k independent random variables with the same distribution as U. As I mentioned before, the formula above can hardly be solved analytically. We must rely on approximations, expansions, recursions or numerical algorithms.

If the frequency of operational events is very large, we must imagine that the central limit effect will be dominant. A large-scale approximation like:

$$F_{X(t)}(t) \approx \Phi\left(\frac{x - EX(t)}{\sqrt{\operatorname{Var} X(t)}}\right)$$

where $\Phi(x)$ denotes the standard normal distribution, might be feasible. Nevertheless, these large-scale approximations have often been proven unreliable by actuarial researchers. Practitioners have tried to avoid this shortcoming by applying refined versions of the central limit theory. Examples are applications of Edgeworth expansions and Gram–Charlier series, but they do not always result in satisfying improvements.

6.4.2 Practical Solution

There is no exact solution or simplistic way of aggregating the frequency and severity distribution. There are quite a few solutions for the problem applying fast Fourier transforms to the distributions. The simplest is through a simulation that can be done even in spreadsheets.

Nevertheless, depending on the size of the frequency distributions, spreadsheets running on personal computers might take several hours to solve the aggregation problem. In practice, the analyst will have to run several aggregations (for example, Poisson/lognormal, negative binomial/GEV, etc.) to pick the best one (using the criteria and methods stated in Chapters 3, 4 and 5). After that, as we will see in the next section, several backtest procedures should be run, and these can be quite time-consuming as well. The technical solution for this pitfall is to run these simulations in mainframe computers, although it must be highlighted that this problem would only occur when several thousand data points were available. For small databases a PC would do the job very well.

The simulation can be run in a spreadsheet using a simple VBA[1] code. I provide in Figure 6.2 an example of a Poisson/lognormal aggregation in a spreadsheet. In one column (second from the left—"FREQUENCY"), we generate Poisson random numbers with $\lambda = 1.2$. This can easily be done in spreadsheets by going to *Tools/Data Analysis/Random Number Generation* and choosing Poisson with parameter 1.2. In order to perform the severity we should generate as many uniform random variables as demanded by the frequency. For example, if the frequency states "3", we should generate three uniform random numbers. These uniform random numbers will be equivalent to p, i.e. the probability that helps us find the quantile in the lognormal function. The quantile in the lognormal function is calculated in a spreadsheet by the function " $= loginv$ (p, location, scale)".

After processing this scheme 10,000 or 100,000 times (Run # is stated in the first column), the results need to be summed up. This is done in the "TOTAL" column. The more we perform the runs, the more stable the final aggregated loss distribution will be. Afterwards, we just need to order the results to get the aggregated distribution. The quantiles are obtained simply by dividing the position by the number of runs. For example, the highest quantile for 10,000 runs will be 99.99% (or 1/10,000).

What we are doing in reality is a kind of structured scenario analysis. Supposing that each row is a day, what we are saying with this simulation is that in the next 10,000 or 100,000 days, considering our "past experience" average of 1.2 events per day following a lognormal pattern, we can predict how severe operational losses will be.

6.5   COHERENT MEASURES OF RISK

Measures of risk have been proposed for quite a long time. However, just recently research was done to find desirable properties for such risk measures. Artzner et al. (1999) developed a list of properties for which risk measures can be considered "coherent".

According to Artzner et al., a coherent risk measure ρ assigns a number $\rho(X)$ to each position with future net worth X, in a way that satisfies the following generalization for the properties for the shortfall approach. For each pair of risks X and Y (correlated or not), as well as for each number n and each positive number t, all the following relations must be satisfied.

6.5.1   Sub-Additivity, $\rho(X + Y) \leqslant \rho(X) + \rho(Y)$

This measure tries to guarantee that the risk behaves reasonably when adding two positions. The sum of two or more risks should be less than or equal to the risks individually. This allows for the individual measurement of risks inside the financial institution, as the sum of the individual measures is conservative.

---

[1]Visual Basic Application—a Microsoft software that allows us to run visual basic code in other applications as Excel spreadsheets.

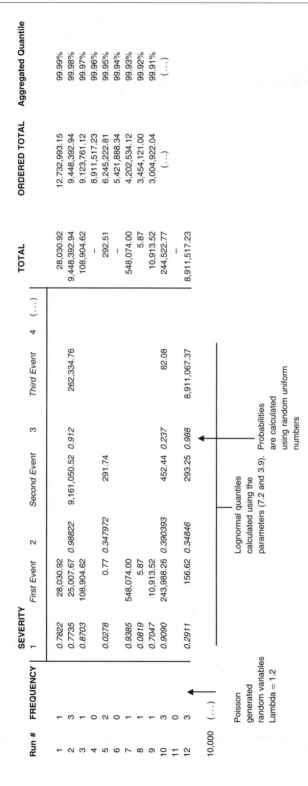

Run #	FREQUENCY	SEVERITY								TOTAL	ORDERED TOTAL	Aggregated Quantile
		First Event 1	2	*Second Event* 3		*Third Event* 4		(…)				
1	1	0.7822	28,030.92							28,030.92	12,732,993.15	99.99%
2	3	0.7735	25,007.67	0.98822	9,161,050.52	0.912	262,334.76			9,448,392.94	9,448,392.94	99.98%
3	1	0.8703	108,904.62							108,904.62	9,123,761.12	99.97%
4	0									–	8,911,517.23	99.96%
5	2	0.0278	0.77	0.347972	291.74					292.51	6,245,222.81	99.95%
6	0									–	5,421,888.34	99.94%
7	1	0.9385	548,074.00							548,074.00	4,202,534.12	99.93%
8	1	0.0819	5.87							5.87	3,454,121.00	99.92%
9	1	0.7047	10,913.52							10,913.52	3,004,922.04	99.91%
10	3	0.9090	243,988.26	0.390393	452.44	0.237	82.08			244,522.77	(…)	(…)
11	0									–		
12	3	0.2911	156.62	0.34846	293.25	0.988	8,911,067.37			8,911,517.23		
10,000	(…)											

Poisson generated random variables Lambda = 1.2

Lognormal quantiles calculated using the parameters (7.2 and 3.9). Probabilities are calculated using random uniform numbers

Figure 6.2   Aggregating frequency and severity by simulation — spreadsheet example

6.5.2   Homogeneity, $\rho(tX) = t\rho(X)$

This property tries to ensure that if you increase your position, you will still have a reliable risk measure.

6.5.3   Risk-Free Condition, $\rho(X + rn) = \rho(X) - n$

This property ensures that when a quantity n, invested at a risk-free rate r, is added to the position under scrutiny, the additional capital requirement is diminished by n.

6.5.4   Monotonicity, $\rho(X) \geqslant \rho(X) - n$

According to the authors, the market VaR will not be a coherent measure as it is not sub-additive. On the other hand, the operational VaR as measured here is coherent since it follows a "shortfall approach". We are measuring the negative of the net worth of several future positions as a scenario analysis.

Artzner et al. (1999) show that the market VaR measure fails to satisfy the sub-additivity property. This becomes evident in the combination of short options positions that can create large losses, with very low probability though, and low VaR aggregated to generate portfolios with larger VaR.

However, the operational VaR as seen in this book is generally based on shortfall distributions like those used in EVT, meaning that the expected loss conditional on exceeding VaR is a "coherent" risk measure.

6.6   BACKTESTING THE OPERATIONAL VaR MODEL

Backtesting, as the name suggests, is the sequential testing of a model against reality to check the accuracy of its predictions. The model outcomes are compared with the actual results during a certain period. The results of the backtest are used to validate a model and in risk management (more specifically in market risk measurement), regulators use them to verify the degree of accuracy of a model, imposing higher multipliers or even rejecting models that do not fit accordingly predetermined minimum standards.

Given the importance of this phase of modeling, some statistics may also help to verify the likelihood of the model not being appropriate, or test the hypothesis that we are either accepting a bad model or rejecting a good one. Basically, we are concerned with four broad types of test that provide us with knowledge of:

(1) *The clustering of the violations*
    This can eventually indicate that the risk model was not able to protect against unexpected losses, or even that a sequence of violations can be explained for one single event.
(2) *The frequency of the violations*
    This must be tested statistically to see whether they are inside acceptable boundaries.
(3) *The size of the violations*
    It is very important to visualize the size of the model error when a violation occurs. For example, if the operational VaR for a certain period was $1 million and the reality shows us losing $3 million, how could we be so wrong? In practice this is very important, particularly in global banks, and especially when we know that the

model is being analyzed by several different analysts. It is important to predefine the boundaries for the acceptance of the model (should a $2 million error in a certain period indicate that the model is bad?).

(4) *The size of the over/under-allocation of capital*
Despite being chosen by the analyst, the balance between risk/capital must be carefully understood and justified. If the average operational losses are in the range of $1 million/day, we eventually do not want to allocate $10 million/day in operational risk capital, as it would probably be overkill. The size of the error matters.

When considering the establishment of a framework for statistical testing, it is sensible to ensure the availability of a large enough set of reliable information on which to base the test. Intuitively, it is obvious that to estimate very unlikely events, one needs a substantial amount of data, especially if the operational VaR is measured for larger holding periods, like monthly or yearly. If the analyst wants to find a "one in 5-year event", the best way is to have a 5-year database. Although some robust statistical techniques deal with such situations (e.g. extreme value theory, structured scenario analysis), a lengthy database is the surest way to affirm that an event just happened once in the last *x* years. It is also relevant to mention that the model violations tend to be reduced the more data we have, because the models tend to get more robust over time. Therefore, a higher than expected number of violations should not be a surprise in the early days of backtesting a model in which the data started to be collected recently.

6.6.1 Backtesting Analytical Framework

The operational VaR model determines that two stochastic processes must initially be fit separately: severity and frequency of the loss distributions. The aggregation of these processes generates the operational VaR that must represent the operational losses during a predetermined period.

These sets of tests should one day be officially responsible for the determination of the capital charges on operational risk at most banks. Therefore, the backtesting and validation of the VaR model (and all its assumptions) are the way to prove that the model is reflecting appropriately the pattern of losses inside the specified period.

As a general rule, models just try to reflect reality, and therefore differences between the prediction and the real outcome must always be expected. We must correct the model based on this reality check to improve the quality of the predictions.

The operational risk backtesting analysis process is composed of two stages. In the first one, the basic, just a summary of the findings is provided to the analyst. If the model is not fitting very well this will be reflected clearly in this summary, and the analyst can go back and change the model assumptions immediately. If the basic test passes, the analyst can go to the second stage, the statistical analysis of the backtest, and double-check if any potential problems exist in the model.

An overview of the stages of the backtesting process is depicted in Figure 6.3.

The steps indicated in the figure are explained below with examples. The basic analysis is explained in Section 6.6.2. There are quite a few statistical tests that might be applied to the operational VaR models. Most of them are already used in backtesting market VaR models. A new test developed by the author based on EVT techniques

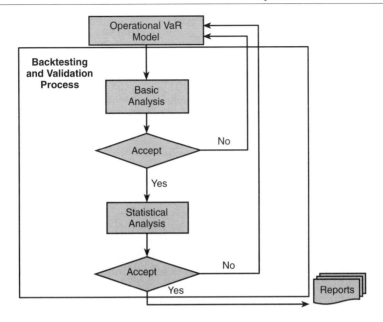

Figure 6.3 Overview of the backtesting process

verifies the clustering of extreme events. We then introduce the Kupiec test and the Crnkovic–Drachman test.

6.6.2 Basic Analysis

This is the initial stage, where a summary of the backtest is reported to the analyst. The basic findings of the backtest are reported, allowing the analyst to have an idea whether the model has an acceptable fit.

The basic report of the database can be seen in Figure 6.4.

The computational demand at this stage can be enormous, especially when the parameters of the frequency distribution of the operational events are very large. The recalculation of each period can take some time. The most important column in this figure is the one that reports the differences between reality and the estimated losses. The analysis will basically be done with the values stated in this column.

The basic statistics necessary at this stage are as below:

Violations $=$ Count[BI $=1$]

Proportion of violations in relation to all observations $=\dfrac{\text{Count[BI}=1]}{\text{Count[BI]}}$

Expected violations $=\alpha\times$period, where $\alpha=(1-$ confidence level)

Sum of the differences between the operational VaR and the verified
operational losses $=C=\sum[R_n-\left(\sum p_n F^X\right)_n]$

An example might help us to understand these concepts. Figure 6.5 is simply a numerical version of Figure 6.4. In this case, we are just comparing the estimated VaR for a certain day against the verified losses for that day.

Time	Operational VaR	Reality	Difference	Binary Indicator (BI)
T_1	$\left(\sum p_n F^X\right)_1$	R_1	$R_1 - \left(\sum p_n F^X\right)_1$	If $R_1 - \left(\sum p_n F^X\right)_1 < 0$ Then BI $= 0$ Otherwise BI $= 1$
T_2	$\left(\sum p_n F^X\right)_2$	R_2	$R_2 - \left(\sum p_n F^X\right)_2$	0–1
T_3	$\left(\sum p_n F^X\right)_3$	R_3	$R_3 - \left(\sum p_n F^X\right)_3$	0–1
(...)	(...)	(...)	(...)	0–1
T_n	$\left(\sum p_n F^X\right)_n$	R_n	$R_n - \left(\sum p_n F^X\right)_n$	0–1

$\left(\sum p_n F^X\right)_n$ is the operational VaR, R_n is the reality at time T_n and BI is the binary indicator for model violations. When BI $= 1$, the actual losses are bigger than those estimated by the VaR.

Figure 6.4   Basic backtest stage

In the case represented in Figure 6.5, there were four violations in 26 days, i.e. a 15.38% rate of violations. The expected number of violations at 95% confidence level is 1.5 (30 observations). Therefore, it seems likely our basic analysis would reject the model. Nevertheless, it must be highlighted that the observation period was too short and the power of any statistical test would be very small. Regularly, we would need larger periods to perform the backtest.

Date	Operational VaR	Operational Losses	Difference	Binary Indicator
20-Jul-01	5,152,037.96	1,645,505.46	3,506,532.50	0
23-Jul-01	5,237,801.03	1,881,693.27	3,356,107.76	0
24-Jul-01	4,360,466.06	1,436,871.92	2,923,594.14	0
25-Jul-01	4,638,549.75	4,608,881.35	29,668.40	0
26-Jul-01	5,048,211.18	4,973,986.63	74,224.55	0
27-Jul-01	4,875,032.02	5,626,391.05	(751,359.03)	1
30-Jul-01	4,751,954.65	6,106,518.31	(1,354,563.67)	1
31-Jul-01	4,456,442.77	5,545,537.21	(1,089,094.44)	1
1-Aug-01	4,807,897.67	1,242,078.62	3,565,819.05	0
2-Aug-01	4,118,811.05	2,869.194.77	1,249,616.28	0
3-Aug-01	4,659,302.15	4,695,814.26	(36,512.11)	1
6-Aug-01	5,069,357.50	3,552,043.96	1,517,313.54	0
7-Aug-01	4,221,968.21	3,245,092.22	976,875.99	0
8-Aug-01	4,302,219.75	208,315.00	4,093,904.75	0
9-Aug-01	4,952,096.35	1,023,281.48	3,928,814.87	0
10-Aug-01	4,777,971.88	4,452,812.06	325,159.82	0
13-Aug-01	4,533,047.23	2,327,452.54	2,205,594.69	0
14-Aug-01	4,853,201.87	2,288,523.90	2,564,677.98	0
15-Aug-01	5,322,069.13	3,406,481.04	1,915,588.09	0
16-Aug-01	5,032,476.92	2,756,530.54	2,275,946.38	0
17-Aug-01	5,259,180.98	5,114,827.57	144,353.41	0
20-Aug-01	5,482,745.01	4,696,250.82	786,494.19	0
21-Aug-01	4,681,218.70	2,395,797.66	2,285,421.04	0
22-Aug-01	5,144,004.84	4,456,669.45	687,335.39	0
23-Aug-01	5,295,681.28	3,004,532.69	2,291,148.58	0
24-Aug-01	4,510,753.24	4,434,670.36	76,082.88	0
(...)	(...)	(...)	(...)	(...)

Figure 6.5   Operational VaR vs. verified operational losses

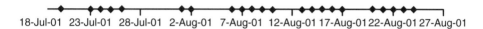

Figure 6.6   Spotting cluster of violations

It would also be interesting to perform a few plots at this stage to help us to visualize the analysis. I will plot two graphs just as an illustration. The first one (Figure 6.6) is the time series of the binary indicator 0–1. The objective of such a graph is to provide a view of the clustering of events. The second plot (Figure 6.7) just depicts the discrepancies between the operational VaR and the real losses during the period.

(1) *Time series of BI = 1 for the purposes of cluster verification*
    As we can see from the plot, there is a clustering of losses around the end of July. This needs to be investigated in further detail. We will see how to do this in the next section.
(2) *Time series of operational VaR and reality in the same graph*
    From Figure 6.7 we can verify that the model works quite well, apart from the clustering around the end of July. The model was not too conservative, but it was too close to be violated in several days. Maybe a more conservative severity distribution is needed.

Basel Model Acceptance Rules (For Market Risk Models)

Since 1996, when the Basel Committee started to accept VaR models in market risk measurement, a few rules for accepting models have been suggested. In Figure 6.8 we show the conditions for VaR model acceptance suggested by the Basel Committee.

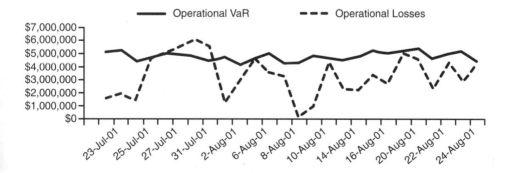

Figure 6.7   Operational VaR vs. operational losses

VaR Confidence Level	$T = 255$ days	$T = 510$ days	$T = 1000$ days
99%	$N < 7$	$1 < N < 7$	$4 < N < 17$
97.5%	$2 < N < 12$	$6 < N < 21$	$15 < N < 36$
95%	$6 < N < 21$	$16 < N < 36$	$37 < N < 65$
92.5%	$11 < N < 28$	$27 < N < 51$	$59 < N < 92$
90%	$16 < N < 36$	$38 < N < 65$	$81 < N < 120$

$N =$ number of violations.

Figure 6.8   VaR confidence levels in market risk

Although the regulators have not established proper rules for accepting the operational VaR, we might follow the same rules for guidance at least.

6.6.3 Statistical Analysis

Clustering of Extreme Events — The Extremal Index

One very important issue that we need to check is the clustering of extreme events. This clustering might influence the stochastic process followed by the operational losses. Extreme value distributions are very sensitive to the value of the shape parameter that, in turn, can be influenced by an event well beyond the average. If, during the course of testing, one large event happens, this must influence forward estimates. Several large events together may indicate a different pattern of loss events that needs to be more carefully understood. Therefore, it is very important to examine whether the model errors (the differences between the operational VaR and reality) are independent of each other or, at least, if this dependence is negligible.

Fortunately, there are tools to estimate this clustering. The extremal index is a useful statistic for describing the clustering of extreme events. The index belongs to the interval [0,1]. The closer the index is to 0 the more clustered the time series.

There are a few methods of estimating the extremal index. We will be interested in two of them, mean cluster size and blocks. They are described below.

Mean Cluster Size   Given $d_1, \ldots, d_n$ let $d_{I(1)}, \ldots, d_{n(k)}$ denote the exceedances over a predetermined threshold u. For some choice of positive integer r, called the run length, define clusters of exceedance times $i(j)$ in the following manner.

Any run of at least r consecutive observations d_I below the threshold u separates two clusters. Hence, there is a minimal gap of length r between two consecutive clusters of exceedance times. A parameter is introduced that characterizes clusters to some extent. Let $n(u, r)$ denote the number of clusters over u. The mean cluster size, relative to u and the run length r, is:

$$\text{Mean cluster size}(u, r) = \frac{k}{n(u, r)}$$

$$\text{Extremal index}(u, r) = \frac{1}{\text{Mean cluster size}(u, r)}$$

where:

k = number of exceedances;

$n(u, r)$ = number of clusters above the threshold.

The parameters are determined as:

u = the same threshold as chosen in the model estimation;
r allows the user to choose. Always start with "10".

Useful Plots:

• Mean cluster size against several thresholds;
• Extremal index against several thresholds.

Blocks Method   Another method to estimate extreme clustering is the blocks method. It is estimated by the equation below:

$$\text{Extremal index} = \frac{K}{N}$$

where K is the number of blocks with one or more exceedances and N is the number of exceedances.

An example might help our understanding. Suppose that we have the database in Figure 6.9 and want to test for extreme clustering via the blocks method.

In this case we separate the time series of differences between the operational VaR and the real operational losses into blocks of five. Therefore, the first block would be (369.98, 272.23, 424.23, 527.65, 519.84). In this case, there was no excess above 600 and $k = 0$. Just two blocks will present events above 600 and the total number of events > 600 is three. Therefore, the extremal index is 0.66. Indeed, there is some degree of clustering as two out of the three events happened in the same block.

The Practical Use of the Extremal Index   One of the advantages of estimating the extremal index is that it also offers alternatives to overcome a poor prediction caused by a strong dependence problem. We do not show the mathematical derivation here, but the correction in the prediction is made as below:

$$P^\alpha = (P^n)^\theta$$

where α is the initial confidence interval, e.g. 95%, and θ is the extremal index.

For example, let us suppose that the 95% quantile used in VaR was prejudiced by some clustering event (e.g. a huge breakdown in the system). Suppose that the extremal index found was 0.213, indicating indeed a reasonable level of clustering. This might be fixed by increasing the quantile using the formula above, hence $95\%^{0.213} = 98.91\%$. Therefore, a higher figure to cover against operational risk is needed due to clustering.

Threshold   600
Run (Block Size)   5

| 369.98 |
| 272.23 |
| 424.43 |
| 527.65 |
| 519.84 |

K   2◄——— Number of Blocks with one or more Exceedances
N   3◄——— Total Number of Exceedances

| 573.31 |
| 181.64 |
| 376.58 |
| 509.50 |
| 1291.76 |

Ext index 0.6667

| 330.98 |
| 230.96 |
| 215.31 |
| 302.24 |
| 322.65 |

| 188.21 |
| 1543.23 |
| 359.60 |
| 413.49 |
| 987.65 |

| 367.30 |
| 362.98 |
| 534.26 |
| 391.47 |
| 277.34 |

| 545.67 |
| 463.18 |
| 302.52 |
| 527.60 |
| 369.53 |

| 298.12 |
| 513.69 |
| 195.29 |
| 531.04 |
| 241.75 |

| 349.52 |
| 418.22 |
| 496.21 |
| 256.57 |
| 316.93 |

| 579.44 |
| 425.26 |
| 375.33 |
| 584.44 |
| 407.98 |

| 202.62 |
| 426.13 |
| 364.13 |
| 436.78 |

Figure 6.9 Extremal index — blocks method

Kupiec Test

The Kupiec test (1995) is mentioned in the text of the Basel Committee paper on MRAs (accepting internal models). Despite its drawbacks, namely low power and dealing just with the frequency of the exceptions, the test can be useful to indicate a bad model.

Basically the Kupiec test tries to check if the violations ratio (number of exceptions/total sample) of the model matches the confidence level determined.

Let:

V = number of violations, i.e. the number of losses in excess of VaR;
T = total number of observations;
p = VaR confidence level.

Then the probability of observing V failures out of T observations is $(1-p)^{T-V}p^V$ and a test of H$_0$: $p = p^*$ is given by the likelihood ratio test statistic:

$$\mathrm{LR_{UC}} = 2\ln[(1-p^*)^{T-V}p^{*V}] + 2\ln\left[\left(1-\frac{T}{V}\right)^{T-V}\left(\frac{V}{T}\right)^V\right]$$

which is distributed as $\chi^2(1)$ under H$_0$.

An example might help to clarify this test. Let the variables be:

p	$0.01 \leftarrow$	VaR confidence level
T	$255 \leftarrow$	Number of days
V	$6 \leftarrow$	Violations

LR$_{UC}$	$3.415358 \leftarrow$	$\mathrm{LR_{UC}} = 2\ln[(1-p^*)^{T-V}\,p^{*V}] + 2\ln[(1-\frac{T}{V})^{T-V}(\frac{V}{T})^V]$
p-test	0.636232	

In the example above, for 1 year of data (T = 255 days) at 99% confidence level, we would expect $1\% \times 255 = 2.5 < 3$ violations, but six happened. However, we would reject the null hypothesis if LR > 3.84 and the LR is smaller. This is reflected in the high *p*-values of the test. We might use the Kupiec test to verify the probability that we are accepting an incorrect model or rejecting a good one.

Q-Test (Crnkovic–Drachman Test)

This test aims at finding the fitness of the predictions to the real impact by comparing the probability distribution function of the prediction with the uniform distribution. The test should be performed in the following manner:

(1) For each day (or period), verify how the PDF performed by noting in which percentile (*p*) of the predictive distribution the reality would be.
(2) Over a period of *N* consecutive days, keep track of the values of *p* that have occurred. The deviation of the distribution of the percentiles from the uniform distribution is a first measure of the quality of the PDF forecast, and therefore of the risk measurement system that uses the forecast. The smaller the deviation, the higher the quality.

	VaR-12.Oct.00	Indicator
0.1	191,234.90	1
0.2	200,090.01	1
0.3	235,675.71	1
0.4	567,911.11	1
0.5	775,678.98	1
0.6	876,567.12	1
0.7	1,113,567.88	1
0.8	1,546,789.01	
0.9	3,213,456.78	
0.999	12,345,678.02	

Losses 12.Oct.00   1,213,456.78

For 0.1, considering that we are measuring a period of 250 days,

$$F(0.1) = \frac{228}{250} = 0.912$$

g(x)	f(x)	f(x)–g(x)	g(x)–f(x)
0.1	0.912	0.812	−0.812
0.2	0.898	0.698	−0.698
0.3	0.888	0.588	−0.588
0.4	0.775	0.375	−0.375
0.5	0.634	0.134	−0.134
0.6	0.544	−0.056	0.056
0.7	0.444	−0.256	0.256
0.8	0.378	−0.422	0.422
0.9	0.301	−0.599	0.599
1	0.291	−0.709	0.709
		MAX ⟶ *0.812*	*0.709*
		K	**0.103**

Figure 6.10   Crnkovic–Drachman test

(3) Let $n(t)$ be the number of observed percentiles p that are less than or equal to t, where $0 \leqslant t \leqslant 1$. Then $F(t) = n(t)/N$. The quality Q of the PDF forecast is then given by:

$$K(f(x), g(x)) = \max_{0 \leqslant x \leqslant 1} \{f(x) - g(x)\} + \max_{0 \leqslant x \leqslant 1} \{g(x) - f(x)\}$$

K is known as the Kuiper statistic and is basically a measure of the distance between two cumulative distribution functions. So Q is a measure of how far away $F(t)$ is from being uniform.

An example can be carried out in a spreadsheet, as in Figure 6.10. An acceptable level for $T = 250$ is $K = 0.109$, therefore, this model can be considered good.

6.7   DIFFERENCES BETWEEN BACKTESTING MARKET AND OPERATIONAL VaR MODELS

For those with a market VaR background, it is always useful to highlight the similarities and differences in the model validation process. As the models follow different stochastic processes (one continuous — the market VaR — and other discrete — the operational VaR), despite the fact that both models use statistical inference and predict the losses for a determined period for a certain confidence interval, their processing is significantly distinct.

Market VaR models in general use the history of a certain number of risk factors and see how they affect the profitability of the position of a bank. The subsequent estimates of the VaR model are validated usually against the daily managerial P&L. As operational losses in general are not reflected in this report, the outcome of the operational VaR model needs to be tested against the losses themselves.

Another important difference is related to the time lag between the event taking place and the effective impact on the earnings. Some events in operational risk can take years to reach a definite amount, as is the case for legal events. The way we should deal with this can be seen in Chapter 2. The market position can be validated every day by marking-to-market, while the operational losses are, in general, detected and measured one or more days later. The operational VaR is also more subject to jumps than the market VaR.

REFERENCES

Artzner, P., Delbaen, F., Eber, J.M. and Heath, D. (1999), "Coherent Measures of Risk", *Mathematical Finance*, 9, 203–228.

Crnkovic, C. and Drachman, J. (1996), "Quality Control", *Risk*, 9, 139–143,

Klugman, S., Panjer, H. and Wilmot, G. (1997), *Loss Models*, Wiley Series in Probability and Statistics, Wiley, New York.

Kupiec, P. (1995), "Techniques for Verifying the Accuracy of Risk Management Models", *Journal of Derivatives*, 7, 41–52.

7
Stochastic Processes in Operational Risk

7.1 INTRODUCTION

In previous chapters we saw how to estimate for operational VaR the aggregation of two probabilistic models: frequency and severity. Nevertheless, there are a few models that are perhaps not directly relevant to the calculation of VaR, but whose understanding facilitates the comprehension of several problems in operational risk.

I show in this chapter some stochastic processes and models that, directly or indirectly, are involved in the modeling of operational risk. In Sections 7.2 and 7.3 we develop an adapted version of risk theory and ruin process models for operational risk. Ruin processes are the bread and butter of insurance and actuarial models. In Section 7.4 we review Markov chain models and then, in Section 7.5, renewal counting processes focusing on the Poisson model, with a simple example. In Section 7.6 queuing theory is briefly introduced, with an example of how it can be used in operational risk. Section 7.7 covers briefly the topic of reliability theory. In Sections 7.8 and 7.9 we summarize the topics of stopping times and mixtures of distributions, respectively.

7.2 RISK THEORY AND RUIN PROCESS

One of the basic stochastic processes in insurance and risk theory is the so-called ruin problem or ruin process. The study of ruin processes helps insurers to define the degree of risk of their portfolio and influences portfolio hedging decisions. The process has the following format:

$$R_n = u + \beta n - \sum_{j=1}^{n} X_i$$

where R is the reserve necessary to cover the losses, u is the initial reserve, β is the premium rate and $\sum_{j=1}^{n} X_i$ is the aggregate losses amount.

Ruin occurs at the time when the reserve variable (R_n) becomes negative. Let τ_s be the ruin time (assuming $\tau_s = \infty$ if no ruin occurs) of the reserve process. Ruin time can be represented by:

$$\tau_s = \inf\left\{t: R_n < 0\right\}$$

We can also consider the ruin time distribution function $H_s(x) = \Pr(\tau_s \leqslant x)$. The ultimate ruin probability can be represented by $\psi(s) = \Pr(\tau_s < \infty)$.

More detailed definitions of risk theory and ruin process can be seen in Rolski et al. (1999) and Embrechts et al. (1997).

7.3   RUIN THEORY APPLIED TO HEDGING AN OR PORTFOLIO

An interesting adaptation of ruin theory can be made for operational risk. This model may be useful to understand the hedging needs. A similar idea used in risk theory can be adapted to operational risk.

The process to estimate R (in this case deemed operational risk capital) would look like:

$$R_n = \kappa + \alpha_n - \sum_{j=1}^{n} X_i$$

In such a model, the initial operational risk capital is represented by κ, α is a percentage of the gross income allocated to operational risk and the X_i are operational losses.

This type of model is very useful to simulate hedging in the long term. For example, if you know that your losses follow a $GEV(\theta_n)$ process, you can simulate the amount necessary to cover future losses given arbitrarily allocated initial capital and a certain percentage of the gross revenue allocated against operational risk. The study of such stochastic processes may be helpful in pricing operational risk derivatives in the near future (see Chapters 13 and 14 and my forthcoming book "Hedging Operational Risk and Integrated Risk Management", to be published by John Wiley).

Again, as in insurance, we want to avoid ruin, i.e. to ensure that during the course of n months ahead we always have enough economic capital to cover unexpected losses.

Some examples might help us to clarify the situation. I developed a few simulations to see whether the economic capital envisaged would be enough for the proposed period. Almost all elements in the process are stochastic, including the parameters (which I made stochastic using a Bayesian-like technique called Markov chain Monte Carlo — see Chapter 12 — based on gamma distributions). The bank revenues also fluctuated following an economic cycle, and could go as low as $300 million/month to $1.6 billion. α and κ were kept fixed during the simulation. The 99% quantile of the aggregated lognormal–Poisson distribution was also used.

In the first simulation I initially allocated $15 million and charged 2.3% of the $1 billion monthly revenues to cover against operational risk. The losses follow an aggregated lognormal (12.5,2.1)–Poisson (8) process. The results can be seen in Figure 7.1.

Typically, if the operational losses follow the pattern simulated, it would be inadvisable to use this level of α and κ. At this level, $\tau = 27$, i.e. in 27 months out of 300 the economic capital was not enough to cover the losses and the first cluster of negative capital was reached in the 15th month, when the economic cycle was good and the revenues from trading were increasing.

Given that, I decided to increase α to $20 million and reduce κ to 2%. I kept the quantile levels and the aggregate loss process unaltered. This is seen in Figure 7.2.

The results were indeed better this time. Nevertheless, τ is still high at 25, but the first ruin time occurred at the 87th month, a clear effect from a higher initial capital.

We still need to find a totally safe process and therefore κ was increased to 3% to see what happened. The simulation results are given in Figure 7.3.

This time we finally succeeded. The capital increased constantly at this level and $\tau = 0$, meaning that the standards set for determining economic capital are high enough

Simulation 1

α = \$15 million

κ = 2.3%

Loss Process $= S(N_t) = \sum\limits_{j=1}^{n} X_i$ = Lognormal (12.5,2.1)–Poisson (8)

99% Quantile

Period $=300$ months

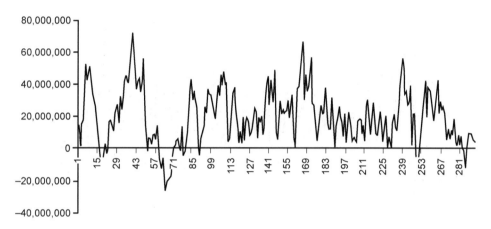

Figure 7.1   First simulation [lognormal (12.5,2.1)–Poisson (8)], $\alpha = \$15$ million, $\kappa = 2.3\%$

and ruin never happened. Maybe we are even on the safe side and some calibration might be done, but the model worked efficiently in covering against operational losses.

It must be highlighted that such models may be a bit more complex to design in some special cases, with several restrictions, but are definitely worth it in terms of understanding the hedging needs of a financial institution.

7.4 MARKOV CHAINS

Markov chains are a special type of discrete-time stochastic process. A Markov chain can be represented by:

$$\Pr(X_{t+1} = i_{t+1}/X_t = i_t, X_{t-1} = i_{t-1}, \ldots, X_1 = i_1, X_0 = i_0) = \Pr(X_{t+1} = i_{t+1}/X_t = i_t)$$

Basically, the formula above states that the probability distribution of the state at time $t+i$ depends on the state at time $t(i_t)$ and does not depend on the states the chain passed through on the way to i_t at time t.

We can also make the assumption that for all states i and j and all t, $\Pr(X_{t+1} = i_{t+1}/X_t = i_t)$ is independent of t. By assuming this, we can write in formulaic terms that $\Pr(X_{t+1} = i_{t+1}/X_t = i_t) = p_{ij}$, where p_{ij} is the probability that, given the system is in state i at time t, it will be in a different state j at time $t+i$. If the system

Simulation 2

$\alpha = \$20$ million

$\kappa = 2\%$

Loss Process = $S(N_t)$ = Lognormal (12.5,2.1)–Poisson (8) 99% Confidence

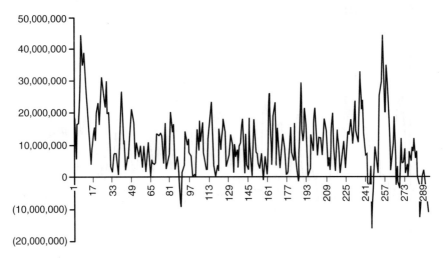

Figure 7.2   Second simulation [lognormal (12.5,2.1)–Poisson (8)], $\alpha = \$20$ million, $\kappa = 2\%$

moves from one state to another during one period, we say that a transition has occurred. The p_{ij} are often referred to as the transition probabilities for the Markov chains. The transition probability matrix can be written as:

$$M = \begin{bmatrix} p_{qq} & p_{12} & \cdots & p_{1s} \\ p_{21} & p_{22} & \cdots & p_{2s} \\ \cdots & \cdots & & \cdots \\ p_{s1} & p_{s2} & & p_{ss} \end{bmatrix}$$

Each entry in the M matrix must be non-negative. Also, the entries in each row must sum to 1.

It will be useful to learn some of the nomenclature used when dealing with Markov chains. A state i is an absorbing state if $p_{ij} = 1$. A state i is considered transient if there exists a state j that is reachable from i, but with state i not reachable from state j. Otherwise, if a state is not transient, it is called a recurrent state.

It is always better to explain concepts with examples. One such is developed below.

Suppose that a financial institution rates its transaction processing states from 1 to 6 in terms of the length of time to settle, following Table 7.1. The transactions in the back-office can be placed in one of these six categories (states).

The financial institution has a reasonable time series of data, and these data indicate that the following Markov chain describes how the states change:

Simulation 3

$\alpha = \$20$ million

$\kappa = 3\%$

Loss Process = $S(N_t)$ = Lognormal (12.5,2.1)–Poisson (8)

99% Confidence

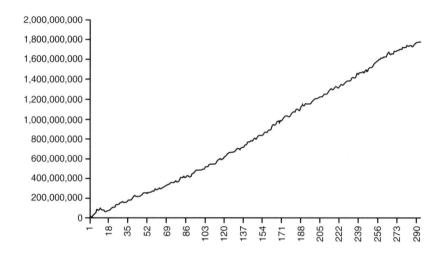

Figure 7.3   Third simulation [lognormal (12.5,2.1)–Poisson (8)], $\alpha = \$20$ million, $\kappa = 3\%$

$$
\begin{array}{c}
 \quad \begin{array}{cccccc} S1 & S2 & S3 & S4 & S5 & S6 \end{array} \\
\begin{array}{c} S1 \\ S2 \\ S3 \\ S4 \\ S5 \\ S6 \end{array}
\begin{bmatrix}
0 & 0.6 & 0 & 0 & 0.4 & 0 \\
0 & 0 & 0.6 & 0 & 0.4 & 0 \\
0 & 0 & 0 & 0.4 & 0.6 & 0 \\
0 & 0 & 0 & 0 & 0.8 & 0.2 \\
0 & 0 & 0 & 0 & 1 & 0 \\
0 & 0 & 0 & 0 & 0 & 1
\end{bmatrix}
\end{array}
$$

What the matrix above says is that if a transaction settlement is 2 days late (state 3), there is a 40% chance that the account will not reach settlement on this day. Also, there is a 60% chance that the settlement will occur on this day. Once a transaction falls

Table 7.1   Transaction processing environment states

State 1	Transaction settled properly on $T+1$
State 2	Transaction settled 1 day late ($T+2$)
State 3	Transaction settled 2 days late ($T+3$)
State 4	Transaction settled 3 days late ($T+4$)
State 5	Transaction settled
State 6	Transaction settled 4 days late or more

Table 7.2   New representation of the states

c_1	Transaction settled properly on $T+1$
c_2	Transaction settled 1 day late $(T+2)$
c_3	Transaction settled 2 days late $(T+3)$
c_4	Transaction settled 3 days late $(T+4)$
a_1	Transaction settled
a_2	Transaction settled 4 days late or more

into states 5 or 6, no further state changes occur as the transaction is settled or moves into a "very late settlement" category. Therefore, these states are considered absorbing.

For any absorbing chain, two issues are important to understand. The first is if the chain starts in a certain transient state what is the expected number of times that each state will be entered before reaching an absorbing state. In other words, how long should a transaction spend in a given absorption state before it ends up in any of the absorbing states? The second issue is to know the probability of ending up in any absorbing state, given that a transaction starts in a certain transient state.

In order to solve this, the transition matrix needs to be written with the transient states first and then the absorbing states. For definition purposes, we define that there are $c - d$ transient states $(c_1, c_2, \ldots, c_{c-d})$ and d absorbing states $(a_1, a_2, \ldots, a_d)$. The transition matrix can then be represented by:

$$
\begin{array}{cc}
c - d & d \\
\text{columns} & \text{columns}
\end{array}
$$

$$
M = \left[\begin{array}{c|c} T & A \\ \hline 0 & F \end{array}\right] \begin{array}{l} c - d \text{ rows} \\ d \text{ rows} \end{array}
$$

The rows and columns of M correspond to the states $(c_1, c_2, \ldots, c_{c-d})$ and $(a_1, a_2, \ldots, a_d)$. F is a $d \times d$ identity matrix reflecting that an absorbing state can never be left. T is a $(c-d) \times (c-d)$ matrix that represents transitions between transient states. A is a $(c-d) \times d$ matrix representing transitions from transient states to absorbing ones. 0 is a $d \times (c-d)$ matrix consisting entirely of zeros, representing the fact that it is impossible to go from an absorbing state to a transient state.

Coming back to our example, we might represent the states as in Table 7.2.

The transition probability matrix (M) can again be depicted as:

	S1	S2	S3	S4	Settled	Very late
S1	0	0.6	0	0	0.4	0
S2	0	0	0.6	0	0.4	0
S3	0	0	0	0.4	0.6	0
S4	0	0	0	0	0.8	0.2
Settled	0	0	0	0	1	0
Very late	0	0	0	0	0	1

Then, $c=6$ and $s=2$, and the following matrices can be represented:

$$T = \begin{bmatrix} 0 & 0.6 & 0 & 0 \\ 0 & 0 & 0.6 & 0 \\ 0 & 0 & 0 & 0.4 \\ 0 & 0 & 0 & 0 \end{bmatrix}$$

$$A = \begin{bmatrix} 0.4 & 0 \\ 0.4 & 0 \\ 0.6 & 0 \\ 0.8 & 0.2 \end{bmatrix}$$

At this stage, we might come back to the issues presented above. These are:

(a) If the chain starts in a certain transient state, and before we reach an absorbing state, what is the expected number of times that each state will be entered? How long should we wait until the absorption takes place?
(b) If the chain begins in a given transient state m_{ij}, what is the probability that we will eventually end up in any absorbing state?

Both questions can be answered by what is often referred to as the Markov chain fundamental matrix, or $(F - T)^{-1}$, where F is the identity matrix. Put another way, if we are in transient state c_i, the probability that we will eventually be absorbed in absorbing state a_j is the ijth element of the matrix $(F - T)^{-1}A$.

Eventually, it would be easier to adapt these questions for our example by rephrasing them. Therefore, the previous questions can be formulated as:

(a) What is the probability that a new transaction will eventually be settled?
(b) What is the probability that a transaction that is 1 day late (state 2) will still be unresolved after 5 days?

In order to answer these questions, we need to follow the methodology explained above. From our previous results, we have:

$$T = \begin{bmatrix} 0 & 0.6 & 0 & 0 \\ 0 & 0 & 0.6 & 0 \\ 0 & 0 & 0 & 0.4 \\ 0 & 0 & 0 & 0 \end{bmatrix} \quad \text{and} \quad A = \begin{bmatrix} 0.4 & 0 \\ 0.4 & 0 \\ 0.6 & 0 \\ 0.8 & 0.2 \end{bmatrix}$$

Following the methodology above, we now subtract T from the identity matrix F:

$$(F - T) = \begin{bmatrix} 1 & -0.6 & 0 & 0 \\ 0 & 1 & -0.5 & 0 \\ 0 & 0 & 1 & -0.4 \\ 0 & 0 & 0 & 1 \end{bmatrix}$$

Now we have to invert the matrix as below (finding the "Markov chain fundamental matrix"):

$$(F - T)^{-1} = \begin{bmatrix} 1 & 0.6 & 0.3 & 0.12 \\ 0 & 1 & 0.5 & 0.20 \\ 0 & 0 & 1 & 0.40 \\ 0 & 0 & 0 & 1 \end{bmatrix}$$

Finally, we have to multiply the matrix above by A (or the absorbing states matrix):

$$(F - T)^{-1} A = \begin{bmatrix} 1 & 0.6 & 0.3 & 0.12 \\ 0 & 1 & 0.5 & 0.20 \\ 0 & 0 & 1 & 0.40 \\ 0 & 0 & 0 & 1 \end{bmatrix} \cdot \begin{bmatrix} 0.4 & 0 \\ 0.5 & 0 \\ 0.6 & 0 \\ 0.7 & 0.3 \end{bmatrix} = \begin{bmatrix} 0.09712 & 0.0288 \\ 0.0952 & 0.0480 \\ 0.920 & 0.080 \\ 0.800 & 0.200 \end{bmatrix}$$

Now we are able to answer the questions formulated above. The probability that a new transaction will eventually be settled is 97.12%. The probability that a transaction that is 1 day late already will go to the latest absorbing state, or 5+ days late, is 4.8%.

Other interesting estimates can be made using this exercise. Looking at the final matrix, we realize that 2.8% of the transactions go to stage 6 or 5+ days late. If we consider the average ticket to be, say, $1,000,000, the business unit to process 1000 transactions per day, the average penalty paid to the counterparty per day to be 0.01% and, for these late transactions, the settlement on average to happen 8 days late, it can be inferred that this business line loses by poor settlement an estimate of $22,400 a day. Considering 22 business days a month, that means almost $500,000!

7.5 RENEWAL PROCESSES

A series of different assumptions can be made on the sequence of losses between occurrence times $\{T_n, n \geqslant 1\}$. In a few cases, it can be assumed that such sequences are generated by a *renewal process* $\{\sigma_n, n \geqslant 1\}$ of arrival claim epochs, i.e. the random variables T_n are non-negative, independent and have the same distribution as a generic random variable T. The distribution function of the inter-occurrence time is then denoted by $F_T(x) = \Pr(T \leqslant x)$. Any counting process that is generated by an iid sum process is called a *renewal counting process*.

The commonest renewal process is the Poisson process, where the generic random variable is exponentially distributed. Poisson processes have particular properties that distinguish them from other renewal properties, since the exponential distribution presents a lack of memory property. I briefly describe below three types of Poisson process: homogeneous, non-homogeneous and mixed or compound.

7.5.1 Homogeneous Poisson Process

The homogeneous Poisson process has the following properties:

(1) It starts at zero, i.e. $N(0) = 0$;
(2) It has independent and stationary increments;
(3) For every $t > 0$, $N(t)$ is a Poisson random variable with parameter λt:

$$\Pr(N(t) = n) = \frac{(\lambda t)^n}{n!} e^{-\lambda t} \quad n = 0, 1, 2, \ldots$$

The Poisson process is probably the most important stochastic process in insurance and operational risk.

As usual, an exercise might help us to clarify the concept. Suppose that the number of transactions processed by the back-office of a business unit follows a Poisson distribution with an average of 30 transactions per hour arriving. Given that, we are asked to:

(1) Find the probability that exactly 60 transactions arrive between 10am and 12noon.
(2) Find the mean and standard deviation of the number of transactions processed between 9am and 1pm.
(3) Find the probability that the time between two consecutive transactions processed is between 1 and 3 minutes.

To answer the first question, we realize that $\lambda t = 2(30) = 60$. The probability is then calculated from: $e^{-60}\, 60^{60}/60! = 5.143\%$. For the second question, the parameter is $\lambda t = 4(30) = 120$. The standard deviation is simply $\sqrt{120} = 10.95$. A little algebra is necessary to answer the third question. Let Y be the time (in minutes) between successive transactions processed. The mean order per minute is exponential with rate $30/60 = 0.5$ transactions per minute. Hence, the PDF of the time between transactions arriving is $0.5e^{-0.5t}$. Therefore:

$$\Pr(1 \leqslant Y \leqslant 3) = \int_1^3 (0.5e^{-0.5t})\mathrm{d}t = e^{-0.5} - e^{-1.5} = 0.38$$

7.5.2   Non-homogeneous Poisson Process

The Poisson process can be extended by replacing the parameter λ with a mean value function Λ. Let $0 \leqslant T_1 \leqslant T_2 \leqslant \cdots \leqslant T_n$ be a Poisson process with intensity $\lambda = 1$. Then, we let Λ be a non-decreasing function, having as generalized inverse Λ^{-1}. Then, $\tau_i = \Lambda^{-1}(T_i)$, $i \geqslant 1$ can be called a non-homogeneous Poisson process with mean value function Λ. For more details on this process refer to Rolski et al. (1999).

7.5.3   Cox Process (Doubly Stochastic)

Researching real cases with real data on the frequency of operational events in a certain time interval, it might happen that the Poisson assumption is not always the best one. As I mentioned before in Chapter 5, it is often possible to fit a negative binomial to the data. The negative binomial distribution can be obtained by mixing the Poisson distribution with a gamma distribution, i.e. by letting the Poisson parameter be gamma distributed (mixture distributions — see Section 7.9). As an alternative, we might also let the Poisson parameter of the homogeneous Poisson process be stochastic (i.e. a mixed Poisson process). Suppose that what we need in reality is more variability in the events arrival process. In a mixed Poisson process, this changeability will diminish as time progresses. In order not to lose this variability, the basic idea is to let the expected number of events $\Lambda((a,b])$ in a given time interval $(a,b]$ be generated by a random measure $\{\Lambda(B), B \in \beta(\Re)\}$.

Following Rolski et al.'s notation, a counting measure $\{N(B)\}$ is called a Cox process or doubly stochastic Poisson process if there exists an intensity process $\lambda(t), n = 1, 2, \ldots$; $k_1, \ldots, k_n \in N$ that can be represented by:

$$\Pr\left(\bigcap_{i=1}^{n}\{N((a_i, b_i]) = k_i\right) = E\left(\prod_{i=1}^{n}\frac{\left[\int_{a_i}^{b_i}\lambda(v)\mathrm{d}v\right]^{k_i}}{k_i!}\ \exp\left[-\int_{a_i}^{b_i}\lambda(v)\mathrm{d}v\right]\right)$$

7.6   QUEUING THEORY

The study of processes is quite important in operational risk, since most operational events arise from errors or lack of capacity in processing transactions from clients. In queuing theory, the input process is called the arrival process. Arrivals might be customers, transactions, etc. An important area within this theory is the so-called "birth–death process". This process is a continuous-time stochastic process for which the system's state at any time is a non-negative integer. In birth–death processes, arrivals are called births and deaths are the end of the process of service provision.

Most queuing systems with exponential inter-arrival times and exponential service times may be modeled as birth–death processes. It is beyond the scope of this book to derive the formulas pertinent to these processes; therefore, I will briefly explain the most important ones below and present a simple example.

Defining the variables of the process, π_j is the probability that at an instant in the future, j arrivals will take place. Alternatively, π_j can be seen as the fraction of time that j arrivals are present. The queuing system has exponential inter-arrival times with parameter λ and the service times are exponentially distributed with parameter μ.

Theoretically:

$$\frac{\text{Expected no. of departures from state } j}{\text{Unit time}} = \frac{\text{Expected no. of entrances into state } j}{\text{Unit time}}$$

Using the variables above, we might see that:

$$\frac{\text{Expected no. of departures from state } j}{\text{Unit time}} = \pi_j(\lambda_j + \mu_j)$$

Since for $j \geqslant 1$ state j can only be entered from state $j-1$ or $j+1$:

$$\frac{\text{Expected no. of entrances into state } j}{\text{Unit time}} = \pi_{j-1}\lambda_{j-1} + \pi_{j+1}\mu_{j+1}$$

Solving the set of equations above we get:

$$\pi_{j-1}\lambda_{j-1} + \pi_{j+1}\mu_{j+1} = \pi_j(\lambda_j + \mu_j)$$

For $j = 0$, $\mu_0 = \pi_{-1} = 0$, therefore we have:

$$\pi_1\mu_1 = \pi_0\lambda_0$$

The equations above are generally known as the conservation of flow equations for a birth–death process. From these equations, we conclude that:

$$\pi_0 = \frac{1}{1 + \sum_{1}^{\infty} c_j}$$

$$\pi_1 = \frac{\pi_0 \lambda_0}{\mu_1}$$

$$\pi_2 = \frac{\pi_0 (\lambda_0 \lambda_1)}{\mu_1 \mu_2}$$

We could define a ratio c as:

$$c_j = \frac{\lambda_0 \lambda_1 \ldots \lambda_{j-1}}{\mu_1 \mu_2 \ldots \mu_j}$$

Or, put another way:

$$\pi_j = \pi_0 c_j \quad \text{i.e.} \quad c_1 = \frac{\lambda_0}{\mu_1}$$

We are now ready for a simple exercise that can be solved in a spreadsheet. Suppose that a business unit processes an average of 2500 transactions per hour. The time between transactions processed follows an exponential distribution. A person in the back-office can handle an average of 30 transactions per hour. The time required to handle a transaction is also exponentially distributed. This business unit can put up to 25 transactions on hold, beyond that a transaction will certainly be late for settlement. This business unit has 75 personnel to process the transactions.

(a) What fraction of time are all processing officers busy?
(b) What fraction of transactions are late being processed and will fail to be settled on time?

I developed a spreadsheet in Figure 7.4 to facilitate the comprehension of this problem. The answer to the first question is simply the sum of the probabilities $\pi_{75} + \cdots + \pi_{100}$. We obtain here, for 2500 transactions that the officers are busy 82.75% of the time. Given this level of transactions, just 0.8615% of the transactions will have some problem in settling. Therefore, the conclusion is that the department is reasonably well dimensioned and structured for this level of transactions, i.e. the department's capacity is proper at this level.

However, we know that the financial market is not that stable and neither are the volumes traded. Suppose that in one tense day the number of transactions processed increased to 3000. The officers would be busy 99.25% of the time, and the fraction of transactions late for settlement would increase to 7.57%. If the market becomes even more dynamic one day due to a rumor, for example, and the transactions double to 5000, the officers would not be able to cope with the demand and the number of transactions lost would be as high as 40%!

This clearly shows the importance of capacity studies in financial institutions. In other industries the demand tends to be much more stable in short periods, like intra-day. The dynamics of the banking system are much higher and so are the risks. A financial institution has immediate cash impacts, reflected in operational losses, when it is not prepared to cope with the demand.

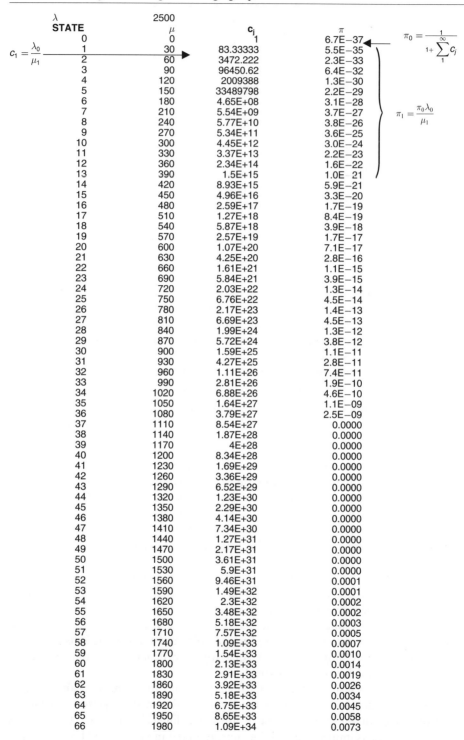

Figure 7.4 Queuing theory — birth–death process example

7.7   RELIABILITY AND MEAN TIME BETWEEN FAILURES

Reliability is a branch of operational research that basically studies the trustworthiness of elements in a system. It is particularly important in building airplanes, for example, where systems and parts can never fail. Reliability tries to provide a statistical background to evaluate the probability that a component or system will operate satisfactorily, either at any particular instant at which it is required or for a certain length of time.

One method reliability uses to describe the occurrence of failures is to state the *mean time between failures* (MTBF). If we define $F(t)$ as the probability that an event will occur before time t, it can be stated that:

$$F(t) = 1 - \exp(-\lambda t)$$

which is basically the exponential distribution CDF with mean $1/\lambda$. Consequently, $1/\lambda$ is the MTBF of events. I provide an example below that might help to explain this idea. We use a state-space representation to illustrate this example (refer to Chapter 8 for a description). Suppose that a transactions processing system is backed up by another system when it fails. State A means the regular system is working, state B means the backup system is working and state C represents a system failure. The state space can be represented as in Figure 7.5.

When the regular system fails it is offset and, while it is repaired, a standby unit is switched on to keep the system flowing. The switching mechanism that links the main system to the backup system has probability p of working when called upon, and the systems have exponential lifetimes with rate parameter λ.

The probabilities of the system can be seen as:

$$P_0(t) = \lambda P_0(t)$$
$$P_1(t) = p\lambda P_0(t) - \lambda P_1(t)$$
$$P_2(t) = (1 - p)\lambda P_0(t) + \lambda P_1(t)$$
$$R(t) = (1 - p)\lambda P_0(t) + \lambda P_1(t)$$

where $R(t)$ is the reliability of the system at time t.

Now suppose that the main system fails and takes 3 hours to fix. The system downtime would be minimized the higher the probability that the standby system works

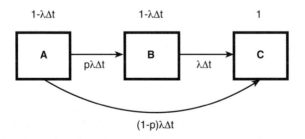

Figure 7.5   Reliability in transactions processing systems

until the main system is put back online. Assuming that the value of p is 90% and that the standby system has a mean working time of 50 hours, the probability that the standby system fails while the main system is under repair is calculated by:

$$P_t = \text{Pr(switch works and standby system working time} < 3 \text{ hours)} + \text{Pr(switch fails)}$$

$$= 0.90 \left[1 - \exp\left(-\frac{3}{50}\right) \right] + 0.05 = 0.1024$$

One day a system vendor arrives in your office and offers a switch that works with 99% reliability and another one that offers a backup system with working time of 100 hours instead of 50. How would this affect the calculation?

In the first case (buying the more reliable switch), $p = 99\%$:

$$P_t = 0.99 \left[1 - \exp\left(-\frac{3}{50}\right) \right] + 0.01 = 0.0676$$

In the second case (buying the new backup system), $t = 100$:

$$P_t = 0.90 \left[1 - \exp\left(-\frac{3}{100}\right) \right] + 0.01 = 0.0765$$

If both are bought:

$$P_t = 0.99 \left[1 - \exp\left(-\frac{3}{100}\right) \right] + 0.01 = 0.03925$$

The advantages are clear; both cases bring good opportunities. By doing a little bit of arithmetic (and knowing the volumes that are processed per day), we can calculate the possible financial advantage of changing the switch or the backup system, or even both.

7.8   STOPPING TIMES

Stopping times are special types of random variables that assume as values a particular time period t. They are usually represented by τ. τ being a stopping time means that it is random and the range of its possible values is the same as $t \in [0,T]$. When an event is observed, it will be in the form $\tau = t$. In reality, the outcome is a particular time period.

As for market and credit derivatives, there are many derivatives in operational risk for which the pricing of the stopping time of a security will be a very important variable. This is the case for American-type securities, in which an early exercise can be represented. The own end date of the security is a random variable as it can be exercised at any time.

Hence, let τ represent the day an operational event will take place and the security will cease to exist (or will be exercised). Given an information set I_t, we will be able to tell whether the security (or option) has been exercised or not. Put another way, given I_t, we can differentiate between the possibilities $\tau \leqslant t$, which means that the security has been exercised, or $\tau > t$, which means the early exercise clause (or the operational risk event embedded in the security) has not yet been utilized.

7.9 MIXTURE DISTRIBUTIONS

Frequently, random variables might not be perfectly explained by one single distribution and we need another one (or a combination of distributions) to explain the process. These types of distributions are commonly referred to as "mixture distributions". This topic is too complex for the scope of this book, but it is useful to mention its existence.

The situation might happen, for example, where transaction processing failures at a business unit could be considered Poisson, but the mean number of transaction processing failures (or the Poisson's λ) might also be considered a variable. Perhaps the rate at which the events happen is dependent on system quality, for instance. In such cases, the number of operational events in a particular period will follow a mixture of Poisson and a distribution for λ.

These mixtures are usually represented by:

$$F_A \underset{\Theta}{\wedge} F_B$$

where F_A represents the base distribution and F_B the mixing distribution, or the distribution of Θ. Therefore, we could have something like:

$$\text{Poisson } (\lambda) \underset{\lambda}{\wedge} \text{Beta } (\alpha, \beta)$$

i.e. a beta mixture of Poisson distributions.

REFERENCES

Embrechts, P., Kluppelberg, C. and Mikosch, T. (1997), *Modelling Extremal Events*, Applications of Mathematics: Stochastic Modeling and Applied Probability, Springer-Verlag, Berlin.

Rolski, T., Schmidli, H., Schmidt, V. and Teugels, J. (1999), *Stochastic Processes for Insurance and Finance*, Wiley Series in Probability and Statistics, Wiley, Berlin.

Part III
Causal Modeling

Causal Models: Applying Econometrics and Time Series Statistics to Operational Risk

8.1 INTRODUCTION

Until now we have just been concerned with using loss data information to estimate the operational VaR for an institution or a particular business area. In practice, this is sufficient to *measure* operational risk but not to *manage* it. Given that we have a VaR measure we, as risk managers, need to learn what drives the process with the objective of managing and reducing operational risk. At this stage, we will move from *operational risk measurement* to *operational risk management*. We need to start to understand the influence of manageable factors like systems and/or people in the operational VaR. This is similar to what market risk managers do when studying, for example, the influence of an increase in interest rates on a bank's VaR and positioning. In this chapter I present a few models that might prove useful in linking control environment factors and key risk indicators to losses, generating models to explain the relationship between them.

In terms of this chapter's organization, the basics of multiple regression and multivariate analysis are briefly shown in Sections 8.2–8.6 and then an operational risk multifactor model is introduced in Section 8.7 to explain losses inside a bank. More sophisticated models in state space, using Kalman filters and Markov chains, are also briefly shown in Sections 8.8 and 8.9. I end up by showing in Section 8.10 an application of discriminant analysis that can be used either inside an organization or between organizations and, similarly to credit risk, how an operational risk migration matrix can be developed.

8.2 BASICS OF MULTIPLE REGRESSION

Francis Galton (1886) introduced the term "regression". In his famous paper, he discovered that although there was a tendency for tall parents to have tall children and likewise for short parents to have short children, the average height of children born to parents of a given height has a tendency to "regress" toward the average height of the population as a whole. Today, regression analysis studies the dependence of one variable, called dependent, on one or more variables, deemed independent.

In a two-variable regression, the regression model will be represented by:

$$Y_i = \alpha_1 + \alpha_2 X_i + \varepsilon_i$$

where Y_i is the dependent variable, X_i is the independent variable and ε_i is the error component. The α's are the parameters of the equation.

That brings us to the problem of estimating the parameters of this equation. There

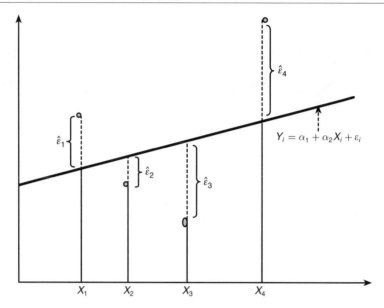

Figure 8.1   Regression line fitting

are many approaches, but one of the most popular is the OLS (ordinary least squares) method. In this method we basically solve the equation for ε_i and minimize:

$$\hat{\varepsilon}_i = Y_i - \hat{\alpha}_1 - \hat{\alpha}_2 X_i \quad \text{or} \quad \hat{\varepsilon}_i = Y_i - \hat{Y}_i$$

As we can see in Figure 8.1, the regression is basically a best linear estimate of a set of data points.

The OLS method squares the residuals and minimizes their sum by solving the problem:

$$\min \sum \hat{\varepsilon}_i = \sum (Y_i - \hat{\alpha}_1 - \hat{\alpha}_2 X_i)^2$$

The parameters that solve the above equation for the minimum value of the residuals are picked.

8.2.1   Goodness-of-Fit or R^2 Coefficient

The coefficient of determination R^2 is a summary measure that tells us how well the regression fits the data. In multiple regression it is important to highlight the fact that the coefficient will always increase as a new explanatory variable is included. Therefore, tests should be used to verify the need to include new variables in the model. The coefficient of determination is given by the formula below:

$$R^2 = 1 - \frac{\sum \hat{u}_i^2}{\sum (Y_i - \bar{Y})^2}$$

This formula is found in virtually any spreadsheet or statistical package.

8.2.2   *F*-Test

A question that is usually of interest is whether the regression equation as a whole is significant. One important test to verify this significance is the *F*-test. The *F*-test is part of the analysis of variance (ANOVA) tests. It verifies the ratio of the variation of the regression caused by the regression itself to the variation caused by the residuals. The *F*-test is basically a joint test of the hypothesis that all the coefficients except the constant term are zero. If all the slopes are zero, the multiple correlation coefficients are zero as well, so the test of this hypothesis can be based on the value of R^2. The *F*-test is calculated by:

$$F = \frac{\left(\hat{\alpha}_2 \sum y_i x_{2i} + \hat{\alpha}_3 \sum y_i x_{3i}\right)/2}{\sum \hat{u}_i^2/(n-3)}$$

and is distributed as an *F* distribution with 2 and $(n-3)$ degrees of freedom. Note that a large *F* is induced by a large value of R^2.

8.2.3   Standard Errors and *t*-Ratios

The standard error is the simple standard deviation of the Y values about the estimated regression line. Put another way, the standard error of the estimate is the standard deviation of the sampling distribution of the statistic. The formula below estimates the standard error:

$$\hat{\sigma} = \sqrt{\frac{\sum \hat{u}_i^2}{n-2}}$$

This is a very important reference to identify if the parameter belongs to a model which estimates coefficient intervals for the parameters as well. The *t*-ratio is an alternative but complementary approach to the coefficient interval method of testing the significance of a model. The *t*-ratio is just the coefficient divided by the standard error and can be represented by:

$$t = \frac{\hat{\beta}_1}{\hat{\sigma}_1}$$

8.2.4   Correlation vs. Regression

Regression and correlation are closely related but conceptually different. In regression analysis, there is an asymmetry in dealing with the dependent and explanatory variables. The dependent variable is assumed to be stochastic, i.e. we have a statistical distribution of its values. The explanatory or independent variables are assumed to have fixed values (although this hypothesis might be relaxed, as we will see in state-space models). In correlation analysis, the variables are treated symmetrically. Furthermore, there is no distinction between dependent and explanatory variables. Both variables are deemed to be stochastic.

   The coefficient of correlation *r* for two variables X and Y is calculated by the formula below:

$$r = \frac{n \sum X_i Y_i - \left(\sum X_i\right)\left(\sum Y_i\right)}{\sqrt{\left[n \sum X_i^2 - \left(\sum X_i\right)^2\right]\left[n \sum Y_i^2 - \left(\sum Y_i\right)^2\right]}}$$

This formula can be found in virtually any spreadsheet or statistical package.

8.3   ECONOMETRIC MODELS: USUAL PROBLEMS

There are several problems that could arise when running an econometric model. There is vast literature on the subject; the less advanced reader might refer to Gujarati (1995) and the more mathematically inclined can refer to Greene (1993) or Hamilton (1994). Below are listed some of the most common problems in identification techniques and a few suggestions on how to fix them. The situations below violate the assumptions of the classical regression models, while a lack of detection and correction might affect the parameters and therefore the quality of the prediction.

8.3.1   Autocorrelation

Autocorrelation can be defined as the lag correlation of a given series with itself. The term is sometimes also used synonymously with serial correlation. In the classical regression model, it is assumed that the disturbance term (the error) of one observation is not influenced by the disturbance of another. Should this not be the case, then the parameter estimation may be seriously compromised.

One way of detecting autocorrelation is through the Durbin–Watson d test. This statistic is defined by the formula below:

$$d = \frac{\sum\limits_{t=2}^{n} (\hat{u}_t - \hat{u}_{t-1})^2}{\sum\limits_{t=2}^{n} \hat{u}_t^2}$$

This ratio is just the ratio of the sum of the squared differences in successive residuals to the residual sum of squares. Any statistical package has this statistic as basic information from the regression, and the analysis is quite straightforward.

Autocorrelation can be fixed by running a special kind of regression called "Cochrane–Orcutt" (see example below; for more theoretical details see, for example, Gujarati 1995). This type of regression estimates the coefficients of autocorrelation iteratively until they differ by a very small amount.

8.3.2   Multicollinearity

It is possible to have a regression with a high R^2 but very low significance of t-ratios. When such a situation occurs, it may be caused by multicollinearity. This means the existence of an exact linear relationship between some or several variables of the model. In this case, very little can be done, as the multicollinearity is a sample problem, i.e. the sample has this characteristic.

8.3.3   Heteroscedasticity

Another important assumption of the classical regression model is that the variance of the error term (or the disturbances) is constant. This is called homoscedasticity. Heteroscedasticity occurs when the variance of the error term varies. Once again, this problem will affect the parameter estimation and needs to be detected.

One formal way to detect heteroscedasticity is through Spearman's rank correlation test. This test is quite simple and based on the following formula:

$$r_{\text{Spearman}} = 1 - 6\left[\frac{\sum d_i^2}{n(n^2 - 1)}\right]$$

where d_i is the rank difference assigned to two different characteristics of the ith element and n is the number of individuals ranked.

The test is run initially by fitting the regression and getting the residuals $\hat{u}_i$ (most software does this automatically). Take the absolute value of $\hat{u}_i$ and rank both $|\hat{u}_i|$ and X_i in ascending or descending order. Using the formula above, find the Spearman correlation index. The significance of the sample r_{Spearman} can be tested via the t-test, using the formula below (with 2 degrees of freedom):

$$t = \frac{r_{\text{Spearman}}\sqrt{n - 2}}{\sqrt{1 - r_{\text{Spearman}}^2}}$$

Comparing with the t-table (available in most spreadsheet and basic statistic books), if the computed t-value exceeds the critical t-value, the hypothesis of heteroscedasticity is accepted. Otherwise, it is rejected.

8.4   MODEL SELECTION CRITERIA

Accepting a model in econometric analysis will involve both statistical and non-statistical considerations. It will depend on the objective of the analysis. The factor usually used to accept a model is the goodness-of-fit coefficient, but this alone is clearly not enough.

Two popular criteria are the Akaike information criterion (AIC) and the Schwarz Bayesian criterion (SBC). They are briefly defined below.

8.4.1   Akaike Information Criterion

Assuming $l_n(\tilde{\theta})$ to be the maximized log-likelihood function of an econometric model, the AIC for this model is defined in general as:

$$\text{AIC} = l_n(\tilde{\theta}) - d$$

where d is the dimension and θ represents the parameters of the model.

For a single-equation regression model, the AIC can be written as:

$$\text{AIC}_\sigma = \log(\tilde{\sigma}^2) + \frac{2d}{n}$$

where $\tilde{\sigma}^2$ is the ML estimator of the variance of regression disturbances.

8.4.2 Schwarz Bayesian Criterion

The SBC provides a large-sample approximation to the posterior odds ratio of models under consideration. It is defined by:

$$\text{SBC}_\sigma = l_n(\tilde{\theta}) - \tfrac{1}{2}d \log n$$

The model with the highest SBC value is selected.

8.5 SPECTRAL ANALYSIS

Spectral analysis allows us to investigate the properties of time series in the frequency domain. The main objective of spectral analysis is to determine how important cycles of different frequency are in determining the behavior of a univariate covariance stationary process.

Assuming that autocovariances are absolutely summable, the population spectrum can be written as:

$$f(\omega) = \frac{1}{\pi}\left[\gamma_0 + 2\sum_{k=1}^{\infty} \gamma_k \cos(\omega k)\right] \quad 0 \leqslant \omega < \pi$$

There are a few methods based on "lag windows" (a set of weights) used to estimate the spectral density of the residuals. Basically the formula is:

$$\hat{f}(\omega_j) = \left(\lambda_0 + 2\sum_{k=1}^{m} \lambda_k R_k \cos(k\omega)\right)$$

where m is the window size and R_k is the autocorrelation coefficient of order k, defined by:

$$R_k = \frac{\left(\sum_{t=k+1}^{n}(x_t - \bar{x})(x_{t-k} - \bar{x})\right)}{\sum_{t=1}^{n}(x_t - \bar{x})^2}$$

λ_k represents the lag windows (the weights) and can be calculated by a few methods, such as Tukey, Bartlett and Panzer. Below we show the Panzer window formula:

$$\lambda_k = \begin{cases} 1 - 6\left(\frac{k}{m}\right)^2 + 6\left(\frac{k}{m}\right)^3 & 0 \leqslant k \leqslant \frac{m}{2} \\ 2\left(1 - \frac{k}{m}\right)^3 & \frac{m}{2} \leqslant k \leqslant m \end{cases}$$

8.6 MULTIVARIATE ANALYSIS

Due to the fact that several factors might explain the operational losses or operational VaR, we probably need to find a way to optimize their use and/or find any possible existing correlation. There are quite a few techniques to perform such an analysis within the area of "multivariate analysis". Below I show two of them, factor analysis (Section 8.6.1) and canonical correlation (Section 8.6.2).

8.6.1 Factor Analysis

Factor analysis is a procedure that takes a large number of variables and verifies whether they have a small number of factors in common that account for their intercorrelation. There are some uses of factor analysis in causal models:

(1) *Data reduction and transformation.* A huge number of factors can be reduced to a manageable level. As an example, an analyst might have collected 36 factors explaining transaction processing losses. After the factor analysis, we might learn that just four or five factors explain 80% of the variance and the remaining factors are almost irrelevant.
(2) *Scaling.* Factor analysis might help in a process of scaling by dividing the variables into independent factors. In this case, each factor might represent a scale measure of some underlying variable. Factor analysis also provides the weights to use for each variable when combining them into a scale.

There are basically three steps in solving a factor analysis problem. Initially, a set of correlations between all combinations of the variables of interest is developed. The next step is to extract a set of initial factors from the correlation matrix generated in the first step, then rotate the initial factors to find the final solution.

Regarding the calculation of the correlation matrix, two broad classes of factor analysis might be distinguished: *R*-factor analysis (calculated between variables) and *Q*-factor analysis (calculated between cases).

In order to proceed with the second step, extracting initial factors, there are quite a few ways to advance, such as the principal component method. The objective of factor extraction is to find a set of factors that are formed as a linear combination of the variables in the correlation matrix. Therefore, if the variables X_1, X_2 and X_3 were highly correlated with one another, they could be put together to form one factor. A linear combination might be defined as follows:

$$z = a_1 X_1 + a_2 X_2 + a_3 X_3 + \cdots + a_n X_n$$

where z is a linear combination. This is called a principal component. The methodology involves searching for the values of a above, which form a linear combination that explains more variance in the correlation matrix than any other set of a values. This is called the first principal component. The explained variance is then subtracted from the original input matrix to yield a residual matrix. A second component is extracted from the matrix, and so on until there is little variance to be explained. As the initial components are usually difficult to explain, the initial solution is rotated to facilitate the interpretation. There are two basic types of rotation: orthogonal rotation, in which the components are kept uncorrelated with one another and oblique rotation, that allows the factors to be correlated with one another. There are several statistical packages that perform this analysis in a very straightforward way.

8.6.2 Canonical Correlation

A canonical correlation is the correlation of two canonical (latent) variables, one representing a set of independent variables, the other a set of dependent variables. Whereas multiple regressions are used for many-to-one relationships, canonical correlation is used for many-to-many relationships. A canonical correlation, also called a *characteristic root*, is a form of correlation relating two sets of variables. As with factor analysis, there may be more than one significant dimension (more than one canonical correlation), each representing an orthogonally separate pattern of relationships between the two latent variables. The maximum number of canonical correlations between two sets of variables is the number of variables in the smaller set.

The first canonical correlation is always the one that explains most of the relationship. The canonical correlations are interpreted the same as Pearson's r: their square is the percentage of variance in one set of variables explained by the other set along the dimension represented by the given canonical correlation (usually the first). Another way to put it is to say that R_c^2 is the percentage of shared variance along this dimension.

Analogous with ordinary correlation, canonical correlation squared is the percentage of variance in the dependent set explained by the independent set of variables along a given dimension. There may be more than one such linear correlation relating the two sets of variables, with each such correlation representing a different dimension by which the independent set of variables is related to the dependent set. The purpose of canonical correlation is to explain the relation of the two sets of variables, not to model the individual variables. The canonical correlation is optimized such that the linear correlation between the two latent variables is maximized. Wilks's lambda is commonly used to test the significance of canonical correlation.

Canonical correlation is a member of the multiple general linear methods family and shares many of the assumptions of multiple regression, such as linearity of relationships, homoscedasticity (same level of relationship for the full range of the data), interval or near-interval data, untruncated variables, proper specification of the model, lack of high multicollinearity and multivariate normality for the purposes of hypothesis testing. It also shares with factor analysis the need to impute labels for the canonical variables based on structure correlations, which function as a form of canonical factor loading. Researchers may well impute different labels based on the same data.

Let us look at the case where only one pair of basis vectors is sought, namely those corresponding to the largest canonical correlation. Consider the linear combinations $x = x^T \hat{w}_x$ and $y = y^T \hat{w}_y$ of the two variables respectively. This means that the function to be maximized is:

$$\rho = \frac{E[xy]}{\sqrt{E[x^2]E[y^2]}} = \frac{E[\hat{w}_x^T xy^T \hat{w}_y]}{\sqrt{E[\hat{w}_x^T xx^T \hat{w}_x]E[\hat{w}_y^T yy^T \hat{w}_y]}}$$

$$= \frac{w_x^T C_{xy} w_y}{\sqrt{w_x^T C_{xx} w_x w_y^T C_{yy} w_y}}$$

The maximum of ρ with respect to w_x and w_y is the maximum canonical correlation. The subsequent canonical correlations are uncorrelated for different solutions, i.e.:

$$\begin{cases} E[x_i x_j] = E[w_{x_i}^T x x^T w_{x_j}] = w_{x_i}^T C_{xx} w_{x_j} = 0 \\ E[y_i y_j] = E[w_{y_i}^T y y^T w_{y_j}] = w_{y_i}^T C_{yy} w_{y_j} = 0 \quad \text{for } i \neq j \\ E[x_i y_j] = E[w_{x_i}^T x y^T w_{y_j}] = w_{x_i}^T C_{xy} w_{y_j} = 0 \end{cases}$$

The projections onto w_x and w_y, i.e. x and y, are called *canonical variates*.

Given that several factors may often be used to explain operational losses, canonical correlation is certainly an eligible technique to deal with this problem. However, this technique still assumes a linear relationship between the factors. In order to allow non-linearities in correlation, one eligible technique will be copulas (see Chapter 11).

8.7   MULTIFACTOR MODELING IN OR — CAUSAL MODELING

As mentioned before, the fact that we have an operational VaR figure is useful but does not help in managing operational risk. There is a clear need for a model that supplements the VaR analysis, explaining the sensitivity of the aggregate losses to manageable factors. As a comparison, with market VaR there are several factors that can be isolated to explain the final composition of the figure. For instance, we can decompose the market VaR in fixed income, equity, FX, etc. By understanding the effect that, for example, macroeconomic variables like inflation, M1, interest rates have on fixed income products, we might analyze how the VaR is affected, for example, by an increase in interest rates.

Likewise, it would be interesting to do the same in operational risk. The difference is that most of the factors that influence operational risk are internal and could be managed by the bank. We might be able to develop causal models that explain the influence of certain variables on the operational risk.

One approach to deal with these causal models is to consider them as linear and use multifactor models to explain losses. That is what I do in this section. The factors (control environment factors, key risk indicators, etc.) are chosen as defined in Chapter 2. Any factors might be used, with their importance to the analysis tested by factor, or principal component, analysis.

Basically, the model tries to explain operational losses with several different control environment factors as below:

$$Y_t = \alpha_t + \beta_{1_t} X_{1_t} + \cdots + \beta_{n_t} x_{n_t} + \varepsilon_t$$

where Y_t represents the operational losses (or operational VaR) in a particular business unit or area in a certain period (day, month, etc.) and X_{n_t} represents the control environment factors. The α's and β's are the estimated parameters.

As a reminder and as covered in Chapter 2, it is important to link operational events to the date they were generated. The importance of this can clearly be seen now. Operational losses in transaction processing crystallize in a few days. In this causal model, it is very important that we locate which transaction caused the loss and when it was originated. Therefore, we can backtrack and examine the control environment at the precise time the event happened. Consider the situation where, on a given day, the

| | Operational Loss Data | | Control Environment Factors | | | |
| | | Number | System | | Data | |
Date	Losses	of Losses	Downtime	Employees	Quality	Transactions
(···)						
2-Jul	$234,412	10,004	3	22	94%	250,096
3-Jul	$91,234	7284	1	24	96%	208,111
4-Jul	$2,734,009	17,972	10	19	88%	345,611
5-Jul	$345,661	8613	3	24	95%	210,075
6-Jul	$545	5745	0	24	98%	185,321
9-Jul	$115,912	9745	1	24	97%	249,876
10-Jul	$1234	8075	0	24	98%	252,345
11-Jul	$91,233	9287	1	24	98%	250,987
12-Jul	$55,908	8879	1	24	98%	236,765
13-Jul	$12,002	9079	0	24	98%	238,911
16-Jul	$23,456	9078	0	24	98%	237,654
17-Jul	$1,787,634	13,514	8	21	89%	293,778
18-Jul	$7,233,704	24,510	16	17	81%	415,422
19-Jul	$2891	8054	0	24	97%	250,912
22-Jul	$122	6061	0	24	98%	191,210
23-Jul	$0	5360	0	24	99%	172,901
24-Jul	$0	5283	0	24	99%	170,415
25-Jul	$200,786	8387	1	24	95%	221,876
26-Jul	$1456	6604	0	24	97%	200,121
27-Jul	$918	5934	0	24	98%	191,435
30-Jul	$1,234,095	11,438	5	22	95%	278,987
31-Jul	$17,654	7287	0	24	96%	238,908
1-Aug	$9871	7549	0	24	97%	235,908
2-Aug	$1,095,033	10,988	3	22	96%	268,001
3-Aug	$1200	6492	0	23	99%	199,761
(···)	(···)					

Figure 8.2 Data set with losses and control environment factors

system crashed for a long time, with many transactions not settled and interest claims due to counterparties. These expenses will be paid on different days. How would we know the real impact if we considered the operational event on the date we paid the expenses?

Here is a practical example. Suppose we have the data set in Figure 8.2, in which four control environment factors are selected to explain the losses: system downtime (measured in minutes per day); employees (number of employees in the back-office on that particular day); data quality (in reality a key performance indicator, the ratio of the number of transactions with no input errors to the total number of transactions); total number of transactions.

Before commencing the development of the multifactor model, we can see that just this collection of factors is an important tool for the analysis of operational risk. For example, during the period shown, we can see that the average cost of error per transaction is $1.81, with standard deviation $3.89. The average cost of error per day (the average loss) is $36.96, with standard deviation $70.22. This can be seen in Figure 8.3.

In Figure 8.3 the error ($) per transaction is calculated by dividing the total cost of errors on that day by the number of transactions processed, for example, for 2-July-2001 it is ($234,412/250,096) = $0.94. We can also calculate the loss ratio in the period, which has an average value of 3.72%. This is extremely high, considering other industries that are more concerned with cost control and operational flow achieve near

	Error($)/ transaction	Cost/ error
2-Jul	0.94	23.43
3-Jul	0.44	12.53
4-Jul	7.91	152.13
5-Jul	1.65	40.13
6-Jul	0.00	0.09
9-Jul	0.46	11.89
10-Jul	0.00	0.15
11-Jul	0.36	9.82
12-Jul	0.24	6.30
13-Jul	0.05	1.32
16-Jul	0.10	2.58
17-Jul	6.08	132.28
18-Jul	17.41	295.13
19-Jul	0.01	0.36
22-Jul	0.00	0.02
23-Jul	0.00	–
24-Jul	0.00	–
25-Jul	0.90	23.94
26-Jul	0.01	0.22
27-Jul	0.00	0.15
30-Jul	4.42	107.89
31-Jul	0.07	2.42
1-Aug	0.04	1.31
2-Aug	4.09	99.66
3-Aug	0.01	0.18
Average	1.81	36.96
Standard Deviation	3.89	70.22

Figure 8.3 Cost of errors per transaction and per error

zero errors (a cell phone manufacturer recently reported an error ratio of 0.03%!). Understanding the source of the errors is fundamental to fixing them and getting lower error ratios.

Using the data set given, we might relate these environmental factors to the operational losses. Figure 8.4 shows the results for the multifactor model (using Microfit software).

The multifactor model equation can be written as:

$$\text{Operational losses} = 7,465,731 + 238,411.5 \times \text{System downtime} - 156,136.4$$
$$\times \text{Employees} - 4,375,915 \times \text{Data quality} + 1.8378$$
$$\times \text{Transactions} + \varepsilon$$

Plotting the predicted against the real results confirms the extremely good fit of the model (see Figure 8.5).

Despite the good fit, some problems are apparent in the regression. The first is that, despite this extremely high fit of the model (approximately 90%), the t-ratios are small (i.e. less than 2 in each case), showing that there is some correlation between the data. This problem, known as multicollinearity (see Section 8.3.2), might be happening. It

Dependent variable is LOSSES
25 observations used for estimation from 2.Jul.2001 to 3.Aug.2001

Regressor	Coefficient	Standard Error	T-Ratio[Prob]
α	7465731	1.26E+07	0.59117[0.561]
System Downtime	238411.5	156304.2	1.5253[0.143]
Employees	−156136.4	227224.5	−0.68715[0.500]
Data Quality	−4375915	1.05E+07	−0.41738[0.681]
Transactions	1.8378	4.2622	0.43118[0.671]

R-Squared	0.90975	R-Bar-Squared	0.89170
S.E. of Regression	505438.0	F-stat. F(4, 20)	50.4038[0.000]
Mean of Dependent Variable	611638.8	S.D. of Dependent Variable	1535897
Residual Sum of Squares	5.11E+12	Equation Log-likelihood	−361.0137
Akaike Info. Criterion	−366.0137	Schwarz Bayesian Criterion	−369.0609
DW-statistic	2.2274		

Diagnostic Tests

Test Statistics	LM Version	F Version
A: Serial Correlation	CHSQ(12) = 8.8504[0.716]	F(12, 8) = 0.36535[0.943]
B: Functional Form	CHSQ(1) = 21.5556[0.000]	F(1, 19) = 118.9054[0.000]
C: Normality	CHSQ(2) = 7.3928[0.025]	Not applicable
D: Heteroscedasticity	CHSQ(1) = 21.8557[0.000]	F(1, 23) = 159.8703[0.000]

A: Lagrange multiplier test of residual serial correlation
B: Ramsey's RESET test using the square of the fitted values
C: Based on a test of skewness and kurtosis of residuals
D: Based on the regression of squared residuals on squared fitted values

Figure 8.4   Multifactor model for operational losses using four control environment factors

means that the factors probably have a reasonable degree of correlation between them. There is not much we can do about it, as this is a sample problem (and we obviously cannot change the data). Multicollinearity is not necessarily bad, especially if the objective of the model is prediction only.

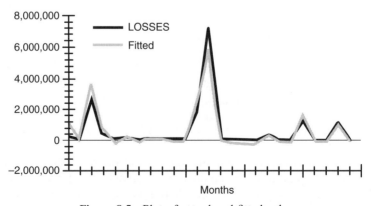

Figure 8.5   Plot of actual and fitted values

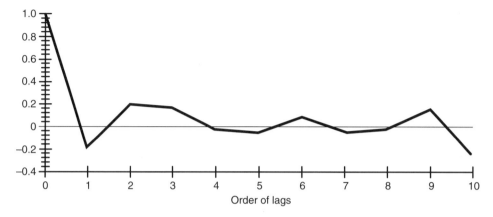

Figure 8.6. Autocorrelation function of residuals

The other problem is that the tests for serial correlation are not good. The LM (Lagrange multiplier) version, for example, presents a p-value of 0.716. If the autocorrelation graph is plotted, as in Figure 8.6, a pattern in the initial lags can clearly be seen.

We also plotted the spectral density of the residuals in Figure 8.7.

In interpreting a plot such as Figure 8.7, it is often more convenient to think in terms of the period of a cyclic function rather than its frequency. Recall from Section 8.5 that if the frequency of a cycle is ω, the period of the cycle is $2\pi/\omega$. Hence, a frequency of $\omega_j = 2\pi/T$ (where T = number of days, months, etc.) corresponds to a period of $2\pi/\omega_j = T/j$. The sample size in our example is too small ($T = 26$ days) to perform any meaningful spectral analysis, and the plot in Figure 8.7 does not say much. However, using a larger sample of the same problem (starting in January 1999 with $T = 426$), we verify that the first peak occurs with frequency $j = 26$. This corresponds to a cycle of $426/26 = 16.38$, or about 1 year and 4 months. When dealing with economic data, this is known as a "business cycle frequency", and the area "under the hill" might tell us how much of the variability in daily growth rates is due, for example, to economic

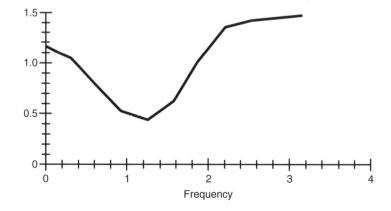

Figure 8.7 Standardized spectral density of residuals (Parzen window)

Test of Serial Correlation of Residuals (OLS case)—1 Lag

Dependent variable is LOSSES
List of variables in OLS regression:
α System Downtime   Employees   Data Quality   Transactions
25 observations used for estimation from 2.Jul.2001 to 3.Aug.2001

Regressor	Coefficient	Standard Error	T-Ratio[Prob]
OLS RES(−1)	−0.26039	0.26439	−0.98485[0.335]

Lagrange Multiplier Statistic	CHSQ(1) = 1.2142[0.270]
F Statistic	F(1, 19) = 0.96994[0.337]

Figure 8.8   Test of serial correlation of residuals

Cochrane–Orcutt Method AR(1) converged after 3 iterations

Dependent variable is LOSSES
25 observations used for estimation from 2.Jul.2001 to 3.Aug.2001

Regressor	Coefficient	Standard Error	T-Ratio[Prob]
α	1.61E+07	1.22E+07	1.3266[0.200]
System Downtime	115081.2	158053.6	0.72812[0.475]
Employees	−338917.4	232879.8	−1.4553[0.161]
Transactions	1.6213	3.7891	0.42789[0.673]
Data Quality	−8642021	9767640	−0.88476[0.387]
R-Squared	0.92913	R-Bar-Squared	0.90944
S.E. of Regression	471510.6	F-stat. F(5,18)	47.1977[0.000]
Mean of Dependent Variable	611638.8	S.D. of Dependent Variable	1535897
Residual Sum of Squares	4.00E+12	Equation Log-likelihood	−344.1311
Akaike Info. Criterion	−350.1311	Schwarz Bayesian Criterion	−353.7877
DW-statistic	2.0155		

Parameters of the Autoregressive Error Specification

$U = -0.19509 {}^{*}U(-1) + E$
(*NONE*)
T-ratio(s) based on asymptotic standard errors in brackets

Figure 8.9   Cochrane–Orcutt method regression

recessions. In our case, this period might indicate a cyclical deterioration of the control environment. This analysis is therefore important and should be performed in larger databases.

Just to confirm that autocorrelation was a problem, a first-order test of residual serial correlation was completed. The result, shown in Figure 8.8, confirms that there are problems in this respect.

Given these serial correlation problems, we need to follow the Cochrane–Orcutt procedure to run the regression. The Cochrane–Orcutt (1949) iterative procedure uses the estimated residuals $\hat{u}_t$ to obtain information about the unknown level of autocorrelation. Details of this procedure can be found in Gujarati (1995). The results of the procedure are seen in Figure 8.9.

Having overcome the serial correlation of the residuals problem, the model can now be analyzed. We write it as:

$$Y = 1.61E + 07 + 115{,}081.20 X_{\text{SystemDowntime}} - 338{,}917.4 X_{\text{Employees}} + 1.62 X_{\text{Transactions}} - 8{,}642{,}021 X_{\text{DataQuality}} + \varepsilon$$
$$R^2 = 93\%$$

The first thing to notice is that all the signs of the coefficients are as expected, i.e. those variables that we expect to be negatively correlated with the losses bear a negative sign. For example, the higher the data quality, the lower the losses; the same relationship is valid for the number of employees. As for system downtime and number of transactions, the higher the value of those variables, the bigger the losses, as expected.

The goodness-of-fit of the model is even higher after correcting for the serial correlation problem, reaching 93% and meaning that the model can be used with a very high degree of confidence. This is an extremely high fit, and will probably not happen frequently, but there are reasons to believe that, to a very high extent, there is a linear correlation between these variables and the losses. In general, the fit of such models should be high.

Knowing the coefficients of these variables, or the sensitivity of the impact on the operational losses of the fluctuation of these variables, we can "price" individual units of the variables. For example, the cost of 1 minute of system downtime in a day reflected in operational losses is $151,081.20. Therefore, any decision that leads to an improvement of the processing systems might use such figures as a benchmark.

If, for example, we consider all variables stable at 3 minutes downtime, 220,000 transactions and 20 employees a day, an improvement of one percentage point (from 98% to 99%) in the quality of the input data will mean a decrease in losses of $86,420.21.

$$Y_1 = 1.61E + 07 + 115{,}081.20 \times 3 - 338{,}917.4 \times 20 + 1.62 \times 220{,}000 - 8{,}642{,}021 \times 98\% = \$1{,}554{,}401.02$$
$$Y_2 = 1.61E + 07 + 115{,}081.20 \times 3 - 338{,}917.4 \times 20 + 1.62 \times 220{,}000 - 8{,}642{,}021 \times 99\% = \$1{,}467{,}980.81$$
$$Y_2 - Y_1 = \$86{,}420.21$$

Another example of how useful these types of model are can be seen in the following case. Suppose that the front-office, due to the profitability of the products traded in this area, decides to increase the daily volume negotiated by 30%. The board then asks the operational risk management unit to evaluate the operational impact of this decision, simultaneously stating that no employees can be hired, as the bank wants to reduce the headcount.

The average number of trades during the period 2-July to 3-August was 239,815. This 30% increase will mean that the average will move to 311,760. Using the above model we realize that, keeping all variables constant, the daily extra cost will be at the significant level of $116,643.62. As no employees can be hired, we should find ways to improve the system, or even improve the average data quality of 95.76%. If an internal quality program is developed and the quality of the input is increased to an average of 97.1%, then the impact on costs of this growth in number of transactions will be zero.

Another application can be made using KCIs (key control indicators; some prefer to call them KPIs, key performance indicators). Keeping to the same example of transaction processing, one factor that most banks collect is the so-called "nostro breaks", i.e. the breaks in the bank's own account (e.g. payments received without clear origin, etc.). In general, when such a situation happens, a proportional number of losses are bound to happen, as transactions cannot be settled when no proper information is provided. The example in Figure 8.10 shows a database that counts the number of

Date	# Nostro Breaks	# Losses
2-Feb-01	1380	330
3-Feb-01	989	1234
4-Feb-01	1598	1289
5-Feb-01	2011	1002
6-Feb-01	1979	1521
7-Feb-01	2193	1875
8-Feb-01	627	1901
9-Feb-01	1406	1712
10-Feb-01	1938	345
11-Feb-01	1065	901
12-Feb-01	1224	1834
13-Feb-01	824	621
14-Feb-01	761	910
15-Feb-01	1109	632
16-Feb-01	1191	234
17-Feb-01	653	872
18-Feb-01	1273	761
19-Feb-01	1338	311
20-Feb-01	1554	899
21-Feb-01	300	871
22-Feb-01	1369	1105
23-Feb-01	1352	102
24-Feb-01	2037	912
25-Feb-01	650	908
26-Feb-01	1426	1239
27-Feb-01	1295	234
28-Feb-01	2289	1182
1-Mar-01	1846	876
2-Mar-01	2450	1512

Figure 8.10   Data set with KCIs and operational losses

nostro breaks and the losses (in this example we are considering the date they happen, not the date they were originated).

Based on this database, we might run a model to check the lag (if any) between the number of nostro breaks and operational losses. The best result was achieved with time lag (2) as seen in Figure 8.11.

Ordinary Least Squares Estimation

Dependent variable is LOSSES
27 observations used for estimation

Regressor	Coefficient	Standard Error	T-Ratio[Prob]
KCI(-2)	0.36726	0.28639	1.2824[0.211]

R-Squared	-0.86290	R-Bar-Squared	-0.86290
S.E. of Regression	540.9852	F-stat.	*NONE*
Mean of Dependent Variable	385.1852	S.D. of Dependent Variable	396.3606
Residual Sum of Squares	7609291	Equation Log-likelihood	-207.7234
Akaike Info. Criterion	-208.7234	Schwarz Bayesian Criterion	-209.3713

Figure 8.11   Regression results for Lag(2) with no intercept

R^2 is negative, due to the fact that no intercept was used in this regression, but it is still very high (86%). This proves a clear correlation between the nostro breaks happening one day and an operational loss happening 2 days later, via the model #Losses $= 0.36726 \times$ #Nostro breaks$_{t-2} + \varepsilon$. This type of model can be very useful in estimating losses when very few factors are available.

A few more applications of this model will be discussed in Chapters 11 and 12.

8.8   KALMAN FILTER

In the previous section a model was presented that was deterministic, with the parameters fixed across time. This model works well, but not without a few theoretical shortcomings. One, for example, is that dynamic systems are driven not only by these control inputs, but also by disturbances that we can neither control nor model deterministically. Another is that, in addition, the control indicators also introduce their own system dynamics and distortions.

A way to overcome these shortcomings must be found in order to improve our model. For example, given incomplete or "noise-corrupted" data and some disturbances that are beyond our control, how is a system optimally controlled to provide optimal information on the state of the controls?

An answer might come from moving the econometric system to one represented in state space and solving via a Kalman filter.

A simple example of the state-space representation of a dynamic econometric model is a univariate MA(1) process:

$$y_t = \mu + \varepsilon_t + \theta \varepsilon_{t-1}$$

This model can be written in state-space form as follows (using the Hamilton 1994 example):

State equation ($r = 2$)

$$\begin{bmatrix} \varepsilon_{t+1} \\ \varepsilon \end{bmatrix} = \begin{bmatrix} 0 & 0 \\ 0 & 0 \end{bmatrix} \begin{bmatrix} \varepsilon_t \\ \varepsilon_{t-1} \end{bmatrix} + \begin{bmatrix} \varepsilon_{t+1} \\ 0 \end{bmatrix}$$

Observation equation ($n = 1$)

$$y_t = \mu + [1 \ \theta] \begin{bmatrix} \varepsilon_t \\ \varepsilon_{t-1} \end{bmatrix}$$

Such models are called "structured" and are nothing more than regression models in which the explanatory variables are functions of time and the parameters are time-varying. The way to handle these structural time-series models is via the state-space form. Once in state-space form, the Kalman filter provides the means of updating the state, as new observations become available. Extrapolating these components into the future makes the necessary system predictions.

An important feature of the state-space form is that it can deal with missing observations. These types of model can also be extended to allow for more subtle data irregularities, such as those arising from data revisions, which is something that often occurs in operational risk.

Setting up models in state space also improves flexibility by allowing irregularly spaced observations to be dealt with, which is definitely the case in operational risk. These state-space models can be solved using the Kalman filter.

The Kalman filter is actually an optimal recursive data processing algorithm. The filter incorporates all available information and processes it to estimate the current level of the variables of interest, essentially via:

- The statistical description of the system noises, measurement errors and any uncertainties.
- Information about the system dynamics.
- Any available information about the variables of interest.

Basically, the Kalman filter combines all available measurement data, plus some prior knowledge about the system and measurement model, to produce an estimate of the desired variables in such a manner that the error is minimized statistically. In general, what filters aim to do (any type) is to get an optimal (minimize errors) estimate of desired quantities from data provided by a noisy environment.

There are a few assumptions that underlie the Kalman filter. The first is that the Kalman filter works for linear models in systems where noises are white and Gaussian. I explain these assumptions below.

Linear systems are much easier to work with than non-linear systems, and the linear system theory (solved by differential equations) is also much more developed. This is essentially the problem to be examined in Chapter 9, when non-linear models are considered. They are much harder to explain and work with.

White noise means that the prediction errors of the system (or the "noises") are not correlated in time. In other words, if the noise is known today, it does not mean that it can be better predicted tomorrow. The Gaussian assumption means that the noise, at any one time, will have the shape of a bell curve.

A simple example will suffice to understand the functioning of the Kalman filter. This example is not numeric, but simply a step-by-step derivation of the filter.

Suppose the operational risk level in a particular business unit is to be estimated. One particular factor is taken to determine the risk level. At time t_1 the risk is considered to be r_1. Nevertheless, because operational risk is complex, and because of human error, etc., the result of the measurement is obviously uncertain. Hence, a measure of the uncertainty of the estimate is its standard deviation σ_{r_1}. The conditional probability of $x(t_1)$, the operational risk at time t_1, can be determined, conditioned on the observed value of the estimate being r_1, as seen in Figure 8.12.

Based on the above, the best estimate of the risk level is:

$$\hat{x}(t_1) = r_1$$

and the variance of the error in the risk estimate would be:

$$\sigma_x^2(t_1) = \sigma_{r_1}^2$$

Given this risk estimate, ask an experienced practitioner in the business area for his risk level estimate immediately afterwards at time $t_2 \cong t_1$, and get from him a measurement r_2 with a variance σ_{r_2}. Because the practitioner should be more

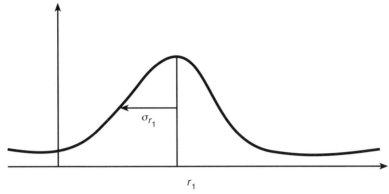

Figure 8.12 Conditional density of operational risk estimate based on measured factor r_1

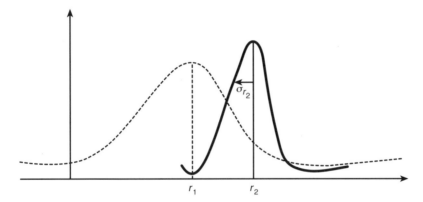

Figure 8.13 Conditional density of operational risk estimate based on measured factor r_2

experienced in this business area, it is assumed that the variance of his estimate will be less than that derived. Therefore, graphically (as shown in Figure 8.13), his estimates will have a narrower distribution (due to the smaller variance).

Now two estimates are available for the risk. The issue is how to combine them. Following the conditional probability approach shown above, the position at time $t_2 \cong t_1$, $x(t_2)$, given both r_1 and r_2, is Gaussian with mean μ and variance σ^2 defined as:

$$\mu = \left[\frac{\sigma_{r_2}^2}{\sigma_{r_1}^2 + \sigma_{r_2}^2} \right] r_1 + \left[\frac{\sigma_{r_1}^2}{\sigma_{r_1}^2 + \sigma_{r_2}^2} \right] r_2$$

and

$$\frac{1}{\sigma^2} = \frac{1}{\sigma_{r_1}^2} + \frac{1}{\sigma_{r_2}^2}$$

Notice that σ is less than σ_{r_1} and σ_{r_2}, as the uncertainty was reduced by combining the two estimates. Therefore, the best estimate is now:

$$\hat{x}(t_2) = \mu$$

The above estimate is the best possible to estimate operational risk given the information currently available. However, as noticed above, if σ_{r_1} is larger than σ_{r_2}, which means that the uncertainty of estimate r_1 is greater than that of r_2, then the formula for μ above will weight r_2 more heavily than r_1. Also, the variance of the estimate is less than σ_{r_1} even if σ_{r_2} is very large, meaning that even poor quality data provides some information and should thus increase the precision of the filter output. The equation $\hat{x}(t_2) = \mu$ can be rewritten as:

$$\hat{x}(t_2) = \left[\frac{\sigma_{r_2}^2}{\sigma_{r_1}^2 + \sigma_{r_2}^2}\right] r_1 + \left[\frac{\sigma_{r_1}^2}{\sigma_{r_1}^2 + \sigma_{r_2}^2}\right] r_2$$

$$= r_1 + \left[\frac{\sigma_{r_1}^2}{\sigma_{r_1}^2 + \sigma_{r_2}^2}\right] [r_2 - r_1]$$

which is almost the final form of the Kalman filter. The filter equation can be written:

$$\hat{x}(t_2) = \hat{x}(t_1) + K(t_2)[r_2 - \hat{x}(t_1)]$$

where:

$$K(t_2) = \frac{\sigma_{r_1}^2}{\sigma_{r_1}^2 + \sigma_{r_2}^2}$$

The set of equations above simply states that the optimal estimate at time t_2, $\hat{x}(t_2)$, is equal to the best prediction of its value before r_2 is taken, $\hat{x}(t_1)$, adjusted by an optimal weighting value times the difference between r_2 and the best prediction.

Basically what the filter does, based on all previous information, is predict the value that the desired variables and measurement will have at the next measurement time. The variance can be rewritten as:

$$\sigma_x^2(t_2) = \sigma_x^2(t_1) - K(t_2)\sigma_x^2(t_1)$$

Extending the measurement to t_3, we assume that a new measurement is taken with value r_3 and variance $\sigma_{r_3}^2$. We now need, as before, to combine the two Gaussian densities available, one containing all information prior to the measurement and the other being r_3. Using the same method as before leads to (considering $t_{\bar{3}}$ as the time just before the measurement is taken at t_3):

$$\hat{x}(t_3) = \hat{x}(t_{\bar{3}}) + K(t_3)\lfloor r_3 - \hat{x}(t_{\bar{3}})\rfloor$$

with variance:

$$\sigma_x^2(t_3) = \sigma_x^2(t_{\bar{3}}) - K(t_3)\sigma_x^2(t_{\bar{3}})$$

The gain of the filter $K(t_3)$ is represented by:

$$K(t_3) = \frac{\sigma_x^2(t_{\bar{3}})}{\sigma_x^2(t_{\bar{3}}) + \sigma_{r_3}^2}$$

From the equation above, if σ_{r_3} is large, then $K(t_3)$ is small. This means that little confidence can be put in a very noisy measurement, and so it is lightly weighted. In the

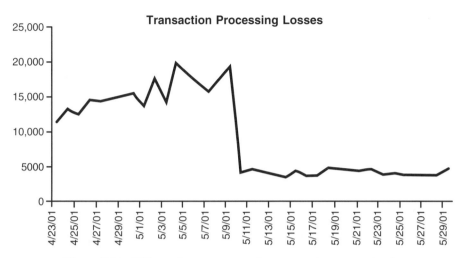

Figure 8.14   Effects of a new transaction processing system in place

limit of absolutely no confidence in the system model output, the optimal policy is to ignore the output and use the new measurement as the optimal update.

The representation of operational risk models in state space and the use of the Kalman filter can be very helpful in allowing, for example, transformation of the model shown in Section 8.7 to a real-time model and, therefore, allowing its use to enforce intra-day operational limit policies. More details can be seen in Chapter 11.

8.9   REGIME SWITCHING MODELS

Often in operational risk (and most certainly in other sciences, particularly economics) the behavior of time series can change quite dramatically. For example, this could arise when a new back-office system is installed that decreases the number of fails by 50%, or if there is a change in regulation that makes an institution more sensitive to a certain event. Figure 8.14 illustrates the case of losses in transaction processing after the implementation of a new system.

The figure shows that there is quite a dramatic break when the new system started on May 10, 2001. We need to see how such changes are modeled. Should the events prior to the new system implementation be ignored? If the data, as plotted above, is used, the model prior to May 10 can be represented by:

$$y_t - \mu_1 = \psi(y_{t\;1} - \mu_1) + \varepsilon_t$$

and the model after May 10 can be represented by:

$$y_t - \mu_2 = \psi(y_{t-1} - \mu_2) + \varepsilon_t$$

where $\mu_2 < \mu_1$.

The specification given by these equations may seem a plausible description of the data above, but it is not adequate as a time-series model. One can assume that if the system has changed in the past it can obviously change again in the future, and this should be considered when making future predictions. It would be much better if instead of treating the change as deterministic, it was considered to be stochastic. A more complete model would therefore include a description of the probability law that governs the change from μ_1 to μ_2.

With that aim, consider including a random variable c_t^*, which can be called the state or regime that the process was in at time t. If $c_t^* = 1$, for example, then the process is in regime 1 (in the example, the losses under the old back-office system), while $c_t^* = 2$ when the process is in regime 2 (the losses under the new back-office system). We can rewrite the equations as:

$$y_t - \mu_{c_t^*} = \psi(y_{t-1} - \mu_{c_{t-1}^*}) + \varepsilon_t$$

where $\mu_{c_t^*}$ indicates μ_1 when $c_t^* = 1$ and μ_2 when $c_t^* = 2$.

As c_t^* takes only discrete values (in our case 1 or 2), a more proper model will have to follow these characteristics. One of the simplest time-series models for a discrete-valued random variable is a Markov chain (see Chapter 7). We can rewrite the autoregressive equation as:

$$y_t = a_{c_t} + \psi_{c_t} y_{t-1} + \varepsilon_t$$

The objective will be to model the regime c_t^* as the outcome of an unobserved N-state Markov chain with the c_t^* independent of ε_t for all t.

By using the Markov chain to model our time series, even if we assume that the change in the regime is definitive, the change might be modeled with a two-stage Markov chain in which stage 2 is an absorbing state. Markov chain modeling allows us to generate forecasts prior to any change, but considering the possibility of a change from regime 1 to regime 2.

The benefits of applying such a model are that we might avoid discarding large chunks of data because the environment changed radically from one day to another. We are able to incorporate in the model larger amounts of data, and also to understand changes in the system. If we assume that one day in the future this "new" system will be replaced by another updated one, this is the type of modeling that would help us to understand the possible benefits.

8.10   DISCRIMINANT ANALYSIS: DEVELOPING OPERATIONAL RISK SCORES

Transforming the qualitative analysis of operational risk into a more quantitative approach is one of the key problems facing operational risk managers. How can risk managers identify the relevant quantitative risk indicators? How can they weight risk factors to produce a more accurate risk rating for a business line or company? This section will show how to achieve this by means of a robust statistical technique known as discriminant analysis.

Solving this problem is important because qualitative risk scoring is being widely adopted by institutions as the most practical way of assessing operational environments across different business units. Several of the indicators used to score the risks of a unit — KRIs — have been inherited or adapted from internal audit functions. These and other operational risk indicators differ from financial risk measures in that they are mostly based on subjective opinions. Often managers are simply asked to rank risks on a scale of, say, 1 to 5.

Even where quantitative risk indicators are employed, the usual methodologies adopted limit the risk analysis because they are univariate. That is, the manager examines each risk indicator in isolation and then arrives at the — essentially qualitative — aggregate risk score or rating. It is thus not possible to determine the correlation between the indicators used by the manager to arrive at the score, or to examine how these indicators relate to the operational losses of a particular business unit over a period of time. This means that it is difficult to adjust the relative value of each indicator as an input to the final score. It is also difficult to work backwards to find out why some business lines do so much better than others in preventing operational losses or risks.

Discriminant analysis is a statistical classification technique that has been used for some time in the world of credit risk management to solve similar problems. In particular, Altman and Beaver (1968) employed the technique to develop one of the dominant models for predicting the likelihood of bankruptcy in firms. To build their model, they extracted 22 financial ratios from the financial statements of 66 companies (some of them bankrupt). Using discriminant analysis, they then identified the five ratios that contributed most to the accuracy of the model's predictions.

To apply the technique to operational risk, we must first devise a risk map that encompasses all types of operational risk (legal, compliance, operations, security, systems, etc.). This exercise is important because of the multidimensional nature of operational risk. For each dimension of risk, specify several quantitative risk indicators (for the sake of the discriminant model we might call them "factors" too). For example, two key factors in a system risk analysis might be "system downtime" (measured in minutes per day) and "system support" (the number of staff supporting a particular system). The same type of "conversion" from qualitative to quantitative should be done for each dimension of OR. It does not matter how many factors are developed, as the number can later be reduced using statistical techniques such as factor analysis or principal component analysis. (Alternatively, the multifactor model itself will discard those factors that are not representative in explaining the variance of the model.)

For example, suppose that we wish to rank the business units of a financial institution in terms of the quality and risk level of the transaction processing in each business. As a first step, we might decide to make a daily record of the number of transactions that exhibited nostro breaks[1] in each of the business units. We could then create a very simple rating for the business lines using the ratio of nostro breaks to the total number of transactions. Business units that exhibited a 0% to 1.5% ratio might be deemed AAA, those with a 1.51% to 3% ratio might be considered AA, and so on. Figure 8.15 shows how three simplified operational environments can be rated using three factors: systems, capacity and people. The idea is to use the "real" measure — the level of nostro breaks — to define the rating, and then attempt to use various factors/indicators to explain this rating.

---

[1]It would be better to use operational losses as our real measure, rather than the "loss proxy" of nostro breaks, but most banks do not have sufficient data to attempt this.

		SYSTEMS		CAPACITY		PEOPLE	
Breaks/volume (%)	Rating	System downtime min/week	System factor	Volume/employee	Capacity factor	% Total employees present	People factor
0–1.5	AAA	$\vec{X}_{AAA}$	$(\cdots)$	$\vec{Y}_{AAA}$	$(\cdots)$	$\vec{Z}_{AAA}$	$(\cdots)$
1.51–3	AA	$\vec{X}_{AA}$		$\vec{Y}_{AA}$		$\vec{Z}_{AA}$	
3.01–4.5	Rating n	$\vec{X}_n$		$\vec{Y}_n$		$\vec{Z}_n$	

DEFINE RATING

PREDICT RATINGS BASED ON FACTORS

Figure 8.15 Operational risk factors/indicators

The table in Figure 8.15 displays the factors characteristic of each rating in terms of the vectors of factors, $\vec{X}_{AAA}$, $\vec{Y}_{AAA}$, $\vec{Z}_{AAA}$ and/or any other extra factor that represents any of the three environments. For example, if a financial institution has six business units, a possible description of system downtime might be $\vec{X}_{AAA} = \{6, 3, 10, 5, 4, 11\}$. The next step is to use discriminant analysis to identify the operational environment and indicators that are associated with good (or poor) operational risk ratings. We might expect an AAA-rated business unit to present lower system downtime, a higher ratio of employee presence, and so on — but without discriminant analysis we will not be able to weight or relate these factors to nostro breaks (or loss) in any formal manner. Performing discriminant analysis, which is no more than a multiple factor econometric model, having as dependent variable the ratings, leads to a discriminant function (OR$_{\text{Rating } n}$) equivalent to:

$$\text{OR score} = \beta_1 x + \beta_2 y + \beta_3 z + \beta_n n$$

Here x is the system downtime factor, y is the volume/employee factor, z is the employees' presence ratio, and n can be any other factor. The next step is to define the scores associated with each rating by analyzing the scores across the full spectrum of business units. For example, we might look at the range of scores and decide that a business has to score higher than, say, 0.957 to achieve a rating of AAA. Units with scores lower than this, down to, say, 0.756 might then be ranked AA, and so on. This allows us to rate business lines for which the "real" measure is unavailable. Suppose, for example, that the analysis of the business units for which data is available suggests that the operational risk score of a business unit can be estimated by the relationship:

$$\text{OR score} = 0.12x + 0.0009y + 0.12z$$

This suggests that a further business unit exhibiting risk indicator scores of, say, $x = 3$ (min/week), $y = 900$ (employees) and $z = 90$ (% of the total) should be awarded a score of 1.278. It would be estimated as AAA even if we do not know the nostro breaks/number of transactions figures.

The main benefits of such a model are:

- The firm can begin to develop an understanding of the weight that should be attributed to the different risk factors/indicators and an understanding of the correlation between them (i.e. the method helps firms understand the statistical relationships between the indicators).
- If the institution is unable to produce loss data (or nostro breaks information, in the context of our example), then the risk indicators/factors, derived previously from loss experiences within the organization, can be used in the model to estimate the rating (and the level of losses).
- Many firms already collect information on certain risk indicators. The approach outlined above allows a firm to use an incomplete loss record from certain business units to calibrate the model, and to estimate the likely size and frequency of losses.

The quantitative indicators that a firm needs to develop for this kind of analysis can also be used in other kinds of statistical models. For example, the frequency or severity of losses can be analyzed using multiple regression techniques. Cluster analysis could be employed to check which factors seem to determine when losses happen. Lastly, a methodology such as this has implications for the whole industry. It could be used to generate operational risk rankings for bank sectors. Rating agencies might use the methodology to rank financial institutions according to their operational environment. In turn, reliable ratings might improve the pricing of operational risk insurance or even support the pricing of operational risk derivatives (Cruz 1999).

8.11   DEVELOPING A MATRIX OF PROBABILITY MIGRATION OF OPERATIONAL RISK RATINGS

A different way to work with the operational risk ratings mentioned in the previous section is in a similar fashion to that for credit risk. In this case, estimate the volatility of value due to changes in the control environment, reflected in the probability of the OR scores changing in the next period.

Hence, it is important to estimate the chance of a business unit with given rate r migrating to any possible control environment (and a different rate) at the risk horizon. The model presented is exactly the same as used in credit risk, but obviously using different factors to rate the control environment.

An example of the matrix of probabilities of migration of operational risk can be seen in Figure 8.16. In this case the traditional approach followed by rating agencies is used, but the rating can be something simpler, such as ranking from 1 to 10.

Current Rate	Rating in the Next Period (%)						
	AAA	AA	A	BBB	BB	B	CCC
AAA	90.81%	8.33%	0.68%	0.06%	0.12%	0.00%	0.00%
AA	0.70%	90.65%	7.79%	0.64%	0.06%	0.14%	0.02%
A	0.15%	2.27%	91.05%	5.52%	0.74%	0.26%	0.01%
BBB	0.12%	0.33%	5.95%	86.93%	5.30%	1.17%	1.12%
BB	0.10%	0.14%	0.67%	7.73%	80.53%	8.84%	1.00%
B	0.60%	0.11%	0.24%	0.43%	6.48%	83.46%	4.07%
CCC	0.22%	0.00%	0.22%	1.30%	2.38%	11.24%	64.86%

Figure 8.16   Probability migration of operational risk ratings

In the example above a business unit deemed "A" has a probability of improving to "AA" of 2.27%, and of being downgraded to "BBB" of 5.57%. The reason for such changes might be forecast changes in the control environment as new regulation is implemented, or new market environments like the implementation of the Euro currency.

As in the previous section, the ratings will be determined by a series of factors, indicators or variables but, bearing in mind the Markovian theory that the next period will depend on this one, some inference might be made on the future state of the controls. For instance, a business may be rated under the "people factor" as BB, due to the relative inexperience of its employees. If an intense training plan is implemented, or if more experienced employees from other areas are transferred, then there is a probability that the business will be ranked better (e.g. "BBB" or "A") in the next period.

This type of approach is a way of looking forward in terms of control, and thus provides incentives for control improvement inside the organization. It would be interesting if rating agencies were to develop an interest in measuring the control environment of banks as part of their assessment. This would assist with pricing operational risk insurance and derivatives. For example, if a bank is deemed "AA" in operational risk terms (no relation with the credit rating), it could make a case for cheaper insurance and operational risk derivatives than for a "B" rated bank.

REFERENCES

Altman, E. and Beaver, W. (1968), "Alternative Accounting Measures as Predictors of Failure", *Accounting Review*, 43, 113–122.

Cochrane, D. and Orcutt, G.H. (1949), "Application of Least Squares Regressions to Relationships Containing Error Terms", *Journal of the American Statistical Association*, 44, 32–61.

Cruz, M. (1999), "Taking Risk to Market", *Risk Magazine*, November.

Galton, F. (1886), "Family Likeness in Stature", *Proceedings of the Royal Society, London*, 40, 42–72.

Greene, W. (1993), *Econometric Analysis*, Prentice-Hall, Englewood Cliffs, NJ.

Gujarati, R. (1995), *Basic Econometrics*, McGraw-Hill International Editions, New York.

Hamilton, J. (1994), *Time Series*, Princeton University Press, Princeton, NJ.

9
Non-Linear Models in Operational Risk

9.1 INTRODUCTION

As an alternative to the linear models presented in the previous chapter, there is also a set of models, generally based on artificial intelligence, that tries to capture non-linearities in operational risk. Some of these techniques generate products already available in the market as Bayesian belief networks.

Such non-linear models come with a warning. Despite what vendors claim they can achieve, there are a few pitfalls in working with them. The most important of these is that they are complicated in comparison with linear models. In general, when some non-linearity exists in a model, the first attempt is to linearize it about some nominal point achieving (and accepting it as) a perturbation or even a model error. Linear systems are much easier to manipulate, and a system of linear differential equations has much more complete theoretical grounds, with the added benefit that it is more practical to use. Given these characteristics, artificial intelligence models have been used in the background in the financial industry. In credit risk, for example, these models are used to evaluate the creditworthiness of consumers, or even in credit risk scoring. Nevertheless, regulators refuse to accept these models in the economic capital definition, due to their characteristics.

Having said that, non-linear models might be able to help, even in the background, operational risk managers to deal with very difficult measurement problems. Furthermore, the technology in these models is increasing at a very fast pace, which raises considerably the reliability of such products. If the intention of the user is not to generate an operational VaR but to use non-linear models as auxiliary systems to understand risk correlations and causalities, the models introduced in this chapter might be very interesting for operational risk management.

In terms of the structure of this chapter, Section 9.2 depicts the functioning of neural networks, with an example of an application to operational risk. In Section 9.3 we mention the Bayesian belief networks. Section 9.4 shows a technique called data mining, whose use will certainly be very important in operational risk. In Section 9.5 we see a fuzzy logic model applied to a couple of operational risk examples.

9.2 NEURAL NETWORKS

As we saw in Chapter 2, KRIs are activity/value-based measures that allow senior managers to track progress toward certain risk objectives. We could have a set of, say, 10 to 12 individual KRIs and CEFs describing the control environment of a business unit. For example, in order to justify transaction processing losses, a few KCIs or CEFs can be established as the "number of transactions processed/employee ratio", "amount spent in control", etc. This scheme gives possible parameters for measuring transaction processing risk in the business unit. If in the next measurement period the "number of transactions processed/employee ratio" declines, we can assume that the risk declined in a certain proportion that might eventually not follow a linear pattern. A scheme like that presented above also allows for the implementation of a neural network that could estimate figures for operational risk based on the volatility of the factors, this time assuming that they do not hold a linear relation among them.

Neural networks are an alternative to non-parametric regressions. Because neural networks are derived from the physiology of nerve cells, they have a distinct research literature, although a few applications to finance do exist. An artificial neural network is a computational structure that mimics the structure of a human brain — a network of "neurons" that can learn and ultimately predict patterns of data. It is beyond the scope of this work to delve into the subject, but the works of Hutchinson et al. (1994) or Campbell et al. (1997) are recommended for a better understanding of basic types of neural networks.

The building block of a neural network is a single "neuron", an analogy with the basic cells that make up the human brain. Each of these neurons accepts various inputs (such as "average employee/business unit", etc.), then weights and sums them, producing an output according to some threshold function. The network is defined by the matrix of the weights of the neurons, their transfer functions and the topology of the connections between the neurons. The first neural networks to be built, single-layered networks, dubbed "perceptrons", could only store a limited number of patterns. In the 1980s, it was demonstrated that a multilayer perceptron network, with hidden layers of neurons between the inputs and outputs, could recognize a much greater range of patterns.

To demonstrate a simple application of a neural network, use a multilayer perceptron (MLP), with logistic transfer function $f(x) = (1 + \exp(-x))^{-1}$, three input units, one hidden layer including two neurons, and one output neuron.

Such an MLP would have the following functional form:

$$Y(I) = f\left[\sum_{j=1}^{J} w2_{(j)} f\left[\sum_{i=1}^{3} w1_{(i,j)} I(i) + \theta_{1(j)}\right] + \theta_{2(j)}\right]$$

where:

Y = output of the net;
f, g = smooth monotonically increasing transfer function;
$w1_{(i,j)}$ = weight between unit i of input layer and unit j of hidden layer;
$w2_{(j)}$ = weight between unit j of hidden layer and output layer;
$I(i)$ = parameter i of input vector I (KCIs or CEFs);
$\theta_{1(j)}$ = bias of unit j of hidden layer;
$\theta_{2(j)}$ = bias of output unit.

One of the advantages of neural networks is that, in contrast to more traditional models, they do not require assumptions to be made about the function to be estimated. As they do not rely on restrictive parameter assumptions, they are more robust to problems that typically affect parametric methods. The objective is to develop a

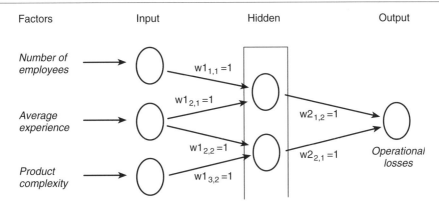

Factors   Input   Hidden   Output

Number of employees $w1_{1,1} = 1$

                          $w1_{2,1} = 1$
Average experience $w2_{1,2} = 1$

                          $w1_{2,2} = 1$ $w2_{2,1} = 1$ *Operational losses*
Product complexity $w1_{3,2} = 1$

$wk_{i,j}$ = weight from *i*th layer, *j*th node to *k*th node of next layer.

Figure 9.1   Neural network: transaction risk example

functional relationship between input factors and risk capital without guessing the form of the relationship in advance.

In Figure 9.1 a simple example of a neural net to estimate risk capital for transaction risk is presented. In this case, the inputs determined by the factors are connected to multiple hidden nodes, and at each hidden node they are weighted (usually differently at each node) and transformed by an activation function $f(\cdot)$. The output of each hidden unit is then weighted yet again, before the value at the output node is transformed by a second activation function $g(\cdot)$.

For a given set of inputs and outputs, MLP approximation amounts to estimating the parameters of the MLP network, through "training" the network. Most nets are trained by "back propagation", which reweights all coefficients based on each succeeding observation of the output relative to the value of a known output, given a set of inputs.

In back propagation the performance function generally used is the sum of squared errors, where the sum is taken with respect to both the number of available patterns and the number of output neurons.

Suppose we have a problem with P patterns (and O respective outputs) and a network structure that includes I inputs, H hidden and J outputs. The objective function of the problem might be seen as:

$$E(W) = \frac{1}{2}\sum_{p=1}^{P}\sum_{j=1}^{J}(P_{pj} - O_{pj})^2$$

The multiplication by 1/2 is applied only for simplification of the expression of the derivatives that are computed in the learning algorithm.

The algorithm starts by generating a set of weights randomly from a uniform distribution. After that, a pattern p is introduced to the network and propagated through the network as follows:

$$\text{Network}_{ph} = w_{h0} + w_{h1} S_{p1} + \cdots + w_{hI} S_{pI} \quad h = 1, \ldots, H$$

The equation above describes how the signals S_p, obtained from the outside, are transmitted to the hidden neurons. These hidden neurons perform a non-linear transformation by applying the logistic function mentioned above and repeated below for convenience:

$$H_{ph} = \left[1 + \exp(-\text{network}_{ph})\right]^{-1} \quad h = 1, \ldots, H$$

Subsequently, the network needs to compute linear combinations of the outputs of the hidden neurons that are then transmitted to the output neurons. This can be represented by:

$$\text{Network}_{pj} = w_{j0} + w_{j1}\,H_{p1} + w_{j2}\,H_{p2} + \cdots + w_{jH}\,H_{pH} \quad j = 1, \ldots, J$$

The outputs are then computed by the output neurons with the same non-linear transformation through the logistic function. A set of J errors $(P_{pj} - O_{pj})^2$ is calculated from a comparison between the target and the output for the pattern p. The errors are used to calculate $E_p(W)$, and the general formula is:

$$E_p(W) = \frac{1}{2}\sum_{p=1}^{P}(T_{pj} - O_{pj})^2$$

The error term is used to modify the weights connecting all the various layers. The general rule for modification of the weights is:

$$\Delta_p w_{ji} = -\alpha\frac{\partial E_t(W)}{\partial w_{ji}}$$

where α is a gradient that represents the learning rate, which regulates the speed of learning.

Based on the above equation, the global error can be derived with respect to weights connecting hidden to output. The following can denote these derivatives in general:

$$\frac{\partial E_p(W)}{\partial w_{ji}} = \frac{\partial E_p(W)}{\partial O_{pj}} \times \frac{\partial O_{pj}}{\partial w_{ji}}$$

which can be modified to $\Delta_p w_{ji} = -\alpha[\partial E_p(W)/\partial w_{ji}] + \omega\Delta_{p-1}w_{ji}$, where ω is the *momentum* that represents the degree of persistence in the modification of weights, since one change will depend on the previous one. When the momentum is added to the model, the value of α can be kept higher than usual in order to speed up the convergence process, since ω provides more stability to the search process.

In sequence with these steps, a cycle needs to be followed to compute the global error until it reaches a specified value.

As seen above, neural networks are basically functions that adapt to any environmental situation. However, as noted in the introduction, it is unlikely that such networks will point out extreme losses and also, due to the difficulty of explaining the calibration and sensitivity in more complex networks, might be hard to sell internally to businesses and externally to regulators. Neural networks should be used just in the case that the models presented in Chapter 8 do not work well.

9.3 BAYESIAN BELIEF NETWORKS

Bayesian belief networks (also known as belief networks, causal probabilistic networks, causal nets, graphical probability networks, probabilistic cause–effect models and probabilistic influence diagrams) have attracted much attention recently as a possible solution to the problems of decision support under uncertainty.

A *Bayesian network* (BN) is a set of nodes representing random variables and a set of arrows connecting these nodes in an acyclic manner. Each node has assigned a function that describes how the state of the node depends on the parents of the node. When used in conjunction with statistical techniques, this graphical model has several benefits for data analysis. The first is due to the fact that the model encodes dependencies among all variables; it readily handles situations where some data entries are missing.

Another benefit is that a Bayesian network can be used to learn causal relationships, and hence can be used to gain an understanding of problem domains and to predict the consequences of intervention. This type of modeling is also a good representation for combining prior knowledge (which often comes in causal form) and data, because the model has both causal and probabilistic semantics. Finally, Bayesian statistical methods in conjunction with Bayesian networks offer an efficient and principled approach to avoiding data overfitting.

To date, Bayesian belief networks have proven useful in practical applications such as medical and mechanical failure diagnosis. Their latest, and certainly most celebrated, use has been by Microsoft, where Bayesian belief nets underlie the help wizards in Microsoft Office. Also the "intelligent" printer fault diagnostic system which runs when logged onto Microsoft's web site is in fact a BN which, as a result of the problem symptoms entered, identifies the most likely fault.

A few authors have written on the application of such networks to operational risk. The reader can refer to King (2001) for examples.

Once again the same pitfalls mentioned in the previous sections apply to BNs. These networks are difficult to model for complex processes in large organizations. Nevertheless, BNs might be used in the background if carefully modeled, and for smaller processes.

9.4 DATA MINING

Data mining is the process of analyzing data from different perspectives and summarizing it into useful information — information that can be used to increase revenue, cut costs or even reduce risk. Data mining software is one of a number of analytical tools for analyzing data. It allows users to analyze data from many different dimensions or angles, categorize it and summarize the relationships identified. Technically, data mining is the process of finding correlations or patterns among dozens of fields in large relational databases.

Data mining can be extremely useful in estimating hidden correlations and patterns of losses related to operational risk in large organizations, where these operational losses can be correlated to a number of unimaginable factors. Although data mining is a relatively new term, the technology is not. Several industries have been using powerful computers to sift through, for example, volumes of supermarket scanner data and develop market research reports. Nevertheless, continuous innovations in computer processing power, disk storage and statistical software are dramatically increasing the accuracy of analysis while driving down the processing cost.

Any type of operational risk data can be bundled to verify any possible relationship or pattern. An increase in employees' average age in a certain business, for example, might represent a decrease in number of legal losses. These types of relationships would be very hard to discover empirically. Basically, data mining consists of four elements:

(1) Extract, transform and load transaction data into a data warehouse system.
(2) Analyze the data by application software.
(3) Provide data access to business analysts and information technology professionals.
(4) Perform plots and graphs of the patterns and relationships. Store and manage the data in a multidimensional database system.

In general, companies with a strong consumer focus — retail, financial, communication and marketing organizations, are the primary users of data mining today. It enables them to determine relationships among "internal" factors such as price, product positioning or staff skills and "external" factors such as economic indicators, competition and customer demographics. Furthermore, it enables them to determine the impact on sales, customer satisfaction and corporate profits. Finally, it enables them to "drill down" into summary information to view detailed transactional data.

One of the most popular (and publicly available) examples of data mining use is in the retail chain Wal-Mart. This retail chain pioneered massive data mining to transform its supplier relationships. Wal-Mart captures point-of-sale transactions from over 2900 stores in six countries and continuously transmits this data to its massive 7.5-terabyte data warehouse. Wal-Mart allows more than 3500 suppliers to access data on their products and perform data analyses. These suppliers use this data to identify customer buying patterns at the store display level. They use this information to manage local store inventories and identify new merchandizing opportunities. In 1995 alone, for example, Wal-Mart computers processed over 1 million complex data queries.

While large-scale information technology has been evolving separate transaction and analytical systems, data mining provides the link between the two. In general, data mining software analyzes relationships and patterns in stored transaction data based on open-ended user queries. Several types of analytical software are available: statistical, machine learning and neural networks. Generally, any of four types of relationship are sought:

(1) *Classes*. Stored data is used to locate data in predetermined groups. For example, a restaurant chain could mine customer purchase data to determine when customers visit and what they typically order. This information could be used to increase traffic by having daily specials.
(2) *Clusters*. Data items are grouped according to logical relationships or consumer preferences. For example, data can be mined to identify market segments or consumer affinities.
(3) *Associations*. Data can be mined to identify associations. The employees' average age–legal losses example is one of associative mining.
(4) *Sequential patterns*. Data is mined to anticipate behavior patterns and trends. For example, an outdoor equipment retailer could predict the likelihood of a backpack being purchased based on a consumer's purchase of sleeping bags and hiking shoes.

Several different levels of analysis are available: artificial neural networks; genetic algorithms; decision trees; nearest-neighbor method (a technique that classifies each record in a data set based on a combination of the classes of the k record(s) most similar to it in a historical data set (where $k > 1$) — sometimes called the k-nearest neighbor technique); rule induction (the extraction of useful if–then rules from data based on statistical significance); data visualization (the visual interpretation of complex relationships in multidimensional data, graphics tools are used to illustrate data relationships).

Data mining is a very important technique in operational risk as it is fundamental to understand the relationship of many different factors to operational losses and the simplest correlation techniques might not work efficiently or uncover hidden patterns or correlations.

9.5 FUZZY LOGIC[1]

Many banks are just beginning to undertake quantitative analysis in the area of operational risk and, as a consequence, several measurement techniques in use still rely on simplistic approaches like self-assessment, "traffic lights" or other, similarly unsophisticated, methodologies. The purpose of this section is to show how the application of fuzzy logic can help to provide a less expensive and more structured view of operational risk inside a bank. By no means is it implied here that fuzzy logic can replace robust statistical methods in measuring operational risk (Cruz 1998), but it can certainly provide a more rigorous framework than the subjective approaches mentioned above. Fuzzy logic does not compete with mathematical probability theory as a means of evaluating random events, but rather can be viewed as a complement to probability theory for dealing with real-world problems in which the available information is subjective, incomplete or unreliable, which may be the case in many manifestations of operational risk.

Fuzzy set theory is a branch of mathematics introduced by Lofti Zadeh (1965). His paper applied multivalued (i.e. fuzzy) logic to sets or groups of objects, thereby allowing for the concept of "intermediate" membership of a set, this being an advance on the binary logic of classical set theory where an element is either a full member of a set or not. On this basis a framework can be established in which the concept of multivalence or "vagueness" can be treated using methods analogous to those used in classical set theory. In essence, the concept of intermediate membership states that everything is a matter of degree; it helps us to work with characteristics that exist in the real world which are of different tones of gray (multivalence), instead of being distinctly black or white (bivalence).

An important feature of fuzzy logic, therefore, is its ability to facilitate decision-making where there are vague or subjective judgements as inputs to the decision process. Fuzzy logic has been applied extensively in the real world, mostly in an engineering context, to control systems where the timing and level of the inputs are at least to some extent uncertain, but also in the social sciences. (For example, one

---

[1]An early version of this chapter was published in *Risk Magazine*. This section is co-authored by John Carroll, Ph.D. in Mathematical Finance, Imperial College, University of London.

manufacturer uses a fuzzy system with over 500 fuzzy rules to evaluate employees' health and fitness.)

9.5.1 Fuzzy Sets

In order to illustrate the concept of a "fuzzy set", as distinct from a classical set, we might consider membership of the set of "Acceptable Number of Breaks". While we presume that the noun in this phrase is unambiguously defined in the context (e.g. number of errors in transaction processing — "nostro breaks"), the adjective "acceptable" requires a subjective interpretation in relation to the current context. In classical set theory, such a set will have a sharply defined ("crisp") membership criterion, e.g. *"Are there 400 breaks or less observed?"* If the answer is *"yes"* then that observation belongs to the set of "Acceptable Number of Breaks", otherwise it does not. The binary condition of membership does not allow any intermediate level. Therefore, an observation of 401 breaks (or, if the variable is continuous, however arbitrarily close to 400 we may choose the level of breaks to be) will not pass the test for membership, whereas 400 breaks or fewer will have full membership of the set (see Figure 9.2). (In this example, we assume that the variable is discrete and the membership function likewise. For the sake of convenience, however, the membership function is shown as continuous in the figure, as will be the case where the variable is continuous.)

If the analogous fuzzy set of "Acceptable Number of Breaks" were to be considered, however, we could define a more diffuse, less discrete boundary by considering any level of breaks in the range from 401 to 599 inclusive to have intermediate membership of the set. Associated with this interval of intermediate membership is a sliding scale of membership from 1 for full membership (number of breaks $\leqslant 400$) to 0 for non-membership (number of breaks $\geqslant 600$), with the degree (or grade) of membership taking intermediate values on the closed interval [0,1] (see Figure 9.3). This need not necessarily be linear, but must be strictly monotonically decreasing over the interval with respect to the number of breaks if there is decreasing acceptance of an increasing

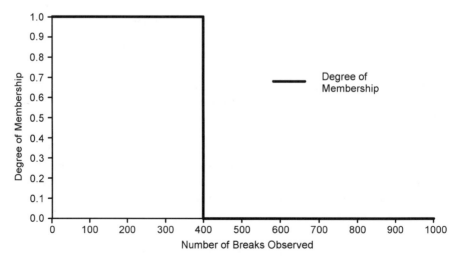

Figure 9.2   Crisp set of "Acceptable Number of Breaks"

number of breaks. (It may be seen that as the interval of intermediate membership tends to zero, so the fuzzy set comes to resemble a crisp counterpart.)

9.5.2 Context Dependency and Intersection of Fuzzy Sets

The use of fuzzy sets also allows differing perceptions between different observers of a descriptive qualifier such as "acceptable" to be represented without the need to set a single, hard benchmark for the test of set membership. The subset containing members deemed to meet simultaneously the differing criteria for multiple observers, i.e. the intersection of the sets, is also more satisfactorily represented using fuzzy set theory which allows for compensatory aggregation of sets, more adequately representing the trade-off involved in human decision-making between conflicting objectives.

For example, under the conditions of classical set theory, when considering an observation for membership of the crisp set of "Acceptable Number of Breaks", person A might ask the question *"Are there 400 breaks or less observed?"* which is represented in Figure 9.2. For person B (having a higher threshold for the acceptable level of breaks), however, the question might be *"Are there 500 breaks or less observed?"*. The set of observations that both A *and* B consider to be acceptable, i.e. the only set upon which they unambiguously agree, is given by the intersection ("and") of these sets, namely observations of 400 or fewer breaks being members. This thereby excludes some of the observations that person B considers to be acceptable (in this case those observations with between 401 and 500 breaks inclusive). There are, therefore, some observations that person B considers to be "acceptable" but which do not qualify for membership of the subset. In the world of non-compensatory aggregation (hard intersection), the subset will be identical to that defined by the stricter standalone test for membership, i.e. the set of observations that person A considers to be "acceptable", illustrated in Figure 9.2.

The use of the fuzzy paradigm, however, allows the strict binary membership condition to be relaxed. If we consider person A to have the membership function shown in

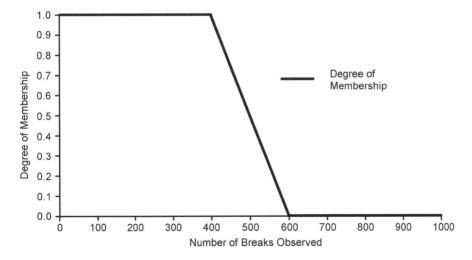

Figure 9.3 Fuzzy set of "Acceptable Number of Breaks"

Figure 9.3, with intermediate grades of membership being associated with those observations having 401 to 599 breaks inclusive, and person B associating intermediate grades of membership with those observations having 501 to 899 breaks inclusive, the observations of between 401 and 899 breaks will also have some intermediate degree of membership in the set that both A *and* B consider to be acceptable. The degree of membership of the intersection will be dependent upon the fuzzy "aggregator" used (e.g. the "fuzzy and", the "compensatory and"). In Figure 9.4, the "fuzzy and" is used, allowing for compensation between the membership functions of the two fuzzy sets.

9.5.3 Use of Fuzzy Logic in Operational Risk

Given the multidimensional and frequently vague characteristics of operational risk, we see two possibilities for the application of the techniques described above, especially in these early stages, as described below.

Cheaper Processing of Subjective OR Techniques

Many banks assess the level of operational risk in their business by applying either subjective indicators (or opinions), or even by just using a few objective indicators that are immediately available, but may not be proven to be causally related to the level of operational risk. In order to assess the OR profile, many analysts may be needed for data collection, in formulating and assessing scenarios, in assigning a "severity" grade (low–medium–high or similar) and preparing the resulting reports. In the final analysis this process may be resource-intensive without providing any special benefit such as risk pricing, optimal allocation of capital, etc. that could be delivered by thorough data collection and mathematical modeling. In this situation, a fuzzy system may be able to perform the same task with minimal human interference, saving the ongoing manual task of collating information, analyzing it and developing reports. (Such a system may

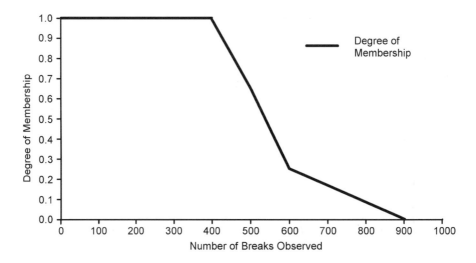

Figure 9.4 Fuzzy set of "Acceptable Number of Breaks" for both A and B: "fuzzy and"

also provide the basis for the development of a "smart" approach, e.g. a neural network, to assess the level of operational risk in an organization.) As mentioned before, the idea of "fuzzifying" a set is to acknowledge that gray areas may exist in the classification of subjective criteria. An example may make the visualization easier.

Let us imagine that the level of operational risk in an institution is deemed low, medium or high (the fuzzy set) based on the opinion of the analyst. In arriving at his/ her decision on the level of operational risk, for the purposes of simplicity suppose that the analyst considers just three contributory factors:

- The number of process fails;
- The number of losses;
- The audit score of the business.

The first two of these are quantitative factors and help in getting to a decision, as seen in Figure 9.5. The final evaluation of the level of operational risk will depend on the perception of the analyst of the interaction of the three factors; this will be reflected in the choice of an appropriate aggregator (and associated parameters if required). In final analysis, we will be able to teach the system to see the world as the analyst does. (Instead of having just three levels of grading (low, medium and high), we may have many more or even a continuum[2].)

Evaluating the Risk Embedded in Complex Situations — Causal Modeling

One of the challenges in assessing the level of operational risk is that in many cases we need to:

- Connect qualitative facts and processes to quantitative values or objectives;
- Understand how complex events interact.

An example of this might be the case of estimating the level of operational risk embedded in a complex corporate finance transaction. Used in a neural network, fuzzy logic may help in the determination of a figure for the level of operational risk by performing an appropriate aggregation of the fuzzy sets representing the drivers for operational failures. The first step is to draw a fuzzy cognitive map that gives us a causal representation of the situation.

A simple example might help in understanding how fuzzy logic works in this case. Suppose an analyst is attempting to measure the effects of system "slowtime" on the level of operational risk (see Figure 9.6). As a first step, several causes and effects are identified and linked to the event of a system slowtime. For example, system slowtime is expected to reduce employee satisfaction, which in turn will result in a decreased number of transactions processed, these being links in a chain of events that will increase the operational risk of a certain business. The same logic can be used to support the assessment of the level of operational risk embedded in, for example,

---

[2]For example, in the fuzzy set defined by the statement "Tall Men".

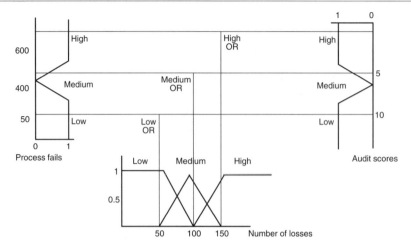

Figure 9.5   Fuzzy logic in OR: first example

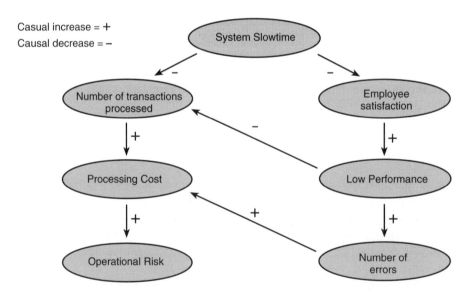

Figure 9.6   Fuzzy map for measuring system slowtime

advising on a merger transaction. Ultimately, the outcome is similar to an automated and "intelligent" scenario analysis.

9.5.4   Conclusion

In banks in which less sophisticated techniques have been put in place, fuzzy logic can help in optimizing tasks such as the classification or ranking of operational risk, or even in allocating a figure to complex transactions where a history of losses may be very difficult to collate. The use of a system such as the one presented here will always be in the background of risk management, as the level of subjectivity involved in the determination of appropriate fuzzy sets and their associated membership functions is greater than in statistical models (e.g. VaR-like models).

REFERENCES

Campbell, J., Lo, A. and McKinley, A. (1997), *The Econometrics of Financial Markets*, Princeton University Press, Princeton, NJ.

Cruz, M. (1998), "Modelling and Measuring Operational Risk", *Journal of Risk*, 1(1), 63–72.

Hutchinson, J., Lo, A. and Poggio, T. (1994), "A Nonparametric Approach to the Pricing and Hedging of Derivatives Securities via Learning Networks", *Journal of Finance*, 49, 851–889.

King, J. (2001), *Measuring and Modeling Operational Risk*, Wiley, London.

Zadeh, L.A. (1965), "Fuzzy Sets", *Information and Control*, 8, 338–353.

Bayesian Techniques in Operational Risk

10.1 INTRODUCTION TO BAYESIAN THEORY

The ideas behind Bayesian theory are very tempting for operational risk, especially in the early days of measurement when data is not available or scarce. Bayesian theory accepts some degree of subjectivity in estimating the parameters of distributions. When very few operational events are available, such a theory seems appealing. It does not come without warnings though. In statistics there is a division between "frequentists" and "Bayesians". Frequentists insist that the parameters must be estimated based on the data available. Many academics believe that science must be totally objective, and reject methods that incorporate subjective judgement.

Bayes (1763), an English clergyman and statistician, developed his theory long ago. Recently, Bayes theory has enjoyed a renaissance among academics, mostly due to advances in the computational techniques to solve the complex problems and formulas presented.

From a Bayesian perspective, there is no essential distinction between observables and parameters of a statistical model, since they are all deemed to be random. Let X be the observed data (operational losses) and θ represent the model parameters and missing data. Formal Bayesian inference then requires the setting up of a joint probability distribution $p(X, \theta)$ over all random quantities. This joint distribution encompasses two parts: $p(\theta)$ and a likelihood $p(X|\theta)$. Identifying $p(\theta)$ and $p(X|\theta)$ gives a full probability model, in which:

$$p(X, \theta) = p(X|\theta)p(\theta)$$

Bayes theorem is used, after having observed the data X, to determine the distribution of θ conditional on X. In general this can be represented by:

$$p(\theta|X) = \frac{p(\theta)p(X|\theta)}{\int p(\theta)p(X|\theta)\mathrm{d}\theta}$$

The above is known as the *posterior* distribution of θ and is the objective of the Bayesian theory. All statistics of the posterior distribution are legitimized by the Bayesian inference.

The Bayesian problems are solved by the following general equation:

Posterior distribution $\propto$ *Prior* distribution $\times$ Likelihood function

---

The prior distribution is the density function of the prior belief about the parameter value θ before observing the data. Put another way, the prior is not a real probability distribution of θ but an uncertainty distribution. It represents the best knowledge (or estimate, or even guess) about θ before the data has been observed. The description of

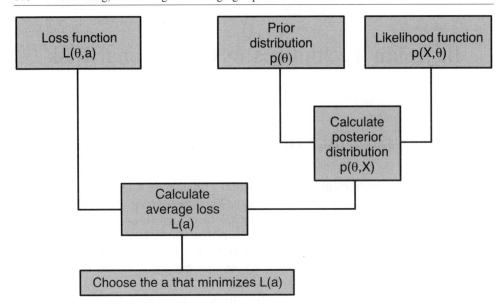

Figure 10.1 Bayesian decision and inference

the knowledge of θ after the observation of data is depicted by the posterior distribution. The likelihood function minimizes the loss caused by the prior distribution and is basically the calculated probability of randomly observing the data for a given value of θ. The Bayesian approach can be depicted as in Figure 10.1.

Basically the Bayesian decision process tries to optimize the utilization of the data available with some prior opinion on the behavior of the parameters and the state of the problem.

A couple of examples might help to clarify the theory, which is a bit complex and technical. In the first example, we calculate the posterior probabilities. Suppose that in a certain business unit, the operational risk is estimated on a daily basis using both the collected operational losses and management opinion. Suppose also that, after some time of observation, it is known that on 40% of business days some kind of operational problem will occur, and on 60% of days no problem whatsoever will occur. Nevertheless, the variation in these figures is considerable, and the Chief Risk Officer would like a more reliable measure[1].

Therefore, in addition to these figures, the operational risk manager for the business unit was asked to collect predictions (X_1 that a problem will occur, or X_2 that a problem will not occur) every morning from the management of the back-office. He observed that, although the estimates are in general reliable, mistakes are obviously committed. The observations collected from the management predict that a day will have no operational problems (X_2), they actually happen (θ_1) 10% of the time. Also, on 30% of days the management estimates problems will occur (X_1), they are incorrect and the day is problem-free (θ_2). Hence, we might represent the prior probabilities as in Table 10.1.

---

[1]At this stage "frequentists" would try to fit a more suitable distribution to the data.

Table 10.1 Prior probabilities

State θ	$p(\theta)$
θ_1 (Some operational problems will occur)	40%
θ_2 (No operational problems will occur)	60%

Table 10.2 Conditional probabilities

State θ	X_1 (Some operational problems will occur)	X_2 (No operational problems will occur)	Σ
θ_1 (Some operational problems will occur)	90%	10%	100%
θ_2 (No operational problems will occur)	30%	70%	100%

The best prediction for the next day, before talking to the management, would be Table 10.1. Nevertheless, after consulting the management and realizing that they estimate we are going to have operational problems on this day, what is the *posterior* distribution? In other words, having the management opinion available in the morning, should we not have a better estimate? Table 10.2 shows the conditional probabilities.

Consider now the proportion of days that the state of operational risk is "*with problems*" and the prediction X is also "*problems*". Put in figures, 40% of the time the state of operational risk is "*with problems*" and, when this happens, there is a 90% probability that the management prediction was "*problems*". Hence, this combination occurs 90% of 40% of the time, or 36% of the time, as can be represented below:

$$p(\theta_1, X_1) = p(\theta_1)p(X_1|\theta_1) = (40\%) \times (90\%) = 36\%$$

Similarly, the probability of "no problems" and the prediction of problems during the day can be represented as:

$$p(\theta_2, X_1) = p(\theta_2)p(X_1|\theta_2) = (60\%) \times (30\%) = 18\%$$

Now, we are able to calculate the probability of having operational problems in a day $p(X_1)$, i.e. $36\% + 18\% = 54\%$. By using the conditional probabilities, we are able to calculate the posterior probabilities as below:

$$p(\theta_1|X_1) = \frac{p(\theta_1, X_1)}{p(X_1)} = \frac{36\%}{54\%} = 67\%$$

$$p(\theta_2|X_1) = \frac{p(\theta_2, X_1)}{p(X_1)} = \frac{18\%}{54\%} = 33\%$$

The posterior probabilities can be seen in Table 10.3.

One can realize that the *posterior* probabilities, after the management opinion is given that a problem will occur, are substantially different from the *prior* probabilities (before their opinion was considered in the analysis).

We can now extend the example to the field of Bayesian decision analysis. Suppose that, given the situation above, we have three actions to take in the back-office (see Table 10.4).

Table 10.3 Posterior probabilities

State θ	$p(\theta|X_1)$
θ_1 (Some operational problems will occur)	67%
θ_2 (No operational problems will occur)	33%

Table 10.4 Actions to be taken given a situation

Action	Description
a_1	To allow the front-office to increase substantially the number of transactions in a day
a_2	To allow the front-office to increase moderately the number of transactions and improve the controls and processing capacity
a_3	To improve the controls and processing capacity

Table 10.5 Loss functions

State θ	a_1	a_2	a_3
θ_1 (Some operational problems will occur)	$70	$40	$20
θ_2 (No operational problems will occur)	$10	$40	$50

Hence, at the beginning of the day the back-office managers would have to decide, based on the best information available, whether they will allow the front-office to increase the transactions and by how much, or if they will improve the controls and capacity by reallocating personnel from other areas.

From a strictly back-office point of view, all these decisions imply costs. These are given in Table 10.5.

Therefore, if action a_1 is taken, and no operational problems occur during the day, the cost will be $10, otherwise it will be $70. Given the prior distribution, the losses would be:

$$L(a_1) = 70(40\%) + 10(60\%) = 34$$
$$L(a_2) = 40(40\%) + 40(60\%) = 40$$
$$L(a_3) = 20(40\%) + 50(60\%) = 38$$

Naturally, we would choose the action that minimizes the losses. In this case, a_1. In practice, we could also increase the number of states to avoid working with three limiting states.

However, as we have seen before, the posterior distribution after using the management observation is substantially different from the prior. If we use the posterior probabilities, the losses would be:

Transactions with Problems	Number of Days	Prior	Likelihood	Prior×Likelihood	Posterior
0%	2	1.00%	0.00%	0.00%	0.00%
10%	30	15.00%	0.81%	0.12%	0.75%
20%	40	20.00%	5.12%	1.02%	6.36%
30%	42	21.00%	13.23%	2.78%	17.25%
40%	34	17.00%	23.04%	3.92%	24.32%
50%	26	13.00%	31.25%	4.06%	25.22%
60%	16	8.00%	34.56%	2.76%	17.16%
70%	8	4.00%	30.87%	1.23%	7.67%
80%	2	1.00%	20.48%	0.20%	1.27%
90%	0	0.00%	7.29%	0.00%	0.00%
100%	0	0.00%	0.00%	0.00%	0.00%
	200			0.161075	

Figure 10.2   Bayesian inference: example 2. Verifying the proportion of problematic transactions

$$L(a_1) = 50$$
$$L(a_2) = 40$$
$$L(a_3) = 30$$

$$L(a_1) = 70(67\%) + 10(33\%) = 50$$
$$L(a_2) = 40(67\%) + 40(33\%) = 40$$
$$L(a_3) = 20(67\%) + 50(33\%) = 30$$

In this case, the better option would be a_3 (the most conservative of the actions).

A second example can be given using transaction processing risk and introducing the likelihood.

Suppose that a business unit starts counting its errors in processing transactions and finds the relation as stated in Figure 10.2. As an example, on 40 days 20% of the transactions have some problem in processing, on 42 days 30%, and so on. The quality of the processing is very poor indeed. Suppose that in order to start dealing with the problem, the operational risk manager picks five transactions randomly to get sample evidence of the likelihood, and three transactions out of these five had problems[2]. What would be the posterior distribution?

The prior distribution is just a result of the relative distribution of the days considering their total. In order to get the posterior distribution this time we will use a likelihood function based on the binomial distribution. As the OR manager examined five transactions and verified that three were wrong, we can just use a spreadsheet with the function =BINOMDIST (3, 5, 20%; False), for example, and get 5.12%. Multiplying the prior times the likelihood gives the posterior, as in the relation we mentioned before. In the last column, we adjust the posterior relative to the number of

---

[2]This type of situation, where a random sample is picked to represent an entire population, can be extremely realistic in the case, for example, of a bank that processes 1 million transactions a day and has no proper system to analyze them individually.

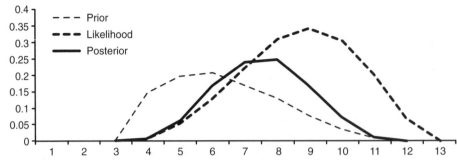

Figure 10.3 Posterior, prior and likelihood plots

days, dividing each probability by 0.161075. A plot of the prior, posterior and likelihood probabilities can be seen in Figure 10.3.

Suppose that the Chief Risk Officer decides to establish a benchmark of 25% of the total transactions as the limit for incorrect processing. What would be the odds of staying inside the boundaries considering the prior and posterior distributions?

The prior would be calculated by:

$$p(\text{errors} < 25\%) = 0.01 + 0.15 + 0.20 = 0.36$$

The posterior is calculated by:

$$p(\text{errors} < 25\%) = 0.00 + 0.075 + 0.0636 = 0.0711$$

Given that, we can notice the influence of the sample with its three wrongfully processed transactions affecting the determination of the whole probability of wrongful events.

10.2 MORE ADVANCED TOPICS IN BAYESIAN THEORY

As Bayesian inference is different from ordinary statistical inference, the understanding of a few topics might be of interest. I start by showing a few techniques to choose a prior distribution (Section 10.2.1) then describe briefly hierarchical models (Section 10.2.2). As we are always concerned with model validation, it would be useful to give a few ideas on Bayesian model validation.

10.2.1 Choosing a Prior Distribution

As we saw in Section 10.1, the prior distributions represent a description of knowledge or opinion about the parameter of a certain distribution prior to the observation of the data. In the prior resides most of the criticism of Bayesian inference, and the analyst must be very reasonable in choosing one prior over another. There are a few types of prior distributions that are regularly mentioned in Bayesian texts, and these are worth mentioning here.

A very common prior in operational risk modeling is the so-called *elicited prior*. This prior is basically the subjective opinion of the value of parameters before any data is available (or if only limited data is available). At the current stage in OR, few

Quantile	Average opinion
99%	4,090,772.99
97.50%	2,540,698.01
95%	1,686,741.13
90%	1,051,802.62

Figure 10.4 Elicited opinion of operational losses in a certain business unit

measurement software packages are available in the market, but those using Bayesian techniques use subjective opinion to evaluate the parameters.

An example might clarify how to convert expert opinion into an elicited prior. Suppose that several senior executives are asked to fill in their opinions about the quantiles of a certain kind of operational event in a business unit. The result can be seen in Figure 10.4.

Given the results above, we might fit a lognormal (12.2, 1.3) prior based on the elicited opinion from experts.

The *uninformed prior* is based on a distribution that is deemed to attribute no information to the Bayesian inference, but only to provide a possible range for the parameters in question. A very popular distribution in this case is the uniform (0,1).

Another commonly referred to prior is the *Jeffreys prior*. Jeffreys (1961) developed a prior that is invariant under any transformation, and hence simulates a version of an uninformed prior. The basis of his method is that one finds a likelihood function to produce the same shape for all data sets, just changing the location of its peak. Therefore, a non-informative prior in this translation would be ambiguous, or flat. Even though it is hard to find such a function, Jeffreys' approximation is given by:

$$\pi(\theta) = \sqrt{I(\theta)}$$

where $I(\theta)$ is the expected Fisher information in the model:

$$I(\theta) = -E_{\frac{X}{\theta}}\left[\frac{\partial^2}{\partial\theta^2}\log l(X|\theta)\right]$$

In reality what the formula is doing is working with the second partial derivative of the log-likelihood function. In this case the prior is influenced just by the shape of the likelihood, and not by the data.

A *conjugate prior* is one with the same functional form as the likelihood function, leading to a posterior distribution belonging to the same family as the prior. Another type of prior is seen when we specify this prior to leave one or more undefined parameters. This type of prior is called a *hyperprior*. One could go adding hyperpriors on hyperpriors, but then the uncertainty increases. These types of Bayesian models are, in general, called hierarchical. We will discuss them next.

10.2.2 Hierarchical Models

In Bayesian applications several parameters can often be connected in some way by the structure of the problem, suggesting that a joint probability model for these parameters should reflect the dependence amongst them. An example in OR can be given for those who believe in external databases. In such hierarchical models it is assumed that, given the probability of losses in Bank A, it might be reasonable to expect the same level of losses in Bank B. The parameters would be related to each other, and the set of parameters θ of Bank B can be seen as a sample from the total population distribution.

These types of problems can be modeled hierarchically, with observable outcomes modeled conditional on certain parameters, which are also given probabilistic specification in terms of further parameters that are called *hyperparameters*. In general, it is sensible to fit hierarchical models with more parameters than there are data points. This is because with few parameters it is difficult to fit large data sets accurately. In hierarchical models several parameters can be used to fit the data well, whilst using a population distribution to structure some dependence in the parameters. A typical structure for a hierarchical model can be seen in Figure 10.5.

In this example, we assumed a prior distribution with parameters α, β and ξ for the model parameters θ_n to estimate the data vectors x_n.

More on hierarchical models can be seen in Gelman et al. (1995).

10.2.3 Model Checking and Sensitivity Analysis in Bayesian Models

Throughout this book I have been paying special attention to model validation and sensitivity analysis. There is no difference here. Models are just an attempt to reflect reality, and Bayesian models are particular in the sense that they accept some degree of subjectivity. Bayesian prior-to-posterior inferences assume the whole structure of a probability model and can result in false inferences when the model is invalid. Hence, a reliable Bayesian analysis should include checks of the adequacy of the fit of the model to the data and the plausibility of the model for the purposes for which it will be used.

The basic question in sensitivity analysis of Bayesian models is to understand the impact of using different probabilistic models in the posterior distribution. These different probabilistic models might diverge in terms of prior specification, sampling distribution, etc. It might be the case that the current model works well, providing an adequate fit to the data, but that posterior inferences diverge under plausible alternative models.

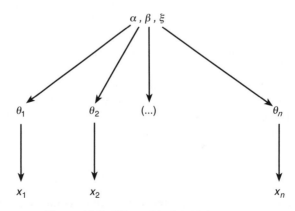

Figure 10.5 Hierarchical model structure

There are several different ways to perform model checking in Bayesian inference. I would like to discuss further the comparison of the posterior predictive distribution of future observations with the data for the events that really occurred. Other ways of checking a Bayesian model include, for example, comparing the posterior distribution of parameters with substantive knowledge of other data. I suggest the interested reader refer to Gelman et al. (1995) for more detail on these models.

The basic fit-checking technique of a model to the data is to draw simulated values from the posterior predictive distribution of replicated data and compare these samples with the observed data. Finding a systematic divergence between the data and the simulations would indicate potential failings of the model. Below we describe a couple of test quantities.

Bayesian p-Values

The *p*-value, in a Bayesian sense, is defined as the probability that the replicated data could be more extreme than the observed data, as measured by:

$$\text{Bayes } p\text{-value} = p(T(x_{\text{rep}}, \theta) \geqslant T(x, \theta)|x)$$

where x_{rep} are the replicated data and θ the parameters of the model.

In the Bayesian approach the *p*-value can be a function of an unknown parameter as well as data, because the test quantity is evaluated over draws from the posterior distribution of the unknown parameters.

Bayes Factors

The Bayes factor is the ratio of the marginal likelihood under one model to the marginal likelihood under another model. If we have two competing models F_1 and F_2, then the ratio of their posterior probabilities is:

$$\text{Bayes factor}(F_2, F_1) \times \frac{p(F_2)}{p(F_1)} = \frac{p(F_2|x)}{p(F_1|x)}$$

where the Bayes factor is given by:

$$\text{Bayes factor}(F_2, F_1) = \frac{p(x|F_2)}{p(x|F_1)} = \frac{\int p(\theta_2|F_2)p(x|\theta_2, F_2)d\theta_2}{\int p(\theta_1|F_1)p(x|\theta_1, F_1)d\theta_1}$$

The objective of using Bayes factors is to choose a single model F_i or average over a set using their posterior distributions, $p(F_i|x)$.

10.3   BAYESIAN SAMPLING TECHNIQUES

Some Bayesian sampling techniques can be interesting even for those who do not appreciate Bayesian theory. These techniques are useful in situations where we have missing data or even complex models to solve. I describe a few of them below.

10.3.1   The Data Augmentation Algorithm

Suppose that the joint density of a sample of x's of size n is given by:

$$\prod_{i=1}^{n} f(x_i|\theta)$$

Regularly our interest would be in making inferences about the parameter θ using a random sample of x. In a Bayesian sense, we would eventually have some feelings about the parameters even before making any measurement. However, if expressing these feelings in terms of quantiles is easier, representing them in terms of parameters is much harder. Someone can always say that $100 million would represent 95% of our losses, however, they would hardly express this in terms of the parameters of the lognormal or exponential distribution. It is hard to represent these prior beliefs in terms of PDFs. A solution might be to require that the prior density function is such that the functional form will remain unchanged by the addition of data, putting the prior and posterior in the same functional form. An example was presented by Thompson (2000) using exponentially distributed failure times. The function can be represented by:

$$f(x_n|\theta) = \theta^n \exp\left(-\theta\sum_{j=1}^{n} x_j\right)$$

Suppose that, absent any data, it is assumed that the prior density of θ is a gamma distribution:

$$p(\theta) = \frac{e^{-\lambda\theta}\lambda^\alpha\theta^{\alpha-1}}{\Gamma(\alpha)}$$

Consequently:

$$E(\theta) = \frac{\alpha}{\lambda} \quad \text{and} \quad \text{Var}(\theta) = \frac{\alpha}{\lambda^2}$$

It is hard to imagine that we would have a good notion of the mean and variance of θ. Furthermore, it will often be the case that many events are missing for many reasons. We had observed operational losses $x_1, \ldots, x_{n-m}$ but are missing $\{x_j\}_{j=n-m+1}^{n}$, since these individuals were lost at times $\{t_j\}_{j=n-m+1}^{n}$. The data augmentation algorithm as described in Thompson (2000) can be developed as:

Step 1. Sample θ_j from $p(\theta_j|x_1, \ldots, x_n)$.
Step 2. Generate $x_{n-m+i}, \ldots, x_n$ from $\theta_j \exp(-\theta_j x_{n-m+i})$.
Step 3. Repeat step 2 N times.
Step 4. Compute $\bar{T} = (1/N) \sum_{i=1}^{N} \sum_{j=1}^{n} x_{ji}$.
Step 5. Let $\lambda^* = \lambda + \bar{T}$ and $\alpha^* = \alpha + n$.
Step 6. The new iterate for the posterior distribution for θ is given by:

$$p(\theta|x_n) = \frac{e^{\theta\lambda^*}(\lambda^*)^{\alpha^*}\theta^{\alpha^*-1}}{\Gamma(\alpha^*)}$$

Step 7. Return to step 1 and repeat the cycle M times until the estimates stabilize.

10.3.2   Bayesian Bootstrapping

In Chapter 4 we saw that bootstrapping can be useful, among other things, to calculate confidence intervals for parameters using regular statistical inference. The Bayesian bootstrap can be viewed as a Bayesian's justification for using bootstrapping. The theory for the Bayesian bootstrap can be seen in Rubin (1981) and Chernick (1999).

Suppose that $x_1, \ldots, x_n$ are n iid realizations of a random variable X with distribution G (empirical distribution represented by $\hat{G}$). Let θ be a parameter (suppose that we are dealing with a single-parameter distribution) of the distribution G. Let $\hat{\theta}$ be an estimate of θ based on $x_1, \ldots, x_n$.

In the case of the Bayesian bootstrap, instead of sampling each x_i with replacement and equal probability $1/n$, the posterior distribution of x_i is used. In this case, the posterior distribution is centered at $1/n$ for each x_i but varies from one Bayesian bootstrap to another.

According to Chernick (1999), the Bayesian bootstrap can be defined as follows:

Step 1. Draw $n - 1$ uniform random variables from the interval [0,1].
Step 2. Let $u_1, \ldots, u_{n-1}$ be their values in increasing order, where $u_0 = 0$ and $u_n = 1$.
Step 3. Define the gaps between uniform order statistics $g_i = u_i - u_{i-1}$ for $i = 1, 2, \ldots, n$.
Step 4. The vector $g = (g_1, \ldots, g_n)$ is used to assign probabilities to the Bayesian bootstrap sample.

That is to say n observations are chosen by sampling with replacement from $x_1, \ldots, x_n$ but instead of each x_i having exactly probability $1/n$ of being selected each time, x_1 is picked with probability g_1, x_n with probability g_n, and so on.

10.3.3   Markov Chain Monte Carlo Algorithms

A new set of techniques based on Markov chain Monte Carlo (MCMC) algorithms made the solution of complex Bayesian problems much easier. These techniques are generally computer-intensive, but with the continuous advance of power in computing even that is no longer an obstacle.

In Bayesian inference, as we have seen, we are trying to evaluate the expectation:

$$E[f(x)] = \frac{\int f(x)\pi(x)\mathrm{d}x}{\int \pi(x)\mathrm{d}x}$$

where $\pi(x)$ is the posterior distribution.

Monte Carlo integration evaluates $E[f(x)]$ by drawing samples from $\pi(x)$ and then approximating:

$$E[f(x)] \approx \frac{1}{n}\sum_{t=1}^{n} f(X_t)$$

Nevertheless, in general, drawing samples from $\pi(x)$ is not feasible, since many times $\pi(x)$ can be non-standard. However, the drawing of samples does not necessarily have to be independent. They can be generated by any process that draws samples throughout the support of $\pi(x)$ in the correct proportions. A popular way of performing this is through a Markov chain having $\pi(x)$ as the stationary distribution. Hence the term MCMC.

Two algorithms are very popular, and I briefly describe them below. Quite a few references relating to MCMC have been released in the last couple of years, but one of the best is still Gilks et al. (1996).

Metropolis–Hastings Algorithm

The Metropolis algorithm (Metropolis et al. 1953) has the form $q(X/Y) = q(Y/X)$ for all X and Y. It is often proper to choose a proposal that generates each component of Y conditionally and independently, given X_t. For the Metropolis algorithm, the acceptance probability reduces to:

$$\alpha(X, Y) = \min\left(1, \frac{\omega(Y)}{\omega(X)}\right) \quad \text{where} \quad \omega(X) = \frac{\pi(X)}{q(X)}$$

Hastings (1970) generalized the above method in the so-called Metropolis–Hastings algorithm. For this algorithm, at each time t, the next state X_{t+1} is chosen by initially sampling a candidate point Y from a proposed distribution $q(\cdot/X_t)$. The proposed distribution may depend on the current point X_t. The candidate point Y is then accepted with probability $\alpha(X_t, Y)$ where:

$$\alpha(X, Y) = \min\left(1, \frac{\pi(Y)q\left(\frac{X}{Y}\right)}{\pi(X)q\left(\frac{Y}{X}\right)}\right)$$

If Y is accepted, the next state becomes $X_{t+1} = Y$. If the candidate point is not accepted, the Markov chain does not move, i.e. Gilks et al. (1996) provide a simple "pseudo-code" for the Metropolis–Hastings algorithm as below:

```
Initialize X₀; set t = 0.
Repeat {
    Sample a point Y from q (./Xt)
    Sample a Uniform (0,1) random variable U
    If U ≤ α(Xt, Y) set Xt+1 = Y
        Otherwise set Xt+1 = Xt
    Increment t
}
```

Gibbs Sampling

The Gibbs sampler is a special case of the Metropolis–Hastings algorithm. The method was developed by Geman and Geman (1984), who used it to analyze Gibbs distributions on lattices. Nevertheless, it is important to notice that the algorithm is not limited to Gibbs distributions.

Gibbs sampling consists purely of sampling from full conditional distributions. Gilks et al. (1996) provide a simple "pseudo-code" for the algorithm:

```
Repeat {
    Sample a point Y from G(.);
    Sample a Uniform (0,1) random variable U;
    If U ≤ g(Y)/G(Y) accept Y; }
Until one Y is accepted.
```

10.4 BAYESIAN EVT

The Bayesian analysis of extreme value data is in general related to the primary concern about the behavior beyond the range of the observed data, namely that the prior may fail to dominate the data. Furthermore, as the likelihood function in Bayesian analysis is itself an asymptotic approximation, it might not be necessary to include more data in the likelihood for an optimal procedure. Eventually, as Kotz and Nadarajah (2000) observed, just raising the threshold in the distribution of threshold exceedances might be conservative enough.

Due to a series of limitations of the application of Bayesian techniques in extreme distributions, the number of studies and research in this field is not large. The hurdles in using the Bayesian approach in EVT are that the value of additional prior information is likely to be substantial, while the feasibility of formulating this kind of knowledge may be questionable for extremal behavior.

As Kotz and Nadarajah (2000) noticed, the application of Bayesian methodology should strive to employ Bayesian procedures as a means to incorporate genuine scientific belief in data analysis, rather than using the Bayesian approach as a formal technical inferential device. As they observe, unfortunately it is the second approach that is often taken in applications.

A model like the GEV that we saw in Chapter 4 will not admit conjugate priors (except when the GEV is fit with one single parameter). Ashour and El-Adl (1980) derived a conjugate prior for the case when $\xi \to 0$, the joint conjugate prior is:

$$f(\mu, \psi) = \psi^{-H} \exp\left[-\frac{G}{\psi} + \frac{H\mu}{\psi} - \frac{D \exp(\mu - \delta)}{\psi} \right]$$

with parameters D, G, H and δ.

An application of Bayesian EVT in insurance can be seen in Smith (2000).

REFERENCES

Ashour, S.K. and El-Adl, Y.M. (1980), "Bayesian Estimation of the Parameters of the Extreme Value Distribution", *Egyptian Statistical Journal*, 24, 140–152.

Bayes, T. (1763), "An Essay Towards Solving a Problem in the Doctrine of Chances", *Philosophical Transactions Royal Society of London*, 53, 370–418.

Chernick, M. (1999), *Bootstrap Methods: A Practitioner's Guide*, Wiley Series in Probability and Statistics, Wiley, New York.

Gelman, A., Carlin, J., Stern, H. and Rubin, D. (1995), *Bayesian Data Analysis*, Chapman & Hall/CRC, New York.

Geman, S. and Geman, D. (1984), "Stochastic Relaxation, Gibbs Distributions and the Bayesian Restoration of Images", *IEEE Transactions on Pattern Analysis and Machine Intelligence*, 6, 721–741.

Gilks, W.R., Richardson, S. and Spielgelhalter, D.J. (1996), *Markov Chain Monte Carlo in Practice*, Chapman & Hall, London.

Hastings, W.K. (1970), "Monte Carlo Sampling Methods using Markov Chains and their Applications", *Biometrika*, 57, 97–109.

Jeffreys, H. (1961), *Theory of Probability*, Oxford University Press, Oxford.

Kotz, S. and Nadarajah, S. (2000), "*Extreme Value Distributions: Theory and Applications*", Imperial College Press, London.

Metropolis, N., Rosenbluth, A.W., Rosenbluth, M.N., Teller, A.H. and Teller, E. (1953), "Equation of State Calculations by Fast Computing Machines", *Journal of Chemical Physics*, 21, 1087–1092.

Rubin, D. (1981), "The Bayesian Bootstrap", *Annals of Statistics*, 9, 130–134.

Smith, R. (2000), "Bayesian Risk Analysis", in *Extremes and Integrated Risk Management*, P. Embrechts (ed.), Risk Publications, London, Chapter 17, pp. 235–252.

Thompson, J.R. (2000). *Simulation: A Modeler's Approach*, Wiley Series in Probability and Statistics, Wiley, New York.

Part IV
Operational Risk Management

11
Operational Risk Reporting, Control and Management

11.1 INTRODUCTION

At this stage, we have seen measurement models that provide an operational VaR figure as well as causal models that help in understanding the factors that generate losses. We are now able to start using this information to provide results for the organization.

The first phase in risk management is generally passive, with the risk managers identifying risks, defining risk policies (including measurement risk policy) and beginning to collect data. Typically, initial reports containing numbers and drawing attention to the newly identified risks will have limited distribution until the organization has sufficient confidence in the numbers. In the second phase, a more refined analysis is undertaken in order to understand the causes and make a first attempt to limit the risks, through implementing a risk control process. In the last phase, which can be defined as the active phase, the organization has a high level of confidence in the risk measures and models and therefore starts using these models to influence the pricing processes, insurance pricing and performance measurement.

In this chapter, I will place more emphasis on the last two phases in the development of a risk management project (i.e. the defensive and the active phases). I will also show how a more thorough operational risk analysis can be used in strategic planning for a bank and even in due diligence for merger and acquisition processes. The chapter starts by showing a few straightforward samples of operational risk reports. I will then show how to implement a highly technical operational risk limit policy, and finish by talking about performance measurement and risk capital. Figure 11.1 shows a generic process of risk management development that can also be applied to operational risk.

11.2 OPERATIONAL RISK REPORTING

Still on the first phase of risk management development (the passive phase), the organization has evolved a few steps, having identified the sources of operational risk, defined a risk policy and begun to undertake the first steps in operational risk measurement. These initial phases were covered in previous chapters of this book. The last stage in the "passive phase" is reporting. This is where the operational risk technical team begins showing the results obtained to other members of the organization and discusses the figures with them. This is a very important step, and in most cases will be the first time that senior executives have a real notion of the size of the potential operational loss exposures.

In general a risk system should include a flexible, interactive reporting module that permits the risk control group to view the results and rerun the analysis if needed. It is

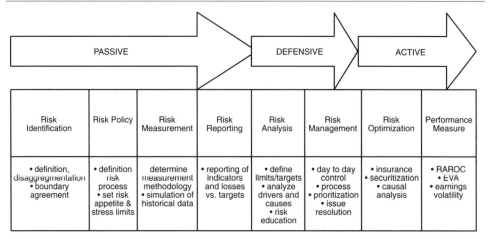

Figure 11.1   Generic process of risk management development

important also that the risk system isolates data collection from risk modeling and establishes a common interface for risk models. This feature would support the use of multiple risk models (operational VaR, OR management model, etc.) and allow easy inclusion in the risk system as they are developed (internally or even vendor-developed). The model interface is really a fundamental part of the risk system. At this stage, all inputs into the models and how the data is used within the models must be fully understood. As the people within the bank who should see some or all the risk reports can reasonably be scattered around the globe, the use of password-protected intra-web technology is necessary. Figure 11.2 shows an overview of the risk system.

Below we list a few examples of the types of reports that might be used by operational risk managers, split by type of user. I start with the reports for market and credit risk management, and then progress to reports for businesses (OR management reports), hedgers and regulators.

11.2.1   Reports for Market and Credit Risk

One of the first reports that can be issued is that related to operational VaR, embedded in market and credit risks (refer to Chapter 2 for more details). Finding the correct market and credit positions, after all errors have been cleared (or if not at least considering that a certain percentage of the market position will be wrong due to operational errors), will improve the internal and external reliability of the VaR models. As can be seen in Figure 11.3, the market VaR curve tends to flatten out when small errors are discarded. The benefits of this are several, including a more reliable RAPM (risk-adjusted performance measurement), for example.

A similar report should be produced for credit risk. Another important report of this type is that showing the adjusted positions and the predicted operational changes at several levels of confidence. For example, imagine that today our equity position is $1 billion. Due to the usual operational errors (using the business unit's pattern of errors shown in Figure 11.3), the operational VaR estimates that a 95% confidence interval for operational errors impacting the $1 billion position would be (−$96.7, $115.2). By

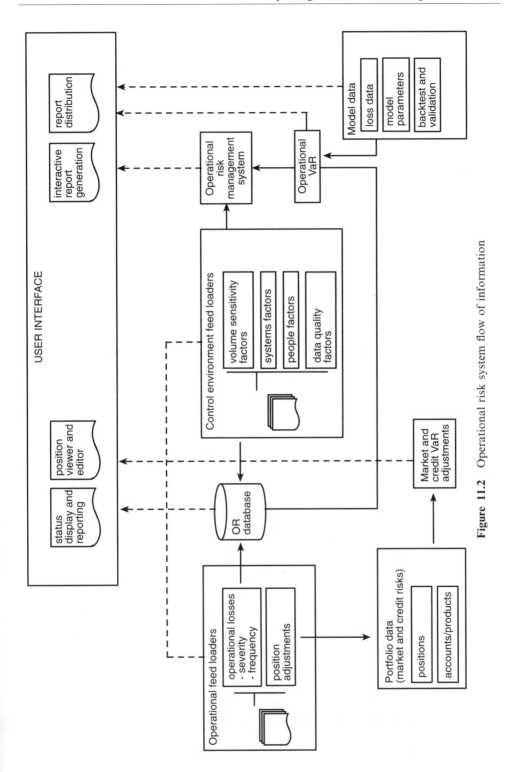

Figure 11.2 Operational risk system flow of information

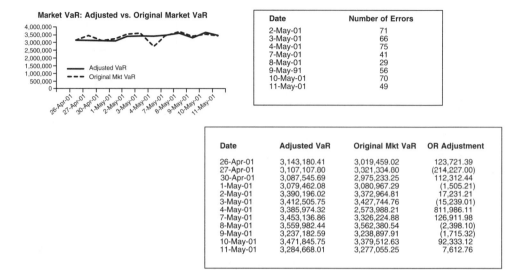

Date	Number of Errors
2-May-01	71
3-May-01	66
4-May-01	75
7-May-01	41
8-May-01	29
9-May-91	56
10-May-01	70
11-May-01	49

Date	Adjusted VaR	Original Mkt VaR	OR Adjustment
26-Apr-01	3,143,180.41	3,019,459.02	123,721.39
27-Apr-01	3,107,107.00	3,321,334.00	(214,227.00)
30-Apr-01	3,087,545.69	2,975,233.25	112,312.44
1-May-01	3,079,462.08	3,080,967.29	(1,505.21)
2-May-01	3,390,196.02	3,372,964.81	17,231.21
3-May-01	3,412,505.75	3,427,744.76	(15,239.01)
4-May-01	3,385,974.32	2,573,988.21	811,986.11
7-May-01	3,453,136.86	3,326,224.88	126,911.98
8-May-01	3,559,982.44	3,562,380.54	(2,398.10)
9-May-01	3,237,182.59	3,238,897.91	(1,715.32)
10-May-01	3,471,845.75	3,379,512.63	92,333.12
11-May-01	3,284,668.01	3,277,055.25	7,612.76

Figure 11.3   Report on the operational VaR embedded in the market VaR

including this "operational risk position" in the market VaR, the market risk flattens out, as theoretically expected. In this case we are just provisioning a certain portion of the position, knowing that there will always be something wrong.

11.2.2   OR Management Reports

A second group of users will be the businesses themselves. The businesses will receive the operational VaR figures and will need to know what to do to manage them. The type of report, in this case, should be less technical and much more practical. I suggest using an intra-net web-design report where the users can play with the results,

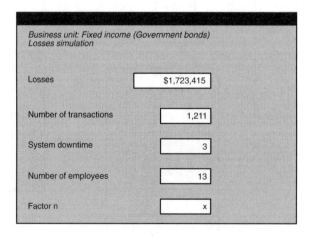

Figure 11.4   OR management report based on the intra-net web

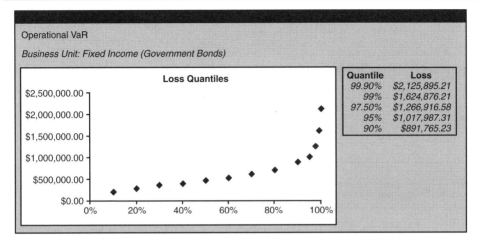

Figure 11.5   Report to the OR hedgers — operational VaR

stressing the factors according to what they think might happen. Figure 11.4 shows an example.

In the example given, we simulate the losses for the business unit *"Fixed Income (Government Bonds)"* within an investment bank. The interactive report allows the user to play with the report, changing the factors to current or stressed values, and hence see how the losses would behave. Obviously some security access must be used at this stage — just a few senior executives might be allowed to see and play with the model.

Other types of "hot spot reports" might be envisaged, which show the businesses their limitations and capacities, helping them to minimize their operational risk exposure.

11.2.3   Reports to the Operational Risk Hedgers

A third type of user of operational risk reports would be the "hedgers", i.e. the insurance department and/or those who are envisaging more sophisticated schemes to hedge OR. These reports would vary depending on the necessity and final objectives of the user. A simple example can be seen in Figure 11.5, which just shows a report of the operational VaR for a single business unit. For the OR hedger, it would be better to have this type of report for the entire fixed income division, or even for the entire group, depending on the type of insurance or structure envisaged. More discussions on the subject can be seen in Chapters 13 and 14.

Based on such reports the OR hedger can determine the appropriate risk premium, coverage and price for transferring risk to the market.

11.2.4   Reports to the Regulators

Whilst the New Basel Accord has stimulated discussions on the quantification of operational risk and thus promoted the development of more sophisticated measures, it has left unresolved the issue of operational VaR. Nevertheless, for the advanced stages of operational risk management banks will have to move toward developing internal models and testing them against reality. The regulators will have to be kept clearly

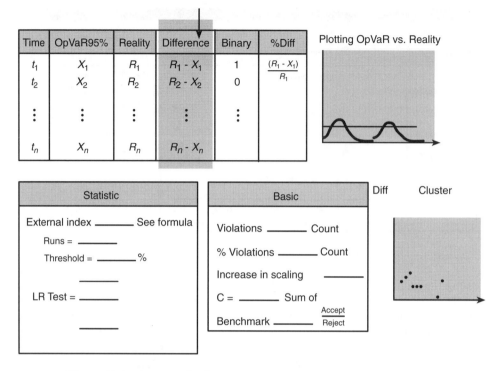

Figure 11.6 Framework of report on model validation to the regulators

informed of the levels of success in testing models against real losses, including backtesting. If several banks start reporting good results then the acceptance process will be much faster. A simple example of a regulatory report can be seen in Figure 11.6 (based on the techniques explained in Chapter 6).

Other appropriate reports for regulators use the methods stated in Chapter 15. Please refer to this chapter for more comments.

The reports shown above are meant to be indicative rather than extensive. I am sure that banks will develop their own set of operational risk reports, showing information deemed important for their particular organization. The list above might therefore be seen as simply providing some suggestions.

11.3 OPERATIONAL RISK CONTROL — INTRA-DAY (REAL-TIME) OR CONTROL

The first step when entering the second phase of developing a risk management process is "defensive". At this stage the risk managers, being aware of the risks they are running, try to establish limits and controls.

In this section, I will try to demonstrate the establishment of a mathematical model-based operational risk limit policy by giving an example. This particular example is based on transaction processing risk within the trading desk of an investment bank.

Time	# Employees	System	Transactions			Projected Operational Losses
			Arriving	Processed	Backlog	
9:00	14	0	56	56	0	721.19
10:00	14	0	91	84	7	1,814.66
11:00	14	0	112	84	35	6,188.54
12:00	14	0	23	58	0	721.19
13:00	13	0	41	41	0	721.19
14:00	13	0	122	78	44	7,594.43
15:00	13	0	165	78	131	21,184.70
16:00	13	10	176	78	229	91,004.58
17:00	13	0	148	78	299	47,427.98
18:00	13	0	11	78	232	*36,961.91*

Figure 11.7   Data set for intra-day transaction processing risk

In Chapter 8, I mentioned that more sophisticated econometric models (state-space models using the Kalman filter) are able to give online best estimates of the factors. These types of models are very reliable and are traditionally used in the airplane industry, for example.

In our case, modern processing systems are able to provide online information about system downtime, system slowtime, number of transactions being processed in real time, etc. As this information can be used within a causal model, a relationship between these variables and the losses can be established in real time. Figure 11.7 shows an example of hourly information for a few factors.

By running a model using past data, showing the number of employees present each hour, the number of transactions arriving every hour, and the backlog of late processed transactions, we get the following model that explains the losses:

$$Y = 721.19 + 5451.3\gamma + 156.21\psi + \varepsilon$$

where γ is the system downtime and ψ is the number of transactions in backlog. This model has R^2 (goodness-of-fit) of 82%.

Suppose that this business unit has an end-of-business operational risk limit of $10,000 and the supervision is being especially rigorous in these early days of implementation, trying to improve the awareness of traders and back-officers of the importance of keeping OR inside the established risk appetite.

By using our model and considering the way the factors behave during the day, we can use this figure as an estimate of our transaction processing VaR. Keep in mind that this model has a very high fitness (82%).

Until lunchtime the situation of backlogs is very well managed, showing that the department is well structured for this level of transaction processing. The number of arriving transactions fluctuates during the day, tending to be higher at the beginning and toward the end of the day. During lunchtime the number of incoming transactions is significantly reduced.

In this example, in the afternoon one employee in the back-office has to leave, reducing the headcount to 13. Given a certain complexity of the product, each back-officer is able to process six transactions per hour, on average. The capacity is therefore significantly diminished in the afternoon and just to aggravate matters at 4pm the system, when the backlog is already 229, crashes and stays offline for 10 minutes. The resulting expected operational loss is almost $100,000 (10 times the limit!) at this stage and, despite the fact that the 13 remaining employees work beyond their limits, the end-of-business projected VaR is $36,961, leaving the management concerned, since the limit for operational losses is $10,000.

To avoid such situations, the management decides to establish an operational risk limit policy that has to be followed by everyone. As the only controllable variable in the model is the number of transactions, in order to avoid exceeding the bank's operational risk appetite in this area the operational risk manager supporting this unit has the authority to stop or reduce trading if necessary to avoid exceeding the limit at the end of the day.

If we consider the example again, but in this case at 4pm the operational risk manager calls a halt to trading until the system is back online and the backlog is reduced to a manageable level of 53, the losses at the end of the business day would be right inside the risk appetite level. This can be seen in Figure 11.8.

The benefits of such modeling can be very significant, especially for trading desks. Different mathematical models, possibly even using non-linear artificial intelligence, might be used for other types of operational risk.

11.4   OPERATIONAL COST CONTROL — DEVELOPING OPERATIONAL RISK STRATEGIES

Traditionally, banks have never been as careful with costs as other industries. In several industries, like electronic hardware for example, the error ratio is extremely low and very well controlled by highly sophisticated cost control departments, which are possibly one of the most complex areas inside an organization (with the exception of R&D — research and development). On the other hand, in the financial services industry, the most sophisticated departments are located in the front-office, on the revenue side. Financial derivatives are priced solely by considering the market opportunity cost. Transaction costs are rarely considered, but where they are, the depth of analysis is not very great. In the portfolio aggregation of these products, the final effect of processing them is never considered.

Time	# Employees	System	Transactions			Projected Operational Losses
			Arriving	Processed	Backlog	
9:00	14	0	56	56	0	721.19
10:00	14	0	91	84	7	1,814.66
11:00	14	0	112	84	35	6,188.54
12:00	14	0	23	58	0	721.19
13:00	13	0	41	41	0	721.19
14:00	13	0	122	78	44	7,594.43
15:00	13	0	165	78	131	21,184.70
16:00	13	10	0	78	53	63,511.62
17:00	13	0	148	78	123	19,935.02
18:00	13	0	11	78	56	*9,468.95*

Figure 11.8   Intra-day operational risk control — establishing limits

In this section, I will try to briefly show how a more sophisticated cost analysis can be developed for financial products based on traditional microeconomic analysis.

Economic theory postulates that for a firm to maximize its results it is necessary for it to continue production up to that point at which equilibrium exists between the variation of the total cost and the variation of the total revenue. In economic terms, the revenue can be classified in three types: total, average and marginal. The total (or gross) revenue is simply the result of the multiplication of the price p of a certain product by the quantity q. It can be represented by:

$$R_{\text{Gross}} = p \times q$$

The average revenue is defined as the result of the division between the total revenue and the total quantity. It is represented analytically by:

$$R_{\text{Average}} = \frac{R_{\text{Gross}}}{q}$$

or:

$$R_{\text{Average}} = \frac{p \times q}{q} = p$$

The last representation of revenue, the marginal, corresponds to the variation of the total revenue in relation to the quantity sold. It is represented by:

$$R_{\text{Mg}} = \frac{\Delta R_{\text{Gross}}}{\Delta q}$$

Supposing that the variations in quantity and gross revenue are infinitesimal (this is acceptable in theory but hardly likely to happen in actual business practice), then the marginal revenue can be determined by the first derivative of the gross revenue in relation to the quantity sold:

$$R_{\text{Mg}} = \frac{\text{d} R_{\text{Gross}}}{\text{d} q}$$

or, for the sale of q units, we have the following relation:

$$R_{\text{Gross}} = \int_{0}^{q} R_{\text{Mg}} \text{d} q$$

An example might help to clarify the relationship between average and marginal revenue. Suppose that the revenue[1] varies according to the number of employees, as shown in Figure 11.9.

It is important to notice that both curves initially rise, reach a maximum and subsequently decline. When the average production (revenue) reaches the maximum, the average and marginal revenue are the same. At this point the profits will also be maximized. This level of production is what every efficient production line aims to achieve. This is one of the main reasons why the revenue and cost decisions must be taken conjointly, particularly in merger and acquisition processes.

---

[1] Just for clarity's sake, it is assumed that revenue and production are the same.

Number of Employees	Gross Revenue	Avg Revenue	Mg Revenue
1	10	10	0
2	24	12	14
3	39	13	15
4	52	13	13
5	61	12.2	9
6	66	11	5
7	66	9.43	0
8	64	8	−2

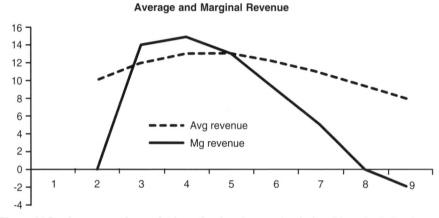

Figure 11.9   Average and marginal production (revenue) relationship — includes data table

From the operational risk perspective it is much more important to understand the costs. From the economic theory point of view, costs can be differentiated between short and long-term, fixed and variable, as well as average and marginal. Since the calculations for marginal and average costs are the same as those used to calculate the average and marginal revenues, we will refrain from restating them here. Nevertheless, an example may prove useful. Consider the data given in Figure 11.10 for this exercise.

Notice that the costs have been divided into fixed and variable. The fixed costs are those you have to pay to operate, like renting the building. The variable costs are those that vary depending on the level of production activity. In the example, the variable cost is nine times bigger than the fixed cost when 20 units are produced, and therefore the marginal cost increases substantially as production grows.

It is important in a bank's strategy to know these figures in detail when planning for growth or when considering buying another organization. Sometimes the cost of increasing the number of trades can result in the returns from the transactions decreasing.

In a bank, the increased number of transactions (the "production") will bring an additional variable cost, due to an increase in operational errors. The relationship for the increase in operational errors can be estimated based on the multifactor models seen in Chapter 8. The (micro)economic theory of revenues, production and costs is complex and there is a vast amount of literature on the subject. We will not go into any more

Quantity	Fixed Cost	Variable Cost	Total Cost	Avg Fixed Cost	Avg Variable Cost	Avg Cost	Mg Cost
1	100	10	110	100	10	110	
2	100	16	116	50.00	8.0	58.0	6
3	100	21	121	33.33	7.0	40.3	5.0
4	100	26	126	25.00	6.5	31.5	5.0
5	100	30	130	20.00	6.0	26.0	4.0
6	100	36	136	16.67	6.0	22.7	6.0
7	100	45.5	145.5	14.29	6.5	20.8	9.5
8	100	56	156	12.50	7.0	19.5	10.5
9	100	72	172	11.11	8.0	19.1	16.0
10	100	90	190	10.00	9.0	19.0	18.0
11	100	109	209	9.09	9.9	19.0	19.0
12	100	130.4	230.4	8.33	10.9	19.2	21.4
13	100	160	260	7.69	12.3	20.0	29.6
14	100	198.2	298.2	7.14	14.2	21.3	38.2
15	100	249.5	349.5	6.67	16.6	23.3	51.3
16	100	324	424	6.25	20.3	26.5	74.5
17	100	418.5	518.5	5.88	24.6	30.5	94.5
18	100	539	639	5.56	29.9	35.5	120.5
19	100	698	798	5.26	36.7	42.0	159.0
20	100	900	1000	5.00	45.0	50.0	202.0

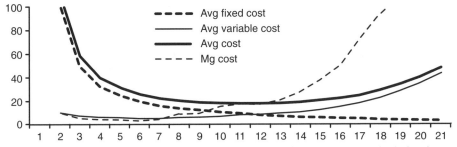

Figure 11.10   Calculation and relationship of marginal and average costs — includes data table

detail in this section, but I strongly suggest a thorough understanding of these relationships when performing any growth strategy. It is worth noticing that perhaps the most important conclusion from these relationships is that the profit will be maximized when the marginal cost and the marginal revenue are exactly the same, i.e. when:

$$C_{Mg} = R_{Mg}$$

This relation will hold for all cases and should be the objective of the strategy of the firm.

I have developed a simple example, based on the same data used in Chapter 8, that might help to illustrate the above theory (see Figure 11.11). Suppose a business unit trades one single product, which has a margin that is very tight and stable at 0.006% per unit trade. The notional value of one unit is $100,000. We can now calculate the revenue, which we do for quantities from 200,000 to 700,000 units per day. In general,

Quantity	Profit	Revenue	Revenue Mg Revenue	Avg Revenue	COSTS Total Cost	Total Mg Cost	Total Avg Cost	Processing Cost	Error Cost	Marginal Error Cost
200,000	138,497	1,200,000			1,061,503	5.31	5.31	1,000,000.00	61,503.20	0.308
205,000	140,842	1,230,000	6.00	6.00	1,089,158	5.53	5.31	1,025,000.00	64,157.88	0.531
210,000	143,133	1,260,000	6.00	6.00	1,116,867	5.54	5.32	1,050,000.00	66,867.06	0.542
220,000	147,551	1,320,000	6.00	6.00	1,172,449	5.56	5.33	1,100,000.00	72,448.89	0.558
230,000	151,751	1,380,000	6.00	6.00	1,228,249	5.58	5.34	1,150,000.00	78,248.69	0.580
240,000	155,734	1,440,000	6.00	6.00	1,284,266	5.60	5.35	1,200,000.00	84,266.46	0.602
250,000	159,498	1,500,000	6.00	6.00	1,340,502	5.62	5.36	1,250,000.00	90,502.21	0.624
260,000	163,044	1,560,000	6.00	6.00	1,396,956	5.65	5.37	1,300,000.00	96,955.92	0.645
270,000	166,372	1,620,000	6.00	6.00	1,453,628	5.67	5.38	1,350,000.50	103,627.61	0.667
280,000	169,483	1,680,000	6.00	6.00	1,510,517	5.69	5.39	1,400,000.00	110,517.27	0.689
290,000	172,375	1,740,000	6.00	6.00	1,567,625	5.71	5.41	1,450,000.00	117,624.90	0.711
300,000	175,049	1,800,000	6.00	6.00	1,624,951	5.73	5.42	1,500,000.00	124,950.50	0.733
310,000	177,506	1,860,000	6.00	6.00	1,682,494	5.75	5.43	1,550,000.00	132,494.08	0.754
320,000	179,744	1,920,000	6.00	6.00	1,740,256	5.78	5.44	1,600,000.00	140,255.62	0.776
330,000	181,765	1,980,000	6.00	6.00	1,798,235	5.80	5.45	1,650,000.00	148,235.14	0.798
350,000	185,152	2,100,000	6.00	6.00	1,914,848	5.83	5.47	1,750,000.00	164,848.09	0.831
400,000	189,805	2,400,000	6.00	6.00	2,210,195	5.91	5.53	2,000,000.00	210,194.95	0.907
427,000	**190,052**	2,562,000	**6.00**	6.00	2,371,948	**5.99**	5.55	2,135,000.00	236,948.08	0.991
450,000	189,009	2,700,000	6.00	6.00	2,510,991	6.02	5.58	2,250,000.00	260,991.11	1.016
500,000	182,763	3,000,000	6.00	6.00	2,817,237	6.12	5.63	2,500,000.00	317,236.54	1.125
600,000	153,925	3,600,000	6.00	6.00	3,446,075	6.29	5.74	3,000,000.00	446,075.27	1.288
700,000	103,289	4,200,000	6.00	6.00	4,096,711	6.51	5.85	3,500,000.00	596,711.15	1.506

Figure 11.11   Cost structure for a business unit — initial case

the business unit trader would only see the trades from the revenue side and be happy to see the revenues grow to $4,200,000 when 700,000 units are traded. Typically, revenue generators will be very happy to see the revenue increase and will not care about the costs involved.

Let us now analyze the costs by dividing them into two types: processing costs and error costs. The processing cost is deemed to be stable at $5 per transaction. The error cost, following the data from the exercise in Chapter 8, is $1.81, with standard deviation of 3.89. Developing a 95% confidence interval for the error cost, we find that it would be $9.43. Therefore, on average it would cost you $5 to process correctly a transaction and $12.43 to reprocess due to errors.

In Chapter 8 we also calculated a loss ratio. For this exercise I developed a simple linear model to relate the loss ratio to the number of transactions processed. The model is given by:

$$\text{Loss ratio} = 0.0094957 + 1.15573\text{E} - 07 \times \text{Transactions}$$
$$R^2 = 89.12\%$$

By using the model above, we are able to verify that if the loss ratio is estimated to be 3.26% when the number of transactions is 200,000, then when the number of transactions grows to 700,000 the error rate climbs to 9.04%!

Following the traditional optimization analysis, the maximum profit condition, $C_{\text{Mg}} = R_{\text{Mg}}$, will be reached at 427,000 units traded, given the current costs and margins. If we trade more than that, we will have declining profits and will need to adjust our processing capacity. This type of modeling allows us to vary our capacity and see how an improvement in the process (system improvement, training process, hiring employees, etc.) will benefit the organization.

In the case of the example, $C_{Mg} = R_{Mg} = \$6$, the profit will be maximized at $190,052. Therefore, although in the exercise in Chapter 8 the average number of transactions was 239,815, given our current environment and capacity conditions, we would maximize our potential by trading 427,000 units per day. If the bank has any intention of trading more than that, it will have to take into consideration the associated costs and eventually hire more people or adapt the processing systems.

I decided to perform an additional simulation with this data, assuming that it was possible to cut the processing costs from $5 to $4 per transaction. The result of this modification is substantial. The maximum profit condition in this case is reached at 900,000 units per day, more than doubling our optimal capacity, as can be seen in Figure 11.12.

In another simulation, the loss ratio was cut proportionally to around 3% through such actions as training the employees and improving the systems, whilst the error cost was reduced proportionally throughout the table. The maximum profit condition was reached at around 600,000 units per day. Therefore, simply by reducing the operational risk within a business unit the optimal capacity was increased by 40%. Hence, it can be seen that very significant productivity gains can be achieved through improving the management of operational risk. See Figure 11.13 for more details of the simulation.

The same type of problem can be formulated in such a way that it can be solved by differentiation. Suppose that a bank has performed an analysis of the structure of the capacity for processing transactions in a certain business unit. Given the current state of the organizational development and the level of resources available (number of employees, systems, etc.) the business unit can process 3000 transactions a day. It is estimated that, without any change in the process or systems, the ratio Δtransactions processed/Δnumber of additional employees is given by $80 - 6\sqrt{x}$ where x is the number of additional employees. Suppose that the Chief Risk Officer asked you what the number of transactions processed would be if 25 employees were hired.

Let y be the number of units produced per day, so:

$$\frac{dy}{dx} = 80 - 6\sqrt{x}$$

which can be transformed into:

$$dy = (80 - 6\sqrt{x})dx$$

This is a differential equation, which can be solved by integration, i.e.:

$$y = 80x - 4x^{\frac{3}{2}} + C$$

As $y = 3000$ when $x = 0$, then $C = 3000$. Therefore:

$$y = 80x - 4x^{\frac{3}{2}} + 3000$$

Taking y_{25} as the value of y when $x = 25$, we have:

$$y_{25} = 2000 - 500 + 3000 = 4500$$

Consequently, 4500 transactions per day will be processed when the number of employees is increased by 25, i.e. an extra 1500 transactions over the current capacity (increasing the capacity by 50%).

		Revenue			COSTS					
Quantity	Profit	Revenue	Mg Revenue	Avg Revenue	Total Cost	Total Mg Cost	Total Avg Cost	Processing Cost	Error Cost	Marginal Error Cost
200,000	338,497	1,200,000			861,503	4.31	4.31	800,000.00	61,503.20	0.308
205,000	345,842	1,230,000	6.00	6.00	884,158	4.53	4.31	820,000.00	64,157.88	0.531
210,000	353,133	1,260,000	6.00	6.00	906,867	4.54	4.32	840,000.00	66,867.06	0.542
220,000	367,551	1,320,000	6.00	6.00	952,449	4.56	4.33	880,000.00	72,448.89	0.558
230,000	381,751	1,380,000	6.00	6.00	998,249	4.58	4.34	920,000.00	78,248.69	0.580
240,000	395,734	1,440,000	6.00	6.00	1,044,266	4.60	4.35	960,000.00	84,266.46	0.602
250,000	409,498	1,500,000	6.00	6.00	1,090,502	4.62	4.36	1,000,000.00	90,502.21	0.624
260,000	423,044	1,560,000	6.00	6.00	1,136,956	4.65	4.37	1,040,000.00	96,955.92	0.645
270,000	436,372	1,620,000	6.00	6.00	1,183,628	4.67	4.38	1,080,000.00	103,627.61	0.667
280,000	449,483	1,680,000	6.00	6.00	1,230,517	4.69	4.39	1,120,000.00	110,517.27	0.689
290,000	462,375	1,740,000	6.00	6.00	1,277,625	4.71	4.41	1,160,000.00	117,624.90	0.711
300,000	475,049	1,800,000	6.00	6.00	1,324,951	4.73	4.42	1,200,000.00	124,950.50	0.733
310,000	487,506	1,860,000	6.00	6.00	1,372,494	4.75	4.43	1,240,000.00	132,494.08	0.754
320,000	499,744	1,920,000	6.00	6.00	1,420,256	4.78	4.44	1,280,000.00	140,255.62	0.776
330,000	511,765	1,980,000	6.00	6.00	1,468,235	4.80	4.45	1,320,000.00	148,235.14	0.798
350,000	535,152	2,100,000	6.00	6.00	1,564,848	4.83	4.47	1,400,000.00	164,848.09	0.831
400,000	589,805	2,400,000	6.00	6.00	1,810,195	4.91	4.53	1,600,000.00	210,194.95	0.907
427,000	617,052	2,562,000	6.00	6.00	1,944,948	4.99	4.55	1,708,000.00	236,948.05	0.991
450,000	639,009	2,700,000	6.00	6.00	2,060,991	5.02	4.58	1,800,000.00	260,991.11	1.016
500,000	682,763	3,000,000	6.00	6.00	2,317,237	5.12	4.63	2,000,000.00	317,236.54	1.125
600,000	753,925	3,600,000	6.00	6.00	2,846,075	5.29	4.74	2,400,000.00	446,075.27	1.288
700,000	803,289	4,200,000	6.00	6.00	3,396,711	5.51	4.85	2,800,000.00	596,711.15	1.506
800,000	830,856	4,800,000	6.00	6.00	3,969,144	5.72	4.96	3,200,000.00	769,144.16	1.724
850,000	836,465	5,100,000	6.00	6.00	4,263,535	5.89	5.02	3,400,000.00	863,534.59	1.888
900,000	**836,626**	5,400,000	**6.00**	6.00	4,563,374	6.00	5.07	3,600,000.00	963,374.31	1.997
950,000	831,337	5,700,000	6.00	6.00	4,868,663	6.11	5.12	3,800,000.00	1,068,663.31	2.106
1,000,000	820,598	6,000,000	6.00	6.00	5,179,402	6.21	5.18	4,000,000.00	1,179,401.60	2.215

Figure 11.12   Cost structure for a business unit — reducing processing costs to $4 per transaction

		Revenue			COSTS					
Quantity	Profit	Revenue	Mg Revenue	Avg Revenue	Total Cost	Total Mg Cost	Total Avg Cost	Processing Cost	Error Cost	Marginal Error Cost
200,000	195,077	1,200,000			1,004,923	5.02	5.02	1,000,000.00	4923.20	0.025
205,000	198,837	1,230,000	6.00	6.00	1,031,163	5.25	5.03	1,025,000.00	6163.38	0.248
210,000	202,542	1,260,000	6.00	6.00	1,057,458	5.26	5.04	1,050,000.00	7458.06	0.259
220,000	209,789	1,320,000	6.00	6.00	1,110,211	5.28	5.05	1,100,000.00	10,210.89	0.275
230,000	216,818	1,380,000	6.00	6.00	1,163,182	5.30	5.06	1,150,000.00	13,181.69	0.297
240,000	223,630	1,440,000	6.00	6.00	1,216,370	5.32	5.07	1,200,000.00	16,370.46	0.319
250,000	230,223	1,500,000	6.00	6.00	1,269,777	5.34	5.08	1,250,000.00	19,777.21	0.341
260,000	236,598	1,560,000	6.00	6.00	1,323,402	5.36	5.09	1,300,000.00	23,401.92	0.362
270,000	242,755	1,620,000	6.00	6.00	1,377,245	5.38	5.10	1,350,000.00	27,244.61	0.384
280,000	248,695	1,680,000	6.00	6.00	1,431,305	5.41	5.11	1,400,000.00	31,305.27	0.406
290,000	254,416	1,740,000	6.00	6.00	1,485,584	5.43	5.12	1,450,000.00	35,583.90	0.428
300,000	259,919	1,800,000	6.00	6.00	1,540,081	5.45	5.13	1,500,000.00	40,080.50	0.450
310,000	265,205	1,860,000	6.00	6.00	1,594,795	5.47	5.14	1,550,000.00	44,795.08	0.471
320,000	270,272	1,920,000	6.00	6.00	1,649,728	5.49	5.16	1,600,000.00	49,727.62	0.493
330,000	275,122	1,980,000	6.00	6.00	1,704,878	5.52	5.17	1,650,000.00	54,878.14	0.515
350,000	284,167	2,100,000	6.00	6.00	1,815,833	5.55	5.19	1,750,000.00	65,833.09	0.548
400,000	302,965	2,400,000	6.00	6.00	2,097,035	5.62	5.24	2,000,000.00	97,034.95	0.624
427,000	310,850	2,562,000	6.00	6.00	2,251,150	5.71	5.27	2,135,000.00	116,149.78	0.708
450,000	316,314	2,700,000	6.00	6.00	2,383,686	5.73	5.30	2,250,000.00	133,686.11	0.733
500,000	324,213	3,000,000	6.00	6.00	2,675,787	5.84	5.35	2,500,000.00	175,786.54	0.842
550,000	326,664	3,300,000	6.00	6.00	2,973,336	5.95	5.41	2,750,000.00	223,336.27	0.951
600,000	323,665	3,600,000	6.00	6.00	3,276,335	6.01	5.46	3,000,000.00	276,335.27	1.005
700,000	301,319	4,200,000	6.00	6.00	3,898,681	6.22	5.57	3,500,000.00	398,681.15	1.223
800,000	257,176	4,800,000	6.00	6.00	4,542,824	6.44	5.68	4,000,000.00	542,824.16	1.441
850,000	226,930	5,100,000	6.00	6.00	4,873,070	6.60	5.73	4,250,000.00	623,069.59	1.605
900,000	**191,236**	5,400,000	**6.00**	6.00	5,208,764	**6.71**	5.79	4,500,000.00	708,764.31	1.714
950,000	150,092	5,700,000	6.00	6.00	5,549,908	6.82	5.84	4,750,000.00	799,908.31	1.823
1,000,000	103,498	6,000,000	6.00	6.00	5,896,502	6.93	5.90	5,000,000.00	896,501.60	1.932

Figure 11.13   Cost structure for a business unit — reducing the cost of errors

11.5 ACTIVE OPERATIONAL RISK MANAGEMENT — RISK CAPITAL, CAPITAL ALLOCATION AND PERFORMANCE MEASUREMENT

The third and final phase of the risk management program is called the "active" phase. Having reached this stage of development the organization will already be comfortable with the figures generated by the models and will be ready to introduce them into its strategy. The operational VaR in this phase may start to be called "operational risk economic capital" (at a certain confidence level).

Capital allocation processes can also be divided into two classes: a "passive" approach and an "active" approach. Under the passive approach are grouped all capital allocation processes that derive an amount of capital attributable to a firm (or business) but do not attempt to steer this number. In many cases, the bank just uses this figure by, for example, submitting the statement of regulatory capital to the financial authorities. A more advanced stage in the evolution of the process might be the application of the input capital in a performance measurement context.

Hence, the "active" approach to capital allocation uses the process to influence business results. The economic capital is then used to adjust the capital allocated to particular businesses, encouraging managers to maximize returns on this allocated capital. This approach allows the management to adjust, for example, the risk capital available to the business. Without this advanced stage, the calculation of economic capital for a business becomes an academic exercise, since business heads will not feel bound by the capital and any attempt to steer the performance of the bank by changing the allocation will have no impact on the organization.

The inclusion of operational risk into the general framework of capital allocation changes the picture substantially. Understanding that the results of individual transactions might be affected by operational errors makes the risk-adjusted return figures valid even for the back-office. See the example in Figure 11.14.

In general the transaction control is done on a daily basis, and gets just the good performance of a trade. In the case above, the trader has done a good deal and made a $50,000 profit in buying US$ against GB£ at 1.3005 and selling almost instantaneously at 1.301. However, the prices and quantities were wrongly booked at first, and a series of mistakes made the transactions settle later than they should, incurring penalties to the counterparties for this reason. The final result of the transaction, considering everything and measuring over a week later when the transaction was totally settled, is

FX Transactions Control							REVENUE SIDE ⇐	COST SIDE ⇒			
Transaction Ticket #	Date	BUY	SELL	Amount (US$)	FX Rate	Counter-party	Transaction Result	Processing Cost	Operational Errors Cost	Final Settlement Date	Final Result
17-0192	18-Jul-01	X		100,000,000.00	1.3005	Bank B		5	32,500.00	27-Jul-01	
17-0193	18-Jul-01		X	100,000,000.00	1.3010	Bank C	50,000.00	5	19,350.00	25-Jul-01	
							$50,000.00		**$51,850.00**		**($1,850.00)**

↑
Most Visible Side

↑
Real Result

Figure 11.14   FX transactions results — accounting for operational errors

Month	Earnings
1	215
2	191
3	245
4	121
5	202
6	310
7	272
8	288
9	134
10	210
11	221
12	253
Average	221.83
Std Dev.	56.88

Figure 11.15   Earnings volatility of a bank

negative at $1850. If this exercise is done for every single transaction, the importance of a reliable back-office is clearly shown and the need to balance the returns with operational risk capital, in addition to market and credit risk capital, becomes clear.

At this stage, organizations will insert the operational risk capital figure into performance measures through RAPM models. In the following subsections, a few approaches will be shown to estimate risk adjusted measures: earnings volatility-based, operational VaR-based and the shareholders' value approach.

11.5.1   Earnings Volatility-Based Methods

One alternative to capital-based models is the approach based on the volatility of earnings. Several early operational risk models adopted this approach, which is illustrated in the following example. Suppose that a bank has monthly earnings as given in Figure 11.15. The definition of earnings at risk will have to do with the volatility. Therefore, we will be dealing with the traditional measure of volatility, the standard deviation. Stating a 99% confidence level on the standard deviation (which is 2.32 based on the normal distribution), the earnings at risk can be considered to be $132.32. The risk capital calculation in this case (supposing a risk-free rate of 5%) can be calculated as:

$$\text{Risk capital} = \frac{\text{Earnings at risk}}{\text{Risk-free rate}} = \frac{\$132.32}{5\%} = \$2646.48$$

The idea of this method is that the risk capital is the amount that should be put aside (invested in a risk-free instrument) so that the yield from this application is enough to cover the volatility of earnings.

This approach has many pitfalls. The first is that the volatility of earnings occurs as a result of many reasons other than just operational ones. The results might have fluctuated due to credit problems (defaults) or asset price fluctuations. Another problem with such an approach is that it assumes the earnings fluctuate in a normal fashion, when in fact this will not be true in many cases.

Month: March

Expected	300
Actual	220
Difference	(80)

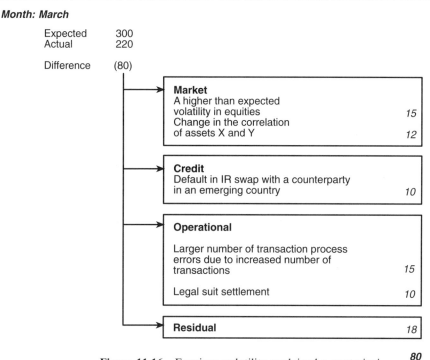

Figure 11.16 Earnings volatility explained a posteriori

The risk capital allocated also does not take into account any unusual events (whether catastrophic or not) that may occasionally affect the earnings. Examples could include a huge legal case lost or extreme market price movements.

Once operational risk can be measured in isolation, this approach might again be reconsidered, using the credit, market and operational measurement techniques to explain the volatility of earnings.

In this case the bank would have an expected level of earnings, due to such factors as positioning, credit exposure and expected operational inefficiencies. The difference between the expected and the actual levels might be explained by several unexpected events in the three types of risk. An example can be seen in Figure 11.16. The difference of earnings in March could be explained by: a higher volatility in equities, that negatively affected the position; a default in a swap with an emerging market bank; an increased number of transactions being processed, thus increasing the number of operational losses.

The disadvantage of such an approach is that it is done a posteriori (after the event). Nevertheless, this type of report might be useful to the board. Variance analysis reports are particularly useful, over a period of time, for identifying recurring events and the cumulative costs of such events.

11.5.2 Operational VaR-Based Methods

Probably the most popular approach in performance measurement is the one developed by Bankers Trust (now Deutsche Bank) in the 1980s. It is usually known as RAROC,

Quantity	Profit	Mg Profit	OpVaR	Mg OpVaR	Mg RAROC
200,000	195,076.80		61,503.20		
205,000	198,836.62	3759.82	64,157.88	2654.68	141.63%
210,000	202,541.94	3705.32	66,867.06	2709.18	136.77%
220,000	209,789.11	7247.17	72,448.89	5581.83	129.83%
230,000	216,818.31	7029.20	78,248.69	5799.80	121.20%
240,000	223,629.54	6811.23	84,266.46	6017.77	113.19%
250,000	230,222.79	6593.25	90,502.21	6235.75	105.73%
260,000	236,598.08	6375.28	96,955.92	6453.72	98.78%
270,000	242,755.39	6157.31	103,627.61	6671.69	92.29%
280,000	248,694.73	5939.34	110,517.27	6889.66	86.21%
290,000	254,416.10	5721.37	117,624.90	7107.63	80.50%
300,000	259,919.50	5503.40	124,950.50	7325.60	75.13%
310,000	265,204.92	5285.43	132,494.08	7543.57	70.07%
320,000	270,272.38	5067.45	140,255.62	7761.55	65.29%
330,000	275,121.86	4849.48	148,235.14	7979.52	60.77%
350,000	284,166.91	9045.05	164,848.09	16,612.95	54.45%
400,000	302,965.05	18,798.13	210,194.95	45,346.87	41.45%
427,000	310,850.22	7885.18	236,948.08	26,753.12	29.47%
450,000	316,313.89	5463.67	260,991.11	24,043.03	22.72%
500,000	324,213.46	7899.56	317,236.54	56,245.44	14.04%
550,000	326,663.73	2450.28	446,075.27	128,838.73	1.90%
600,000	323,664.73	(2999.01)	596,711.15	150,635.87	−1.99%
700,000	301,318.85	(22,345.87)	713,216.78	116,505.63	−19.18%
800,000	257,175.84	(44,143.01)	854,218.91	141,002.13	−31.31%
850,000	226,930.41	(30,245.43)	970,911.12	116,692.21	−25.92%
900,000	191,235.69	(35,694.72)	1,101,876.22	130,965.10	−27.26%
950,000	150,091.69	(41,144.00)	1,211,911.34	110,035.12	−37.39%
1,000,000	103,498.40	(46,593.29)	1,399,321.11	187,409.77	−24.86%

Figure 11.17 Marginal RAPM application to operational risk

but a few acronyms can be used as follows:

Ratio	Note
RAROC	Risk-Adjusted Return on Capital
RORAC	Return on Risk-Adjusted Capital
RAROA	Risk-Adjusted Return on Assets
RARORAC	Risk-Adjusted Return on Risk-Adjusted Capital

Basically the RARORAC formula can be seen as:

$$\text{RARORAC} = \frac{\text{Risk-adjusted return}}{\text{Risk-adjusted capital}}$$
$$= \frac{\text{Revenues} - \text{Expenses} - \text{Transfer prices} - \text{Expected losses}}{\text{VaR}}$$

In the above formula we have simply adjusted the returns (earnings) taking into consideration the expected losses, then divided by the risk capital represented by the VaR figure. One of the main advantages of using such an approach is that all elements can be calculated ex ante, i.e. we are dealing with "expected" losses instead of realized

Box 11.1   Risk-Adjusted Pricing of Swaps

The methodologies used for determining risk-adjusted performance measurement can be adapted and used for pricing swaps and other derivatives. An example might be useful to show how operational risk can influence the pricing of a swap transaction. Basically the risk-adjusted decision would follow the ratio:

RARORAC

$$= \frac{\text{Net income}}{\text{Risk-adjusted capital}}$$

$$= \frac{\text{Revenue} + \text{Fees} - \text{Credit line} - \text{Expenses} - \text{Reserve capital} - \text{Reserve taxes}}{\text{Market} + \text{Credit} + \text{Operational (volatility, correlations, etc.)}}$$

Suppose that we need to price a $100 million swap (for the same credit risk level counterparty — AA equivalent) and we are able to use the operational risk figure for dealing purposes. How would a higher operational risk influence the price of the swap? By reversing the calculation of RARORAC above, we can get the required revenue, given that the total VaR (market+credit+operational) for a swap of 1 basis point is 2.15.

Now imagine that the Chief Risk Officer and the Head of the Swaps Trading Business Unit agree that the benchmark RARORAC for an individual trade will be 8.40%, as given in the figure below. Suppose that in the afternoon the business unit back-office suffers from systems problems and a bottleneck happens in processing the transactions. This poorer operational risk environment makes the VaR change to 2 basis points (keeping market and credit risk constant). In order to adjust to this higher risk level, caused by operational risk problems, the required revenue for the swap would be 2.29. In this case, the required revenue would be 2.29 basis points per swap to match this higher level of risk. Instead of completely stopping the swap trading, management should accept trades that reward the current level of risk.

Situation 1

Required Revenue	2.15
-Funding Cost	0.7
- Credit Reserve	0.31
- Expense Reserve	1
Pre-tax Revenue	0.14
-Tax(40%)	0.06
Net Income	0.08
VaR (Total)	1
Net Cost of Capital	8%
RARORAC	8.40%
VaR*Net Cost of Capital	0.08

Situation 2

Required Revenue	2.29
-Funding Cost	0.7
- Credit Reserve	0.31
- Expense Reserve	1
Pre-tax Revenue	0.28
-Tax(40%)	0.11
Net Income	0.17
VaR (Total)	2
Net Cost of Capital	8%
RARORAC	8.40%
VaR*Net Cost of Capital	0.16

In bps of Notional

ones and VaR is also a measure of estimated losses in a certain period given a certain degree of confidence. For this reason, the approach is generally used for performance measurement.

An important concept within RAPM, which helps in decision-making, is the "marginal RAPM". The marginal RAPM is calculated by:

$$\text{Marginal RAPM} = \frac{\Delta\text{Profit}}{\Delta\text{VaR}}$$

This kind of calculation might also be extremely useful for establishing limit policies. Consider the example in Figure 11.17, where the risk can be estimated using an econometric model having as variables the number of transactions, the minutes of system downtime (not shown) and the number of employees (also not shown). The business unit has a certain limit for processing transactions and the profit is seen to be marginally decreasing after a certain number of transactions. The operational VaR is also marginally increasing, making the marginal RAROC decrease until it becomes negative at approximately 600,000 units.

The basis of the RAPM model is to exactly reward the investment decisions being taken based on (weighted by) the risk. The incorporation of operational risk into the model brings the whole process closer to reality. The challenge is to educate the organization to understand and acknowledge the importance of this new risk and incorporate it into the RAPM process. This might also imply redesigning the structure of the business units, since in general back-office functions have no direct revenue. Eventually, for RAPM purposes, the back-office of a certain product might have to be integrated with the front desk.

11.5.3   Shareholders' Value Approaches

The main objective of shareholder value analysis (SVA) is to maximize the value of the organization to the shareholders. SVA basically states that any venture inside the organization must be undertaken only if a positive net present value (NPV) is obtained. Otherwise, the firm should just return capital to its shareholders in the form of dividends, share buybacks or even acquisitions. A key factor in the analysis is to find a proper discount rate.

A derivative of the SVA is the EVA (economic value added) developed by Stern Stewart & Co. EVA is based on the creation of value during a particular period, measuring the economic profits as:

$$\text{EVA} = \text{Profit} - (\text{Capital} \times d)$$

where d is the discount rate.

SVA is, in essence, no more than the traditional discounted cash flow analysis. The value of any asset or investment is defined as the NPV of the expected cash flows, discounted by, for example, the cost of capital.

I will not delve too much into this subject, but the reader who is interested in an alternative analysis to the SVA approach should refer to Chapter 18, where I apply real options analysis to operational risk.

Stress Tests and Scenario Analysis

12.1 INTRODUCTION

Despite being very conservative in all steps of measurement (through using heavy-tail distributions and even extreme value theory in modeling) there is still the possibility of a few large unexpected events occurring due to the unpredictable characteristic of OR events. Therefore it would be particularly useful to have a few structured models that can be used to perform stress tests and also to generate scenario analyses. In this chapter I present a few such models. In my view, there are two broad methods to perform structured stress tests and scenario analysis in operational risk. The first is based on the VaR model and involves stressing the parameters based on several different premises. The second is based on the multifactor model and uses the control environment to generate stress scenarios.

Figure 12.1 illustrates the possibilities that will be shown in this chapter.

The choice between models is basically dependent upon the data available to the analyst. However, where possible I would strongly advocate the use of multifactor-based models, as they are based on manageable operational variables and are clearly understandable to other individuals within the organization.

This chapter initially introduces a few basic concepts on simulation, including the development of a few random variates from statistical distributions and the important concepts of copulas and Latin hypercubes. In Section 12.3 we see how to develop scenarios and stress test a model through the use of the multifactor models shown in Chapter 8. In Sections 12.4 and 12.5, the development of an add-in to the operational VaR model is also introduced. The first add-in is calculated based on the volatility of the control environment, the second add-in uses a matrix of probabilities of control rate migration. Section 12.6 introduces a model that generates scenarios based on the trends of parameters of the operational VaR model. Several numerical examples of stress test/ scenario analysis models are shown throughout the chapter.

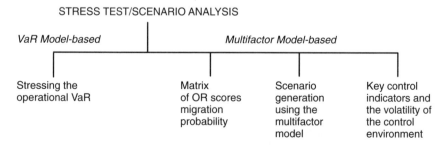

Figure 12.1 Overview of stress tests/scenario analysis models

12.2   USEFUL TOOLS IN OPERATIONAL RISK SIMULATION

A few basic concepts relating to simulation are presented in the next subsections, which might be useful in understanding the techniques used in this chapter and throughout the book. Initially, a few useful random number generators are presented. I then discuss the important concept of copulas of distributions, before finally considering a simulation technique known as the Latin hypercube.

12.2.1   Random Uniform Variates Generation

As random numbers are fundamental in simulation and scenario analysis, it would be useful to have a list of important random number generators for several distributions. By simply changing the value of u with a uniform random number, as done in Table 12.1, random numbers can be generated.

I provide below an example of an exponential distribution with $\lambda = 0.00003$, as shown in Table 12.2. Using Excel, we simply go to *Tools/Data Analysis/Random Number Generation/Uniform* and generate a series of random numbers in the interval [0,1] on the left. On the right we use the formula u/λ to generate the random exponential numbers.

Table 12.1   Random uniform variates for a few distributions

Distribution	Random number function
Weibull	$u^{1/\alpha}\beta$
Exponential	u/λ
Cauchy	$\alpha + u\beta$
Lognormal	$e^{\alpha+u\beta}$
Normal	$\alpha - u\beta$
Rayleigh	$u\lambda$

Table 12.2   Random number generation for the exponential distribution, $\lambda = 0.00003$

Uniform random numbers (u)	Exponential random numbers
0.382000183	127,333.39
0.100680563	33,560.19
0.596484268	198,828.09
0.899105808	299,701.94
0.884609516	294,869.84
0.958464309	319,488.10
0.014496292	4832.10
0.407422102	135,807.37
0.863246559	287,748.85
0.138584552	46,194.85
0.245033113	81,677.70
0.045472579	15,157.53

12.2.2   Copulas and Multivariate Extreme Value Distributions

In Chapter 4 we discussed univariate extreme value distributions, where each type of loss has its own distribution curve. However, in reality there is a theory of multivariate extreme value theory, which is still in its infancy. This can be used to model the tails of multivariate distributions supported by reasonable theoretical assumptions. Multivariate EVT is basically about understanding the dependence structure of extreme events. Dependence relations between random variables are one of the most widely studied subjects in statistics. Without understanding these dependent relationships, no meaningful statistical model can be developed.

Obviously, the understanding of dependent risks will also be very important in operational risk. One of the objectives of risk investigations in operational risk is to measure the volatility in the results caused by a set of predefined operational events. In many cases the operational events might be a function of (or correlated to) another risk. For example, a bank might be trying to protect itself against huge aggregated interest expenses. Suppose that after some research, it is determined that interest expenses risk is correlated with large system crashes. Hence, there are two risks involved: one is that the system crashes for a reasonably long period of time and the second is that this crash will cause a large impact in the results. Often a bank will be prepared for the financial consequences of a major system crash and will have a backup system in place. In which case the two events will be independent.

One way to perform the analysis above is through multivariate EVT analysis by using copulas. Copulas are functions that join or "couple" multivariate distribution functions to their one-dimensional marginal functions. Put another way, copulas are multivariate distribution functions whose one-dimensional margins are uniform in the interval (0,1).

In terms of formally building a copula, let's suppose we have a random vector $X = (X_1, \ldots, X_n)$ that represents operational losses of n different kinds measured at the same point in time. We might assume that these losses have joint distributions $F(X_1, \ldots, X_n) = C[F_1(X_1), \ldots, F_n(X_n)]$ for a unique function C that is called the *copula* of F. A copula might be seen as a multivariate distribution function with standard uniform marginal distributions, or simply as a function. As the copula C does not vary under increasing transformations of the operational losses, we can use C as the dependence structure of X or F.

Therefore, copulas are built by combining the marginal distributions of two different random variables. There are quite a few models of copulas. Below I show two: the Gumbel and the Marshall–Olkin. The fitting of these models should be performed in a similar way to the fitness tests used in Part II of this book (estimate parameters, fit the data, plot graphs, verify the fitness, etc.).

Gumbel Copula

The Gumbel copula is represented by:

$$C_\beta^{\text{Gumbel}}(x, y) = \exp\left\{ - \left[(-\log x)^{1/\beta} + (-\log y)^{1/\beta} \right]^\beta \right\} \quad 0 < \beta \leqslant 1$$

where β is estimated by the sample correlation coefficient.

The Marshall–Olkin Model

The standard Marshall–Olkin distributions M_λ are bivariate extreme value distributions with exponential marginals, where the dependence parameter λ ranges from 0 to 1. For $\lambda = 0$ there is independence, and for $\lambda = 1$ total dependence. It can be represented by:

$$M_\lambda(x, y) = \exp\left((1 - \lambda)(x + y) + \lambda \min\{x, y\}\right) \quad x, y < 0$$

The parameter estimation in this model is given by:

$$\hat{\lambda}_k = \frac{2 + k}{\sum_{i \leqslant k} \max\{x_i, y_i\}}$$

Copulas and Dependence

Copulas are also commonly used to measure correlation among variables (see Embrechts 2000). Dependence properties and measures of association are interrelated; the most widely known scale-invariant measures of association are Kendall's τ and Spearman's ρ (see Chapter 8). Both coefficients measure a form of dependence known as concordance. It is important in the calculation of Kendall's coefficient to understand the concept of concordance.

Let (x_i, y_i) and (x_j, y_j) denote two observations from a vector (X, Y) of continuous random variables. It can be said that (x_i, y_i) and (x_j, y_j) are concordant if $x_i < x_j$ and $y_i < y_j$ or $x_i > x_j$ and $y_i > y_j$, i.e. if they move in the same direction, up or down. Otherwise they would be deemed discordant.

Having determined this simple concept, the calculation of the Kendall's coefficient is straightforward. Let a denote the number of concordant pairs and b the number of discordant pairs. Then Kendall's coefficient is calculated by:

$$\tau = \frac{a - b}{a + b} = \frac{a - b}{\binom{n}{2}}$$

This coefficient is very important in the study of copulas. An important reference in this field is the work of Nelson (1999).

Another important use that we can make of copulas is to generate random variates from them, in this way generating dependent random variate numbers. There are a few methods to do this (refer to Nelson 1999). These methods, which are similar to those based on univariate random numbers, are based on the uniform distribution. One such method can be seen below:

(1) Generate two independent uniform (0,1) variates u and t.
(2) Set $v = u\sqrt{t}/[1 - (1 - u)\sqrt{t}]$
(3) Set $x = 2u - 1$ and $y = -\ln(1 - v)$.
(4) The expected pair is (x, y).

The whole benefit of copulas in dependence studies is that they bring a non-linear solution to the problem of estimating correlations. For example, if instead of linear correlations we use so-called rank correlations, then the problem of consistency with the marginal distributions should not appear. Given a proper rank correlation matrix, it is often not difficult to find a copula with a parameterization that gives this rank correlation matrix.

The study of risk interdependencies is still at an early stage in operational risk due to the lack of data. However, there should be significant progress in the next few years. The use of copulas will be very important in defining the interrelationship between these extreme risks.

12.2.3 Latin Hypercube

The Latin hypercube sampling technique for simulation is basically a more structured method of performing a Monte Carlo simulation, that improves the performance of the algorithm. The major difference between the two approaches is that the Latin hypercube has a memory of the process while the Monte Carlo simulation does not. For this reason, the Latin hypercube method will consistently generate values that are nearer to the theoretical values of the input distribution than the regular simulation. Nowadays most software and spreadsheets have the required functionality, which works basically as follows:

(1) The probability distribution is split into n intervals of identical probability, with n being the number of iterations to be performed in the model.
(2) One of these intervals is randomly picked using a random number.
(3) After that a second random number is picked to determine where, within the interval, $G(x)$ should lie.
(4) Then $x = F(G(x))$ is calculated for that value of $G(x)$.
(5) The whole process is repeated, but the interval used in the first iteration is registered and is not selected in the next or future iterations.
(6) The process is repeated for all iterations. As the number of intervals is also the same as the number of iterations, each interval will only be sampled once.

The Latin hypercube method can also be used in the aggregation of severity and frequency distributions in estimating the operational VaR instead of the plain vanilla Monte Carlo simulation. The Latin hypercube reduces considerably the simulation time.

12.3 SCENARIO GENERATIONS USING THE MULTIFACTOR MODEL

The stress scenario model developed in this section is particularly good for those banks that already collect control environment factors. This is perhaps the most technical approach of all in this chapter, and it is very similar to those used by the market and credit risk models.

In this approach we basically take the multifactor estimated for a particular business or area inside the bank (as below) and assume the independent random variables are stochastic, fitting distributions to them. In Chapter 8 we saw that:

$$Y_t = \alpha_t + \beta_{1_t} X_{1_t} + \cdots + \beta_{n_t} X_{n_t} + \varepsilon_t$$

where Y_t represents the operational losses in a particular area and X_{n_t} represents the control environment factors. The α's and β's are the estimated parameters.

The model works very well, as shown in Chapter 8, and allows many sensitivity analyses to be carried out (e.g. with the variables simulating an increase of 30% in the volume of transactions, reducing the number of employees, etc.). Nevertheless, the model used in Chapter 8 is deterministic (i.e. we are not considering the possibility that the parameters and the random variables might vary). In reality, our model could be seen as in Figure 12.2.

This means that we could let the independent variables of the model be stochastic whilst also finding confidence intervals for the parameters. Then see how the results vary, performing a stress test in a model with a good fit. Here, we are basically stressing (or developing scenarios) using the sets of variables of the model, namely the coefficients and the independent variables:

$$\text{Parameter coefficients} = \alpha, \beta_{\text{SystemDowntime}}, \beta_{\text{Employees}}, \beta_{\text{DataQuality}}, \beta_{\text{Transactions}} \quad (1)$$

$$\text{Independent variables} = X_{\text{SystemDowntime}}, X_{\text{Employees}}, X_{\text{DataQuality}}, X_{\text{Transactions}} \quad (2)$$

I show below an example using both methods. The data set is that shown in Chapter 8, reproduced in Figure 12.3 for convenience.

This data sample will be used in the examples in the next few sections, in which scenario generation methods are presented. In Section 12.3.1, the independent variables are made stochastic (using (2) above) and in Section 12.3.2, we calculate coefficient intervals for the model parameters (using (1) above).

12.3.1 Stochastic Independent Variables

In this model, instead of considering the independent variables to have one single value [for example, $X_{\text{SystemDowntime}} = 3$], we fit a distribution to the variable $X_{\text{SystemDowntime}}$ allowing it to have several values at different quantiles.

More formally, this structured exercise might fit distributions to variables, for example:

$$X_{n_t} \sim \text{Poisson}(\lambda) \quad \text{or} \quad X_{n_t} \sim \text{Lognormal}(\alpha, \beta)$$

We might be able to fit distributions to these random variables using the same techniques applied before in Part II. For example, the time series of *number of employees working per day* seems to follow a Gaussian pattern (normal distribution with mean

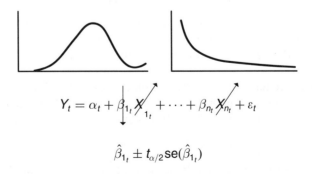

$$Y_t = \alpha_t + \beta_{1_t} X_{1_t} + \cdots + \beta_{n_t} X_{n_t} + \varepsilon_t$$

$$\hat{\beta}_{1_t} \pm t_{\alpha/2} \text{se}(\hat{\beta}_{1_t})$$

Figure 12.2 Multifactor model-based scenario generation and stress testing

Operational Loss Data			Control Environment Factors			
Date	Losses	Number of Losses	System Downtime	Employees	Data Quality	Transaction
(...)						
2-Jul	$234,412	10,004	3	22	94%	250,096
3-Jul	$91,234	7284	1	24	96%	208,111
4-Jul	$2,734,009	17,972	10	19	88%	345,611
5-Jul	$345,661	8613	3	24	95%	210,075
6-Jul	$545	5745	0	24	98%	185,321
9-Jul	$115,912	9745	1	24	97%	249,876
10-Jul	$1234	8075	0	24	98%	252,345
11-Jul	$91,233	9287	1	24	98%	250,987
12-Jul	$55,908	8879	1	24	98%	236,765
13-Jul	$12,002	9079	0	24	98%	238,911
16-Jul	$23,456	9078	0	24	98%	237,654
17-Jul	$1,787,634	13,514	8	21	89%	293,778
18-Jul	$7,233,704	24,510	16	17	81%	415,422
19-Jul	$2891	8054	0	24	97%	250,912
22-Jul	$122	6061	0	24	98%	191,210
23-Jul	$0	5360	0	24	99%	172,901
24-Jul	$0	5283	0	24	99%	170,415
25-Jul	$200,786	8,387	1	24	95%	221,876
26-Jul	$1456	6604	0	24	97%	200,121
27-Jul	$918	5934	0	24	98%	191,435
30-Jul	$1,234,095	11,438	5	22	95%	278,987
31-Jul	$17,654	7287	0	24	96%	238,908
1-Aug	$9871	7549	0	24	97%	235,908
2-Aug	$1,095,033	10,988	3	22	96%	268,001
3-Aug	$1200	6492	0	23	99%	199,761
(...)	(...)					

Figure 12.3   Data set from Chapter 8

	System Downtime [Poisson (2.12)]	Employees [Normal (23.12, 1.786)]	Data Quality [Beta (3.3, 1.7, 0, 1)]	Transactions [Lognormal (12.36, 0.2054)]
99.99%	10	17.6	5%	504,062.45
99%	6	18.96	18.52%	378,592.09
97.50%	5	19.62	24.26%	351,138.39
95%	4.8	20.18	31.20%	329,124.57

Figure 12.4   Quantiles of the independent variables

23.12 and standard deviation 1.786), system downtime fits a Poisson process, and so on. The results can be seen in Figure 12.4.

Based on the distributions for each independent variable, estimated from the time series, we can replace them in the multifactor model estimated in Chapter 8:

$$Y = 1.61\text{E} + 07 + 115{,}081.20\,X_{\text{SystemDowntime}} - 338{,}917.4\,X_{\text{Employees}}$$
$$+ 1.62\,X_{\text{Transactions}} - 8{,}642{,}021\,X_{\text{DataQuality}} + \varepsilon$$
$$R^2 = 93\%$$

by the respective extreme quantiles in order to stress the model. For example, using the 95% quantile, we have:

$$Y_{95\%} = 1.61\text{E} + 07 + 115{,}081.20 \times 4.8 - 338{,}917.4 \times 20.18 + 1.62 \times 329{,}124$$
$$- 8{,}642{,}021 \times 31.20\% = \$7{,}650{,}335.74$$

The results for the 95%, 97.5%, 99% and 99.99% quantiles can be seen in Figure 12.5.

Backtesting the model against reality, we are able to see that even the 95% confidence level is good enough, as the worst day happened on July 18 and the losses amounted to $7.2 million.

12.3.2 Estimating Confidence Intervals for the Model Parameters

Having played with the explanatory variables, now it would be useful to understand the variability of the parameters of a model and see how they influence the results. This is particularly interesting in the current model, since we have found multicollinearity (see Chapter 8) and the parameters have high standard errors and low t-ratios.

We start by showing the calculation of t-ratios:

$$t = \frac{\text{Estimator} - \text{Parameter}}{\text{Estimated standard error of estimator}} = \frac{\hat{\beta}_n - \beta_n}{\text{se}(\hat{\beta}_n)}$$

The t-ratio, as defined above, follows the t-distribution with $(n - 2)$ degrees of freedom. Hence, we use the t-distribution, instead of using the normal distribution, to establish a confidence interval for β_n as follows:

$$\Pr(-t_{\alpha/2} \leqslant t \leqslant t_{\alpha/2})$$

where the t in the middle of this inequality is the t-value and $t_{\alpha/2}$ is the value of the t-variable obtained from the t-distribution for $\alpha/2$ level of significance and $(n - 2)$ degrees of freedom (usually called the critical t-value at $\alpha/2$ level of significance). This can be solved in a spreadsheet by using the function = TINV (probability, degrees of freedom).

Solving the formula above for our case, we get the confidence interval as:

99.99%	11,671,001.16
99%	9,377,922.36
97.50%	8,498,592.99
95%	7,650,335.74

Figure 12.5 Losses estimated using stochastic variables

$$\Pr\left[-t_{\alpha/2} \leqslant \frac{\hat{\beta}_n - \beta_n}{\mathrm{se}(\hat{\beta}_n)} \leqslant t_{\alpha/2}\right] = 1 - \alpha$$

The confidence interval can then be summarized as:

$$\hat{\beta}_n \pm t_{\alpha/2}\mathrm{se}(\hat{\beta}_n)$$

Applying this theory to our example, we get the t-values for 24 ($= n - 2$ or $26 - 2$) degrees of freedom and several levels of confidence as in Figure 12.6.

Having calculated these values, it becomes very simple to estimate confidence intervals for the parameters of the model, as listed in Figure 12.7 for a few degrees of confidence (95%, 97.5%, 99% and 99.99%).

Having the multifactor model coefficient values in hand ($\alpha = 1.61\mathrm{E} +07$, $\beta_{\mathrm{SystemDowntime}} = 115{,}081.20$, $\beta_{\mathrm{Employee}} = -338{,}917.4$, $\beta_{\mathrm{Transactions}} = 1.62$, $\beta_{\mathrm{DataQuality}} = 8{,}642{,}021$), I have simply replaced the original coefficient values in the model by their upper bound confidence interval (at 95%, 97.5%, 99% and 99.99%). For the independent variables, I have used the average values of the independent variables. The results can be seen in Figure 12.8.

In this particular example, the results obtained are extremely conservative, mostly due to the aforementioned multicollinearity effects that made the parameters vary more. Although this stress model would not be recommended in this case, due to these problems, such results are unlikely to happen in most models. A combination of both models, presented in Section 12.3.1 and in this section (stressing both parameters and independent variables) is also possible.

12.4 KEY CONTROL INDICATORS AND THE VOLATILITY OF LOSSES

In the approach developed in this section, I will calculate an extra factor to be added to the operational VaR in order to account for excess volatility of the control environment. As we have seen before in Chapter 8, volatility in operational losses is already accounted for in the VaR model. Since some key risk indicators denote future losses, it would be interesting if the final capital model accounted for any extra volatility in the control environment. A volatile control environment, reflected by the key risk indicators, might indicate that the predictions embedded in the operational VaR fluctuate more than expected, and therefore an add-in reflecting this volatility might be needed. The scheme in Figure 12.9 shows the idea.

Level of confidence	Critical t-value
99.99%	4.654
99%	2.796
97.5%	2.390
95%	2.063

Figure 12.6 Critical t-values

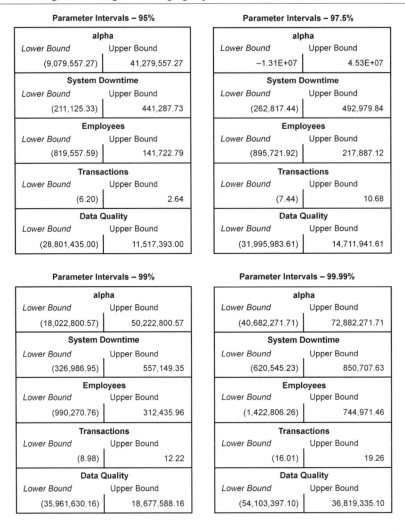

Figure 12.7   Confidence intervals for the parameters of the multifactor model

The calculation of the add-in is very simple and follows the formula below:

$$\text{OR capital} = (1 + \nu) \times \text{OpVaR}$$

where ν is the volatility of the control environment and the operational VaR is calculated as in Chapter 6. This multiplier is similar to the one used successfully by the regulators to multiply the market VaR figure.

There are a few methods available to estimate ν and I show two of them below. The first is the simplest one available, that just calculates the standard deviation of the logarithm of the quantities. The other is the GARCH method.

Parameter Conf. Interval	Losses
95%	57,153,777.43
97.50%	68,000,401.25
99%	96,812,362.88
99.99%	114,411,384.09

Figure 12.8   Losses estimated using the upper bound of the confidence interval

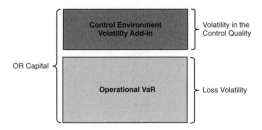

Figure 12.9   Control environment volatility add-in

12.4.1   Simple Calculation of Volatility

A simple method to calculate volatility can be seen in Hull (2000). Basically, we calculate a ratio (u) of the natural logarithm of the variation of prices (or quantities) as shown:

$$u = \ln \left(\frac{Q_i}{Q_{i-1}} \right)$$

The estimate of the standard deviation of u's can be given by:

$$\sigma = \sqrt{\frac{1}{n-1} \sum_{i=1}^{n} (u_i - \bar{u})^2}$$

or:

$$\sigma = \sqrt{\frac{1}{n-1} \sum_{i=1}^{n} u_i^2 - \frac{1}{n(n-1)} \left(\sum_{i=1}^{n} u_i \right)^2}$$

Supposing that the database is given on a daily basis, the extrapolation to a monthly or a yearly level is done by a simple multiplication of the square root of the business days.

An example might help in understanding the approach. For that purpose, consider the data in Figure 12.10.

As can be seen, the data sets from business units A and B are very similar, with the averages being close. Nevertheless, the calculation of the volatility, as indicated by the formulas above, will show otherwise. In Figure 12.11 the daily volatilities are calculated and extrapolated to monthly and yearly figures.

Date	Nostro Breaks Business A	Nostro Breaks Business B
14-Mar-01	692	824
15-Mar-01	778	718
16-Mar-01	807	707
19-Mar-01	737	754
20-Mar-01	749	695
21-Mar-01	667	955
22-Mar-01	801	800
23-Mar-01	742	737
26-Mar-01	703	847
27-Mar-01	755	763
28-Mar-01	833	698
29-Mar-01	738	657
30-Mar-01	739	663
2-Apr-01	778	694
3-Apr-01	880	738
4-Apr-01	766	714
5-Apr-01	755	816
6-Apr-01	905	598
9-Apr-01	764	877
10-Apr-01	748	622
11-Apr-01	717	744
12-Apr-01	829	791
13-Apr-01	877	698
16-Apr-01	802	809
Average	773	747

Figure 12.10   Data set of nostro breaks (KCIs)

Business A

Volatility	0.102537
Year	163%
Month	48%

Business B

Volatility	0.170777
Year	271%
Month	80%

Figure 12.11   Volatilities of business units A and B

As we can see from the tables in Figure 12.11, the volatility of the control environment, as measured by the number of nostro breaks, is much higher in business B than in business A, and so too is the uncertainty relating to quality control. Therefore, the multiplier for B will be higher than for A.

Following the method presented here, and supposing a monthly VaR of $30 million for both units, the final economic capital figure can be estimated as 2.63 × $30 = $78.9 for business unit A and 3.71 × $30 = $111.3 for the more volatile business unit B.

12.4.2 GARCH Model to Calculate the Volatility

With regard to financial asset returns, it is observed that large market plunges, for example, tend to be followed by even larger returns. Put another way, the volatility of asset returns tends to be serially correlated. To capture this serial correlation, Engle (1982) proposed a class of autoregressive conditional heteroscedasticity (ARCH) models. Extending these models to a more general one, based on an analogy with ARMA models, Bollerslev (1986) developed a model that measures persistent movements in volatility without estimating a very large number of parameters. This model is called a GARCH(p, q) model. The GARCH(1,1) model can be represented as:

$$\sigma_n^2 = \gamma V + \alpha u_{n-1}^2 + \beta \sigma_{n-1}^2$$

where γ is the weight assigned to V, α is the weight assigned to u_{n-1}^2, and β is the weight assigned to σ_{n-1}^2. The weights must sum to 1, i.e. $\gamma + \alpha + \beta = 1$.

GARCH(1,1) means that σ_n^2 is based on the most recent observations of u^2 and the most recent estimate of the variance rate.

The GARCH modeling of volatility provides a flexible method for dealing with operational events. Such events might happen due to a large system crash, for example, when there could be clusters of large events. A good reference on the subject is Hull (2000). Most time series and econometrics software presents GARCH models.

12.5 DEVELOPING AN ADD-IN VIA CONTROL MIGRATION PROBABILITIES

A different way of working with operational risk ratings, mentioned in the previous section and also in Chapter 8, is similar to that used in credit risk. Here we also wish to estimate the volatility due to changes in the control environment, not just in the expected loss. However, in the model presented here it is important to estimate the chance of a business unit control environment deteriorating or improving to different control ratings, in a certain time horizon. The model developed here considers the probabilities of migration from one control rating level to the others. A coefficient (c) is developed, ranging (arbitrarily) from 1 to 2 as the control rating[1] (which can be established quantitatively or qualitatively) varies from 0 to 10, as shown below:

$$c = 1 + \frac{\text{Control rating}}{10}$$

Once again, by using the VaR results might be multiplied by $(1 + c)$, however, we can infer more appropriately the required economic capital using a scheme as seen in Figure 12.12. In this example, it is assumed that the operational VaR for a certain business is $77.5 and the current level of control environment is deemed "4".

According to Figure 12.12, this particular business unit has an 89.50% chance of keeping its "4" status in the next audit period, and a 5.50% of improving to "3", etc.

Let p_i be the probability of being in any control rating (state) and μ_i the appropriate economic capital within each state. Given this, it is straightforward to calculate the

---

[1] Where 10 is the worst grade and 0 is the best.

Control Rating	c	Probability (%)	$c \times X_n$
0	1	0.00%	77.5
1	1.1	0.12%	85.25
2	1.2	0.25%	93
3	1.3	5.50%	100.75
4	1.4	89.50%	108.5
5	1.5	3.50%	116.25
6	1.6	1.10%	124
7	1.7	0.02%	131.75
8	1.8	0.01%	139.5
9	1.9	0.00%	147.25
10	2	0.00%	155
		100.00%	

Initial Value: 77.5   ***Weighted Average:*** **108.46**
(Treasury and
Capital Markets)   ***Standard Deviation:*** **29.00**

Figure 12.12   Example of economic capital allocation considering control rating migration probabilities

mean μ and the standard deviation using the formulas below (similar formulas are used in CreditMetrics™):

$$\mu_{Total} = \sum_{i=1}^{s} p_i \mu_i$$

$$\sigma^l_{Total} = \sqrt{\sum_{i=1}^{s} p_i \mu_i^2 - \mu^2_{Total\ i}}$$

Following the example in the figure, in order to allocate economic capital at the $\alpha\%$ level of confidence (by using the normal distribution), one should use the weighted average and sum it to the standard deviation$\times 1.65$. Put in formulaic terms, we have:

$$\text{Operational risk capital}_{\alpha\%} = \mu + (\Phi^{-1} \times \sigma)$$

Using the figures from the example with 95% confidence, we have:

$$\text{Operational risk capital}_{95\%} = \$108.46 + (1.65 \times 29.00) = \$156.31$$

The amount allocated at the 95% confidence level would be approximately $156.31. Compared to the VaR estimate, which is based purely on the losses ($77.5), the final capital more than doubles ($156.31) due to the probability of migration within the control environment. Banks that have started the internal ratings process might find this approach interesting.

12.6   GENERATING SCENARIOS BASED ON THE PARAMETERS OF THE OPERATIONAL VaR MODEL

In Part II of this book I showed how to build the operational risk VaR model. This is composed of several parameters that basically depend on the stochastic processes chosen to represent the severity and frequency models. One way of stressing this model is simply to estimate the confidence intervals of the parameters and use their upper bound (in the case of EVT these can be found by using resampling techniques as shown in Chapter 4). The results will always be very conservative (or perhaps too conservative for EVT, due to the asymptotic characteristic of these distributions).

Another way of dealing with the parameters is seen in Chapter 10, in which we use Bayesian techniques to stress the parameters of a model. However, we can also work with the parameters in a much simpler way, as shown by McNeil (2000). In his article, McNeil created trends for the parameters and then used these to stress a model.

We can, for example, suppose that the frequency parameters would follow a homogeneous Poisson process, non-homogeneous Poisson process, etc. and see how the VaR would behave. Likewise, we might try to fit trends to the severity distribution parameters and see how they could possibly behave in the near future.

In Figure 12.13 are listed possible models for trends (most of them available in spreadsheets, thus making them very easy to play with).

Using the time series presented in Figure 12.14 (with the respective R^2) the graphs using the trendline equations listed in Figure 12.13 are shown (Figure 12.15).

Given the above, the best trend for the Hill (shape) parameter would be the polynomial (apart from the moving average, which in general is the best fit).

Trend	Equation
Linear $$y = mx + b$$	where m is the slope and b is the intercept
Polynomial $$y = b + c_1 x + c_2 x^2 + c_3 x^3 + \cdots + c_6 x^6$$	where b and c are constants
Logarithmic $$y = c \ln x + b$$	where c and b are constants, and ln is the natural logarithm function
Exponential $$y = c e^{bx}$$	where c and b are constants, and e is the base of the natural logarithm
Power $$y = c x^b$$	where c and b are constants
Moving Average $$F_t = \frac{A_t + A_{t-1} + \cdots + A_{t-n+1}}{n}$$	where the number of points in a moving average trendline equals the total number of points in the series less the number specified for the period

Figure 12.13 Equations for estimating trendlines

Shape Parameter	
2-Jul	0.382000183
3-Jul	1.100680563
4-Jul	1.596484268
5-Jul	1.899105808
6-Jul	1.884609516
9-Jul	1.958464309
10-Jul	1.914496292
11-Jul	1.407422102
12-Jul	1.863246559
13-Jul	0.938584552
16-Jul	1.245033113
17-Jul	1.245472579
18-Jul	1.032380139
19-Jul	1.164128544
22-Jul	1.219611194
23-Jul	1.117090365
24-Jul	1.285042879
25-Jul	1.343089084
26-Jul	1.55363628
27-Jul	1.657371746
30-Jul	1.871837519
31-Jul	1.955601672
1-Aug	2.103061007
2-Aug	2.076601764
3-Aug	2.426160466

Figure 12.14   Hill shape parameter time series

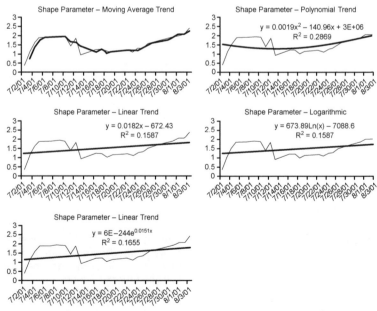

Figure 12.15   Trendline plots with equations and R^2

Scenario 1

Severity Parameters

	Value	Trend	Fitted Trend Equation
Shape	2.11	Polynomial	$y = 0.0019x^2 - 140.96x + 3E - 06$
Scale	102,632.11	Linear	$y = 215.6x - 29.7$
Location	451,266.24	Linear	$y = 1250.1x - 321$

Frequency Parameters

Poisson Non-Homogeneous Process
With parameters x and y

Figure 12.16   Scenario generation using trends and different stochastic models for the parameters

Carrying out the same procedure for all the parameters of a model and then combining them with the various hypotheses for the frequency models provides us with several combined scenarios, as in Figure 12.16.

A certain number of scenarios might be developed using different assumptions for the future behavior of the parameters. The only possible limiting constraint to this approach is that the computational requirement demand can be high.

REFERENCES

Bollerslev, T. (1986), "Generalized Autoregressive Conditional Heteroscedasticity", *Journal of Econometrics*, 31, 307–327.

Embrechts, P. (2000), *Extremes and Integrated Risk Management*, Risk Publications, London.

Engle, R.F. (1982), "Autoregressive Conditional Heteroscedasticity with Estimates of the Variance of UK Inflation", *Econometrica*, 50, 987–1008.

Hull, J. (2000), *Options, Futures and Other Derivatives*, 4th Edition, Prentice Hall, New York.

McNeil, A. (2000), "Developing Scenarios for Future Extreme Losses Using the Peaks Over Threshold Method", in *Extremes and Integrated Risk Management*, P. Embrechts (ed.), Risk Publications, London, Chapter 18, 253–269.

Nelson, R. (1999), *An Introduction to Copulas*, Springer-Verlag, New York.

Part V
Hedging Operational Risk

13
Operational Risk Derivatives

13.1 INTRODUCTION

The topic of hedging operational risk became of particular interest to banks after the Basel Committee determined that a capital charge would be instituted for operational risk.

Currently the hedging alternatives are very limited. Broadly speaking, the operational risk manager has the following options:

(1) Risk mitigation;
(2) Insurance;
(3) Capital allocation.

13.1.1 Risk Mitigation

The first option is not a financial one, although clearly it has a financial impact. Risk mitigation is currently the most commonly used approach, with management decisions typically being based on qualitative or even intuitive measures. Many banks have operational risk managers who work within business lines in order to mitigate operational risks. The problem is that risk mitigation decisions by themselves will not necessarily protect a bank from an operational risk catastrophe. Managerial decisions need to be complemented with some form of financial instrument.

13.1.2 Insurance

The second option, insurance, is already used by banks, but hitherto has played a limited role in risk mitigation/hedging. There are various reasons for this. One is that traditional policies offered by insurance companies address only very specific and limited areas of operational risk. The insurance market itself is very fragmented and the policies and coverage are not uniform. Traditional insurance does not address the multidimensional nature of operational risk. Secondly, risk pricing is not transparent, which is a sensitive question for financial institutions. Insurance requires a large premium to be paid each year, that has a negative effect on cash flow. And thirdly, in the event of an operational risk catastrophe, even if a bank was insured and the loss was clearly covered by the policy, the insurer may take some considerable time to pay the bank. Insurers could represent a credit risk, and it may be considered that they could possibly default on payment of a large loss. Even if this situation does not happen, payment could take much longer than anticipated if there is litigation concerning the origin or cause of the loss. A central bank or a consortium of investors is unlikely to be willing to bail out a financially distressed bank for very long. Given this time constraint, in the case of a catastrophic event insurance may not in fact save an institution, although it does reduce earnings volatility caused by operational losses.

13.1.3 Capital Allocation

The third option is to allocate capital against operational risk. This is probably the most expensive way of protecting a bank against earnings volatility, but can be very effective if used in the context of performance measurement, adjusting returns inside the organization to the appropriate level of risk. Since the frequency and severity of loss events are stochastic, the capital allocated for bearing risk has to be invested in liquid assets and cannot be used operationally. Thus retaining risk internally can tie up corporate capital, which obviously reduces the return. Capital allocation implies having a reliable quantitative measurement model for the organization — capital must be estimated based on a very objective basis using sound statistical/mathematical techniques.

As mentioned before, since the subject matter of this chapter and the following one is so broad, I will be publishing more details in a forthcoming book. In this chapter I will comment on the challenges and alternatives to pricing OR derivatives. I will then show a few products and provide a good idea of how they should be structured and priced (without going too deeply into the actual details of pricing and hedging such instruments).

13.2 BASIC FRAMEWORK AND CHALLENGES IN PRICING OR DERIVATIVES

If modeling regular asset derivatives is complicated enough, the modeling of operational risk offers even more hurdles. Some of these challenges, like moral hazard and adverse selection, are common to pricing insurance. I describe below some of the differences and the challenges in pricing various structures.

13.2.1 Incomplete Markets

The intention in this chapter is to develop ideas about pricing and analyzing operational risk from the issuer's point of view. There are basically two methods currently being considered to price Cat bonds, which could be adopted for ORL bonds: actuarial and financial methods. Embrechts et al. (1997) provide a good summary of the discussion of these alternatives. The aim in derivative pricing is to protect against market conditions and price swings through dynamic hedging.

The distribution under the real-world probability measure of some financial risk is not used for pricing this risk; instead prices are estimated using some artificial martingale measure whose existence is closely associated with the economic notion of no-arbitrage. These models are called *complete*.

For models of the type we are studying here, in general no unique martingale price exists and therefore holding the derivative is a genuinely risky business. This condition is called an *incomplete market*. The pricing of uncertain cash-flow streams under these conditions is substantially weaker in the interpretation of the pricing results that can be obtained than is the case for pricing in complete securities markets. The price can no longer be justified by arbitrage considerations alone (i.e. the cost of a portfolio of existing assets that provides the appropriate payoffs), since there is no such portfolio. The uniqueness of the price is lost. A more simple explanation is that a portfolio of traditional bonds or shares cannot hedge the payments of an ORL bond due to the fact that they are uncorrelated with other economic variables. Therefore the original derivatives pricing scheme cannot be used in the present case.

13.2.2 Utility Theory

Economic theory defines "utility" as a quality that makes a product desirable. This concept was originated in the 19th century mainly by the economists Gossen (1854), Jevons (1871) and Walras (1874). For them utility was seen as a measurable quality of any product, and later it was admitted as an additive quality. In their view any good or service consumed generates utility; the higher the consumption, the higher the total utility associated with the consumption of the product.

At this stage of theoretical development, these authors assumed that utility was measured in a cardinal fashion, in that the utility measure of a product was not affected by the consumption of another product. For example, a piece of bread per day might have 5 units of utility, two pieces of bread 9 units, three pieces 11 units and so on. The amount of, say, cheese consumed was independent of the bread consumed. A piece of cheese might have 20 units of utility, two pieces of cheese 37 units, etc. Therefore, two pieces of bread and two of cheese would have 46 units of utility.

Two problems are very clear with such an approach. Firstly, it is doubtful that utility could be measurable cardinally as numbers like 46, 25, etc. Secondly, even if measurable, considering the utility of products as independent and additive is hardly acceptable for all cases.

A second stream of utility theory came with Edgeworth (1881) and Fisher (1892), where these authors questioned the independence and additive characteristics of utility. They assumed that utility was measurable but, in general, was not additive. The total utility was dependent on the quantity of each product consumed in a certain period of time, but was not the simple sum of the utilities independently measured for each product individually. Nevertheless, these authors still accepted that utility could be measured cardinally.

The work of Pareto (1906) provided the basis for removal of this last obstacle. Pareto's work showed that it is not necessary to measure utility cardinally (although we could still use this option), but instead to order utility by preference and then plot curves of indifference.

Utility theory has been used since then in economics and finance to explain consumer behavior, and even to price assets. Utility theory has also commonly been applied to price insurance as well. I use an example in operational risk hedging to explain the basis of this theory.

Suppose that you wish to hedge your bank headquarters against any physical operational event (fire, riots, etc.). Making the example simple, let the total wealth (a utility concept) of the bank be $200, of which $100 is the value of the headquarters. Making another simplifying assumption, presume that any loss would be total and a fire would reduce your bank's wealth to $100. Now let the probability of fire be 10%. As your bank's final wealth will be either $200 or $100, with respective probabilities

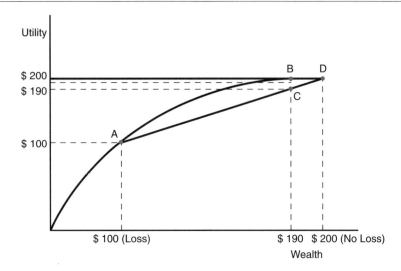

Figure 13.1   Utility curve for hedging OR in a bank headquarters

of 90% and 10%, you can represent your bank's utility in considering hedging OR as:

$$\textit{Expected} \text{ utility} = 90\% \times \$200 + 10\% \times \$100 = \$190$$

The above expression is the utility of the bank if no hedging is bought. The expected value of the loss is $10. A hedge provider (insurer, for example) charging a premium equal to the expected loss would break even if it held a large portfolio of such risks. If the bank purchases the hedge for $10, it changes the uncertainty for a final wealth of $190. Plotting the indifference curve might help us to understand the concept. This is done in Figure 13.1.

The curve is concave, which shows a degree of risk aversion. A cord AD was drawn from the two positions on the utility curve corresponding to alternative wealth levels. The point C, where the cord intercepts the expected money value, traces out the expected utility. As the curve is concave, point C, which represents the final wealth with hedging, would always be a better option than point D, the final wealth with no hedging purchased. This is despite the fact that they have the same value. If the curve were convex, the opposite would happen, as the operational risk hedger would be less averse to risk.

Of course this was a simple example, and much more elaborate utility functions can be developed. Nevertheless, one of the problems in using utility theory is that establishing a utility function for the investor or hedger is, in practice, quite complicated or even impossible.

13.2.3 Moral Hazard

Moral hazard is the term used within the insurance industry to refer to the effect of a reduction in control of losses by an individual insured, due to the protection provided by insurance. When I perform presentations on operational risk derivatives and hedging this is usually one of the first issues to be raised.

Insurers understand that insurance reduces policyholders' incentives to prevent losses. The insurance market obviously has protection against the moral hazard effect, which I will show below. The most important point is that, as a result of moral hazard, insurers are not likely to offer full coverage and, therefore, moral hazard implies that policyholders will have to bear risk. Furthermore, because moral hazard is hardly ever totally eliminated, it leads to an increase in the cost of coverage provided.

Two conditions are required for moral hazard to arise. The first is that expected losses must depend on the insured's behavior after having obtained insurance. For example, suppose that a bank gets protection against interest expenses arising from late settlement, then immediately after purchasing hedging the bank decides to increase the transaction volume by 200% (thus increasing the likelihood of interest claims), simply because they are hedged. A solution to this condition (limiting moral hazard) would be to limit the coverage for a certain number of transactions processed, or increase the premium paid in proportion to the number of transactions.

The second condition for moral hazard is concerned with the difficulty of determining individual behavior. It can be very hard and/or costly to observe and measure the impact of the insured's behavior on expected claim costs. Thus, monitoring will only be used where it is cost-effective.

In general, experience rating and limited coverage are the two major methods of reducing moral hazard, and certainly it will be no different for operational risk derivatives. Another important principle used in derivatives contracts, which will certainly be very important in OR derivatives, is the indemnity principle. This states that an insurance policy cannot pay out more than the financial loss suffered.

13.2.4 Adverse Selection

Adverse selection refers to situations in which the various buyers of insurance have different expected losses, however, the insurer (or the capital market, as the seller of insurance) is unable to distinguish between the different types of buyer and is therefore unable to charge differentiated premiums. This provides one more argument against the external databases consortia for operational risk. It does not matter if you have a reliable database gathering most of the industry's operational events. When the hedger is trying to price a policy or a derivative, the most important issue is to understand a particular bank's level of risk, not the market average.

Adverse selection arises because it is too costly to classify insureds perfectly. In this case, insurers will charge an average premium to all clients. What happens as a result is that those with a level of risk lower than the average would change insurance companies or find another way to hedge the risk (even deciding not to buy the hedge at all), whereas those clients with higher risk, who would obviously benefit from the low premium rate, would buy the protection. The insurer (or hedge seller) would therefore get an adverse selection of clients, because of its inability to differentiate properly between clients.

13.2.5 Actuarial vs. Financial Pricing

Most textbooks on actuarial or insurance mathematics would contain the definition and principles of an insurance premium. A suggestion might be Rolski et al. (1999) or Bowers et al. (1987).

Table 13.1 Actuarial pricing of OR hedging — four principles

Principle	Representation
Expectation	$\Pi = EX + \delta EX$
Variance	$\Pi = EX + \delta \mathrm{VaR}(X)$
Semi-variance	$\Pi = EX + \delta E((X - EX)^+)^2$
Standard deviation	$\Pi = EX + \sqrt{\delta \mathrm{VaR}(X)}$

The risk premium principles can be divided into four broad categories: the net premium; those based on utility theory; VaR-based; and the Esscher principle. I briefly define each of these below. In all cases it is assumed that $\delta > 0$.

Category 1: The Net Premium Principle

The risk premium is equal to the expected losses, i.e. these principles are based on the equivalent principle yielding $\Pi = EX$. The resulting principles are seen in Table 13.1.

Category 2: Utility Theory

In this case the premiums are based on more sophisticated utility functions. One very important function is the exponential, in which the premium principle is represented by:

$$\Pi = \frac{1}{\delta} \ \log E(\mathrm{e}^{\delta X})$$

Category 3: VaR-Based Methods (Quantile)

The premium is defined by a certain quantile (Q) of a risk measure with a certain degree, α, of confidence. The representation can be made as:

$$\Pi = Q(1 - \alpha)$$

Category 4: The Esscher Principle

This principle has been gaining importance in risk theory lately. A few articles have been written (see Christensen 1999, for example) trying to build martingales using the Esscher principle, which can be represented by:

$$\Pi = \frac{E(X\mathrm{e}^{\delta X})}{E(\mathrm{e}^{\delta X})}$$

These relationships are a few of the more important ones used in actuarial pricing of insurance. Nevertheless, lately academics have been paying much more attention to pricing models that consider financial techniques for pricing insurance. The problem usually found is that, as mentioned before, there are *no-arbitrage conditions*, or we

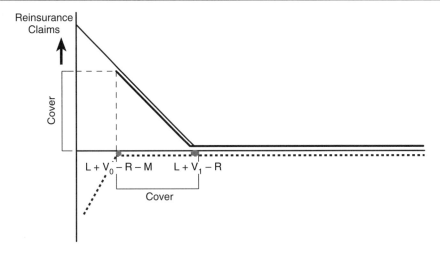

Figure 13.2 Comparing insurance/OR derivatives with regular derivatives strategies

cannot completely hedge the instruments as we could for ordinary options or futures contracts.

I avoid using martingale or stochastic theory to prove this here, but instead use a simple analytical example proving that, in theory, pricing (re)insurance, operational risk derivatives and regular derivatives can be quite similar.

Suppose that the following financial structure (which can be a reinsurance stop-loss policy, for example) is priced using the formula below:

$$P = \min[\max(L + (V_0 - V_1) - R, 0), M]$$

where L is the underwriting loss, V_n is the value of the market stock portfolio, M is the maximum cover and R is the retention or attachment point. P is the loss reimbursement to the hedger. We are covering the losses in excess of R with a limit M.

Figure 13.2 illustrates the transaction.

The graph clearly shows, as can be seen from the formula, that the claims would decrease with increased value of the stock portfolio. Given the graph, we can split P into two distinct parts:

$$P = \max[(L + V_0 - R) - V_1, 0] - \max[(L + V_0 - R - M) - V_1, 0]$$

From a financial pricing point of view the stop-loss can be seen as a bear spread of put options written on the portfolio V_1 with strike prices given by $L + V_0 - R$ and $L + V_0 - R - M$. It turns out that pricing operational risk hedging structures is equivalent to pricing positions, in particular operational loss events contingent on financial option strategies. Consequently, the final price is computed by valuing the different financial options embedded in the agreement. It is worth highlighting that, in contrast to the usual financial market instruments, the traditional risk-neutral techniques cannot be used here directly, but with some adjustments using actuarial methods the results are very similar and reliable.

13.3   OPERATIONAL RISK DERIVATIVES

In this section I list a few products/structures that might be helpful in hedging OR. As I mentioned previously, due to the vastness of the subject, a dedicated book will soon be published describing these products/structures in more detail, indicating how to price and hedge them using different methodologies. Here, I briefly describe the pricing of the ORL bond and an OR swap. I also briefly mention the equity Cat put option and a structure similar to a "first-to-default" swap.

13.3.1   ORL Bonds

In this section I introduce the idea of a derivative that arises from the securitization of operational risk, thus developing operational risk-linked (ORL) bonds. The objective here is to suggest the introduction of this instrument and prove the feasibility and robustness of its pricing. It is beyond the scope of this book to detail any legal aspects, such as the creation of special purpose vehicles (SPV). ORL bonds are inspired by the recent development of insurance and catastrophe-linked bonds. However, the pricing is slightly different, in the sense that the simulations used in insurance and catastrophe-linked bonds consider variables such as extreme weather conditions[1].

The basic structure can be seen in Figure 13.3.

The advantage of ORL bonds over the hedging alternative is that the insurance helps avoid swings in earnings volatility, and may even save the institution in the event of an "operational risk catastrophe". Looking from the bond investor's point of view, ORL bonds offer the same benefits as Cat bonds, since operational risk events are uncorrelated with market or credit occurrences. In contrast, buying regular bonds or even shares in the issuer bank does not bring significant diversification benefits[2]. In this respect ORL bonds offer better diversification opportunities since their expected betas are near zero. A study on the correlation of PCS (property claim service) options, a type of reinsurance-linked security traded at CBOT (Chicago Board of Trade), proved no correlation with the S&P 500 (see Canter et al. 1996). In this case the efficient frontier of the investment is raised with no substantial increase in the risk. Currently, investment institutions are competing more fiercely to produce consistent, high returns on capital, so diversification is becoming one of the hot topics amongst asset managers.

The methodology envisaged here will explore an actuarial parametric approach for pricing ORL bonds. As mentioned before, the pricing of ORL bonds can be very similar to the pricing of insurance Cat bonds, and the parametric approach has been chosen by some issuers of Cat bonds (see Schmock 1998). We are particularly interested in estimating the tails of loss severity and aggregate distributions. In these situations it is essential to find a reliable statistical model for the largest observed operational losses. A model chosen for its overall fit to the whole distribution may not provide a particularly good fit for the large losses, and such a model would therefore fail in pricing ORL

---

[1]Some Cat bond variables could be inflation in building costs, population growth, cost of land, etc.
[2]A recent study showed that if 5% of Cat risk is added to a portfolio of 60% equities and 40% bonds the return of the portfolio increases by 1.25% and the volatility (risk) decreases by 0.25%.

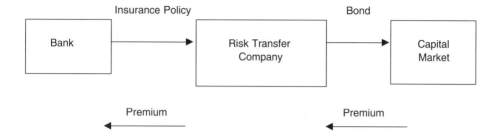

The structure of an ORL bond

AGENT	Financial Institution	Risk Transfer Company or SPV	Capital Market
INSTRUMENT	Insurance Policy offered by RTC	Takes the Risk and issues BOND linked to operational event at the financial institution	Buys the BOND
FINANCIAL RESULTS	Paid a Premium	Receives a Commission	Receives High Yield
RISKS	None up to the limit insured	None	If the operational event described in the BOND happens in the financial institution, loss of some or all the principal or interest

Figure 13.3   Structuring an ORL bond

bonds. Our modeling of catastrophic operational losses is based on EVT. It is important in these models to understand the sensitivity of the price if distributions or parameters, particularly the shape, are changed: the shape parameter can make the loss and the aggregate distribution quite unstable, especially for high quantiles. We try to overcome this problem by testing the results against different distributions and using resampling techniques such as bootstrapping and the jackknife to check the stability of the parameters. The pricing methodology follows four steps.

(1) Estimate the parameters of the frequency and severity distributions

The most common frequency distribution is the Poisson, or normal distribution, in which maximum likelihood can estimate its parameter. However, we will opt to use the "probability weighted" or "L-moments" method in estimating the parameters of the severity distributions. One advantage of L-moments in relation to maximum likelihood is its simplicity and straightforwardness. It also has a better applicability in small samples than ML (see Landwehr et al. 1979). Hosking and Wallis (1987) have demonstrated asymptotic efficiency of the individual L-moments estimators. It is important to recognize that the conclusion they reached was in terms of the small-sample properties of L-moments. Our present interest here is to study small samples of the largest operational losses. As Hosking et al. (1985) noted, although probability weighted estimators are asymptotically inefficient compared to ML estimators, no deficiency is detectable in samples of 100 or less. The biases of L-moment estimators are small and decrease rapidly as the sample size increases. The standard deviations of the L-moment estimators are comparable with those of ML estimators for moderate sample sizes ($n = 50$, 100) and are often substantially less than those of ML for small samples.

(2) *Analyze the sensitivity of the parameters using resampling techniques*

Limiting the analysis to tail events in general means working with small samples. Therefore, the inclusion or exclusion of a single operational loss event may significantly influence the shape of the tail, which is quite crucial in the analysis. Hence, it is important to test the robustness of the parameters estimated. Two techniques may help in this sense: bootstrapping and jackknife (see Efron and Tibshirani 1993).

Bootstrapping is used to obtain a description of the sampling properties of empirical estimators using the sample data themselves, rather than broad theoretical results, which are in general not yet developed for tails of the distribution.

Let $\hat{\Theta}_n$ be the estimate of a parameter vector θ based on a sample of operational loss events $X = (x_1, \ldots, x_n)$. An approximation to the statistical properties of $\hat{\Theta}_n$ can be obtained by studying a sample of bootstrap estimators $\hat{\Theta}(b)_m$, $b = 1, \ldots, B$, obtained by sampling m observations, with replacement, from X and recomputing $\hat{\Theta}$ with each sample. The bootstrap sample size, m, may be larger or smaller than n. This is done a total of B times, and the desired sampling characteristic is computed from $\hat{\Theta} = [\hat{\Theta}(1)_m, \ldots, \hat{\Theta}(B)_m]$. We might approximate the asymptotic covariance matrix of the estimator $\hat{\Theta}$ using:

$$\text{Estimated asymptotic variance } [\hat{\Theta}] = \frac{1}{B} \sum_{b=1}^{B} [\hat{\Theta}(b)_m - \hat{\Theta}_n][\hat{\Theta}(b)_m - \hat{\Theta}_n]'$$

Jackknife is a simulation technique similar to bootstrapping. In this technique we have to re-estimate the parameters by successively dropping a single observation from the operational loss events, getting n alternative parameter estimates $\{\hat{\Theta}_{-1}, \ldots, \hat{\Theta}_{-n}\}$. The pseudo-parameters originating from the jackknife can be useful to estimate the variance (or bias) of the parameters as well as standard errors.

(3) *Find the aggregate distribution through simulation*

In this section we aim to structure and price a bond that covers the aggregate losses during one year. We therefore estimate the aggregate loss distribution. For bonds covering just the largest loss above a certain threshold there is no need to estimate the aggregate distribution. Previously the severity and frequency of the operational losses were estimated. Now we need to aggregate them through simulation. The simulation results are then used to construct an artificial loss experience, which can be used as a substitute for an actual history of losses when necessary. In order to perform a risk and return analysis of the investment, the prospective investor may very well use a forward-looking scenario simulation if a historical database is not available. The bank issuing the bond or the pricing consultant should use the internal historical database of losses as much as possible. The objective with simulation is to obtain the compound distribution of operational losses, considering the number and size of losses. Traditionally, S denotes the aggregate sum of losses associated with a set of n observed claims $X_1, \ldots, X_n$:

$$S = X_1 + X_2 + \cdots + X_n \quad n = 0, 1, 2, \ldots; \quad S = 0 \text{ if } n = 0$$

where n has a counting distribution (such as the Poisson distribution). The random sum S has a distribution function:

$$F_S(x) = \Pr(S \leqslant x)$$

$$= \sum_{n=0}^{\infty} p_n \Pr(S \leqslant x | N = n)$$

$$= \sum_{n=0}^{\infty} p_n F_X^{*n}(x)$$

Here N is the random variable for the number of claims of the period of study, and $F_X^{*n}(x)$ is an n-fold convolution of $F_X(x)$, the distribution function for a typical loss X. In most cases there will be no analytical method to obtain separate expressions for $\{p_n\}$ and $F_X(x)$ from $F_S(x)$, where p_n is the probability of n losses given, for example, by the Poisson or the negative binomial counting distribution and $F_X^{*n}(x)$ is the aggregate claim size distribution function for a fixed number of n claims fitted by extreme value distributions.

(4) Structure of the ORL bond

There are several different possibilities to structure the ORL bond. It all depends on the level of risk and coverage desired. The principal can be totally or partially at risk and similarly for the interest (in the case of coupon bonds). For the purpose of simplicity, in this chapter it will be priced as a zero-coupon ORL bond in which the principal is fully at risk and linked to the risk of yearly aggregated losses higher than a certain threshold. In this case the price of the bond will be defined by the following formula:

$$P = \frac{(1 - \alpha) \text{ Par value}}{(1 + r)^t}$$

where r is the risk-free interest rate, t is the number of years and α is the risk premium for the security equivalent of the operational event risk. The following relation holds:

$$\Pr[\text{bond default}] = \Pr[\text{aggregated (yearly) interest expenses} > X]$$

If the bond is issued for terms longer than 1 year, the probability that an event might happen in the longer term needs to be modified, because the odds of an event occurring obviously grow as the holding period of the bond increases. The return period of the event $\{X > \text{aggregated yearly interest expenses} = Y\}$ can be defined as excess loss $EL(Y) = p^{-1} = (F(Y))^{-1}$. The relevant questions concerning the return period can now

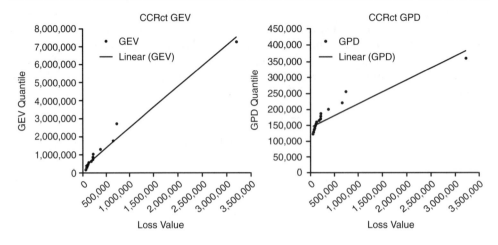

Figure 13.4   QQ-Plot for GEV and GPD

be answered straightforwardly, through the corresponding properties of the geometric distributions (for details see Embrechts et al. 1997). We can then define:

$$\alpha = p_k = p\sum_{i=1}^{k}(1-p)^{i-1} = 1 - (1-p)^k \quad k \in N$$

where α is the probability that there will be at least one exceedance of Y before time k and p is the probability of excess aggregated losses to a certain threshold.

In order to show the pricing of a security for operational risk, we used a database from a medium-sized investment bank. The database contained claims relating to expenses risk[3] for just one location. The expenses happened during the period from 1994 to 1998. Using the methodology above, the first step was to choose a distribution[4] and the level at which we should work. After performing graphical test analysis (QQ and mean excess plots), it is apparent that GEV fits the data slightly better. Figure 13.4 shows the QQ-plot for the GEV and GPD.

Given Figure 13.4, I decided to pursue an analysis of the extreme losses, using the GEV distribution since that fits a little better than GPD. Extreme distributions can be very sensitive to the choice of threshold. For this reason, I estimated the parameters of the distribution choosing different thresholds. The results are seen in Table 13.2.

As can be seen from this table, four parameters were estimated for each of the six different levels of threshold, these being shape, scale and location for GEV, and λ for the Poisson distribution. I aggregated the distributions through Monte Carlo simulation. Each simulation was composed of 10,000 runs, repeated 10 times for

---

[3]Interest claims expenses are charges incurred due to problems in the processing, settlement or clearing of transactions. Banks are expected to compensate the counterparties for these errors.
[4]To test against model risk the analyst might want to test the pricing under other distributions.

Table 13.2   Parameter estimation and excess loss quantiles

Threshold	Shape	Scale	Location	λ	1% Excess loss quantile (US$ M)
10	1.130	313,045.99	587,833.75	6.64	27.3
20	0.953	223,847.22	355,266.93	13.29	22.5
30	0.888	174,187.97	263,982.11	19.94	22.7
40	0.909	139,197.84	208,216.20	26.58	26.2
50	0.941	115,310.81	171,927.33	33.23	26.8
60	0.912	102,538.89	149,677.38	39.88	26.5

each threshold to see if there was any remarkable variance. The quantiles resulting from the runs seem very stable, being independent of the level of threshold chosen. Nevertheless, I performed a Hill plot to test the stability of the shape parameter, which is quite influential in estimating high quantiles of the severity distribution. The relative straight line at the 45–60 levels indicates that this level of threshold would be a reasonable choice. We chose to use the 50 largest events. At this level of threshold the 1% aggregated excess loss probability is estimated to be US$ 26.8 million. As expected, it is a conservative figure since the worst year registered was US$ 3.8 million in accumulated interest expenses.

Following the methodology, I proceed with the jackknife and bootstrap resampling techniques to analyze the sensitivity of the parameters of the severity distribution. The jackknife run shows that the parameters are quite stable, but still influenced by the largest event. The bootstrap 95% confidence intervals were very close to those of the jackknife. Other simulations were run considering the top range of the confidence intervals, and the results were just slightly above the initial ones. The 1% excess loss quantile was US$ 28.2 million, just US$ 1.4 million above the previous estimates.

I then use the 1% level of probability of excess losses to price an ORL bond of US$ 26.8 million. If the aggregate sum of interest expenses paid is higher than the value of the bond, the investors will not receive their principal back. Obviously, if the bond is issued for periods longer than 1 year the probability of losses will increase, as shown previously. The results of issuing the bond for 1 to 5-year periods are shown in Table 13.3. We see that, given the current market conditions, for the issuer it is cheaper to reissue the bond every year than to issue a 5-year one. The rate-on-line is also quite reasonable considering that we are buying insurance against a "catastrophic" bad year (approximately seven times worse than the worst recorded year so far). More important than anything, it must be considered that in this case the money needed to cover this catastrophic unexpected loss is already inside the institution. From the point of view of the investor it is a high-yield bond issued by a high-rated institution in which the risk embedded is not correlated to market or credit events.

I believe that financial institutions should optimize their operational risk hedging decisions by using the four options available. The alternative introduced in this section, the securitization of operational risk through ORL bonds, can be interesting as it allows financial institutions to have cash available right after the operational loss event has happened, thus limiting earnings volatility. In the case of a catastrophic event this may be the only hedge. Banks obviously tend to be secretive about their operational losses.

Table 13.3 Pricing the ORL bond

Holding period (years)	Excess of loss probability	ORL bond price (per 100 face value)	Risk premium (bps above risk-free rate)	ROL[a] equivalent
1	1.00%	94.286	104	1.04%
2	1.99%	88.898	124	2.47%
3	2.97%	83.818	143	4.29%
4	3.94%	79.028	163	6.52%
5	4.90%	74.513	183	9.17%

[a]ROL stands for rate-on-line and is a term used in the insurance industry, meaning the premium divided by the underlying coverage. Just the risk premium (above the regular borrowing cost) is considered as the price here.

As the disclosure of the internal losses database (if one were available) would not always be possible, the structuring and modeling process will need to be thoroughly checked by rating agencies and other third parties such as audit firms. The choice of distribution and parameter estimation needs to be robust enough to avoid high variances in the risk premium and also to reduce model risk.

In the same way that banks have credit ratings and spreads, I believe that these instruments will allow the industry to express its view on the management of operational risk at a particular financial institution, by accepting smaller premiums from those institutions regarded as well managed and by charging an excess for those that are poorly perceived. Possibly this would provide incentives for the banking industry to improve the management of operational risk. These instruments also represent a good opportunity for investors, as they are uncorrelated with market or credit events.

13.3.2 OR Swap

In this section I introduce another product and briefly show how it can be priced. In the last few years several products that securitize credit risk have been launched and some have become very popular. The credit default swap is one of them. The structure envisaged for the OR swap is similar, although the pricing will differ due to the different stochastic processes involved in operational risk.

In a strict sense there are not many differences between a swap and an insurance policy. With an insurance policy we are basically asking a counterparty to hedge a certain type of risk inside our organization. With a swap we are basically doing the same. The difference lies in the agility of the instrument. It offers a wider choice of counterparty through the capital markets. It also provides greater competition for insurers, thus putting pressure on prices. Another advantage might result from these swaps having a differentiated duration (i.e. 6 months, 8 months, 1 year, etc.) while insurance policies are in general pre-established for fixed periods of time. The price of these OR swaps would also fluctuate in the secondary market, as the perception changes in relation to a certain risk, allowing the buyers (banks, insurance companies, etc.) to better manage their risk by selling the swaps if necessary. In this case, the product will also increase competition in the reinsurance market, where insurers are buyers of swaps.

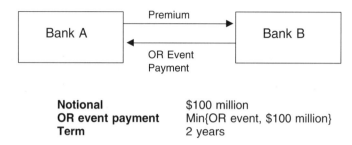

Figure 13.5 OR swap structure

Notional	$100 million
OR event payment	Min{OR event, $100 million}
Term	2 years

The OR swap can be useful if, for example, a bank is migrating from one transaction-processing system to another and this migration will last 4 months, say. Suppose that the management do not want to be exposed to settlement risk above $50 million during this migration. One of the solutions in this case is to issue a swap against late settlement expenses for values above $50 million and pay monthly nettings to the counterparty. As with any swap or insurance policy, the seller of the swap would be exposed to credit risk from the counterparty defaulting on payment. Therefore, this product should be used just for reasonable loss values and not catastrophic ones.

I thought it might be interesting to introduce briefly one structured example showing the pricing. Suppose that a bank wants to buy a hedge against two specific operational risk events: a legal event (a class action, for example) and a liability one. In this case, a loss database is not totally confidential as these events are of public notice. In the actual case upon which this example is based, the bank even decided to release the database of its events thus far to make the swap easier to price. In our example, let the term of the swap be 2 years. The structure of the swap will be as in Figure 13.5.

The structure of the swap is built envisaging that, if an event occurs, the counterparty would pay just the amount of the loss, or $100 million, whichever is the smaller. This reduces the moral hazard problem in the case that issuers make an agreement with the claiming party in a class action settling for a smaller value and sharing the $100 million.

As we have two risks involved in the OR swap (one legal subtype and a liability risk), until the end of the swap the situations listed in Table 13.4 might occur.

If any of the first three situations occur, Bank B would make a fixed payment (*P*) to Bank A. If situation 4 occurs, no payment is due from Bank B to Bank A. We might create an indicator that will help us with pricing. This indicator states that the event situation can be represented by:

Table 13.4 Possible events affecting the OR swap

	Legal event (class action)	Liability event
Situation 1	Happens	Does not happen
Situation 2	Does not happen	Happens
Situation 3	Happens	Happens
Situation 4	Does not happen	Does not happen

Note: We are assuming independence between the events in this example.

$$e(t) = \begin{cases} 0; & \Pr\,[1-p] \\ 1; & \Pr\,[p] \end{cases}$$

The issue is now to calculate the probability (p) of the event happening. Once again EVT might help us in the solution. The Gumbel method of exceedances helps us to predict the number of values in future observations that would exceed past observed records. The Gumbel method (for more details, see Embrechts et al. 1997) assumes that the frequency of the events follows a hypergeometric stochastic process represented by:

$$\Pr(H = j) = \frac{\binom{r+n-\tau+j}{n-\tau}\binom{j+\tau-1}{\tau-1}}{\binom{r+n}{n}} \quad \text{where } j = 0, 1, \ldots, r$$

where τ is the threshold, n is the total number of events, j is the total number of events registered above the chosen threshold and r is the number of future observations $X_{n+1}, \ldots, X_{n+r}$ (or how many periods ahead we would go). Therefore, we could represent by:

$$H_r^n(\tau) = \sum_{i=1}^{r} I_{\{X_{n+i}\} > X_{\tau,n}}$$

the number of exceedances of $X_{\tau,n}$ among the next r observations $X_{n+1}, \ldots, X_{n+r}$.

Coming back to the example, suppose that the number of events in Bank A's database is 31 for the class action event and 82 for the liability event. In the current case, we need to know the probability of an event higher than the threshold (in this case we let the threshold be the highest event) not happening in the next year, so we can price the OR swap. Therefore, for the legal event we have $n = 31$ (number of events in the legal database), $r = 1$ (1 year ahead), $k = 1$ (largest event) and $j = 0$ (such an event never taken place) and we find that:

$$H_1^{31}(1) = 0.01$$

Therefore, the probability that the largest event would be exceeded in the next year is precisely 1.00%. For the second year the probability increases to 1.98%. For the liability event, as we have much less data and more uncertainty, and due to the fact that a few years ago Bank A had a liability event above $100 million, the probability is estimated to be 2.40% (in this case $k = 2$, i.e. the $100 million would be the second largest event) for the first year and the probability increases to 4.73% for the second year.

Given that, we design Table 13.5. Here I priced separately the legal and liability events considering the respective α (probability of the event happening). The basic process during the time of the swap would be as illustrated in Figure 13.6.

Table 13.5   OR swap pricing and term structure data

Maturity (years)	Risk-free		Legal event			Liability event		
	Price	Yield	Price		Yield	Price		Yield
1	0.9524	5.00%	0.93431	1.00%	5.96%	0.90892	2.40%	7.38%
2	0.9036	5.20%	0.90827	1.98%	7.92%	0.86893	4.73%	9.64%

t = 0   t = 1   t = 2

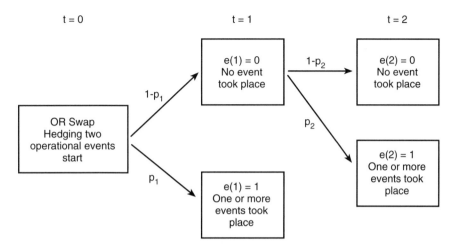

Figure 13.6   OR swap pricing structure

In the present problem, there are two events involved in the swap with two different probabilities (α_1, α_2). Therefore, in this case we have:

$$p_t = \Pr(\alpha_1 \cup \alpha_2) = \Pr(\alpha_1) + \Pr(\alpha_2)$$

Given the above, the probabilities in the problem would be $p_1 = 3.40\%$, $(1 - p_1) = 96.60\%$; $p_2 = 6.71\%$, $(1 - p_2) = 93.29\%$.

The final swap valuation is made simply by finding the present value of the cash flows discounted by the operational loss probabilities.

13.3.3   "First-Loss-to-Happen" Put

An alternative to the OR swap can be derived from the credit derivative instrument "first-to-default put". Suppose that a bank bears the same two risks as in the previous section but wants to hedge just the first event to happen above a certain threshold. The bank's motivation for this type of hedging instrument, for example, might be based on its experience that large legal events do not happen frequently and, therefore, a swap would not be necessary.

A "first-loss-to-happen" (FTH) put gives the bank the chance to reduce its operational risk exposure by being compensated in the case of one of the events embedded in the put happening during a certain pre-specified period. If more than one event above the threshold happens during the period, the FTH just compensates for the largest one.

The structure can be represented as in Figure 13.7. In this structure, above a certain threshold, the hedge buyer pays a premium of x basis points over the risk-free rate to a seller. The threshold should be chosen in such a way that the loss probabilities are reasonably small, making the probability that more than one event will happen over the time of the put very low. In return, the seller provides the buyer with cover for the first event (or the largest in a series) above a predetermined threshold, as specified in the contract.

Figure 13.7   First-to-happen put

13.3.4   Equity OR Cat Put

A form of contingent loss provision can be structured in such a way that a bank arranges a counterparty to provide equity capital under pre-agreed terms and circumstances. An example is the issuing of a put on a bank's own stock. If the option is exercised, the bank can issue new shares and put these to the counterparty at the agreed strike price. This type of hedging can be extremely useful against "other risk" events like strategic decisions resulting in losses.

This type of instrument is basically a put option that is triggered by some risky event related to operational risk (or any other risk management concern). The event could, for example, be a major loss due to a legal event or even devaluation in the share price caused by reputational damage after publicly releasing information on an event. The option can be exercised only when the two triggers are activated. The first is a fall in the share price, making the option "in-the-money". The second is that the loss event must actually occur (the legal event, reputational event, etc.). If the operational loss event happens and the stock price does not suffer any damage, the option is not exercised.

This type of structure may prove extremely interesting for banks wishing to protect shareholder value, after occurrence of an operational loss (or "other risk" events — see Part VII). This structure does increase hedge capacity due to the fact that the exercise of the put to issue preferred shares below their market value results in wealth transfer from the counterparty to the bank right after a major (catastrophic) loss.

REFERENCES

Bowers, N., Gerber, H., Hickman, J., Jones, D. and Nesbitt, C. (1987), *Actuarial Mathematics*, The Society of Actuaries, Schaumburg, IL.

Canter, M., Cole, J. and Sandor, R. (1996), "Insurance Derivatives, a New Asset Class for the Capital Markets and a New Hedging Tool for the Financial Industry", *The Journal of Derivatives*, 4, 89–104.

Christensen, C.V. (1999), "A New Model for Pricing Catastrophe Insurance Derivatives", Working Paper, Department of Mathematical Sciences, University of Aarhus, Denmark.

Edgeworth, F. (1881), *Mathematical Physics*, Kegan Paul, London.

Efron, B. and Tibshirani, R. (1993), *An Introduction to Bootstrap*, Chapman & Hall, New York.

Embrechts, P., Kluppelberg, C. and Mikosch, T. (1997), *Modeling Extreme Events for Insurance and Finance*, Applications of Mathematics, Stochastic Modeling and Applied Probability, No. 33, Springer-Verlag, Berlin.

Fischer, I. (1892), *The Principles of Economics*, London.

Gossen, L. (1854), *The Development of the Laws of Exchange among Men and the Consequences of Human Action*, London.

Hosking, J.R.M., Wallis, J. and Wood, E. (1985), "Estimation of Generalized Extreme Value Distribution by the Method of Probability Weighted Moments", *Technometrics*, 27, 251–261.

Hosking, J.R.M. and Wallis, J. (1987), "Parameter and Quantile Estimation for the Generalized Pareto Distribution", *Technometrics*, 29, 339–349.

Jevons, W. (1871), *Theory of Political Economy*, Macmillan, London.

Landwehr, J., Matalas, N. and Wallis, J. (1979), "Probability Weighted Moments Compared to Some Traditional Techniques in Estimating Gumbel Parameters and Quantiles", *Water Resources Research*, 15, 1055–1064.

Pareto, V. (1906), *Manuale d'economia politica*, Rome.

Rolski, T., Schmidli, H., Schmidt, V. and Teugels, J. (1999), *Stochastic Processes for Insurance and Finance*, Wiley, London.

Schmock, U. (1998), "Estimating the Value of the WinCat coupons of the Winterthur Insurance Convertible Bond: A Study of the Model Risk", working paper, ETH, Zurich.

Walras, L. (1874), *Elements of Pure Economics, or the Theory of Social Wealth*, reprinted by Orion Editions, Philadelphia, VA.

14
Developing a Hedging Program
for Operational Risk

14.1 INTRODUCTION

In the previous chapter we saw how to structure and price a few sophisticated instruments to hedge operational risk. These products may open the gates of the capital markets, leading to acceptance of financial instruments based on operational risk. In this chapter I show how to use these products as well as other more traditional financial instruments such as insurance and internal capital retention in order to develop a hedge program for operational risk.

Currently there are few options available for hedging operational risk. Even insurance, the most established instrument available in the market, does not cover operational risk in all its dimensions. This is due in part to the current low level of demand; however, the number of products and structures is expected to grow substantially as banks advance in their measurement projects.

Presently, the spectrum of products available to hedge operational risk is as shown in Figure 14.1.

I will briefly describe a few of these products in this chapter, and then give an example of how to put them together in a hedging program.

14.2 RETAINING AND QUASI-RETAINING STRUCTURES

The simplest structures, and perhaps the most expensive ones from an opportunity cost point of view, are the retaining and "quasi-retaining" structures. These structures and instruments are basically priced by developing the expected discounted cash flow of losses and the allocated capital or premiums. The best option would be the one that shows the best NPV discounted at the opportunity cost.

Below, I show a few examples giving an idea of costs.

14.2.1 Internal Capital Retention

This option reflects the pure retention of risk. In this case a bank simply allocates a certain amount of capital that it considers sufficient to cover potential losses. With the evolution of operational risk measurement and modeling, the expected losses will probably be embedded in the price of financial products with retained internal capital being a function of the volume of products traded.

The calculation of the cost of this retention is quite simple. Suppose that the risk-free rate is 5% p.a. and that the expected return on the bank's assets including its portfolio is 15% p.a. What is the opportunity cost? The actual level of cost will depend on the

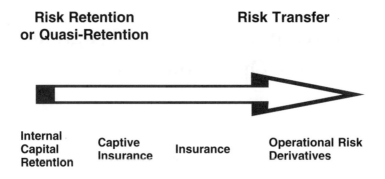

Figure 14.1   Scope of OR hedging

behavior of the loss events (and, therefore, on the use of this allocated fund) during the course of the year. So, if a bank estimates its operational losses to be $25 million in a year, and its opportunity cost of capital is 10%, the expected cost is $2.5 million.

14.2.2   Captive Insurance

A very popular method of hedging operational risk in large banks is through captive insurance companies. These companies are wholly owned subsidiaries that pay the losses. The advantage of having a captive insurance subsidiary is that the company can undertake transactions not just with the parent company, but also with reinsurers (as well as other companies if necessary).

In terms of classification, if a captive only deals with its parent corporation and/or wholly owned subsidiaries of the parent, it is called a pure captive. If many different companies form a captive it is called a group captive.

The financing of losses through pure captives is basically a form of retaining risk. There are also some advantages in using captives, which explains their popularity. The tax advantage provides an incentive for firms to arrange loss-financing transactions that can be treated as insurance for tax purposes. Furthermore, as captive transactions are treated as insurance transactions, banks can reduce expected tax payments relative to retention. Excise taxes, for example, create an incentive to have transactions with foreign insurers treated as reinsurance rather than insurance, since in the UK taxes on foreign transactions amount to 4% in insurance premiums but only 1% in reinsurance premiums. This is the reason why many captives are established as foreign companies in fiscal havens like the Bahamas or the Cayman Islands. Given that very broad strategic issues are involved in the inception of a captive insurance program, the decision to create a captive should be made at corporate level within the bank.

An additional, and perhaps even more important, motivation for establishing a captive insurer is that it allows the group to purchase excess insurance coverage directly from reinsurers. As reinsurance transactions are classically less subject to stringent regulation, having a transaction classified as reinsurance can reduce regulatory constraints on the transaction.

	Year 1	Year 2	Year 3	Year 4
Initial Cost	(1,200,000)			
Administration Fee	(150,000)	(150,000)	(150,000)	(150,000)
Fronting Fee	(200,000)	(200,000)	(200,000)	(200,000)
Reduction in Premiums	1,100,000	1,100,000	1,100,000	1,100,000
Pre-Tax Cash Flow	(450,000)	750,000	750,000	750,000
Income Tax (40%)	—	300,000	300,000	300,000
Cash Flow	(450,000)	450,000	450,000	450,000

Figure 14.2   Example of cash flow of a captive insurance project

An example of the cash flow resulting from the establishment of a captive can be seen in Figure 14.2.

This shows modified cash flow after the introduction of the captive. It is assumed that an initial cost of $1.2 million is payable to consultants and lawyers in order to establish the captive. In addition, there is a regular charge which relates to the administration costs of the captive together with a "fronting fee" paid to the fronting insurer (responsible for management of the captive). The expected reduction in premiums by creating the captive is assumed to be $1.1 million. I am not considering here the tax advantage of doing that. Since operational losses cannot be calculated as "expected" and included in the balance sheet, as is the current practice for credit risk, the expected operational losses are left out. Nevertheless, the insurance premium with the captive can be considered as an expense, and therefore will be a way of providing for the expected operational losses.

As I mentioned at the beginning of this section, the options to hedge OR at this level (retention or quasi-retention) would be better understood from a discounted cash flow point of view. In this case, with a 10% opportunity cost, the NPV would be 608,258 and the IRR of the project would be 84%. Nevertheless, the bank's corporate center must perform a thorough analysis of the possibilities, including an operational losses pattern scenario, to make the best decision.

14.2.3   Finite Risk

The insurance industry offers multiyear self-insurance plans that are commonly called finite risk insurance. The name arises from the fact that the risk transfer is very limited. Therefore, the insured will pay for most (or all) of the losses.

The structure of the contracts is very simple and is generally established for periods ranging from 2 to 5 years. In this scheme the insured pays premiums into a fund managed by the insurer who charges an administration fee. The fund pays an interest (agreed between the parties) and the losses are paid by the fund. If the fund is insufficient to pay all the losses in a given year, then the insurer might pay losses up to a certain limit if this condition was pre-negotiated. Nevertheless, this amount will eventually have to be paid back to the insurer. On the other hand, if the fund has a surplus at the end of the period, it will be returned to the insured.

The advantage of finite risk over simple internal capital allocation is that the payments are smoothed over time. I provide a couple of examples of the finite risk structure that might help to illustrate this. Suppose that an operational risk manager starts a measurement project to estimate the operational losses within a bank. The bank management does not accept internal capital retention. Therefore, the manager has to find other quasi-retaining structures and decides upon finite risk.

We analyze two cases. In the first the manager estimates the expected losses to be around $20–$25 million a year. In this case, he establishes a 3-year finite risk arrangement, paying a premium of $25 million, a fee of 10% of the premium ($2,500,000) and a negotiated interest rate of 5%. The insurer agrees to pay losses up to 20% above the limit, but with a punitive rate of 16% p.a. Suppose that the punitive rate is paid just at the end, in order to simplify the calculations.

The structure can be seen in Figure 14.3. Since the manager estimated correctly the losses (and the volatility of expected losses was low), the structure worked quite well. The losses during the 3-year period were $66 million and the premium paid was $75 million plus $3,750,000 net fees (i.e. fees minus interest earned). In the end the insurer would return $5.3 million back to the bank. In this case, we are incurring opportunity costs by receiving just 5%. Supposing the opportunity cost is 10%, the bank will incur a $22.5 million loss. Therefore, the cost of the structure is given by the opportunity cost of the premiums paid plus the net fees plus the opportunity cost on the balances. Therefore, this first structure has a direct cost of $3.75 million (the net fees) plus a hidden (opportunity) cost of around $8.6 million.

In the second case, the manager estimated the losses to be around $15 million and as we can see, compared to the previous example, the structure does not work efficiently and effectively. The penalty interest rate is applied already in the second year, making the whole structure very costly for the bank. The total cost is decreased by the smaller net fees of $2,250,000 but severely increased by the penalty rates during the course of years 2

Finite Risk—Structure 1

3-Year contract; premium = $25 million; interest rate = 5%

	Year 1	Year 2	Year 3	Total
Premium	25,000,000	25,000,000	25,000,000	75,000,000
Balance Carried from Previous Year	—	1,201,779	5,079,434	—
Fee	(2,500,000)	(2,500,000)	(2,500,000)	(7,500,000)
Op Losses (Year 1)	(22,548,221)	(19,872,345)	(23,499,215)	(65,919,781)
Interest on Balance*	1,250,000	1,250,000	1,250,000	3,750,000
Final Balance	1,201,779	5,079,434	5,330,219	—

*We are assuming that the interest is charged on the full premium to simplify the calculations

Figure 14.3 Cash flow of a finite risk structure—Case 1

Finite Risk — Structure 2

3-Year contract; premium = $15 million; interest rate = 5%

	Year 1	Year 2	Year 3	Total
Premium	15,000,000	15,000,000	15,000,000	45,000,000
Balance Carried from Previous Year	—	(8,298,221)	(13,920,566)	—
Fee	(1,500,000)	(1,500,000)	(1,500,000)	(4,500,000)
Op Losses (Year 1)	(22,548,221)	(19,872,345)	(23,499,215)	(65,919,781)
Interest on Balance*	750,000	750,000	750,000	2,250,000
Final Balance	(8,298,221)	(13,920,566)	(23,169,781)	—

*We are assuming that the interest is charged on the full premium to simplify the calculations

Figure 14.4   Cash flow of a finite risk structure — Case 2

and 3, amounting to $0.96 million. This is a consequence of the conservative estimates of the manager. An extra $16.2 million had to be arranged to pay up the losses. The structure also bears an opportunity cost of around $4.5 million. Figure 14.4 depicts this.

In the third structure (see Figure 14.5), the manager estimated the operational losses to be $15 million but the volatility of the expected losses was so high that both parties decided to increase the premium in the following years to avoid higher penalties. In this case, the cost of the structure was $1.7 million just in penalties alone, and an extra $32.6 million had to be allocated internally to cover the losses.

A more sophisticated and detailed analysis of the cost of these structures would probably discount the penalty fees, using the bank's funding. The objective here is simply to illustrate the structure of finite risk and how the volatilities of the expected operational losses might affect the cost of the product.

Finite Risk — Structure 3

3-Year contract; premium = $15 million; interest rate = 5%

	Year 1	Year 2	Year 3	Total
Premium	15,000,000	20,000,000	35,000,000	70,000,000
Balance Carried from Previous Year	—	(8,298,221)	(33,170,566)	—
Fee	(1,500,000)	(2,000,000)	(3,500,000)	(7,000,000)
Op Losses (Year 1)	(22,548,221)	(43,872,345)	(13,499,215)	(79,919,781)
Interest on Balance*	750,000	1,000,000	1,750,000	3,500,000
Final Balance	(8,298,221)	(33,170,566)	(13,419,781)	—

*We are assuming that the interest is charged on the full premium to simplify the calculations

Figure 14.5   Cash flow of a finite risk structure — Case 3

If considered appropriate, eventually the finite risk structure could be replicated inside the bank by establishing an "internal fund", thus eliminating payment of fees and penalties.

14.2.4 Risk Retention Groups

The idea of risk retention groups (or "mutuals") has been around in the insurance industry for quite some time. The suggestion of creating these groups has been discussed, especially amongst British banks. A mutual has similar characteristics to a group captive, but in reality is a pooling arrangement to protect a number of different organizations, generally in the same sector.

Mutuals might be considered as a further option for hedging operational risk.

14.3 OPERATIONAL RISK INSURANCE

Insurance is one of the most important instruments for hedging OR and, in terms of risk transfer, is currently the only instrument to be widely used. Nevertheless, there are a number of concerns about the use of insurance for the purposes of hedging OR in banks. In this section I briefly summarize the discussions and present the techniques for integrated insurance programs.

14.3.1 Is Insurance a Proper Hedge for OR?

The discussions about the appropriateness of insurance to protect against operational risks have dominated the topic of operational risk hedging. The main issue is that the definition and classification of operational risk varies significantly. Therefore, insurers fear being held liable for losses that have not been factored into their premium calculations. As a result, insurers generally word policies very carefully in order to exclude risks that are not definite in amount, time, place or cause. Consequently, this may lead to gaps in the available cover, preventing the insurance of all risks encompassing OR (although some "business risk types", which are not included in regulatory capital, might be included). In addition, where policies have not been properly worded there is the possibility of lengthy disputes over whether a loss really is covered or not. This can at best lead to long delays in the payment of claims.

Specific policies offered by insurance companies to financial institutions include:

- Bankers Blanket Bond (including cover for computer crime);
- Professional Indemnity;
- Directors and Officers Liability;
- Employment Practices Liability;
- Non-Financial Property — All Risks;
- General & Other Liability.

In addition, new products have recently been introduced for:

- Unauthorized Trading;
- Organizational Liability.

Some types of insurance are compulsory in several developed countries. Typical examples are:

(a) *Depositor Protection Insurance.* Deposit insurance schemes provide broad protection for depositors against the adverse effects of bank insolvency, while providing regulators with the option of refusing to bail out ailing deposit-taking institutions. Hence, deposit insurance is not linked to specific causes; instead, all that is required is insolvency to trigger the payment of compensation.

(b) *Fidelity Insurance.* Bonding or fidelity insurance is designed to protect an employer against dishonesty or default on the part of an employee.

The recent Basel Accord discussions resulted in the Basel Committee pointing out a number of potential pitfalls with operational risk insurance and other forms of outsourcing. Some of these points are:

- The insurance industry is not sufficiently well capitalized. A bank that is transferring risk may be better capitalized than the accepting insurance company.
- Blanket cover is not available. There are many different contracts for different elements, which do not fit together sufficiently well. This leads to uninsured gaps or inefficient overlaps.
- Limiting conditions and exclusion clauses lead to doubt regarding payment in the event of failure.
- Delays in payment could result in serious damage to the claimant.
- It is difficult to determine the true economic value of insurance purchased in the absence of sufficient and appropriate data.

Therefore, although it appears that the Basel Committee is prepared to consider insurance as a mitigant for operational risk, there are a number of issues that need to be addressed by the financial services industry before it is finally accepted. An industry committee has recently been established in London, and several new ideas are being formulated, for example, the development of global master agreements, similar to those for credit derivatives. These would predefine the risks embedded in a policy, thus avoiding the problem of lengthy wording in insurance policies and also reducing costs.

14.3.2 Integrated Insurance Programs

In general, the calculation given in many insurance books presents the situation as just one risk type requiring coverage. In reality there is an emergence in the insurance industry of insurance programs for financial institutions that are in most cases offered as integrated programs that cover more than one risk. These products are so-called basket insurance (or basket options). For example, instead of having separate coverage and limits for property, bankers blanket bond, and directors and officers liability losses, some banks purchase contracts with indemnity payments and limits based on the total losses from all three exposures. Basically, the separate coverage works as illustrated in Figure 14.6.

In this program, the coverage is differentiated by type of risk or exposure. The policies might even be with different insurance companies. Each policy has a different level of deductible (or no deductible at all). See Figure 14.7.

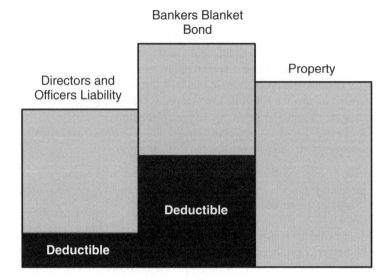

Figure 14.6 Separate coverages — three different policies

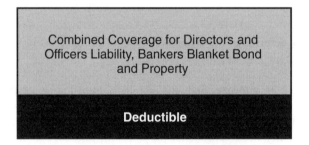

Figure 14.7 Integrated insurance program

The integrated program puts all the various coverages together. In the program, as shown, the basket policy encompasses all three policies into one. The basket insurance approach is an emerging trend in insurance. In this case the insurance companies are trying to mitigate the effects of adverse selection (as there is very limited information on the banking industry's operational losses, and certainly no information on an individual bank's losses, which are treated as confidential) by pooling all risks into one broad policy. These types of coverage might be interesting for a bank that is not measuring OR and has as much information about its risk profile as the insurer, i.e. very little.

A bank that has already started the measurement process and has a structured operational risk database will have a better understanding of its risk profile. Consequently, it may prefer to buy separate policies for each type of risk.

Another classification for insurance programs is into vertical and horizontal programs. In the examples above, typically there is a primary layer (in general the deductibles) and then an excess layer, after which another layer might kick in, and so on. This is called a vertical layering, i.e. each layer is piled on top of the one below.

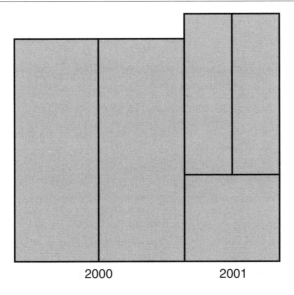

Figure 14.8   Horizontal vs. vertical program

A substitute structure is to arrange the program horizontally, as in Figure 14.8.

In this figure, the primary layer for 2000 was split between two insurers (it could have been more than two). This is called horizontal layering. In 2001 the primary layer was covered by a single insurer and the excess layer by two. The decision between vertical or horizontal layering programs involves issues of risk sharing and certain conditions on the insurance market.

14.4   AUDITING INSURANCE EFFICIENCY

If the operational risk manager followed my suggestions in database modeling by registering each loss event separately, a second step at this stage would be to perform an audit in the efficiency of the insurance coverage with respect to the bank's loss profile. An example with a few events can be seen in Figure 14.9.

In the example, the stolen laptop was totally covered and the insurance company paid it back in 102 days. In the time of this policy expiration, one of the parameters to choose among insurers might be, for example, the reduction in average payment of these events. A bank might verify that, based on its risk profile, it is buying too much insurance for one type of risk and eventually not buying enough for another. This understanding of the operational loss profile will be fundamental for designing a proper hedging program.

14.5   APPLICATION OF DEVELOPING
A SIMPLE HEDGING PROGRAM

In this section I developed a simple application of a hedging program for one type of operational risk (frauds) in a commercial bank. The development of a full program

Operational Loss Event	Loss Amount	OR Type	Event Date	Ins. Pay Date	Paymt Gap	Ins. Policy Coverage	Coverage	Net Loss
Laptop stolen	2345.00	Security Risk	3-Dec-00	15-Mar-01	102	100%	100%	0
Small fire in the cafeteria	17,332.12	Security Risk	4-Dec-00			Below Deductible	0%	17,332.12
Litigation Case #2,371	1,243,990.00	Legal/ Liability Risk	9-Mar-99	17-Mar-01	739	75%	75%	310,997.50
Liability Case #10,789	250,000,00	Legal/ Liability Risk	3-Dec-99	7-Dec-00	370	50%	50%	125,000.00
(...)	(...)							

Figure 14.9 Operational net losses database — verifying insurance efficiency

covering all operational risks would be beyond the scope of this book. However, I hope this exercise (using a real operational losses database) will illustrate the ideas.

The database records the frauds happening within a certain region of a commercial bank. Given the characteristics of the database, I decided to split it into three layers: "$0–$1 million"; "$1–$7 million"; "$7 million + ". The number of events is stated in Figure 14.10.

As this bank buys annual policies instead of multiyear policies, I decided to split the number of events per year, as in Figure 14.11. The number of operational events seems pretty stable in all layers. The smaller frauds, below $1 million, dominate the database and most of the losses are within this category. Only one single event above $7 million took place during these 4 years.

Now it would be interesting to see some basic statistics of the data. Figure 14.12 shows the first four moments of the data for the entire database and the first two layers. If we consider the whole database we verify that it is very extreme. The kurtosis is extremely high (remember from Chapter 4, a normal distribution would accept kurtosis < 3) and very positively skewed. Separating the losses by layers, the situation improves considerably. At this stage, we might have an idea of the model for the stochastic behavior of the frauds.

To complete the basic analysis, Figure 14.13 shows the aggregated loss amounts per year. The figure lost due to fraud in 4 years reaches an impressive $114,773,081! In terms of value, the few events in the second layer almost match those in the primary layer.

We should now be able to design a simple hedging program for these layers. I describe the method for each one below.

Layer	Loss Events
$0–$1 million	3328
$1–$7 million	20
$7 million +	1

Figure 14.10 Number of frauds

Layer	1998	1999	2000	2001
$0–$1 million	781	871	915	761
$1–$7 million	5	3	4	8
$7 million +	—	1	—	—

Figure 14.11   Number of frauds 1998–2001 stated per year

	Average	StDev	Skewness	Kurtosis
Whole Data	31,546	209,567	18	423
$0–$1 million	18,145	59,283	9	97
$1–$7 million	2,155,319	1,414,739	2	4

Figure 14.12   Statistics of the frauds database 1998–2001

	Total	1998	1999	2000	2001
Layer					
Whole Data	$114,773,081	$26,731,821	$29,298,222	$31,555,700	$27,187,338
$0–$1 million	$60,387,491	$13,877,209	$15,502,912	$16,602,931	$14,404,439
$1–$1 million	$45,261,701	$11,632,781	$7,221,990	$9,052,340	$17,354,589
$7 million +	$9,123,889	$0	$9,123,889	$0	$0

Figure 14.13   Aggregated losses per year and layer

14.5.1   First or Primary Layer

The bank might decide to retain this lower level of individual losses (less than $1 million) instead of transferring them. The fraud losses at this level might be considered "operational inefficiencies" or "expected operational losses" for this particular bank, and embedded into the price of a transaction. Figure 14.14 shows this pricing.

As can be seen from this figure, the expected fraud losses per transaction are really very stable, varying from $0.18 to $0.22. Therefore, each transaction should account for this amount to cover against expected frauds. This is certainly an incentive for the bank to improve the controls. Furthermore, with this approach any improvement in the control that results in a reduction of expected frauds can be valued in monetary terms.

14.5.2   Secondary Layer

The bank decided to establish as a deductible (D) $1 million for the first layer. After a few calculations, they established that the risk transfer to an insurance company would

	1998	1999	2000	2001
Number of Transactions	78,336,216	71,915,421	80,333,871	81,900,212
Operational Risk Capital per Transaction	0.18	0.22	0.21	0.18

Figure 14.14   Expected fraud risk in a commercial bank

be limited to $8 million. Therefore, the first simple calculation we have to perform is the relative layer length (R) that is given by:

$$R = \frac{U+D}{D} = \frac{7+1}{1} = 8$$

The next step of the calculation would be to choose the proper statistical distribution for the losses situated at this layer. Just to simplify the analysis, I will perform the statistical calculations using the one-parameter representation of the Pareto distribution, assuming that it is the best fit. From Chapter 3, it will be recalled that the distribution is given by:

$$f(x) = \frac{\alpha\theta^\alpha}{x^{\alpha+1}}$$

The cumulative distribution would be:

$$F(x) = 1 - \left(\frac{\theta}{\alpha}\right)^\alpha$$

The parameter α can be estimated by:

$$\hat{\alpha} = \frac{\dfrac{\sum\limits_{j=1}^{n} x_j}{n}}{\dfrac{\sum\limits_{j=1}^{n} x_j}{n} - \theta}$$

To calculate the risk premium of the second layer, we need to estimate first the expected value of a single loss in the layer, will which then be aggregated with the expected frequency of losses on that layer, as we saw in Part II of this book. The formal result of the expected loss using the one-parameter Pareto distribution will be:

$$\text{Expected loss} = \int_{D}^{EP} (x-D)\alpha y^\alpha x^{-\alpha-1}\,\mathrm{d}x + \int_{EP}^{\infty} U\alpha y^\alpha x^{-\alpha-1}\,\mathrm{d}x$$

where EP is the exit point (upper layer (U) + deductible (D)) and y is an observed point. The formula above can be reduced to (leaving out the derivation here for simplicity):

$$\text{Expected loss} = \frac{D}{1-\alpha}(R^{1-\alpha} - 1) \quad \text{if } \alpha \neq 1$$

From the data, we estimate $\alpha = 0.7$. Therefore, applying the data in the formula above we find that:

$$\text{Expected loss} = \frac{1,000,000}{1 - 0.7} (8^{1-0.7} - 1) = 2,886,886.61$$

The average number of events in the past 4 years is five. Therefore, the Poisson λ will be 5. Using a very simplistic approximation, we could multiply the expected frequency and severity and find that the risk premium would be:

$$\text{Risk premium} = 2,886,886.61 \times 5 = 14,434,433.05$$

Just for convenience, I repeat below the aggregated losses at the layer:

1998	1999	2000	2001
$11,632,781	$7,221,990	$9,052,350	$17,354,789

Given this loss pattern, we may consider that perhaps we would be making a good deal in paying this risk premium, if we believe that the loss pattern will continue as high as in 2001. Otherwise the risk premium will be too high and we would be better off retaining the risk. It must be highlighted that the insurance company would also add to this premium other expenses such as a safety margin, administrative costs, etc.

For the bank, these calculations might be a useful tool to verify whether the premium charged by the insurer is too expensive or cheap based on calculations using the bank's own past experience.

14.5.3 Excess Layer

In this case we have just one single data point. It is obviously impossible to fit statistical distributions to one single point. Very little can be done at this level, with one single event. Nevertheless, one way to use this single data point is by allowing it to roughly estimate how many events of this magnitude have occurred in the last 4 years. We might solve this problem by extrapolation. Insurers frequently apply these techniques to solve such problems.

We might see this largest event as an "empirical quantile" of the total distribution. Empirical distributions are calculated by:

$$F_n^{\text{Quantile}}(t) = X_{k,n} \quad \text{for } 1 - \frac{k}{n} < t \leqslant 1 - \frac{k-1}{n}$$

If we consider our single point above $7 million as the empirical quantile of an empirical distribution, the quantile would be 99.97% considering $n = 3349$.

Given this logic, the observation point might also be seen as a percentage of the total losses, so that it can be fine-tuned to a portfolio of any size. In our case, for 4 years of experience the yearly frequency $\lambda = 0.25$ for losses above $7 million. If we prefer to perform the analysis monthly, $\lambda = 0.021$. In terms of aggregate losses, this represents 7.95% of the total.

Using the one-parameter Pareto, it is practice for actuaries to let $\alpha = 1$ when no database is available. In this case, the expected loss is estimated by:

$$\text{Expected loss} = D \times \ln(LL) \quad LL = 2$$

Letting $D = \$7,000,000$ we find that the expected loss is \$4,852,030.26 for this layer. A simple calculation would give us the risk premium:

$$\text{Risk premium} = 0.25 \times \$4,852,030.26 = \$1,213,007.57$$

Therefore, the risk premium of this layer could be estimated based on statistical grounds, always highlighting that we are doing the best we can given the extremely scarce experience. In practice, as happens in the second layer, other costs need to be added to the risk premium to find the final cost of hedging. If we are issuing an ORL bond, for instance, we need to include agent costs, investment bank structuring costs, commissions, etc.

REFERENCES

Bank of America (1995), "Derivatives and Corporate Risk Management", *Journal of Applied Corporate Finance*, 8(3), 58–75.

Bishop, M. (1996), "Survey of Corporate Risk Management: The Art of Risk Spreading", *The Economist*, 338, Issue 7952.

Black, F. and Scholes, M. (1973), "The Pricing of Options and Corporate Liabilities", *Journal of Political Economy*, 81, 637–654.

Briys, E. and Schlesinger, H. (1990), "Risk Aversion and the Propensities for Self Insurance and Self Protection", *The Geneva Papers on Risk and Insurance Theory*, 16(1), 59–74.

Briys, E., Schlesinger, H. and Schulenburg, J. (1991), "Reliability of Risk Management: Market Insurance, Self-Insurance and Self-Protection Reconsidered", *The Geneva Papers on Risk and Insurance Theory*, 16(1), 45–58.

Cho, D. (1988), "The Impact of Risk Management Decisions on Firm Value: Gordon's Growth Model Approach", *Journal of Risk and Insurance*, 55, 118–131.

Core, J. (1997), "On the Corporate Demand for Directors' and Officers' Insurance", *The Journal of Risk and Insurance*, 64(1), 63–87.

Cornell, B. and Shapiro, A. (1987), "Corporate Stakeholders and Corporate Finance", *Financial Management*, 16, 5–14.

Cummings, J. (1976), "Risk Management and the Theory of the Firm", *Journal of Risk and Insurance*, 43, 587–609.

Cummings, J. and Sommer, D. (1996), "Capital and Risk in Property–Liability Insurance Markets", *Journal of Banking and Finance*, 20, 1069–1092.

Davidson, W., Cross, M. and Thornton, J. (1992), "Corporate Demand for Insurance: Some Empirical and Theoretical Results", *Journal of Financial Services Research*, 6, 61–72.

Dekel, E and Scotchmer, S. (1990), "Collusion Through Insurance: Sharing the Cost of Oil Spill Cleanups", *American Economic Review*, 80(1), 249–252.

Dionne, G. and Eeckhoudt, L. (1985), "Risk Aversion, Self Insurance and Self Protection", *Economic Letters*, 17, 39–57.

Doherty, N. (1985), *Corporate Risk Management: A Financial Exposition*, McGraw-Hill, New York.

Doherty, N. and Schlesinger, H. (1985), "Incomplete Markets for Insurance: An Overview", *The Journal of Risk and Insurance*, 53(3), 402–423.

Doherty, N. and Smith, C. (1993), "Corporate Insurance Strategy: The Case of British Petroleum", *Journal of Applied Corporate Finance*, 6(3), 4–15.

Doherty, N. (2000), *Integrated Risk Management*, McGraw-Hill, New York.

Dolde, W. (1993), "The Trajectory of Corporate Financial Risk Management", *Journal of Applied Corporate Finance*, 6(3), 33–41.

Dolde, W. (1995), "Hedging, Leverage and Primitive Risk", *The Journal of Financial Engineering*, 4, 187–216.

Dufey, G. and Srinivasulu, S. (1983), "The Case for Corporate Management of Foreign Exchange Risk", *Financial Management*, Winter, 54–62.

Easterbrook, F. and Fischel, D. (1985), "Limited Liability and the Corporation", *The University of Chicago Law Review*, 52(1), 89–117.

Eeckhoudt, L. and Gollier, C. (1992), *Risk: Evaluation, Management and Sharing*, Harvester-Wheatsheaf, London.

Eeckhoudt, L., Gollier, C. and Schlesinger, H. (1997), "The No-Loss Offset Provision and the Attitude Towards Risk of a Risk Neutral Firm", *Journal of Public Economics*, 65, 207–217.

Ehrlich, I. and Becker, G. (1972), "Market Insurance, Self Insurance and Self Protection", *Journal of Political Economy*, 80, 623–647.

Eldor, R. and Zilcha, I. (1990), "Oligopoly, Uncertain Demand, and Forward Markets", *Journal of Economics and Business*, 42, 17–26.

Faure, M. and Heine, G. (1991), "The Insurance of Fines: The Case of Oil Pollution", *The Geneva Papers on Risk and Insurance*, 16(58), 39–58.

Freeman, P. and Kunreuther, H. (1996), "The Roles of Insurance and Well-Specified Standards in Dealing with Environmental Risks", *Managerial and Decision Economics*, 17, 517–530.

Froot, K., Scharfstein, D. and Stein, J. (1993), "Risk Management: Coordinating Corporate Investment and Financing Policies", *The Journal of Finance*, 48(5), 1629–1658.

Géczy, C., Minton, B. and Schrand, C. (1997), "Why Firms Use Currency Derivatives", *The Journal of Finance*, 52(4), 1323–1354.

Gollier, C., Koehl, P. and Rochet, J. (1997), "Risk-Taking Behaviour with Limited Liability and Risk Aversion", *The Journal of Risk and Insurance*, 64(2), 347–370.

Grillet, L. (1992), "Corporate Insurance and Corporate Stakeholders: I. Transactions Cost Theory", *Journal of Insurance Regulation*, 11(2), 232–251.

Grillet, L. (1993), "Corporate Insurance and Corporate Stakeholders: Limits of Insurability and Public Policy", *Journal of Insurance Regulation*, 11(3), 291–313.

Haugen, R. and Senbet, L. (1981), "Resolving the Agency Problems of External Capital Through Options", *The Journal of Finance*, 36(3), 629–647.

Haugen, R. and Senbet, L. (1988), "Bankruptcy and Agency Costs: Their Significance to the Theory of Optimal Capital Structure", *Journal of Finance and Quantitative Analysis*, 23, 27–38.

Holderness, C. (1990), "Liability Insurers as Corporate Monitors", *International Review of Law and Economics*, 10, 115–129.

Katzman, M. (1985), *Chemical Catastrophes: Regulating Environmental Risk Through Pollution Liability Insurance*, Richard D. Irwin, Illinois.

Khang, H. (1992), "Determinants of Corporate Insurance Purchases: Empirical Evidence", Ph.D. Thesis, University of Georgia.

Kleffner, A. and Doherty, N. (1996), "Costly Risk Bearing and the Supply of Catastrophic Insurance", *The Journal of Risk and Insurance*, 63(4), 657–671.

Kunreuther, H., Doherty, N. and Kleffner, A. (1993), "On Shaky Ground?: Earthquakes and the Insurance Industry", *Risk Management*, May, 36–48.

Lave, C. and Quigley, J. (1989), "Why is this Man Smiling", mimeo, Graduate School of Public Policy, University of California, Berkeley.

MacMinn, R. (1987), "Insurance and Corporate Risk Management", *Journal of Risk and Insurance*, 54, 659–676.

Main, B. (1982), "Business Insurance and Large, Widely Held Corporations", *The Geneva Papers on Risk and Insurance*, 7(24), 237–247.

Main, B. (1983a), "Risk Management and the Theory of the Firm: Comment", *Journal of Risk and Insurance*, 50, 140–144.

Main, B. (1983b), "Corporate Insurance Purchases and Taxes", *Journal of Risk and Insurance*, 50(2), 197–223.

May, D. (1995), "Do Managerial Motives Influence Firm Risk Reduction Strategies", *The Journal of Finance*, 50(4), 1291–1308.

Mayers, D. and Smith, C. (1982), "On the Corporate Demand for Insurance", *Journal of Business*, 55(2), 281–296.

Mayers, D. and Smith, C. (1983), "The Interdependence of Individual Portfolio Decisions and the Demand for Insurance", *Journal of Political Economy*, 91(2), 304–311.

Mayers, D. and Smith, C. (1987), "Corporate Insurance and the Under-Investment Problem", *Journal of Risk and Insurance*, 54, 45–54.

Mayers, D. and Smith, C. (1990), "On the Corporate Demand for Insurance: Evidence from the Reinsurance Market", *Journal of Business*, 63(1), 19–40.

Mossin, J. (1968), "Aspects of Rational Insurance Purchasing", *Journal of Political Economy*, 76, 553–568.

Nance, D., Smith. C. and Smithson, C. (1993), "On the Determinants of Corporate Hedging", *Journal of Finance*, 48, 267–284.

Parry, M. and Parry, A. (1991), "The Purchase of Insurance by a Risk-Neutral Firm for a Risk Averse Agent", *The Journal of Risk and Insurance*, 58(1), 30–46.

Rawls, S. and Smithson, C. (1990), "Strategic Risk Management", *Journal of Applied Corporate Finance*, 2(4), 6–18.

Razin, A. (1976), "Rational Insurance Purchasing", *The Journal of Finance*, 31(1), 133–137.

Rees, R. (1989), "Uncertainty, Information and Insurance", in J. Hey (ed.), *Current Issues in Microeconomics*, MacMillan, London.

Schoemaker, P. and Kunreuther, H. (1979), "An Experimental Study of Insurance Decisions", *Journal of Risk and Insurance*, 46, 603–618.

Shapiro, A. and Titman, S. (1985), "An Integrated Approach to Corporate Risk Management", *Midland Corporate Finance Journal*, 3, 41–56.

Skogh, G. (1989), "The Transactions Cost Theory of Insurance: Contracting Impediments and Costs", *Journal of Risk and Insurance*, 56, 726–732.

Skogh, G. (1991), "Insurance and the Institutional Economics of Financial Intermediation", *The Geneva Papers on Risk and Insurance*, 16(58), 59–72.

Smith, C. and Stultz, R. (1985), "The Determinants of Firms' Hedging Policies", *Journal of Financial and Quantitative Analysis*, 20(4), 391–405.

Stultz, R. (1996), "Rethinking Risk Management", *Journal of Applied Corporate Finance*, 9(3), 8–24.

Tufano, P. (1996), "Who Manages Risk? An Empirical Examination of Risk Management Practices in the Gold Mining Industry", *The Journal of Finance*, 51(4), 1097–1137.

Williams, C., Smith, M. and Young, P. (1998), *Risk Management and Insurance*, 8th Edition, McGraw-Hill International, New York.

Part VI
Regulatory Capital

Operational Risk Regulatory Capital

15.1 INTRODUCTION

Until a few years ago, operational risk was not seen as a codified risk type but, taking its lead from other industries (nuclear, etc.), the financial services industry has come to recognize it as a distinct risk type and has since devoted increasing resources to detecting, classifying, measuring and managing it. Possibly as a result of this, the Basel Committee of Banking Supervisors[1] (BCBS) decided to include an explicit capital requirement for operational risk when undertaking a revision of the Basel Accord[2], starting in 1998 and publishing a first consultative document in June 1999. (At the time of writing, the revised accord, commonly referred to as "Basel 2", is still undergoing revision, and is scheduled to be implemented at the start of 2005.) The introduction of this capital requirement took by surprise a good part of the financial services industry that did not believe this would happen so quickly (if ever). (Under the current accord, it was assumed that the credit risk charge implicitly covers other risks such as operational.)

Having given notice of its intention, the BCBS defined operational risk as "*the risk of losses resulting from inadequate or failed internal processes, people and systems or from external events*" in a second consultative document[3]. (The BCBS had originally sought to develop a capital requirement for "other" risks, to include risks such as "strategic" or "reputational" risks, but having consulted with the industry, omitted these, as they are more prone to subjective interpretation and, consequently, more difficult to quantify.)

The Basel Committee devised a range of approaches, with input from the industry, to calculate the capital requirement that was designed to reflect the variations in industry risk measurement and management practices. These approaches are intended to be "evolutionary", providing incentives through lower capital requirements for institutions to move to a more sophisticated approach for calculating the capital requirement for operational risk. A financial institution will have to meet certain qualitative and quantitative criteria in order to be allowed to move to a more advanced approach, largely reflecting improved operational risk measurement and management.

In the next section are outlined the three pillars on which the revised accord will be based, and their relationship to operational risk, followed by the proposed approaches,

---

[1]The Committee formulates broad supervisory standards and guidelines and recommends statements of best practice.
[2]A capital measurement system devised in 1988 which provided for the implementation of a credit risk measurement framework with a minimum capital standard of 8% of risk-weighted assets by end-1992.
[3]"Working Paper on the Regulatory Treatment of Operational Risk", Basel Committee on Banking Supervision (September 2001).

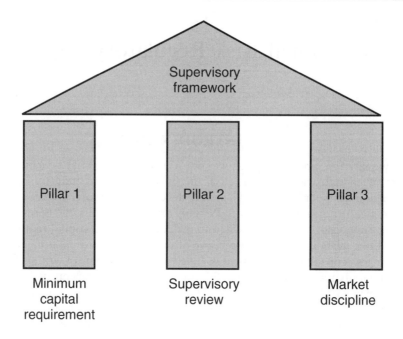

Figure 15.1   The three pillars of the supervisory framework

and a numerical example. Finally, there are comments on some underlying problems that might hinder application of the revised accord.

15.2   SUPERVISORY FRAMEWORK — THE THREE SUPERVISION PILLARS

In order to achieve the objectives[4] of the new accord, the Basel Committee decided to establish a new supervisory framework based on three pillars (see Figure 15.1): minimum capital requirement, supervisory review process and market discipline.

Under the first pillar, a minimum amount of capital will have to be put aside to protect a bank against the credit and operational risks it takes on in the course of its business activities. The supervisory review pillar is designed to ensure that banks follow rigorous processes, measure their risks in a robust and reliable manner, and have enough capital to protect the wider banking community against the systemic implications of the risks they undertake. The third pillar, market discipline, works as

---

[4]Amongst other things, these state that the revised accord should " . . . *at least maintain the current overall level of capital in the system . . . [and] . . . constitute a more comprehensive approach to addressing risks*", "Overview of The New Basel Capital Accord", Basel Committee on Banking Supervision (January 2001).

a lever to reinforce the safety and reliability of the banking system, through better disclosure of risk exposures and capital levels to the market, so that the industry and investors can better assess the solvency level of a bank.

All three pillars of the new accord play an important role in the operational risk framework. As mentioned above, the BCBS intends to lay down a minimum capital requirement and a set of qualitative and quantitative requirements for risk management and measurement that would determine the eligibility to use a particular method for capital assessment.

Pillar 2 will be used to assess the control environment in which a bank operates by setting out a framework in which banks are required to evaluate their economic capital level and the regulators then review this process of assessment. If the capital assessment process is inadequate and/or the determined economic capital is deemed to be insufficient, the regulators will expect the banks to take immediate action to correct the situation.

The third pillar, market discipline, has the potential to reinforce capital regulation and other supervisory efforts to promote safety and soundness in banks and financial systems by employing the scrutiny of external stakeholders such as shareholders, holders of debt securities, etc. In the context of operational risk, this means that regulators might ask banks to disclose operational losses in the process of a fuller review of operational risk measurement and management. The BCBS has indicated that in the longer term such disclosures will be part of the qualifying criteria in order for banks to use more advanced internal measurement approaches. (A summary of the requirements under the three pillars for each of the three approaches is given in Section 15.4.)

15.3 PILLAR 1—REGULATORY MINIMUM CAPITAL APPROACHES

Four approaches have been outlined by the BCBS, all based to some degree on aggregating a proportion of one or more "financial indicators" (such as gross income) to derive the capital requirement. The basic indicator approach (BIA) is the simplest,

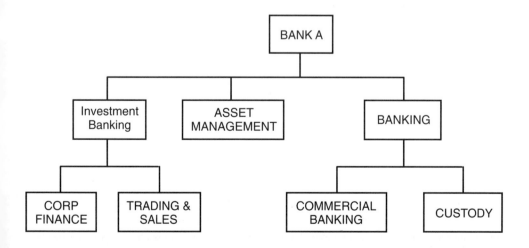

Figure 15.2 Bank A structure

Table 15.1   Bank A gross income (US$ M)

		Gross income
Division	Asset Management	321
Division	Banking	1031
	Commercial Bank	815
	Custody	216
Division	Investment Banking	3137
	Corporate Finance	1002
	Trading & Sales	2135
Consolidated Bank A		**4489**

considering just a single financial indicator across the bank, and it is unlikely that large, internationally diversified banks will be allowed to use this approach. Next along the scale of complexity is the standardized approach (SA) that allows for a number of financial indicators to be used. There is also the internal measurement approach (IMA) that incorporates internal loss data into the calculation of the charge, and banks might have to invest considerable effort to reach the standards necessary to adopt this approach. More recently, in the September 2001 paper, the BCBS decided to also allow banks to use their own internally developed models to measure operational risk under the advanced measurement approaches (AMA). A full description of these approaches can be seen at the BIS site: www.bis.org

In order to illustrate these approaches, consider the simple example of banking group "A" (see Figure 15.2), which has a number of differing and disparate business activities, is of a respectable size and operates in major financial centers across the globe.

In Table 15.2 we consider the gross income[5] associated with the divisions in the banking group. (Additional information that might be used later is that Bank A has $250,000 million of funds under management in its asset management division, $1000 million annual average assets in the commercial bank, and annual settlement throughput of $35,000 million.)

15.3.1   Basic Indicator Approach

In this first approach, gross income has been proposed as a proxy for the operational risk inherent in a bank. Each bank using this approach should calculate its capital requirement for operational risk using the simple formula below:

$$\text{Operational risk charge} = \alpha \times \text{Gross income}$$

---

[5]The BCBS has proposed the following definition, subject to further refinement:

Gross income = Net interest income + Net non-interest income

(including fees and commissions receivable less fees and commissions payable, the net result of financial operations and other gross income). Further details are given in "Operational Risk", Basel Committee on Banking Supervision (January 2001).

where α^6 is the parameter used to transform the gross income into a capital requirement for operational risk, as determined by the regulator.

As a first step, and with input from the industry, the BCBS estimated that, on average, 20% of the economic capital in a bank is attributable to operational risk. Later this figure was revised to 12%. At this stage, in the absence of loss data or any sophisticated operational risk management structure, the BCBS used this figure of 12%, applied to current minimum regulatory capital, as the basis for an initial estimate of the multiplication factor α. An initial calibration for α indicates that it would be around 20%. Therefore, in the case of Bank A, the capital requirement for operational risk across the bank is (US$ M):

$$\text{Operational risk charge} = 20\% \times 4489 = 897.80$$

The capital figure appears to be very high relative to the total gross income across the banking group. (It must be noted that banks deemed to be sophisticated and global, such as Bank A in this example, would find it unlikely that they would be allowed to use this approach.)

15.3.2   Standardized Approach

SA is a refined version of BIA. In order to qualify to use this approach, the bank must be capable of differentiating its business into business units and business lines defined by the regulators, and have the appropriate indicators available, which act as a proxy for the level of activity and, by extension, operational risk.

The rationale behind this approach lies in the recognition that operational risks arising in different businesses have differentiated profiles, and one business unit might be riskier than another. An investment bank, for example, in general might be expected to be riskier than an asset management division. In this approach the business units and business lines will be determined by the regulator, as well as the indicators that will be used to calculate the operational risk charge. The provisional classification is given in Table 15.2, taken from the third consultative paper (September 2001) from the BCBS that considers eight business lines.

In addition, Table 15.3 contains a set of weightings, assigned on the perceived relative riskiness of the business lines, which might act as a first approximation in determining the risk profile of a bank. The initial β's were defined from a pool ("QIS") made from internationally active banks that provided information on the series of indicators.

From this table, trading and sales seems to be, on average, the riskiest activity in banking, with a mean of 0.246 from 26 respondents and also the highest weighted average (0.202).

The total of the relative weightings for the business lines, after specifying a single value in the range, should sum to 100%. The calculation of the β's for each business line i is carried out using the following general formula:

---

[6]In the more advanced approaches outlined in the next two sections, i.e. the standardized and internal measurement approaches, the parameters performing the same role are the β's and γ's respectively, also to be determined by the regulator.

Table 15.2 Basel Committee list of business units for the standardized approach

Business units	Business lines	Indicator
Investment Banking	Corporate Finance	Gross income
	Trading & Sales	Gross income
Banking	Retail Banking	Gross income
	Commercial Banking	Gross income
	Payment & Settlement	Gross income
Others	Retail Brokerage	Gross income
	Agency Services & Custody	Gross income
	Asset Management	Gross income

$$\beta_i = \frac{(12\% \text{ of MRC} \times \text{OpRisk share (\%)})}{\text{Gross income}_i}$$

where OpRisk share is the share of a bank's operational risk economic capital allocated to business line i and MRC is the minimum capital requirement. (We shall use the convention that there are to be m business lines when the proposals are finalized. At the moment there are eight business lines specified, so that $m = 8$.)

It is anticipated that it will be necessary for the BCBS to calibrate the capital factor for each business line, β_i, on a sample of banks. (In an ideal world this would be the entire population of banks using the approach[7], but this would be unfeasible to do, so a smaller sample will probably be taken.) The likely use of different indicators across the business lines introduces some additional complexity into the approach, especially in the derivation of the relative risk weightings contained in Table 15.3. If all the

Table 15.3 Business lines relative weightings

Business line	Median	Mean	Weighted average	Number of banks
Corporate Finance	0.131	0.236	0.12	19
Trading & Sales	0.171	0.241	0.202	26
Retail Banking	0.125	0.127	0.11	24
Commercial Banking	0.132	0.169	0.152	27
Payment & Settlement	0.208	0.203	0.185	15
Retail Brokerage	0.113	0.149	0.161	15
Agency Services & Custody	0.174	0.232	0.183	14
Asset Management	0.133	0.185	0.152	22

Summary of the analysis of the QIS data (based on the BCBS paper).

---

[7]This also raises the question of recalibration of the capital factors over time. As banks move from the BIA to the SA, the characteristics of the member population are likely to change, both in terms of the current minimum capital requirement and the financial indicators—if the capital factors remain unchanged, are they valid for the new banks using this approach? If, however, they are recalibrated, banks previously using the SA might see a step change in their capital requirements even if there was no change in their circumstances.

Table 15.4 The standardized approach—calculated capital charge for Bank A

	β	Gross income	
Asset Management	0.19	321	60.99
Commercial Banking	0.17	815	138.55
Custody	0.245	216	52.92
Corporate Finance	0.15	1002	150.30
Trading & Sales	0.18	2135	384.30
			787.06

indicators were gross income, it is obvious that the risk weightings would sum to 100% as the contribution of each business is the total gross income of the bank. The inclusion of different indicators makes any aggregation of the indicators problematic, and this will have to be reflected in the business line weightings.

The operational risk charge across the bank is then calculated as:

$$\text{Operational risk charge} = \sum_{i=1}^{m} \beta_i \phi_i$$

where β_i is the capital factor for the business line i and ϕ_i is the associated indicator for business line i, summing across the m business lines. (It may be seen that, if an institution does not undertake any business in a given business line, then the relevant indicator will also be zero[8], and the capital requirement for that business line will also be zero.)

In this case, we apply the approach to Bank A, and the results can be seen in Table 15.4. Using the capital factors given with the indicators above, we estimate the charges to be (US$ M):

$$\text{Operational risk charge} = \sum_{i=1}^{m} \beta_i \phi_i = 787.06$$

Compared to the BIA, the charge is substantially smaller using the second approach. Indeed, recognizing that the different businesses in an institution have different risk profiles allows a bank to be required to hold less capital than just setting aside 20% of its gross income under the BIA.

15.3.3 Internal Measurement Approach

A more advanced approach proposed in the second consultative document, IMA is again more sensitive as it incorporates the bank's own internal operational losses as

---

[8]The financial indicators should always be monotonically increasing with increasing level of any business activity that might lead to the presence of operational risk: if a net measure were to be used as an indicator it might be possible for a bank to run considerable operational risk but see a low or zero capital requirement, e.g. taking net income as an example in a loss-making business. As a corollary, if an indicator of this type were not to be used, banks might seek to "game" the regime to lead to a lower (or zero) capital requirement, e.g. booking income in business lines where the capital factor was lower.

Table 15.5 Internal measurement approach indicators

Symbol	Indicator	Definition
σ	Exposure indicator (specified by the regulator[11])	Proxy for the size of operational risk exposure
λ	Probability of a loss event	Based on internal loss data, calculated as: $$\frac{\sum \text{loss events}}{\sum \text{transactions}}$$
ν	Loss given an event	Average loss when an event happens

part of the calculation of the capital requirement. This approach is very similar to that used in credit risk and encompasses the notions of expected and unexpected losses.

As in the area of credit risk, conceptually a capital charge for operational risk should cover only unexpected losses due to events solely attributable to that risk type. (If one expects to lose a certain sum in a given period, based upon historical or anticipated losses, these losses are obviously not the result of risk[9]). Prior to any given accounting period, banks would hope that these expected losses are firstly included in the pricing of deals, and secondly through general provisions, with the crystallization of a loss being recognized in specific provisions[10]. Nevertheless, as mentioned in Chapter 2, accounting rules in most countries do not allow provisioning for operational risk, but do so for long-duration events such as legal cases. Accounting standards generally require measurable estimation tests to be met and losses to be probable before provisions or contingencies are actually booked.

Notwithstanding this, the BCBS is proposing to calibrate the capital requirement for operational risk in this approach based on both expected and unexpected losses, although allowing some recognition for provisioning and loss deduction. (One possibility is that a proportion of end-of-period provisions or contingencies might be deducted from the minimum capital requirement as long as the bank discloses them as such.) Also, the capital charge for a limited list of banking activities where the annual deduction of actual operational losses is prevalent could be based on unexpected losses only, plus an eventual margin for estimation errors.

One of the criteria for a bank to meet in order to use this approach will be the compilation of a historical database on operational losses over a number of years to make the approach feasible. (It is anticipated that supervisors might require 2 or 3 years of reliable data, although the recent focus on operational risk means that, in general, banks have only recently begun to start collecting relevant data.)

The methodology for the IMA extends that for the SA, the first step being to define appropriate generic indicators across business lines (Table 15.5). Using these, the expected operational loss would be:

---

[9]Even allowing for the uncertainty in the identities of the counterparties contributing to the total loss.
[10]Although this is obviously dependent upon the jurisdiction.
[11]At the inception of the revised accord, although there may be some scope for banks to use more appropriate indicators at a later date.

$$\text{Expected operational loss} = \sum_{j=1}^{n} \sum_{i=1}^{m} \left(\sigma_{ij} \times \lambda_{ij} \times \nu_{ij} \right)$$

where m is the number of business units and n the operational loss types, i.e. the same convention as for the SA. (The business lines are given in Table 15.2 and the operational risk loss types are given in Chapter 2.) (As in the SA, where a bank does not undertake business in a particular area, the indicators will equal zero and the consequent capital requirement will also be zero[12]. However, the points raised in footnote 9 should be borne in mind.)

The regulator will derive the γ factor for each business line i and risk type j, i.e. γ_{ij}, which will transform the expected loss for that combination of business line and risk type into a capital requirement for the unexpected loss. The capital charge for a bank will then be the overall sum of all resulting products:

$$\text{Operational risk charge} = \sum_{j=1}^{n} \sum_{i=1}^{m} \gamma_{ij} \times \left(\sigma_{ij} \times \lambda_{ij} \times \nu_{ij} \right)$$

Banks will be expected to provide figures for the individual inputs (indicator, loss probability, loss given event), rather than a composite value to the regulators, as the reliability of the data submitted will be thoroughly scrutinized. The BCBS has also indicated that there might be an adjustment of the γ factor for one or more business line/risk type combination(s) where a comparison of the ratio of the unexpected losses that a bank suffers relative to its expected losses in that area differs significantly from the industry norm, as measured by an RPI (risk profile index). The use of the RPI will be dependent on there being sufficient data available to determine a "standard" industry loss profile. In terms of loss distributions, a higher γ for a business line/risk type combination within a bank (resulting from comparison to the RPI) will reflect a relatively fatter tail with respect to the industry norm, i.e. the difference between the expected and unexpected losses.

We shall now consider the operational risk charge for Bank A in two different scenarios. In the first case the indicators are reported in Table 15.6.

In this first situation, despite Bank A still having some pretty bad probability of loss events in the commercial bank and in the trading and sales unit, it is worth investing in a project to collect data and better manage operational risk, since the capital charge is considerably smaller. The gamma factor is a bit high for trading and sales, at 2.4, which can be expected due to the high level of transactions performed during the year, 42,891 million. The other exposure indicators are represented by: "funds under management" for asset management; "volume of transactions" for custody, commercial bank and trading and sales; "number of new deals" for corporate finance. σ and ν are represented in \$ millions and λ in percentage. The final charge was \$675.35, which is better than the previous approach.

---

[12]Although this raises the question of the treatment of a business line where the bank does undertake business, but has suffered no losses, either arising from no loss events or no loss given that an event has occurred. As the operational risk capital requirement is to be held against both expected and unexpected losses, the validity of the simplistic extrapolation of the expected loss to an unexpected loss is debatable.

Table 15.6 Operational risk charge under the internal measurement approach for Bank A—Situation 1

	Indicators			Expected operational loss	γ
	σ	λ	ν		
Asset Management	250,000	0.02%	2.00	100.00	1.2
Banking					
Commercial Bank	17,231	4.13%	0.20	142.33	1.1
Custody	21,345	1.07%	0.01	2.28	0.9
Investment Banking					
Corporate Finance	0.234	0.25%	3.10	0.00	0.8
Trading & Sales	42,891	4.60%	0.08	157.84	2.4
Operational Risk Charge—Bank A				**657.43**	

Table 15.7 Operational risk charge under the internal measurement approach for Bank A—Situation 2

	Indicators			Expected operational loss	γ
	σ	λ	ν		
Asset Management	250,000	0.02%	2.00	100.00	1.2
Banking					
Commercial Bank	17,231	4.13%	0.20	142.33	1.1
Custody	21,345	1.07%	0.01	2.28	0.9
Investment Banking					
Corporate Finance	0.234	0.25%	3.10	0.00	0.8
Trading & Sales	48,332	5.10%	0.12	295.79	3.6
Operational Risk Charge—Bank A				**1343.47**	

Nevertheless, suppose that, keeping all other business line and risk type loss profiles the same as before, the number of transactions in the trading and sales division of the investment bank is increased to 48,332 million, and due to a few very large events the gamma factor changes from 2.4 to 3.6. Table 15.7 depicts the situation.

In this case, due to a few large events, the capital more than doubled to $1343.47. Bank A would better have stayed in the previous approach in this case, and threw away the money spent on the project to collect loss data. The point here is that if the regulators do not provide a way to include insurance or any kind of operational risk hedging in the analysis, eventually many banks would rather not invest in expensive and thorough data collection projects and see themselves paying out more capital in the end. The discussion on the inclusion of insurance and hedging in the regulatory supervision process should be considered fundamental in the next few years.

15.3.4 Advanced Measurement Approaches

The use of internally developed models to measure OR with respect to regulatory capital was allowed in the September 2001 working paper. By allowing such models the

BCBS recognizes that a variety of potentially credible approaches to quantify OR are currently being developed by the industry, and that these R&D activities should be incentivized. Hence, under AMA the regulatory capital requirement for OR will be based on an estimate of operational risk derived from a bank's internal risk measurement system. This figure would be subject to a floor[13] based on the standardized approach capital charge for OR.

Under this approach banks would be allowed to use the output of their internal operational risk measurement system subject to a long list of qualitative and quantitative standards set by the committee. AMA mirrors the structure used for market risk capital requirements. As much as in the market risk settings, the qualitative standards would address a bank's OR management environment, processes and risk control efforts. The quantitative standards would include a supervisory soundness standard that all internally generated risk estimates have to meet.

15.4   QUALITATIVE REQUIREMENTS UNDER THE THREE PILLARS

A more detailed specification of the impact of the three pillars on operational risk charge can be seen in Table 15.8.

The qualitative requirements for AMA are obviously much more stringent and are still being discussed by the BCBS at the time of writing this book. A few of those so far disclosed suggest that a bank must be able to demonstrate that the risk measure used for regulatory purposes reflects a holding period of 1 year and a confidence interval of 99.9%. The confidence interval suggested by the regulators seems a bit high; as we saw in early chapters of this book, operational risk is not explained by the normal distribution and for fat-tailed distributions such quantiles might indicate very high figures to cover OR. This is even more concerning as the BCBS also suggests banks under AMA might capture the impact of infrequent but potentially severe operational risk events.

Other important requirements are that the internal measurement system must be consistent with the scope of OR as defined by the regulators. Regarding the use of historical data, a minimum of 5 years is suggested unless for the starting period, where 3 years of history will suffice. The validation of parameters and outputs of the model should be used with robust statistical techniques, and shown periodically to the regulators.

In summary, the intention with this kind of evolutionary approach is to provide incentives for banks to invest in operational risk measurement projects, best risk practices and systematic data collection. The intention is that as banks move through the spectrum of approaches, the capital requirement for operational risk is reduced as the monitoring, measurement and management processes become more stringent.

---

[13]The floor is currently estimated as 75% of the SA capital charge.

Table 15.8 Supervisory framework and operational risk

Supervisory impact	BI	SA	IMA
Pillar 1 *Minimum Capital Required*	No prerequisites — this is the default approach. (This approach is intended for smaller local banks and will probably not be available to the larger global banks)	Banks must, at a minimum, satisfy these prerequisites: • Independent audit function • Operational losses are tracked and reported consistently • Business units mapped according to the accord guidelines • Independent OR function for measurement methodology and process	All previous prerequirements plus: • Demonstration of use of OR data and measures in OR management • Operational loss data should be available for a certain number of years • Loss data is validated • The collection of loss data comes from a reliable system • Skilled operational risk staff with knowledge to deal with the technical issues
Pillar 2 *Supervisory Review*	Arrangements for OR management have to be reviewed by the regulator	Regulators will review mapping of business lines	Regulators will examine thoroughly the operational loss data collection process
Pillar 3 *Market Discipline*	Banks should have to disclose: • The level of OR capital approach chosen (basic, standardized, etc.) • OR capital as % of total capital	All previous requirements plus: • Risk exposures by business line	Banks should have to disclose all items as before plus making some supplementary disclosures for aggregated operational losses in a certain period by business line

15.5   CONSIDERATIONS FOR THE CURRENT PROPOSALS FOR OPERATIONAL RISK

At the time of writing, a number of areas of concern exist that have not been adequately addressed by the current proposals from the BCBS, particularly in relation to current market practices.

(1) *Insurance.* As stated before, non-recognition of insurance for, or any form of hedging of, operational risk may encourage banks not to use these mechanisms to reduce immediate risk. Additionally, the appropriate treatment of these methods of risk reduction needs to be considered when providing incentives for banks to move from one of the approaches outlined earlier to the next. Even if insurance is accepted as a risk mitigator, very clear rules should be established.

(2) *Limiting the exposure indicator.* In the IMA, there are a few proxies for the size of the operations on which operational risk will be based. For example, in legal or liability risk, the losses for malpractice or poor advice might be a multiplier of the

gross income of the business. The same might happen in the case of losses in derivatives caused by operational problems.

(3) *Control environment.* Operational risk is very much a function of the internal control environment rather than of the operational losses themselves, i.e. a bank with tighter internal controls is less likely to suffer operational losses than a bank with looser controls. In this respect, the relationship between the minimum capital requirement in pillar 1 of the revised accord and the supervisory element of pillar 2 is not explicitly defined at the time of writing.

(4) *Linearity of relationship between OR and size of the bank.* So far the agreement assumes a relative linearity of operational risk in relation to the size of the institution. This happens due to the charges being based on a certain percentage of an indicator.

(5) *Implementation of systems and controls.* At the time of writing, there are relatively few details available for the implementation of the approaches outlined above. Whilst broad guidance has been given, regulators are not in a position to publish details of the supervisory regime that will accompany the final proposals, since these are still under development. For banks there are obviously systems and data implications with attendant resource and cost considerations to be borne in mind.

15.6 CONCLUSION/WARNING

The views in this chapter and the consequent calculations are based on discussions between the industry and the BCBS until July 2001. As the accord is bound to change significantly until the final publication, the reader should pay attention to the next BCBS papers, that are due to come out soon, and industry seminars.

Part VII
Measuring "Other Risks"

In the previous parts of the book we have seen models that measure the impact of loss events in the cost base. However, loss events also often impact the revenue by decreasing the processing capacity (due to fire or earthquake, for example), reputational issues (loss of customer confidence in the trustworthiness/capability of the bank's management), etc.

Operational Risk *(Cost Base)*	"Other Risks" — Foregone Revenue *(Revenue Base)*
Legal Losses	Reputational Events
Fees and Fines	Departure of Key Personnel
Penalties	e-Risks
Late Settlement Fees	Strategic Events
etc.	etc.

If industry and regulators are defining the loss events as "operational risk", those events that affect basically foregone revenue are being considered "other risks" or "foregone revenue losses". These types of risks are much more difficult to measure. However, this is customarily done by the legal system. For example, when customers buy a product, and it does not work, they might sue the manufacturer to get a replacement. They might also sue for moral damages; because eventually they could not perform their jobs if they depended on this particular product, etc. These figures are calculated at court.

In terms of the organization of Part VII, in Chapter 16 we introduce an enterprise-wide model to measure reputational risk with the study of three cases. Chapter 17 presents a multifactor model that measures key personnel or concentration risk with application to the front and back-offices of an investment bank. Chapter 18 deals with the application of real options to the measurement of operational risk in more sophisticated (or difficult to measure) structures, such as e-banks and strategy risk.

An Enterprise-Wide Model for Measuring Reputational Risk

16.1 WHAT IS REPUTATIONAL RISK?

Reputational events are, in general, the indirect impact of a direct or "real" loss. It is noteworthy that one of the main assets a financial institution may have is the "trust" that consumers and clients put in them. Nobody with a reasonable information level would trust their savings to an institution that is rumored to be in a poor financial condition, or have unreliable employees. There are a number of financial institutions that have failed due to reputational issues. This is different from other industries. If, for example, a shoe factory has financial problems caused by poor management but has good products, a customer is likely to be indifferent to the situation and will purchase a pair of shoes manufactured in this factory. A financial institution, however, needs the trust of the client in order to handle his savings. If the situation is reportedly poor, the difficulties could be aggravated.

Reputational risk can be split into a few sub-types. Among these sub-types may be strategic risk. Strategic risk is related to crucial changes made by the executive board of an institution that can jeopardize its value, such as a decision to enter into a new venture or business. Changes in a financial institution's strategy are in general announced, and analyzed by the market, and transformed into a rise or fall in the share price (in other words, it changes the value of the institution). Strategies badly perceived or poorly communicated to the market provoke a reduction in the price. In the case of a reduction in credit rating, this will certainly raise borrowing costs and consequently reduce the profit. However, these rating changes do not come about unexpectedly, and the share prices will usually anticipate the event over a period of time.

Some businesses may be more sensitive to reputational events than others. For example, a rogue trader in a fund management would probably have a much more serious impact on reputational losses than losses in a lower profile department such as shipping finance.

The idea behind the econometric market model presented here is that, as a financial institution is publicly listed on the stock market, it is very likely that this institution would have full coverage of investment analysts and investors who will evaluate immediately the impact of an operational event on the value of the institution. There is an excellent hint of what is likely to happen with the share price, since these professionals are tracking the institution's financial soundness on a daily basis, and communicate their analyses to a massive number of stockholders. Therefore, the impact on the price is immediate. As a consequence, we avoid the difficult task of measuring separately the direct economic effect of customer or deposit losses, but estimate these losses using the information contained in stock prices.

16.2   BACKGROUND ON ECONOMETRIC EVENT-ANALYSIS MODELS

The objective of this chapter is to present a model which measures reputational risk. This model relates the sensitivity of the market to a bank's strategies and to operational events measured by the impact on the shareholders' value. Some risk management departments of major financial institutions recognize the peculiarity of reputational risk investigation inside OR, with OR seminars and workshops often having separate lectures on the measurement of reputational risk.

Reputational risk can be subdivided into a few sub-types such as "change of management", "political and economic risk" and (perceptions of changes of) "strategy"; all of them related to the perception by the investors of the bank's strategy and reputation. Reputational risk has an "indirect impact" on the institution. Reputational losses might not be tangible, at least initially. They are indirect because they are a consequence of other events that cause flight of clients, depositors, etc.

The justification for an approach based on market data relies on the market efficiency hypothesis. This says that the stock prices are what primarily reflect the opinion of the investors on the strategy and reputation of a bank, in circumstances of an event that affects the result and/or the image of a financial institution. Therefore, a multifactor model approach based on arbitrage price theory (APT) (Ross 1976) can be an appropriate tool for the measurement of the impact of a reputational/company-specific event on a particular share price and, consequently, on the shareholders' value, which is what we want to protect. An econometric model with estimates of the losses for various degrees of confidence can be derived, thereby allowing an appropriate level of economic capital to be allocated against reputational risk.

Similar econometric models have been used in academic studies in order to evaluate the impact of, for example, new market regulations or dividend announcements on security price performance.

After the seminal article of Fama et al. (1969), in which they measured the impact of stock split announcements on stock prices, several articles have explored similar methodologies to measure the impact of several different events on the stock market. Concern with the financial or economic consequences of events has stimulated since then a large body of empirical research that focuses on the impact of such events on a firm's security prices. In econometrics this is known as "event studies".

Ball and Touros (1988) incorporated uncertainty into the event in the analysis of the performance of securities. They did not use a market model, but sought to understand how a rise in the variance affects the share price of a company. Brown and Warner (1985) used daily stock prices, providing a variety of alternative models for measuring abnormal returns.

Another field that has used "event-study" models to evaluate the impact on the value of a firm is merger and acquisitions. Malatesta and Thompson (1985), for example, relaxed the hypothesis of an efficient market, allowing that events could be partially anticipated by insiders. They also used a market model to evaluate the economic impact of acquisitions. One of the differences between the event studies presented above and the "risk management approach" developed here is that event studies use, in general, stock split or stock dividend databases which are larger than those containing operational risk/reputational events. Another important difference is that the approach presented here not only justifies past losses, but also introduces a model in which a risk manager can allocate capital to support the business. With that intention, in addition to measuring the impact of reputational events, a probit/logit model has been developed to measure the estimated likelihood of occurrence. The main objective here is to present a sound econometric model which measures the reputational risk of a financial institution and, by using a comparable methodology to that used in market risk measurement, to determine an appropriate level of capital to be allocated to cover this risk.

In terms of the chapter structure, a more detailed analysis of the concept of reputational risk is presented in Section 16.2. In Section 16.3, the multifactor model measuring the reputational event impact is constructed, and in Section 16.4, the probit/logit model that measures the likelihood is introduced. In Section 16.5, the complete model of economic capital is derived and subsequently, in Section 16.6, the model is applied to some events. Alternative models to hedge reputational risk are suggested in Section 16.7. The conclusion and summary comes in Section 16.8.

16.3   THE MULTIFACTOR MODEL

Based on the efficient financial market hypothesis, security prices adjust immediately to reflect unanticipated information. Therefore, it is assumed that strategic and reputational risk events are reflected instantaneously in the share prices. Also assumed is the unpredictability of events. The model will therefore derive, given current market conditions, an amount of economic capital that would cover unexpected reputational events.

A market model is a statistical model that relates the return of any given security to the return of a market portfolio, and can be seen in its simplest form as:

$$R_{it} = \alpha_i + \beta_i R_{\text{Mkt},t} + \varepsilon_{it} \tag{16.1}$$

where R_{it} and $R_{\text{Mkt},t}$ (we considered during this chapter that all returns have already discounted the risk-free rate) are the epoch-t returns on security i and the market portfolio, respectively, and ε_{it} is the zero mean disturbance term (the residual), that part of the return not explained by the market factor. This is a linear relationship having as parameters α_i and β_i. The latter measures the degree of sensitivity of the share i to the market.

A simple market model such as (16.1) tends to explain less the share return, because it predicts that only one type of non-diversifiable risk influences expected security returns, the "market risk". In contrast, APT explicitly recognizes that a variety of risks may affect expected returns. A factor should be included that would allow us to understand the influence of the events in the financial sector as a whole; therefore, a factor related to the performance of the overall financial sector is introduced.

The equation becomes:

$$R_{it} = \alpha_i + \beta_{i1} R_{\text{Mkt},t} + \beta_{i2} R_{\text{Banks},t} + \varepsilon_{it} \tag{16.2}$$

where $R_{\text{Banks},t}$ is the return of the banking sector in a particular market at epoch t.

The residuals (ε_{it}) in (16.2) still carry non-noise elements related to market or credit risk, which might be extracted by including more factors. As the major interest is in measuring the impact of reputational/strategic events, an indicator $R_{REP,t}$ is introduced, where:

$$R_{REP,t} = 1 \text{ if a reputational event has occurred at epoch } t$$
$$0 \text{ otherwise}$$

Equation (16.2) then becomes:

$$R_{it} = \alpha_i + \beta_{i1} R_{Mkt,t} + \beta_{i2} R_{Banks,t} + \beta_{i3} R_{REP,t} + \varepsilon_{it} \qquad (16.3)$$

The inclusion of $R_{REP,t}$ is also expected to enhance the fitness of the model. The β_{i3} coefficient gives the impact of a reputational event on the share price.

These estimated β coefficients, which measure the three different types of risk, also help in predicting the effect of various scenarios on the excess return for the security.

In the next section, it is shown how the probability of these unexpected reputational returns may be estimated.

16.3.1   Statistical Testing of the Multifactor Model

The usual tests for identifying specification errors, such as omitting a relevant variable, including an irrelevant variable or errors of measurement bias, should be performed. Amongst the best known and used tests are Ramsey's RESET, the Lagrange multiplier test and the Durbin–Watson (DW) d statistic. For the reader with little experience of these tests, the reading of Greene (1993), Gujarati (1993) or Hamilton (1994) is recommended.

16.4   ESTIMATING THE PROBABILITY OF REPUTATIONAL EVENTS

As shown in Section 16.3, the variable $R_{REP,t}$ which measures the sensitivity to reputational events, is a qualitative variable. For risk management purposes, it would be interesting to measure the distribution of the probability of these events occurring.

The CDF can be used to model regressions where the response variable is dichotomous, taking values 0 and 1. For historical as well as practical reasons, the CDFs commonly chosen to represent the probability response models are the logistic and the normal, the former giving rise to the logit model and the latter to the probit model.

Logit and probit models represent particular formulations of the univariate binary quantitative response models, defined by:

$$\Pr(Y_i = 1) = F(\beta' x_i) \quad i = 1, 2, \ldots, n \qquad (16.4)$$

where F is a known CDF and Y_i, $i = 1, 2, \ldots, n$ are independently distributed binary random variables taking the value 1 or 0. x_i is a $k \times 1$ vector of explanatory variables. β' is a $1 \times k$ vector of unknown coefficients, so $\beta' x_i$ is a scalar. Under the probit model, F is specified by:

$$F(z) = \Phi(z) = \int_{-\infty}^{z} \frac{1}{\sqrt{2\pi}} \exp\left\{ -\frac{1}{2} t^2 \right\} dt, \quad z = (\beta' x_i) \qquad (16.5)$$

which is the CDF of the standard normal distribution. Under the logit model, F is specified by:

$$F(z) = \Lambda(z) = \frac{e^z}{1 + e^z} \tag{16.6}$$

16.4.1 Statistical Testing of the Likelihood Model

In order to test the probit/logit model, the Pesaran–Timmerman non-parametric test of predictive performance, proposed by Pesaran and Timmerman (1992), was chosen. As it is beyond the scope of this work to explain the test, we refer the reader to the above book.

16.5 ESTIMATION OF THE REPUTATIONAL VaR (VaR$_{\text{REP}}$)

One of the most common methods of hedging against risks is to allocate economic capital based on capital at risk, defined as the maximum possible loss within a known confidence interval over an orderly liquidation period. In this chapter, we call this VaR$_{\text{REP}}$. As VaR$_{\text{REP}}$ is calculated before the fact, the assumptions made about the time t conditional distribution of epoch $t + 1$ returns plays a crucial role. At this point it is useful to note the similarities and differences between our methodology for evaluating reputational risk and those established for evaluating market positions at risk, the so-called VaR method.

The measurement of the reputational risk embedded in the share price can provide the possibility of applying an approach similar to VaR for measuring the reputational risk. The model proposed thus far aims at finding the reputational risk by discounting some market and sector factors that would affect other institutions as well.

The impact over time could be measured, as in traditional event studies, by the CAR (cumulative abnormal returns). Similar studies can be seen in Campbell et al. (1997). In general, what happens with reputational catastrophes is that, after a sharp negative initial impact, after a while a recovery occurs. This ability to recover will vary considerably between financial institutions. The study of reputational events shows us that most of the reputational impact caused by the bad publicity lasts for a while and then the share price starts to recover a little. This is because either the investors speculate that the share price has become too low, or because the situation (and the consequent losses) that caused the impact become more clear. In fact a reputational event could last more than one day, making a financial institution lose a significant fraction of its market value. This value sometimes cannot be recovered.

In RiskMetrics, the DEaR (daily earnings at risk) for a single position is determined by:

$$\text{DEaR}_t = (\Phi_{1-\alpha}^{-1} \times \hat{\sigma}) \times \text{PV}_Z \times \hat{\beta} R_{\text{REP},t} \tag{16.7}$$

where PV$_Z$ is the present value of the position Z, the term in brackets measures the adverse move per day ($\Phi_{1-\alpha}^{-1}$ is the $100(1 - \alpha)\%$ significant point of the standard normal distribution and σ the volatility), and $\hat{\beta} R_{\text{REP},t}$ is the sensitivity to price move per unit of market value of reputational risk. Likewise, still following the market efficiency hypothesis, it must be considered that reputational events, by affecting a financial institution's deposits, new businesses and so on, will be reflected in the share price. Therefore, the objective of a risk management policy should be to protect the market value of the bank (Y) in relation to eventual reputational losses.

Consider N_{it} as the number of outstanding shares of security i at time t and X_{it} as the share price. Therefore:

$$Y_{it} = N_{it} \times X_{it} \tag{16.8}$$

can be considered our equivalent to the VaR's "present value of the position". It can also be called the shareholders' value. In the present case it is what the risk manager should be concerned with protecting against reputational events. By estimating the reputational impact, we are able to determine how much of this net worth is "under reputational risk".

Depending on the time frame over which the risk manager would like to measure reputational risk, two methods can be devised of performing such calculations: on a real-time basis and on a periodical basis. I describe both in the next subsections.

16.5.1   Real-Time Basis

In order to verify reputational events on a real-time basis, we should use the outcomes of both the multifactor model $\hat{\beta}R_{REP,t}$ and the δ given by the probit/logit models[1]. They should be applied to verify the level of capital necessary, generating the following equation:

$$\text{VaR}_{REP} = \delta \times Y \times \beta_+ \tag{16.9}$$

where $\beta_+ = t_{\alpha/2}\text{se}(\hat{\beta}R_{REP,t})$, $100(1 - \alpha)\%$ is a desired quantile and se is the estimated standard error of the coefficient's estimator.

The model above can measure the reputational risk embedded in the share price on a real-time basis. As the share price of a financial institution starts to lag in relation to other banks and the market index, the model will automatically demand that more capital be allocated to cover reputational risk. Such a model can also help the risk manager to spot an eventual reputational event. In order to avoid high volatility in economic capital allocation (if $\delta = 0\%$, no economic capital for reputational risk will be required), the risk manager can determine a minimum amount by either establishing a floor for δ or using an estimated average, etc.

16.5.2   Periodical Basis

Some risk managers will not be interested in measuring reputational risk on a real-time basis, and for this reason we found it useful to develop a methodology for longer periods.

The methodology is very similar to that used by RiskMetrics[TM] to verify the market risk of a single stock. In order to measure reputational risk, we should apply the following formula:

---

[1]$\delta = F(\hat{\beta}'x_i)$.

$$\text{VaR}_{\text{REP}} = Y \times \beta_+ \times (\Phi_{1-\alpha}^{-1} \times \sigma_{\text{Market index}}) \tag{16.10}$$

where $\Phi_{1-\alpha}^{-1} \times \sigma_{\text{Market index}}$ is the price volatility estimate of the market index at confidence level α (as in (16.7)) and Y is as in (16.8) and (16.9).

By using this method, a risk manager can measure reputational risk on a periodical basis. A summary of the methods can be found in Figure 16.1.

16.6   EMPIRICAL RESULTS ON SOME FINANCIAL INSTITUTIONS

The Japanese financial system has been the stage for several huge operational events which seriously affected the reputation of various institutions. The alleged collusion of members of the board or executives of some of the most important financial institutions in the country with gangsters of the so-called "soskaya" caused severe direct operational losses and indirect losses due to the bad publicity. Furthermore, some large unauthorized trades took place in a couple of banks.

For this reason we decided to analyze some reputational cases for Japanese banks. The widely publicized case of options mispricing in NatWest Markets will also be analyzed. The data were obtained from the Bloomberg historical database.

Following the methodology suggested by the text, we considered as "reputational events", hence having "1" in the indicator variable REP, events that can be classified as "reputational". We then verified the consequent impact for a certain period of 50, 100 and 200 business days following the event. The event must have been reported in major newspapers or by electronic information agents such as Bloomberg or Reuters.

In the three cases presented below reputation played an important role in affecting the value of the institutions. We tested just the "daily" model based on equation (16.9).

16.6.1   Event 1—Daiwa Securities

The so-called "Daiwa case" involved the disguise of loss-making positions. Over an 11-year period (from 1984 to 1995) the total loss amounted to US$ 1.1 billion by way of an estimated 30,000 unauthorized trades—an average loss of US$ 400,000 for every working day. The losses were hidden by selling securities held on behalf of customers. These trades were concealed by hiding the trade confirmations and forging statements of securities holdings, as well as falsifying the statements of securities held by customers. As in the case of Barings, the disguise of losses was possible because the head trader was also in charge of the back-office functions. The fine alone imposed by the Federal Reserve amounted to US$ 340 million. The termination of Daiwa's business in the USA was also decided.

The sampling period is related to the impact of the decision to terminate the American derivatives operations in late May 1996. The strategic decision to terminate US derivatives operations, and the reputational cost generated by these events, is particularly interesting for our study because no specific direct monetary loss was created by this purely strategic decision. This is the event being investigated for Daiwa.

One notable feature was that the investors at first did not understand the implications of the decision, and then when details of the possible losses were released, Daiwa's price plunged deeply.

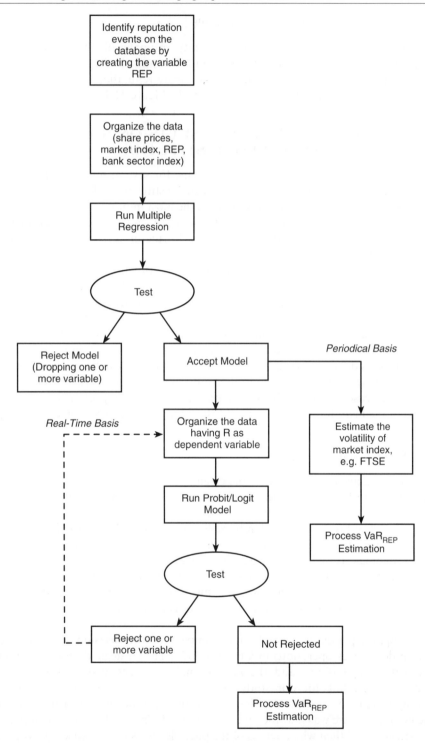

Figure 16.1   Summary of the reputational risk model

In Figure 16.2, we have plotted the CAR for Daiwa after the release of their operational risk event. After a while the share price started to drop steadily. The brokerage firms' reports on Daiwa share performance estimated the impact of business deals and customer losses on the net income. Daiwa's share price had lost approximately 50% of its absolute value by the end of July 1997.

16.6.2   Event 2 — Nomura's Executives' Collusion with Gangsters

The second example is an event that occurred at Nomura Securities. Due to the nature and extent of the event and the evident impact on share prices, this case can be considered exemplar. On March 6, 1997, it was announced in all the leading newspapers in the world that top Nomura executives had colluded with local gangsters.

To model this period, as in any other event study, we consider starting at a time prior to the event. We model the impact for the period of 50, 100 and 200 days after the event.

Nomura's CAR, depicted in Figure 16.3, shows that, even if we consider the poor performance of the Japanese stock market as a whole in the period, the company suffered a large share price fall. Bank analysts released reports and company evaluations stating that several governments as well as large pension funds were refusing to work with Nomura due to the allegedly internal corruption. The new business losses were estimated at US$ 500 million by one bank. The *Financial Times* reported that Nomura was one of the leaders of bond issues in Europe, and that after the scandal their position was threatened. The indirect or reputational impact was very strong. The losses of customers, deposits and new business were being rumored in the financial market.

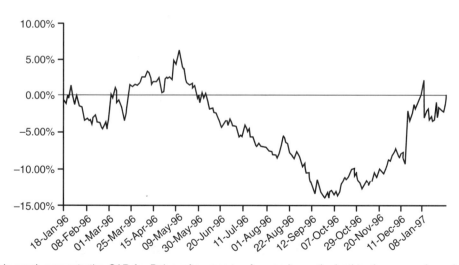

This graph presents the CAR for Daiwa after reports of several unauthorized trades were released on 30-May-1996. The econometric model is for the 200-day basis. Notice that some recovery was initially attempted before the stock price dropped severely.

Figure 16.2   CAR for Daiwa

16.6.3   Event 3—NatWest Options Mispricing

One case that happened towards the end of February 1997 (a few days prior to news of the Nomura event) and led to widespread repercussions was that of options mispricing at NatWest.

On February 27, NatWest called the press, as is usual market practice, to release their results. The market considered these results disappointing. By coincidence, on the next day, it became apparent to the board that several options were being mispriced due to one trader's deliberately low volatility inputs into the model. The direct losses were initially estimated at £90 million. Nevertheless, the bank suffered losses in its market value much sharper than this amount. NatWest had to recall the press and communicate this fact, which caused extremely negative repercussions in the market.

The NatWest situation was different from its Japanese counterpart in an obvious way. The British banking system was not subject to any general credibility problem.

The situation of NatWest was aggravated by the fact that, considering the bank's financial results were below expectations and the reputational event caused by the options mispricing, the board of directors decided to announce their interest in selling NatWest Markets, i.e. their investment banking arm. NatWest share prices dropped immediately as a result.

Nevertheless, NatWest share prices did recover (see Figure 16.4). The options mispricing event affected just a single area of the bank, and did not impact other areas

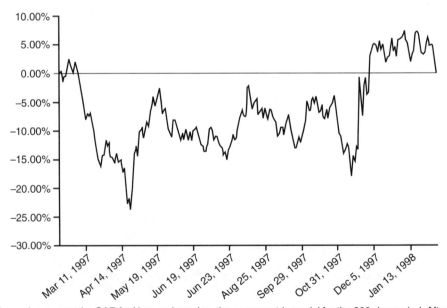

This graph presents the CAR for Nomura based on the econometric model for the 200-day period. After the release of the news, the reputational impact was very strong. Nevertheless, Nomura share prices are seen to be recovering just 10 months after the event.

Figure 16.3   CAR for Nomura

inside the bank. The event was just a sign that the controls on the derivative operations needed tightening further. Some banks reported the same problems after the NatWest event. It is clear that other investment banks decided to perform the same audit to check if they were victims to a similar event. The event was educational in this sense.

We applied the multifactor model explained in Section 16.3 to these three reputational events using share prices, market and banking sector indices and the reputational qualitative variable REP. The risk-free rate (r_f) was considered zero in all cases. The results are presented in Table 16.1.

All regressions present a reasonable goodness-of-fit (R^2) ranging from 0.58 to 0.72, showing that the model is satisfactorily reflecting the share price variance. The diagnostic tests prove that the model is appropriate.

The coefficients of the variable R presented negative signs as expected, since they reflect the "reputational impact" caused by the event on the share price. Obviously the coefficient varies according to the impact felt by each organization. The least strong impact was the one felt by NatWest. The worst was that of Nomura.

It is important to highlight that the results presented above reflect previous adjustments for heteroscedasticity, serial correlation or some variables which presented low significance (verified by means of t-ratios), such as the "Topix" index for Daiwa, and were deleted.

Following the model devised in the previous sections, we need to perform probit/logit to estimate the likelihood of the events. The results are presented in Table 16.2.

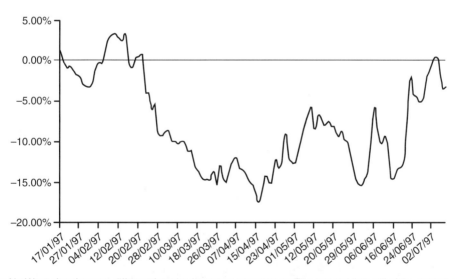

The NatWest situation was different from its Japanese counterpart. The general "mood" of the market was positive in England at that time. The reputational event was strong though because, after the release of the option mispricing, NatWest manifested its wishes to sell its investment bank, NatWest Markets.

Figure 16.4   CAR for NatWest

Table 16.1 Multifactor model for reputational events

(a) The model coefficients

	Daiwa				Nomura				NatWest			
	α	β_{TPX}	β_{Bank}	β_{REP}	α	β_{TPX}	β_{Bank}	β_{REP}	α	β_{ftse}	β_{Bank}	β_{REP}
50-day	0.00386 (2.511 [0.00])	Deleted	0.88935 (7.1722 [0.000])	−0.01902 (−5.795 [0.000])	0.006158 (2.7880 [0.008])	1.0872 (3.2207 [0.000])	0.22613 (2.278 [0.000])	−0.03770 (−9.279 [0.000])	0.00233 (2.062 [0.000])	0.1347 (1.517 [0.00])	0.71601 (3.4182 [0.001])	−0.019453 (−7.1473 [0.000])
100-day	0.00297 (3.0945 [0.000])	Deleted	0.72079 (8.4546 [0.000])	−0.1677 (−7.813 [0.00])	0.007623 (4.5609 [0.000])	0.59618 (2.3909 [0.000])	0.46788 (3.2375 [0.000])	−0.03585 (−10.85 [0.000])	0.00345 (3.202 [0.000])	0.3475 (2.463 [0.00])	0.67132 (5.2746 [0.000])	−0.01921 (−9.1945 [0.000])
200-day	0.00322 (5.1033 [0.000])	Deleted	0.86116 (18.8410 [0.000])	−0.01722 (−12.50 [0.00])	0.009414 (6.8696 [0.000])	0.41147 (2.1908 [0.00])	0.11694 (0.97784 [0.000])	−0.03540 (−12.83 [0.000])	0.0055 (6.9318 [0.000])	0.4956 (3.234 [0.00])	0.83317 (8.5714 [0.000])	−0.02293 (−13.959 [0.000])

β_{TPX} stands for Topix weighted average Japanese stock market index.
β_{ftse} stands for Financial Times Stock Exchange weighted average London stock market index.
β_{REP} stands for reputational. This is the indicator variable that is 1 when a reputational event took place and 0 otherwise.

(b) The regression analysis

	Daiwa				Nomura				NatWest			
	R^2	EL*	F	DW	R^2	EL*	F	DW	R^2	EL*	F	DW
50-day	0.655	162.8833	44.6904 [0.000]	1.83	0.762	148.1599	49.249 [0.000]	1.88	0.711	171.7465	37.71 [0.000]	1.93
100-day	0.580	335.3668	67.237 [0.000]	1.86	0.715	285.4972	80.447 [0.000]	2.11	0.724	331.0657	84.22 [0.000]	1.94
200-day	0.683	848.3651	274.82 [0.000]	1.98	0.451	629.9985	65.87 [0.000]	2.05	0.694	817.6534	198.96 [0.000]	1.85

*Equation likelihood.

(c) Diagnostics of the regression

	Daiwa				Nomura				NatWest			
	SC[1]	FF[2]	NORM[3]	H[4]	SC[1]	FF[2]	NORM[3]	H[4]	SC[1]	FF[2]	NORM[3]	H[4]
50-day	2.234 [0.000]	3.987 [0.000]	CHSQ(2) 7.7109 [0.000]	12.130 [0.000]	1.787 [0.000]	2.116 [0.000]	CHSQ(2) 2.365 [0.000]	3.216 [0.000]	1.812 [0.000]	2.00 [0.00]	CHSQ(2) 21.0662 [0.000]	1.92 [0.00]
100-day	3.271 [0.000]	4.953 [0.000]	CHSQ(2) 44.3297 [0.000]	18.818 [0.000]	2.015 [0.000]	2.894 [0.000]	CHSQ(2) 11.7874 [0.000]	4.112 [0.000]	2.123 [0.000]	2.32 [0.00]	CHSQ(2) 51.485 [0.000]	2.01 [0.00]
200-day	3.865 [0.000]	5.157 [0.000]	CHSQ(2) 725.5765 [0.000]	26.907 [0.000]	2.996 [0.000]	3.234 [0.000]	CHSQ(2) 979.444 [0.000]	4.651 [0.000]	2.912 [0.000]	3.25 [0.00]	CHSQ(2) 119.6825 [0.000]	16.0 [0.00]

[1]SC stands for serial correlation test, Lagrange multiplier test of residual serial correlation.
[2]FF stands for functional form test or Ramsey's RESET test using the square of fitted values.
[3]NORM means normality, the test is based on a test of skewness and kurtosis of residuals.
[4]H stands for heteroscedasticity, this test is based on the regression of squared residuals on squared fitted values.

Table 16.2 Likelihood model for reputational events (probit)

(a) Coefficients

	Daiwa				Nomura				NatWest			
	α	β_{Tpx}	β_{Bank}	$\beta_{\text{REP Daiwa}}$	α	β_{Tpx}	β_{Bank}	$\beta_{\text{REP Nomura}}$	α	β_{ftse}	β_{Bank}	$\beta_{\text{REP NatWest}}$
50-day	−4.944 (−2.088)	243.404 (3.087)	143.893 (13.988)	−565.66 (−2.97)	−3.423 (−2.165)	203.92 (1.825)	61.615 (1.249)	−241.35 (−2.19)	−8.232 (−2.56)	350.32 (1.546)	577.21 (1.821)	−997.21 (−1.989)
100-day	−4.5091 (−3.502)	243.135 (1.640)	105.508 (13.701)	−548.05 (−3.38)	−2.690 (−4.055)	113.27 (2.084)	71.722 (2.244)	−208.74 (−3.87)	−7.003 (−2.08)	339.25 (1.641)	544.59 (1.792)	−1033.00 (−2.01)
200-day	−3.3816 (−6.653)	198.775 (3.050)	118.258 (49.592)	−420.22 (−6.30)	−1.777 (−7.339)	38.30 (1.546)	27.862 (1.661)	−121.04 (−6.89)	−4.863 (−4.69)	294.95 (3.327)	265.56 (4.047)	−600.75 (−4.579)

β_{Tpx} stands for Topix weighted average Japanese stock market index.
β_{ftse} stands for Financial Times Stock Exchange weighted average London stock market index.

(b) Regression analysis

	Daiwa				Nomura				NatWest			
	R^2	EL*	P–T test**	Wald***	R^2	EL*	P–T test**	Wald***	R^2	EL*	P–T test**	Wald***
50-day	0.98	−5.1980	−10.0872 [0.000]	CHSQ(4) 35.785 [0.000]	0.94	−4.4549	−5.6933 [0.000]	CHSQ(3) 5.795 [0.000]	0.98	−3.7623	−6.761 [0.000]	CHSQ(4) 15.7631 [0.000]
100-day	0.97	−9.2424	−16.2041 [0.000]	CHSQ(4) 40.345 [0.000]	0.95	−11.1572	−11.148 [0.000]	CHSQ(3) 6.122 [0.000]	0.96	−4.9621	−9.7996 [0.000]	CHSQ(4) 22.3451 [0.000]
200-day	0.95	−32.1591	−25.3057 [0.000]	CHSQ(4) 49.9651 [0.000]	0.92	−49.2550	−20.078 [0.000]	CHSQ(3) 6.967 [0.000]	0.96	−22.5370	−20.331 [0.000]	CHSQ(4) 28.9773 [0.000]

*Equation likelihood.
**Pesaran–Timmermann test.
***Wald test.

The goodness-of-fit (R^2) for both probit and logit (not shown here) models were very impressive at 0.95. We chose to use the probit model because of its slightly better log-likelihood function and Akaike and Schwarz Bayesian criterion in all three events. The model passed the Pesaran–Timmerman statistics and the Wald test for the joint hypothesis that all coefficients are zero at 95% confidence level for each event. These tests assure both the correctness and the robustness of the model.

16.7   VaR$_{REP}$ AND HEDGING REPUTATIONAL RISK

Having processed the econometric models, we are ready to estimate the economic capital to cover against reputational risk based on the formulas provided for the two different bases, real-time (16.9) and periodical (16.10). Figure 16.5 shows the required economic capital in applying the real-time basis during the time of the events for the three banks.

As expected, the worst situation, in absolute terms, came from Nomura given the size of the bank (in terms of market value). It should be considered that the economic capital in this case will also include the market capitalization, therefore the figures, by themselves, are not comparable given the different sizes of the banks. A more detailed analysis is seen in Figure 16.6. In this figure is shown a comparison of the market value losses due to reputational events with the operational losses that generated the bad image.

The worst proportional loss was felt by NatWest due to their decision to sell unexpectedly the investment bank arm. The impact in the market value reached a low of US$ 11 billion, or 73.3 times worse than the original loss of US$ 150 million, due to strategy problems.

These figures can also provide a basis for discussion about hedging reputational risk. Many insurance companies offer policies against such events, for example. The figures above can serve as an indicator of whether the premium of the policy is appropriate or not.

Another hedging structure that can be envisaged is through the development of a contingent equity scheme. In such schemes the bank makes arrangements for a counterparty to provide equity capital under agreed terms and circumstances. For example, the firm can issue a put option on its own stock. In exercising this option, the bank can issue new shares and put these to a counterparty at an agreed strike price. The design of these instruments usually carries an additional trigger that relates to some risky event of risk management concern. In the present case, the event could be a reputational event within a given range. Hence, the option can only be exercised when two triggers are activated. First, the option must become "in-the-money" (the share price falls below the strike price) and second, the activating event must not be the current market conditions but a reputational event that depresses just this particular bank share price. These two triggers are likely to be positively correlated with each other as a reputational event normally results in a fall in share price.

16.8   CONCLUSIONS

The econometric model presented here aims to allocate economic capital at an appropriate level to cover against reputational events. We believe that this approach is

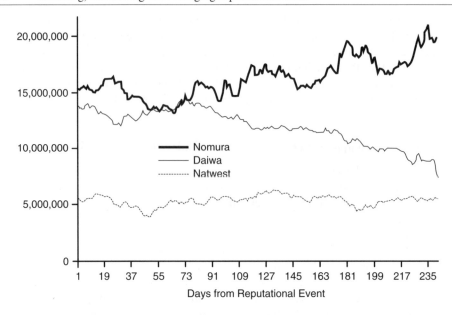

Figure 16.5   VaR$_{REP}$ for Daiwa, Nomura and NatWest using real-time basis (£)

	Trigger Operational Event (Loss in US$)	Maximum Loss in Market Value due to the Event	Multiplier
Daiwa	1.1 Billion	2 Billion	1.8
Nomura	1 Billion	12.5 Billion	12.5
NatWest	150 Million	11 Billion	73.3

Figure 16.6   Comparing market value impact due to reputational events with the size of the original operational loss

a simple and dynamic way to measure reputational risk. It can easily be adapted to an electronic spreadsheet, preferably connected to some electronic data provider like Reuters or Bloomberg, and the measurement can be made on a daily basis.

Despite its scope of dealing with financial institutions, the model could be implemented for any public institution in any sector or country. The example with Japanese financial institutions was provided due to a number of large reputational and company-specific recent events that represented large abnormal returns. All companies and institutions are subject to reputational events and, obviously, to issues that affect just their own performance. It is recommended that a level of economic capital be kept to cover against those risks that can affect the shareholders' value, especially in financial institutions where trust is vital.

The methodology used here is aligned with that used by market risk analysis, making easier its integration inside the risk management function. Also, it is obviously important for a financial institution to have a measure of the reputational risk, to make easier the discussion of buying insurance or allocating/attributing economic capital for hedging purposes.

Some limitations can be seen though. Some problems will appear if a company's share is not liquid enough to be traded every (or almost every) day, even with thin volume. The model could fail to capture the reputational risk in this circumstance also because the application of the indicator R would be compromised in such a case, or even the statistical robustness of the coefficient estimators could be questioned.

Another limitation is that the model, by using share prices, can only be applied to public companies. As most of the financial institutions are listed in stock exchanges, this will not be a major problem.

REFERENCES

Ball, C. and Touros, W. (1988), "Investigating Security Price Performance in the Presence of Event-day Uncertainty", *Journal of Financial Economics*, 22, 123–154.

Brown, S. and Warner, J. (1985), "Using Daily Stock Returns: The Case of Event Studies", *Journal of Financial Economics*, 14, 3–31.

Campbell, J., Lo, A. and MacKinley, A. (1997), *The Econometrics of Financial Markets*, Princeton University Press, Princeton, NJ.

Fama, E., Fisher, L., Jensen, M. and Roll, R. (1969), "The Adjustment of Stock Prices to New Information", *International Economic Review*, 10, 1–21.

Greene, W. (1993), *Econometric Analysis*, 2nd Edition, MacMillan, New York.

Gujarati, R. (1993), *Basic Econometrics*, 3rd Edition, McGraw-Hill International, London.

Hamilton, J. (1994), *Time Series Analysis*, Princeton University Press, Princeton, NJ.

Malatesta, P. and Thompson, R. (1985), "Partially Anticipated Events", *Journal of Financial Economics*, 14, 237–250.

Pesaran, P. and Timmerman, A. (1992), "A Simple Non-parametric Test of Predictive Performance", *Journal of Business and Economics Statistics*, 10, 461–465.

Ross, S. (1976), "Options and Efficiency", *Quarterly Journal of Economics*, 90, 75–89.

17

Measuring Concentration
(or Key Personnel) Risk

17.1 INTRODUCTION

Concentration risk can be interpreted in a number of different ways in risk management, depending on the context in which the term is employed. For example, those concerned with evaluating the level of credit risk in an organization see "concentration risk" arising from the point of view of low or diminishing diversification across industrial sectors, geographical regions, etc. in a loan portfolio. From a risk and stability perspective, this concentration can be a serious problem. If a particular sector in which a bank is excessively exposed experiences economic hardships, this can result in serious financial problems for the bank. From a market and operational risk viewpoint, concentration risk can be seen much more from the "key personnel" side, i.e. concentration risk would be the risk that star producers, revenue generators or even efficient back-officers leave the organization, therefore impacting the results of an organization by being an unexpected source of volatility of earnings.

In this chapter a model is presented that might be used to assess the key personnel risk in the front and back-office of a financial institution by estimating the concentration level and the probability that a key employee might leave the organization. This model may also be used to measure concentration risk in credit loans, but the examples here are based on evaluating concentration risk arising from the presence of key personnel in an organization. The model is first employed to assess this type of concentration risk in the front-office, which is done by estimating the level of revenue generation concentration and the likelihood that certain key players might leave the bank. Second, a method for pinpointing key personnel in the back-office and estimating the financial importance of their presence is developed.

17.2 MEASURING KEY PERSONNEL RISK IN THE FRONT-OFFICE

Obviously when the performance of a trading desk, commercial bank or any other business depends heavily on a relatively small number of "star" traders or business-critical employees, there is a risk of these employees leaving the organization, directly impacting earnings and shareholder value.

Three factors might immediately be identified that contribute to the overall level of risk, namely the gross income generated by the employee, the concentration of income-generation within that employee, and the probability that the employee will leave, i.e.:

$$\text{VaR}_{KP} = f(\text{Gross income, Concentration level, Probability of star employee leaving})$$

As a first attempt at defining this function, we might propose:

$$\text{VaR}_{KP} = \text{Gross income} \times \text{Concentration level}$$
$$\times \text{Probability of star employee leaving}$$

The value at risk deriving from the possibility of key people leaving the organization may be given by the gross income weighted by the concentration level giving the concentration risk in a certain unit, and also the probability of these key employees leaving the organization. Symbolically, this can be represented mathematically by:

$$\text{VaR}_{KP} = \text{Gross income} \times G \times P$$

where G is the Gini concentration index and P is the probability that the employee will leave the bank.

Whilst the gross income attributable to a desk or across a trading/business unit might be relatively straightforward to calculate, we need to derive estimates of the second and third factors in order to estimate the key personnel VaR. Firstly, we consider the dilution of income generation amongst employees by estimating the degree of concentration using the Gini index (G), illustrated in Section 17.2.1. (This index varies from 0 to 1, where 0 means no concentration and 1 means total concentration.)

Secondly, we calculate the probability that an employee will leave an organization by means of a multifactor logit model: this model is presented in Section 17.2.2.

17.2.1 Calculating the Gini Concentration Index

In economic science, the Gini index of income or resource inequality is a measure of the degree to which a population shares a resource unequally. It is based on a statistical concept known as the "mean difference" of a population. The index is scaled to vary from a minimum of zero to a maximum of unity, zero representing no inequality in the distribution of the resource amongst the population, and unity representing the maximum possible degree of inequality.

A simple example will serve to illustrate the concept. We might take, for example, the lowest 20% of the population in terms of per capita income and ask what portion of the total income is attributable to this 20%. If the corresponding proportion of total income is also 20% we might consider the income distribution as fair, and would have a Gini index of zero. If it is less than 20%, however, we might say that there is some degree of income inequality. In general, to estimate inequality in a distribution, we define a function, $G(x)$, to be the fraction of the total value of a certain resource belonging to the lowest $(100x)\%$ of the population, ranked by increasing per capita ownership of that resource. This curve is defined on the interval [0,1] and is known as the Lorenz curve of the resource distribution. Hence, the Gini index of inequality is a measure of the difference between $G(x)$ and the straight line representing a distribution with no inequality. (In this particular example, an egalitarian society would have a Gini index of zero, i.e. each member of the population has an equal income, with the Lorenz curve coinciding perfectly with the 45° line.)

The Gini index measures the gap between the actual line and the 45° line in the Lorenz curve. In the egalitarian society, the Gini would be 0.000, since the Lorenz curve would match the 45° line perfectly; the higher the Gini, then, the greater the distance, and the more unequal the distribution of income. In a perfectly unequal society, in which one member of the population has all the income, the value of the Gini index would be unity.

More formally, the Lorenz curve can be defined by:

$$L(p) = \frac{1}{E[x]} \int_0^p F_X^{-1}(t)\mathrm{d}t$$

where:

$$F_X^{-1} = \inf_x \{x\colon F_X(t) \geqslant t\}$$

Graphically, the Lorenz curve can be represented as in Figure 17.1.

The straight line in Figure 17.1 represents the "perfect equality in distribution" and any deviation from this equality is represented by the Lorenz curve. There are three different measures of inequality linked to the Gini coefficient, derived from the Lorenz curve:

- *Index of dissimilarity.* The maximum vertical deviation between the Lorenz curve and the line of perfect equality, measured along the y-axis, which is represented by:

$$\mathrm{ID} = 0.5 \sum_{i=1}^{N} |X_i - Y_j|$$

- *Gini concentration ratio.* The area of concentration between the Lorenz curve and the line of perfect equality, expressed as a proportion of the area enclosed by the triangle defined by the x-axis, the line $x = 1$ and the "line of equality":

$$\mathrm{GCR} = \sum_{i=1}^{N-1} |X_i Y_{i+1} - X_{i+1} Y_j|$$

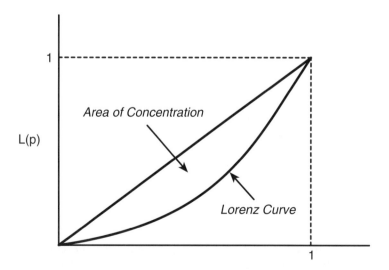

Figure 17.1   The Lorenz curve

- *Gini mean difference*. The mean of the difference between each observation and every other observation that can be represented by:

$$G = \binom{n}{2}^{-1} \sum_{i<j}^{n} \sum^{n} |X_i - X_j|$$

In the case where we are trying to estimate the concentration of gross income generation in a bank, we adapt the Gini index rather than using one of the three traditional Gini measures given above. A more informative Gini-type index in this case is given by:

$$G = \sum_{i=1}^{N} 2(X_i - Y_i)\Delta X_i$$

where:

$$X_i = \frac{1}{N} \quad Y_i = \text{cumulative percentage of income by unit}$$

$$\Delta X_i = X_i - X_{i-1}$$

The above measure also gives values in the [0,1] interval and is basically a comparison between the empirical "perfect equality" and the estimated Lorenz curve.

17.2.2 Multifactor Logit Models—Estimating the Likelihood of Key People Leaving the Bank

There are a number of regression models that have dependent binary variables of the kind (0–1). The most common are the probit models (see Chapter 16) and the logit models. In these types of model, as seen in Chapter 16, we are trying to infer the probability of an event happening given a series of factors. More formally, we let:

$$Z_i = \alpha + \beta_1 X_1 + \cdots + \beta_n X_n$$

where α is the intercept and the β's represent several factors that will be used to explain the probability of an employee leaving the bank, as detailed below.

We can include these factors above in the logistic distribution function represented by:

$$P_i = \frac{1}{1 + e^{-Z_i}}$$

It is readily seen that for all values of Z_i, P_i ranges from 0 to 1 and is a non-linear relation of Z_i. Suppose that P_i is the probability of an employee leaving an organization; the complementary probability (i.e. the employee would not leave the organization) is $(1 - P_i)$. Forming the ratio below gives the relative likelihood of the employee leaving the bank with respect to the employee staying with the bank:

$$\frac{P_i}{1 - P_i} = \frac{1 + e^{Z_i}}{1 + e^{-Z_i}} = e^{Z_i}$$

The ratio is simply the odds ratio in favor of leaving the bank compared with not leaving the bank. (Put another way, if $P_i = 75\%$, the odds are 3 to 1 in favor of an employee leaving the bank.) By taking the natural log of the formula above, we get:

$$L_i = \ln\left(\frac{P_i}{1 - P_i}\right) = Z_i = \alpha + \beta_1 X_1 + \cdots + \beta_n X_n$$

It can be seen that the log of the "odds ratio" is linear, not only in the X_i factors but also in the β_i parameters. L is called the logit function (see Gujarati 1993).

Therefore, the logit model would have m factors as independent variables. In our example, we use the model to attempt to estimate the likelihood of an employee leaving the organization, based on factors in three major categories: work environment, economic environment and personal reasons. Table 17.1 shows a far from exhaustive list of factors.

The whole spectrum of reasons (factors) why an employee might leave an organization is, in general, captured as personnel leave that organization (assuming the real reason[s] is given), and data should be available within the human resources department. Obviously, factors in the third category are subject to much more variability, so data might not be as available in this area. Nevertheless, the results of such a model are reasonably good, since economic or work environment reasons generally determine the satisfaction of a person in a position.

The dependent variable, i.e. whether the person left the organization, is binary, taking a value of either zero or unity (the former where the employee leaves the organization, the latter where the employee remains with the organization).

Therefore, the final model will look like:

$$P = \text{Work environment factors} + \text{Economic factors} + \varepsilon$$

Put another way, the probability of an employee leaving a bank might be estimated by considering a series of factors (collected by the human resources department) based on past experiences of employees who left the bank. This type of modeling also allows operational and human resource managers to reduce key personnel risk by, for example, determining the appropriate time to increase salary in a pre-emptive manner. In the next section an illustration is given.

17.3   FRONT-OFFICE EXAMPLE

In this example I will try to estimate the key personnel (or concentration) risk in two trading desks of a bank. Each desk is composed of 10 traders and the first trading desk is slightly more profitable than the other one. In Figure 17.2 we see the gross income generation by trader in a particular period.

Table 17.1 Examples of factors in three major groups: work environment, economic environment and personal reasons

Work environment	Economic environment	Personal reasons
1. Trading desk staff turnover ratio	1. Salary-to-market-salary ratio	Difficult to measure
2. Time working for the bank	2. Profitability of the trading desk	
3. Team recruitment policy		

Trading Desk 1

A	$919.86
B	$333.39
C	$561.12
D	$1865.88
E	$1819.01
F	$2139.88
G	$210.15
H	$459.49
I	$1757.01
J	$447.98
	$10,513.78

Trading Desk 2

A	$769.98
B	$672.23
C	$824.43
D	$927.65
E	$919.84
F	$973.31
G	$581.64
H	$776.58
I	$909.50
J	$691.33
	$8046.49

Figure 17.2   Traders' gross income generation by desk

It is immediately apparent that the gross income generation is more concentrated for desk 1 than for desk 2. Using the Gini methodology, we can confirm that this is indeed the case, with desk 1 having a Gini index of 0.93 and desk 2 an index of 0.21. Empirically, we can also say that desk 1 is definitely riskier than desk 2 (based on the standard deviation of the income figures), but this gives us no idea of the level of key personnel risk that we are running. The objective here is to present this concentration risk as a quantifiable figure and, therefore, we need to follow the methodology presented above.

The first step is to approach the human resources department to determine the dominant factors, both quantitative and qualitative, given by employees who had previously left the organization and collect relevant data on these factors. In this example the factors in Table 17.2 are found to be material, and an appropriate metric is given.

In other industries and/or cultures different factors might be more dominant, such as "time in the organization" in countries where people tend to stay in the same job for a considerable length of time. (Macroeconomic variables may also be included in the model, but in this example they are less relevant.)

In the present example of two trading desks, the five factors mentioned above explain between 70% and 80% of the resignations. The "turnover ratio" did not influence the results and was not included. Some factors are interesting. For example, if the star traders in a desk were hired together as a team from another organization, they tend to

Table 17.2   Suggested factors

Factor	Measure
Performance measurement	Appraisal grade
Time in the organization	Number of months working for the bank
Salary	Salary–market ratio (comparing the employee salary with the average — this average being provided by one of several market salary pools, e.g. Hay)
Team recruited	1 = Yes 0 = No
Trading desk (or business unit) profitability	Trading desk average ROE for the previous 3 months

leave the bank together as well. If one of the team is fired, for example, and gets a job in another bank, the remainder of the team tends to follow suit.

Based on a real-life example, a logit regression with the factors above was undertaken to determine what factors were important in influencing traders to leave the bank and find out, given the current factor status, the likelihood that they would leave the bank. The logit model results are given in Table 17.3. (Statistically, the R^2 of the model is very high at 93.152% and the model also passed the F-test at 100.66.)

Now we are in a position to calculate the probability that any of the star traders at either trading desk will leave the bank. I start with trading desk 1, that is more concentrated. Consider, first, the position for trading desk 1. The traders D, E, F and I were hired as a team exactly 24 months ago from another institution, and indeed they concentrate most of the revenues of the trading desk. The trading desk is reasonably profitable with an ROE of 30%. The results for a few traders can be seen in Table 17.4. (For the purposes of this model, it should be noted that we have assumed the greater the salary of a trader with respect to the market average, the more difficult it will be to find another opportunity with the same or an improved salary.)

From Table 17.4, trader F, the leader in revenue generation, achieved "1", or the best grade, in his last appraisal but his "salary-to-market ratio" is 0.9, meaning that his salary is approximately 10% below what is accepted as an average in the market. Given these factors, the model estimates that he has a 47.5% chance of leaving the bank. Trader D achieved a "2" in his appraisal, but his salary-to-market ratio is 1.3, meaning that it would be harder for him to find a better opportunity in the market. His chances of leaving the bank are estimated by the model to be 37%. Trader E also had "2" as an appraisal, but is making double the market average and the model estimates his chances of leaving the team as 13.5%. We need to process the likelihood model for each of the traders.

Table 17.3   Logit model results

Factor	Coefficient	Std error	t-Ratio
α	1.240	0.266	4.648
Team recruit	0.096	0.107	0.897
ROE	−1.727	0.373	−4.626
Time in the bank	−0.003	0.001	−2.318
Salary–market ratio	−0.308	0.095	−3.236
Appraisal	0.018	0.047	0.396

Table 17.4   Model results for a few traders

Trader	Salary–market ratio	Appraisal	Pr(will leave)
F	0.9	1	47.5%
D	1.3	2	37%
E	2.0	2	13.5%

Knowing the Gini concentration index for desk 1 and the likelihood of each trader leaving the bank, we can now proceed to estimate the key personnel VaR as below:

$$\text{VaR}_{\text{KP}} = \text{Gross income} \times G \times P$$
$$= \sum_{j=1}^{n} \text{Trader income}_j \times 0.932 \times P_j$$
$$= \$2774$$

The VaR for key personnel risk, after weighting the concentration of the desk and the personnel factor for each trader, is $2774.20. Therefore, the trading desk is running a considerable risk in this area of losing a great part of its revenue. A salary increase for trader F, for example, would reduce the risk significantly. Using the same method for desk 2, we get:

$$\text{VaR}_{\text{KP}} = \text{Gross income} \times G \times P$$
$$= \sum_{j=1}^{n} \text{Trader income}_j \times 0.215 \times P_j$$
$$= \$366$$

The key personnel risk is much smaller in this desk as the income is less concentrated and the human resources management process is being done properly, hence the estimated probability of an employee leaving is also smaller.

A similar model can be applied to credit risk concentration by using, instead of traders' income generation, loans by industry. A more concentrated portfolio will face more risks. Also, instead of probabilities of leaving the bank, we might calculate the probability that economic hardships happen in a certain industry using economic factors.

17.4   MEASURING KEY PERSONNEL RISK IN THE BACK-OFFICE

Another important source of operational risk arises where a few skilled and experienced employees become critical to the smooth processing of transactions. Determining who these key employees are will depend on the bank capturing data on events, e.g. precisely when the event took place, its scale, etc.

As an example, we return to the database previously used in Chapter 8. Instead of counting the number of employees (max $= 22$), a dummy indicator is created, taking the value zero when the employee was absent, and unity when the employee was present.

Table 17.5 shows some of the results.

A regression analysis is now run, similar to that in Chapter 8, but instead of using the variable EMPLOYEES we will be using the variables $E_1, \ldots, E_{22}$ to denote the 22 employees. Adapting the model in Chapter 8, we get:

$$\text{Operational losses} = \alpha + \beta_{\text{SD}} + \beta_{\text{DQ}} + \beta_{\text{Transactions}} + \beta_{E1}E1 + \cdots + \beta_{E22}E22 + \varepsilon$$

In such a model, it is important to verify which parameter is statistically significantly different from zero. We need to test the hypothesis:

Table 17.5 Operational loss data and control environment factors creating dummy variables per individual employee

Operational Loss Data		Control Environment Factors							
Data	Losses	System downtime	E1	E2	E3	(...)	E22	Data quality	Transactions
(...)									
2-Jul	$234,412	3	0	0	0		1	94%	250,096
3-Jul	$91,234	1	0	0	1		0	96%	208,111
4-Jul	$2,734,009	10	1	0	0		0	88%	345,611
5-Jul	$345,661	3	0	0	0		0	95%	210,075
6-Jul	$545	0	0	0	0		0	98%	185,321
9-Jul	$115,912	1	0	0	0		0	97%	249,876
10-Jul	$1234	0	0	0	1		0	98%	252,345
11-Jul	$91,233	1	0	0	0		0	98%	250,987
12-Jul	$55,908	1	0	0	0		0	98%	236,765
13-Jul	$12,002	0	0	0	0		0	98%	238,911
16-Jul	$23,456	0	0	0	0		0	98%	237,654
17-Jul	$1,787,634	8	1	0	0		0	89%	293,778
18-Jul	$7,233,704	16	1	0	0		0	81%	415,422
19-Jul	$2891	0	0	0	0		0	97%	250,912
22-Jul	$122	0	0	0	0		0	98%	191,210
23-Jul	$0	0	0	0	1		0	99%	172,901
24-Jul	$0	0	0	0	0		0	99%	170,415
25-Jul	$200,786	1	0	0	0		0	95%	221,876
26-Jul	$1456	0	0	0	0		0	97%	200,121
27-Jul	$918	0	0	0	0		0	98%	191,435
30-Jul	$1,234,095	5	1	0	0		0	95%	278,987
31-Jul	$17,654	0	0	0	0		0	96%	238,908
1-Aug	$9871	0	0	0	0		0	97%	235,908
2-Aug	$1,095,033	3	0	0	0		0	96%	268,001
3-Aug	$1200	0	0	0	0		1	99%	199,761
(...)	(...)								

$$H_1: \beta_{E1} = \beta_{E2} = \ldots = \beta_{E22} \neq 0$$

In effect, we are determining whether the presence of a certain employee affects significantly the operational losses, testing this through a Wald test (see Greene 1993).

The results for the example above indicate that the coefficients for the effect of employees' presence (β_{En}) are in general very close to zero, with the exception of β_{E4} which is 15,322. This means that the presence of variable E4 (representing employee 4) might be influential in the reduction of operational losses, since the operational losses increase on most days that he is absent. Performing a Wald test for linear and non-linear restrictions on the hypothesis that this parameter would be significantly different from zero gives the result:

$$H_1: \beta_{E4} = 0$$
$$\text{CHSQ}(2) = 25.12[0.000]$$

The Wald statistic for testing the restriction is 25.12, which implies a strong rejection of the hypothesis. The same test for the remaining parameters accepted the hypothesis that they might be zero given that they were really small. The conclusion to be drawn is that the operational efficiency is not particularly affected by the presence of any one employee, with the exception of employee number 4.

In order to proceed with the VaR calculation, we need to multiply β_{E4} by P_{E4}, the probability of employee 4 leaving the bank. The VaR for the back-office can then be formalized as:

$$\text{VaR}_{\text{Back-office}} = \sum_{i=1}^{n} \beta_i \times P_i$$

where n is the number of employees whose model coefficient passed the Wald test, proving that their absence significantly affects the results.

In this example, just one employee out of 22 significantly affected the quality of the processing. Using the same logit model as in the previous sections, we find that the daily key personnel VaR for the back-office is:

$$\text{VaR}_{\text{Back-office}} = 15{,}322 \times 34.2\% = \$5240$$

This means that if employee 4 leaves the bank the results (through an increase in operational errors) would potentially fall in the amount above.

17.5 CONCLUSION

In this chapter we have presented some ideas about the quantification of a specific type of "other risk", so-called "key personnel" risk. The ideas outlined here might provide the basis for a more detailed discussion on operational efficiency and people management. (It would probably not be a good idea to allocate capital against these types of risk, although the measurement would certainly help to manage better these situations.)

REFERENCES

Greene, W. (1993), *Econometric Analysis*, 3rd Edition, Prentice-Hall, Englewood Cliffs, NJ.
Gujarati, R. (1993), *Basic Econometrics*, 3rd Edition, McGraw-Hill International, London.

Using Real Options in Modeling and Measuring Operational and "Other" Risks

18.1 INTRODUCTION

A real option is the right, but not the obligation, to take an action in relation to an investment or business situation (e.g. deferring, expanding, contracting or abandoning an investment or a project) at a predetermined cost called the exercise price, for a determined period of time—the life of the option. Real options use the same tools developed to evaluate financial options, however, applied to "real life" situations.

The real options theory has recently been subject to increasing interest from academics and practitioners, and a few good books and articles have been issued: for example, Copeland and Antikarov (2001) and Trigeorgis (1999). This field of study began in the 1970s, when Myers (1977) realized that part of the value of a firm is accounted for by the present value of options to make further investments on possibly favorable terms. Real options theory addresses the issue that investment valuation based on static discounted cash flow tends to overlook the value of decision flexibility. What Myers (1977) realized is that a firm that is in a position to explore potentially lucrative business opportunities is worth more than a firm that is not.

Under traditional investment analysis, using the NPV or any other technique based on discounted cash flows, the impact of risk is always on the downside. Risk depresses the value of the investment. What real options theory brings is the vision that risk can be influenced through managerial flexibility, and can become a central instrument for value creation. Consequently, under such circumstances risk also increases the value of an investment opportunity.

Given that risk can be a good thing, one can proceed to incorporate other types of corporate real options that capture the inherent value of the active management of the risk factor. The determinants of risk, or the risk factors, can be divided into several groups, but we can simply separate them into the usual broad categories of market, credit and operational risk. Each risk factor should be mapped and understood in relation to its role in managerial flexibility. Operational risk is certainly a key factor. For example, keeping the remaining factors equal, an operating structure characterized by a prevalence of fixed costs is rigid and difficult to modify when production levels or market conditions change. Operational decision errors in such an environment can be costly. As we saw in Chapter 10, the degree of cost structure rigidity substantially conditions the effect that changes in volume might have on operating results. Therefore, decisions like hiring or laying off employees or buying a better operating system might be justified based on real options theory.

High fixed costs would tend to render many corporate decisions difficult to reverse, and often will imply significant reconversion costs. Given that, there is value to the possibility of delaying the implementation of a project under such a level of uncertainty (operational risk level), and conditioning such decisions on a favorable evaluation of the variables.

The potential use of real options in evaluating strategy and business risks and even, in some cases, operational risk, is large. In this chapter I use real options theory to briefly evaluate three cases. In Section 18.2 is evaluated the strategy risk of a managerial decision to purchase a new transaction processing system using switching options. In Section 18.3 is developed a passport option structure to price operational risk, and in Section 18.4 real options are used to estimate the operational risk at an e-bank venture.

18.2   EVALUATING STRATEGY RISK USING SWITCHING OPTIONS

It is a usual business situation to decide between two or more strategies. Every manager is faced with such a situation at least a few times in his/her career, if not every day. Many of these decisions would most certainly have an impact on the earnings of a corporation or bank. Obviously, the expected impact is always desired to be positive but there are risks and uncertainties that the strategy will not be achieved and the results will be negative. The strategic decisions might arise from the board or the CEO in the case of a bank's overall strategy, or even from an IT manager in deciding on the purchase of a new system. An example of strategy risk arising from wrong decisions by the board was seen in Chapter 16, when NatWest's owners decided to communicate their intention to sell NatWest's investment bank arm after a huge operational risk loss. NatWest's share prices dropped considerably, as we have seen, making the bank lose a considerable share of its value, and finally end up being sold to Royal Bank of Scotland for a lower value than it would have achieved if another strategy had been used.

Real options might offer a tool to evaluate strategy risk by modeling the strategic decisions as options to abandon or defer a project or a strategy at a future point, for example. One type of real option that gives the owner the right to switch between two modes of operation at a fixed cost is called "switching options". These options can model, for instance, the option to start up and then shut down a business unit (like starting up a global investment bank and then selling out after a few years), to exit and then re-enter an industry and even to decide between competing technological alternatives.

The pricing of switching options is not simple as they belong to the "path-dependent" family of options. Options with this characteristic are in general priced backwards using dynamic programming techniques. The reader should refer to Copeland and Antikarov (2001) for more details on the pricing of such options.

An example might help to clarify the use of switching options in analyzing the strategy risk on a more "down-to-earth" basis (instead of estimating strategy risk in board decisions). Suppose that an American investment bank decides to open an office in London, focusing basically on fixed income trading, and the operational risk manager decides, in conjunction with the IT manager, to investigate alternatives to installing a fixed income transaction processing system in London. The alternatives being analyzed by the executives are stated in Table 18.1.

The first alternative would be to install the current transaction processing system used in the US in London. There are quite a few adaptations to be made to the local

Table 18.1 Strategies to reduce operational risk in transaction processing

Alternative	Description and cost
A	Use the current US fixed income processing system in the London office. Apart from an extra license, this alternative would also demand buying several add-ins and quite a few adaptations to the local legal and compliance environment
B	Use the services of one of these new transaction processing companies
C	Buy, lease or develop a "switching" system that allows the use of both alternatives A and B. The switching system would allow transactions to be processed in the current US system or at a contractor, whichever is the most convenient in terms of capability and price

environment, and the final cost would be $2 million. One problem with the current fixed income transaction processing system is that it is quite old and cannot cope properly with a higher average of transactions; and the number of failures and crashes happen with discomforting frequency. The idea of upgrading this system has been in mind for quite a while. Therefore, the OR manager sees this decision process as an opportunity to discuss the eventual change of the current transaction processing system, since the level of operational losses caused by system failures is above acceptable levels.

The second alternative is to hire the services of one of these new transaction processing companies. In this case, it would not be necessary to purchase a new system as the transactions would be processed by a contractor. Furthemore, the processing errors caused by the contractor will be fully reimbursed, eliminating a great part of the operational risk. However, as one would expect, the cost per transaction is much higher than with the first alternative.

The third alternative is slightly more sophisticated and includes the purchase (or development) of a switching system that would allow transactions to be processed either internally (eventually even in the US, in this case the US international fixed income transaction would have to be adapted to settle London transactions) or at the contractor, depending on the volume being processed in a particular time and the optimal cost.

The decision here should be based on considering the size of the operations (depending on market conditions), the system's reliability (the cost of eventually purchasing a new system or upgrading/adapting the current one) and, especially, in terms of the operational risk that each system brings. The real option approach in this case would indicate the price that the bank would be indifferent to in taking each of the three strategies for processing fixed income transactions in London, as well as the strategy risk the bank will be running in terms of increasing their operational risk exposure.

The full valuation of the switching option is beyond the scope of this chapter (once again I suggest Copeland and Antikarov 2001 and Trigeorgis 1999 as references). However, the analysis can be based on the net cash flow of each alternative, considering the operational risk embedded in each one as in Figure 18.1.

As expected, alternative A has higher fixed costs and still considerable variable costs, mostly caused by errors in processing. This alternative bears higher operational risk. On

Figure 18.1   Costs and operational risk of the strategic alternatives to process transactions in the London office

the other hand, alternative B has low fixed costs (just the monthly fixed fee charged by the vendor) and higher variable costs (the cost per transaction processed). The issue of valuing alternative C involves the use of the switching option. This option would indicate the conditions (price, volume level, etc.) under which the bank would benefit from using one or another system on an arbitrage-free basis.

18.3   DEVELOPING A PASSPORT OPTION STRUCTURE TO PRICE OPERATIONAL RISK

A passport option is basically a call option on a "trading account", providing the holder with the amount in this account if it is positive, or zero if it is negative. The trading account is defined as the amount of money accumulated in a certain period due to trading in a particular asset. The basic idea of a passport option, as it is traded in the financial market, is that a counterparty sells to an investor an "option on a P&L" that results from a (yet unknown) investment strategy that the investor would otherwise have followed. The payout would either be zero (if the earnings are negative) or the total earnings at the end of the investment strategy. The investor does not necessarily need to execute trades (except on the purchase of the passport), but rather "phones in" the trades he/she would have made otherwise. The counterparty does not necessarily know in advance which (if any) trades the investor will "phone in". From the investor's perspective such a structure could be a reasonable deal, since they need not execute any trades (and thus there are no transaction costs, balance sheet use, etc.), and they get whatever profits they would have made or zero. Put another way, if the trader is good (or lucky) then the amount in the trading account will grow; otherwise the amount will be negative. The passport option represents the price the hedger would pay to be insured against losing money in a certain asset over a given time horizon.

By changing the underlying of the trading account to "operational losses" on a particular account or product line, we arrive at a similar arrangement that might be useful to price operational risk hedging.

Let Φ be the total value of operational losses in a certain business unit in an investment bank. The payoff of the passport option is:

$$\max(\Phi, 0)$$

Suppose that the operational losses satisfy the following stochastic differential equation:

$$d\Phi = (\Phi - \nu L)dt + \nu dL$$

where ν is the number of transactions processed and L is a loss index ratio represented as a percentage of the total volume of transactions processed. The value of the operational passport option is a function of:

$$PO(L,\Phi,t)$$

The value of the passport option (or operational risk[1]) would be given as a function of the loss ratio (L), the past operational losses (Φ) and the time. Hedging this option can be done theoretically by:

$$H = PO - \Delta L$$

Deriving the equation above using Ito's lemma, we find that:

$$dH = \left(\frac{\partial PO}{\partial t} + \frac{1}{2}\sigma^2 L^2 \frac{\partial^2 PO}{\partial L^2} + \nu\sigma^2 L^2 \frac{\partial^2 PO}{\partial L \partial \Phi} + \frac{1}{2}\nu^2\sigma^2 L^2 \frac{\partial^2 PO}{\partial \Phi^2}\right) + \frac{\partial PO}{\partial L}dL + \frac{\partial PO}{\partial \Phi}d\Phi - \Delta dL$$

As $d\Phi$ contains a dL term, the correct hedge ratio is:

$$\Delta = \frac{\partial PO}{\partial L} + \nu\frac{\partial PO}{\partial \Phi}$$

Adapting from the financial market passport option and assuming a no-arbitrage principle, we can find the pricing equation as:

$$\frac{\partial PO}{\partial t} + \frac{1}{2}\sigma^2 L^2 \frac{\partial^2 PO}{\partial L^2} + \nu\sigma^2 L^2 \frac{\partial^2 PO}{\partial L \partial \Phi} + \frac{1}{2}\nu^2\sigma^2 L^2 \frac{\partial^2 PO}{\partial \Phi^2} + L\frac{\partial PO}{\partial L} + \Phi\frac{\partial PO}{\partial \Phi} - PO = 0$$

To solve this we need to use a tool called stochastic control. This is necessary due to the problem of choosing ν, or the number of transactions. We might assume that the holder of the option (or the business unit manager) acts optimally, making the contract values as high as possible, meaning that he/she will eventually choose to limit the transactions to avoid even larger operational losses. This does not mean that the business unit manager would always follow this strategy, because decisions regarding the number of transactions also have a market return perspective and he/she might be obliged to cope with a higher volume of transactions. The highest value for the option will happen when ν is chosen to maximize the terms in the equation above. This can also be represented by:

$$\max_{\nu}\left(\nu\sigma^2 L^2 \frac{\partial^2 PO}{\partial L \partial \Phi} + \frac{1}{2}\nu^2\sigma^2 L^2 \frac{\partial^2 PO}{\partial \Phi^2}\right)$$

It must be re-emphasized that operational risk does not have the same stochastic

---

[1] The stochastic processes in operational risk are in general better represented by Poisson or Cox processes (see Chapter 7). However, the stochastic process above might be seen as a "continuous version" of the transaction processing losses process, for example. This is assumed just for simplification purposes.

Table 18.2 Passport real option for transaction processing losses

Notional amount	$50 million
Term	1 month
Transactions frequency	Up to 10,000 a day
Settlement amount	max(0, total operational losses)
Upfront premium	5.25% of the notional

processes as the financial market. Nevertheless, the pricing of operational risk as a passport option adapted from real option theory, or using option theory to price "real" events, might be a "quick and dirty" way to price and measure operational risk.

An example of the operational risk passport option structure can be seen in Table 18.2.

The calculation of the premium would indicate, following the arbitrage-free principle, how much of the total of transactions processed is lost in operational errors, indicating an appropriate level of risk premium (or insurance price). The use of this real option structure basically helps to indicate to what level a bank would be indifferent between hedging operational risk and not, given the volatility of the operational losses and the transaction processing volume. Such a structure can work well inside the organization to help find a reasonable pricing level for operational risk, or even in more sophisticated schemes where the structure can be sold to a counterparty.

18.4 MEASURING OPERATIONAL RISK AT AN e-BANK VENTURE

One of the key challenges facing new businesses is the evaluation of the potential market for their products and services, and the risks involved in the business. The challenge is particularly significant in completely new markets, like the "virtual banks or brokerages" (respectively "e-banks" and "e-brokers"). Given these particularities, real option theory plays an important role in the valuation of these new e-businesses (for an overview of business networks valuation, see Appendix A).

The decision on which real options must be included in the process, and when they should be exercised, is also critical. The outlook is highly uncertain, especially for start-up companies in a start-up market. In addition to the usual market potential issues, there are doubts related to the effectiveness of the technology behind the e-bank or e-broker; the acceptance by the customers, etc.

Another challenge is that, because these e-banks are relatively new areas (although quite a few already have over a million clients), there is often little historical information of particular relevance to a specific sector or company available. More than ever, external operational loss data is very scarce and could not be used even as a benchmark.

Despite all these shortcomings, it is possible to estimate risks in these ventures using a few mathematical techniques. In this section I briefly show that real options theory might help in the estimation of operational risk in e-banks. Figure 18.2 shows a simple risk architecture for an e-bank venture.

In the structural design of the e-bank business, the future cash flows are originated contingent to a series of risk factors, conveniently split into operational, market and

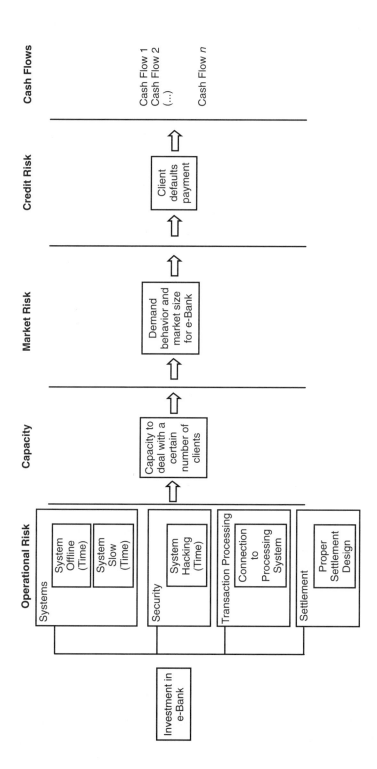

Figure 18.2 Risk architecture for an e-bank venture

credit risk. As our objective is to quantify the operational risk involved in the venture, I split operational risk into four different sub-types: systems, security, transaction processing and settlement. Other factors that could be included might be compliance to SEC rules (in the USA), for example. Operational problems will affect particularly the capability to serve a certain number of clients at the same time. Any problem on the operational side would affect the cash flow (earnings), causing volatility in the results. These operational factors determine the management's ability to react to evolving market conditions such as an unexpected number of clients.

Operational risk might be considered the main risk an e-bank runs, in contrast to a "real" bank where credit risk is in general predominant. In an e-bank, market risk is being considered, not the risk of bearing financial instruments but the market demand risk. Credit risk should be really small or even non-existent, depending on the business design.

In the risk architecture shown, the future cash flows depend on the management's reaction to the particular realization of the uncertainty. Consequently, every type of uncertainty should be open to future business conditions to evaluate how a particular factor would affect the earnings. After all the risk factors are mapped, the calculations can be done by Monte Carlo simulation, or even using more sophisticated techniques such as stochastic dynamic programming.

The net cash flow can be calculated as:

Net cash flow = Revenues − Costs

Net cash flow = Product margin × Demand − Fixed operating costs − Variable costs

Operational events would affect both the revenue side, meaning the e-bank system is prepared to attend to a certain number of clients per hour and any operational error could affect potential revenues, but would also mainly affect the variable costs, in the case of errors in the process that would demand rework or compensation to third parties.

Therefore, the value (V) of the e-bank can be measured roughly by:

$$V = \sum \text{Net cash flows}(M, C, \alpha)$$

where M is the market risk, C is the credit risk and α is the operational risk. Hence, the net cash flows are stated (and V) as a function of market, credit and operational risk. Any change in risk would influence the value of the e-bank.

Operational risk can be represented by the variation in value due to changes in the net cash flows caused by operational risk factors. The formulaic representation can be seen as below:

$$\alpha = \Delta V(\Theta_n)$$

The formula above can be read as operational risk (α) equal to changes in value (ΔV) due to changes in a set of n operational risk factors (Θ). The estimate of operational risk can be done through a structured Monte Carlo simulation, where these operational risk factors would be stressed and the impact in the results would be felt. A simple example might help to clarify the idea.

Suppose that we need to estimate the impact of one operational factor on the results. The operational risk analyst knows that (or there is an estimate that), on average, 2000 customers are connected to the e-bank doing business transactions between 2pm and 3pm. Imagine that we need to calculate the impact of "system offline" for 1 hour at this time. Considering that the average expected revenue in each transaction completed is $20, the impact on the daily revenue of having the system offline for 1 hour between 2pm and 3pm is $40,000. In terms of structured Monte Carlo, we might assume that the factor "system offline" follows a certain statistical pattern (Poisson, hypergeometric, etc.) and perform a certain number of runs where the system crashes for different durations and at different hours of the day. Running these scenarios 10,000 or 100,000 or even a million times, we might have a good estimate of the risks involved in the e-bank venture.

With real options, as the underlying asset is often not traded, a proxy for volatility has to be found. Such a proxy can be the Monte Carlo simulation of V, as above. Finding the volatility (or the potential volatility) of the risk factors and their impact on the results would help us to price and measure any type of risk in an e-bank.

REFERENCES

Copeland, T. and Antikarov, V. (2001), *Real Options: A Practitioners' Guide*, Texere LLC, New York.
Myers, S.C. (1977), "Determinants of Corporate Borrowing", *Journal of Financial Economics*, 5, 147–175.
Trigeorgis, L. (ed.) (1999), *Real Options and Business Strategy*, Risk Publications, London.

APPENDIX A: VALUING NETWORKS

Understanding the Basics of e-Venture Valuation

The new communication networks, such as those of telecoms and the Internet, have changed the way investors evaluate new businesses. These evaluation techniques are based on the premise that "the more people in contact, the more the business possibilities". In order to estimate the net cash flows, investors have to understand thoroughly the demand and calculation of the potential number of customers in each type of network become crucial.

There are quite a few mathematical techniques up to the job of estimating the value of a business network. In this appendix I provide just a few examples for different network complexities.

Suppose we have a more traditional network architecture such as the radio or TV. In these networks, the value is proportional to the audience, i.e. the number of people with the TV or radio turned on to a particular channel or radio station. If the audience is large, it would be reasonable to suppose that more publicity slots will be sold and the value of the network increases. In such systems, where there is one single broadcaster (information generator) and several receptors, the number of possible connections is equal to the number of users (N). Therefore, the value of the network (V) is directly proportional to N (and the business potential it brings to the companies that buy advertising slots). This is known as the "Law of Sarnoff", named after David Sarnoff, founder of the first large American radio broadcaster, RCA.

Now imagine a more sophisticated network, such as those of telecoms. These are a system of several "broadcasters" (information generators) to several receptors. The networks allow a greater number of simultaneous connections than a TV network. If there are N users and they can establish communication with everyone else, another mathematical relation should be established. Such a relation is called "Metcalf's Law" in a tribute to one of the creators of computer networks, Bob Metcalf. In this case, the economic value of the network (V) is proportional to N^2 (or even more precisely, $N(N-1)$). Therefore, the economic value of a telecom network, which allows a larger combination of communications between two participants, is much larger than that of TV or radio. This is easily verified by comparing the gross income of telecom companies with that of TV or radio broadcasters.

For the Internet, the math becomes slightly more complicated, due to the increased possibility of simultaneous connections. Now it is not just two persons that can communicate at the same time[2], as in the telephone system. With the Internet it is possible to put together, in an efficient communication, a very large number of persons (chat lines, etc.). A third "law" can be established in the "Law of Reed" (named after David Reed, former Lotus chief scientist). V in this case is explained by the relation $V = 2^N$, i.e. the economic value of the network grows exponentially with the number of users. This is what makes the Internet so revolutionary for the economy, and led to those almost incredible values for start-up companies. Whether these amazing values are going to become a reality (in terms of revenue generation) is still to be proven, but the investors' expectations (and valuation models) are reasonably justified.

---

[2]Although conference calls are a possibility (limited by the quality and the fact that just one person can speak at a time).

Index